Playing cards that, peeled
back, reveal an escape map
printed inside

Walnut shell hiding a
miniature compass to
aid escape and evasion

Pencil with a secret miniature
compass within, accessed by
unscrewing the eraser

MI9

HELEN FRY

MI9

A History of the Secret Service for Escape and Evasion in World War Two

YALE UNIVERSITY PRESS
NEW HAVEN AND LONDON

For information about this and other Yale University Press publications, please contact:
U.S. Office: sales.press@yale.edu   yalebooks.com
Europe Office: sales@yaleup.co.uk   yalebooks.co.uk

Set in Adobe Garamond Pro by IDSUK (DataConnection) Ltd
Printed in Great Britain by TJ International Ltd, Padstow, Cornwall

Library of Congress Control Number: 2020941218

ISBN 978-0-300-23320-9

A catalogue record for this book is available from the British Library.

10 9 8 7 6 5 4 3 2 1

Dedicated to my grandfather
John J. M. Jeffery
DSC, DFC

RNVR, Fleet Air Arm,
spitfire pilot attached to the RAF in the Battle of Britain,
senior test pilot in the Cold War

A WARNING FROM THE PAST

He was in plain clothes, his instinct was to
escape. Here was the risk; as he appeared
on the top of the wall shots might ring out.
He heaved himself up . . . his waistcoat hooked
on to something . . . he freed it . . .
he saw a sudden glow in the cupped hands of
a sentry lighting his cigarette . . . He dropped
into the garden and crept into some bushes.
To his horror he realised he had left his
food tablets, map and compass on the
wrong side of the wall, as a result of which
he later suffered considerably.
The moral is still the same:
Always Carry Your Escape Aids with You!

This prisoner who escaped in the Boer War became
British Prime Minister Winston Churchill.

(MI9 bulletin, WO 208/3268)

CONTENTS

CONTENTS

ILLUSTRATIONS

In text

All chapter head illustrations by Rui Riccardo.

p. xx: The badge of Intelligence School 9 (Western European) – the executive branch of MI9 – used in the secret missions over Holland in 1944. Courtesy of Barbara Smith.

p. 17: Map of major escape lines in Western Europe.

Headers to Prologue, Chapters 6, 12: Whittington chess set with secret compartments to hide items such as a file and hacksaw.

Headers to Chapters 1, 7, 13: Pencil with a secret miniature compass within, accessed by unscrewing the eraser.

Headers to Chapters 2, 8, 14: Playing cards that, peeled back, reveal an escape map printed inside.

Headers to Chapters 3, 9, 15: Miniature telescope used to observe camp guards when planning escapes, or crossing points on a frontier.

Headers to Chapters 4, 10, 16: 78rpm record concealing an escape map which could be smuggled into POW camps.

Headers to Chapters 5, 11, Epilogue: Walnut shell hiding a miniature compass to aid escape and evasion.

Plates

1. Colditz Castle, Leipzig, Germany. Courtesy of US Military Archives.
2. Christopher Clayton Hutton. Courtesy of the P.M. Froom Collection.

ILLUSTRATIONS

3. (a) A shaving brush and (b) an escape pipe with concealed compasses. Courtesy of the P.M. Froom Collection.

4. Monopoly set. Courtesy of the P.M. Froom Collection.

5. Brigadier Norman Crockatt at MI9 headquarters at Wilton Park, Buckinghamshire, c.1942. Courtesy of the Jestin family, the Jestin archive.

6. MI9 headquarters at Wilton Park, Buckinghamshire, c.1942. Courtesy of the Jestin family, the Jestin archive.

7. Wedding of Jimmy Langley and Peggy van Lier, November 1942. Courtesy of Roddy Langley.

8. Pat O'Leary. Courtesy of *Eye Spy Magazine*.

9. Dédée (Andrée De Jongh). Courtesy of Comète Ligne Remembrance.

10. Janine, Elvire (Tante Go) and Freddie de Greef. Courtesy of the de Greef family.

11. The de Greef family at home at Villa Voisin in Anglet. Courtesy of the de Greef family.

12. The Comet Line, July 1941. Courtesy of the de Greef family.

13. Bidassoa bridge. Chronicle / Alamy Stock Photo.

14. The Vatican, Rome. De Agostini / Getty Images.

15. Sam Derry. Courtesy of Claire Derry.

16. Renata Faccincani della Torre. Courtesy of Vanessa Clewes.

17. The opening entry in the first of the Little Black Books, 1941. Courtesy of the de Greef family.

18. Some of the airmen saved by the Comet Line. Courtesy of the de Greef family.

19. Airmen about to be repatriated back to Britain. Courtesy of the de Greef family.

20. Airmen being repatriated to Britain by Michael Creswell for MI9. Courtesy of the de Greef family.

21. Georges d'Oultremont. Courtesy of the d'Oultremont family.

22. Lieutenant Airey Neave. Courtesy of the Neave family.

23. The tented camp at Forêt de Fréteval. Courtesy of the Neave family.

24. Kim Philby. Bettmann / Getty Images.

25. A transcript from Room 900. Author's collection.

AUTHOR'S NOTE

A history of MI9 was first provided by Airey Neave (*Saturday at MI9*) in 1969. His account, followed by those of Donald Darling and then M.R.D. Foot with Jimmy Langley, closely matches the history and development of MI9 as seen in the official MI9 histories, training lectures and manuals and MI9 bulletins.[1] The types of escape aids, and the amounts of these sent in to POW camps, were also detailed in their books prior to declassification of the official MI9 war diary.[2] There are limiting factors with the MI9 files which contain no historical accounts of the formation and history of the Comet Line, Pat Line or sea evacuations. MI9 was running its operations in the context of a war that needed to be won and therefore was clearly not collecting information to write an official history of the escape lines later. The reconstructions by Foot and Langley, Darling and Neave from eyewitness accounts, leaders of the escape lines, helpers and MI9 agents provide the first detailed histories of escape lines that cannot be reconstructed from material in MI9 files.

New material will emerge in this book on the role of MI9's women who worked at its headquarters, first in London and then at Wilton Park in Beaconsfield. MI9 used female interrogators – a job traditionally reserved only for men. I also uncover new evidence related to women's intelligence work in occupied Europe. Through simple and ordinary acts of resistance, they made a significant contribution to saving Allied airmen and soldiers. Their stories in Italy are a good example of this. Material is included on the Rome Escape Organisation under Sam Derry and Monsignor O'Flaherty – a story which, although published in 1960, is often forgotten in books on MI9. It is now possible to include this escape line with the benefit of declassified Foreign Office files. Highlighted for the first time, too, are certain stories of escape into Switzerland and the role of the Vatican in MI9's work. The Vatican is rarely, if ever, included in historical accounts of MI9,[3] but it supported the intelligence unit and the Rome Escape Organisation which operated from within the Vatican precincts. During the course of this book I raise questions about the traditional understanding of the Vatican's neutrality during the war.[4]

Another area I explore in depth is the contribution of Varian Fry, the American who rescued Jews and intelligentsia from Marseille and smuggled them over the Pyrenees into Spain during 1940-41. Fry, who is no relation to the author, worked in this period for British intelligence as a spy. I look at the under-cover work of former Austrian émigré Fritz Molden who established networks for British and American intelligence from Italy, into Switzerland and Austria. Included, too, are accounts of the sea evacuations in support of MI9, Special Operations Executive (SOE) and MI6.[5] Access to the family papers of helpers in Britain and Belgium provides more detail to the traditional stories as told by Foot and Langley, and Neave. This is particularly true for the 'Maréchal affair', when the Belgian Maréchal family was betrayed, and the personal accounts reveal the subsequent implications of that denouncement for the Comet Line.

If there is a strong theme that emerges in MI9's history, it concerns the commitment and courage of the thousands of helpers, couriers and guides in Europe. They were prepared to work for a secret, unnamed organisation in Britain and were united in the concerted effort to free Europe from Nazi occu-pation. British Prime Minister Winston Churchill, himself a POW and escaper in the Boer War, understood the difficulties which prisoners had to bear. He sent a rallying message to British POWs to boost their morale:

In this great struggle in which we are engaged, my thoughts are often with you who have had the misfortune to fall into the hands of the Nazi. Your lot is a hard one, but it will help you to keep your courage up to know that all is well at home. Never has the country been so completely united in its determination to exterminate Nazidom and re-establish freedom in the world . . . We press forward steadily along the road to certain victory. Keep yourselves fit in mind and body, so that you may the better serve our land, and, when peace comes, play your part in establishing a happier, safer homeland. God bless you all.[6]

Churchill was an advocate of unorthodox methods of warfare and whole-heartedly supported the work of MI9.[7] His order for the establishment of the most unorthodox organisation of them all – Special Operations Executive (SOE) – to 'set Europe ablaze', caused great anxiety in MI6 and especially for its deputy chief, Claude Dansey. SOE was carrying out acts of sabotage too close to MI6 agents and escape lines, hence drawing attention to areas within occupied Europe where MI6 would rather quietly carry out its work undisturbed. But occasionally, SOE and MI6 agents had to be evacuated via MI9's sea operations, and these are a good example of rare cooperation; generally, SOE operated separately from MI9 and MI6.[8] The tales of audacious escapes soon found their way into popular culture and became amongst some of the best-loved stories of the Second World War, inspiring major films such as *The Great Escape*. But MI9 was as much about the eclectic characters who ran this secret service for escape and evasion as the Allied airmen and soldiers who escaped with the assistance of many known and unknown helpers across Europe.

The challenge in writing this book has been marshalling the sheer volume of research material now available – from thousands of declassified MI9 files at the National Archives, to published and unpublished memoirs, biographies, papers in family possession, military archives abroad and primary interviews with former helpers and descendants of MI9 personnel. The quantity of files on MI9 in all theatres of the war would require several published volumes to do it justice, so the main focus of the book is on escape and evasion in Western Europe.

The book is able to provide an updated history of MI9 using declassified files from the National Archives alongside new material released from the Military Archives in Belgium (VSSE), unpublished papers and memoirs, and interviews with families of MI9 and escape line personnel, and a surviving veteran of the Comet Line. By unearthing hitherto unpublished material, I hope to provide an account of the human stories of MI9 alongside the organisation and its operations.

It is important to clarify what kind of material is contained in the MI9 files. These files consist of thousands of escape and evasion reports from the interrogation of returning Allied personnel, as well as historical MI9 bulletins, MI9 and IS9 histories which set out the scope of MI9's work and training, and a small number of files containing citations for the awards to helpers. A limited number of official memos and correspondence is available. This is the extent of the currently declassified MI9 files. The individual files for the helpers have not been released to protect their identity even now, although some names are already known from the citations for their awards, or from their autobiographies. The accounts of MI9 by Foot and Langley, Neave and Darling were written with no apparent access to the then classified files. This is clear from a comment by Foot and Langley that 'whether escapers and evaders provided a significant body of intelligence remains an official secret'.[9] It is my intention over the course of the following pages to answer this question and show how MI9's escapers and evaders did make an important contribution to intelligence.

An area that has always been difficult to elucidate has been the historical and operational relationship between MI9 and MI6, both of which ran escape lines and agents. Historically, the lines between these two secret services have appeared blurred. Although MI6 files are not publicly accessible, and a full evaluation of its relationship to MI9 is limited, evidence emerges for the first time here that enables a new analysis of the relationship between MI9 and MI6. Declassified MI9 files, not available to Foot and Langley or Neave, establish that MI9 was in fact involved in intelligence gathering. But this astonishing new discovery goes further than commenting on whether escapers and evaders provided intelligence for MI9; for the first time this book can reveal the extraordinary role that spy (and later traitor) Kim Philby played in Room 900 – the most fiercely protected and highly secret section of MI9. From that previously unpublished material, it is also now possible to understand the type of intelligence that was being collected by Room 900. Traditionally it has been thought that MI9 /Room 900 was solely running escape lines and agents in support of those lines. But it is possible to see that its role went beyond escape and evasion. The biggest disclosure is the fact that MI9's Room 900 was engaged in intelligence and counter-espionage work on a par with MI6 and, the evidence suggests, even placing it within a section of MI6. This will transform the traditional understanding that MI9 was solely an administrative organisation for the rescue of escapers and evaders. This exciting new thread to the history of MI9 firmly places MI9 as an intelligence organisation on a level with MI5, MI6, Bletchley Park and today's GCHQ – something which had previously not been discovered. It means that MI9 was, in fact, a major player in the history of espionage.

ACKNOWLEDGEMENTS

Huge thanks must go to Heather McCallum, the Managing Director at Yale's London office and commissioning editor, for publishing this book and for her enthusiasm and support. She has an amazing team who are dedicated to ensuring the book can be the best possible. I have been working very closely with my editor Marika Lysandrou at Yale who has been meticulous with the final edits and has pushed me in areas where she believes there is more analysis to be undertaken. She gave me confidence to stride out with my own analysis of new research material. This has definitely enhanced the book – thank you. I am equally grateful to my agent Andrew Lownie for his immense support throughout.

There have been so many individuals, relatives of MI9 personnel and professional historians who have generously and patiently helped with my questions and research. It has been clear that they all care passionately about MI9's history. I am exceedingly grateful to John Howes, Michael Bottenheim, Roger Stanton, Phil Froom, Dr Barbara Bond, Lee Richards, Roddy Langley, Patrick Neave, William Neave and Sebastian Neave, Chris Lyth and Anne Lyth, Graham Withers, Keith Janes, Claire Derry, Vanessa Clewes, David Margulies, James Barshall, Barbara Smith and Sarah Hardcastle, Dick Smith, David Hewson, Angela Hammond, Mark Scoble, Neil Fearn, Nigel Morgan, Barbara Lloyd, Phil Tomaselli, Steve Kippax, Sarah Paterson, Kay Heather, Rolf Steiner, Terry Brace, Emac Macaulay and Dr Paul Stewart.

In Belgium, my sincere thanks to Comtesse Brigitte d'Oultremont, Elsie Maréchal and Monique Hanotte for being interviewed for the book and for their hospitality during my visit. Thanks, too, go to Dr Peter Verstraeten who secured the release of files from the Belgian Military Archives (VSSE).

I am grateful to ELMS (WW2 Escape Lines Memorial Society), the Colditz Society and Comète Line Remembrance who have supported this research. Huge support has also been given by Mark Birdsall and Deborah McDonald of *Eye Spy Intelligence Magazine*, Fred Judge and Joyce Hutton at the Military Intelligence Museum (Chicksands), National Army Museum, staff at the National Archives, the RAF Medmenham Collection and Imperial War Museum. My thanks to the Trustees of the Museum of Military Intelligence for the honour of being able to serve as one of their ambassadors. I am grateful, too, to fellow trustees of the Friends of the Intelligence Corps Museum for their support.

My final thanks are for my family, for their loyal and practical support over the years, and to my sons who provide so much encouragement and are an inspiration themselves.

ABBREVIATIONS

BCRA	Bureau Central des Renseignements et d'Action - French intelligence service
BEF	British Expeditionary Force
CIA	Central Intelligence Agency (US)
CQMS	Company Quartermaster Sergeant
CSDIC	Combined Services Detailed Interrogation Centre
CSDIC (CMF)	Combined Services Detailed Interrogation Centre, Central Mediterranean Force, Italy
CU	Code Users
CWF	Coastal Watching Flotilla
DMI	Director of Military Intelligence
DSO	Distinguished Service Order
IS9	Intelligence School 9
IS9(CMF)	Intelligence School 9 (Central Mediterranean Force)
IS9(ME)	Intelligence School 9 (Middle East)
IS9(WEA)	Intelligence School 9 (Western European)
IS9(X)	Section of Intelligence School 9 which planned and facilitated escape and evasion from POW camps
IS9(Y)	Section of Intelligence School 9 which dealt with codes and communications
IS9(Z)	A technical section of Intelligence School 9, responsible for the production and despatch of escape and evasion devices

ABBREVIATIONS

MGB	motor gun boat
MI5	Military intelligence for national security within Britain
MI6	Military intelligence for Britain's security aboard
MI9	Military intelligence for prisoners of war
MIS(X)	American equivalent of MI9 which dealt with escape and evasion
MIS-Y	American equivalent of MI9(a) which interrogated Germans POWs and bugged their conversations
MNB	Mouvement national belge
MTB	motor torpedo boat
NCO	Non-commissioned officer
OSS	Office of Strategic Services (US)
POWs	Prisoners of war
RANVR	Royal Australian Naval Volunteer Reserve
RASC	Royal Army Service Corps
RNVR	Royal Navy Reserve
SAS	Special Air Service
SBO	senior British officer
SHAEF	Supreme Headquarters Allied Expeditionary Force
SOE	Special Operations Executive
SS	Schutzstaffel
USAF	United States Air Force
USAAF	United States Army Air Force
WAAF	Women's Auxiliary Air Force

The badge of Intelligence School 9 (Western European) – the executive branch of MI9 – used in the secret missions over Holland in 1944

PROLOGUE
RED CARNATION

London: March 1941

Jimmy Langley crossed the foyer of London's exclusive Savoy Hotel. At a glance it was evident that he had been wounded in action. The amputation of his left arm had marked the end of his military service. For this wounded soldier, who had been taken prisoner by the Germans in France and recently escaped, there was still an important role to play in the war working for British intelligence. Langley was to attend a meeting scheduled for 12.30 p.m. He had been given clear instructions from the War Office to approach a man wearing a red carnation in his jacket buttonhole and with a folded copy of *The Times* newspaper upside down on the table in front of him. Langley approached an older man seated in a wing-back chair, a red carnation slipped through his buttonhole. His first impression was of 'a benign uncle, with white hair, blue eyes and general air of benevolence'. But this was quickly erased as the man abruptly looked him up and down and grunted: 'Hmm – F.O.L's son [Frederick Oswald Langley] and wounded. What a bit of luck.'[1]

Frederick Langley had worked in espionage for this man in Switzerland in the First World War in 1917/18.[2] Now Jimmy Langley came face to face with his father's former boss, Claude Dansey – deputy head of MI6 – and arguably one of the most powerful characters in an organisation that officially did not exist. Dansey had a formidable reputation as a difficult and controversial figure, with an intelligence career that stretched back to the Boer War.[3] He always operated by his own dictum: 'Every man has his price, and every woman is seducible.' It was said that Stewart Menzies (the new 'C', head of MI6) deferred

1

to Dansey on decisions, giving Dansey the real power within MI6. Langley recalled: 'Dansey was one of those powerful men who prefer to keep their power hidden . . . What Dansey wanted done was done, and what he wanted undone was undone.'[4]

This was another war, and Dansey was given the task of overseeing covert escape lines out of Nazi-occupied Europe for MI9 – a branch of intelligence as secret as MI5 and MI6. Within MI9 few had the comprehensive knowledge to see how its influence and work extended to every corner of Europe occupied by the Third Reich. The main concern for MI6 was not to blur the demarcation lines between MI9's escape lines and its own. As Dansey worked for both MI6 and MI9, he could maintain overall control of the escape lines and enable MI6 to keep a tight rein on MI9's operations in France, the Low Countries, Denmark and the Iberian Peninsula. Dansey believed that the young man standing in front of him would serve him well in that task, but their casual chat revealed nothing as they enjoyed two dry martinis and lunch. 'Uncle Claude', as Dansey was affectionately known in close circles, preferred not to talk about clandestine matters in public. At the end of lunch, Langley was no wiser about the real purpose of their meeting. Dansey instructed him to report to Broadway Buildings near St James's Park on Monday morning.

Broadway Buildings was in fact the secret headquarters of MI6. A plaque at the main entrance indicated the offices of the Minimax Fire Extinguisher Company, but this masked its real identity. Little did Langley realise when he met Dansey that day in March 1941 that it marked the beginning of his wartime career with two branches of military intelligence – MI9 and MI6 – and his entry into the world of espionage. It was a recruitment move perhaps typical of the unorthodox methods used then by the intelligence services to take on new officers. Langley would soon become head of a new and even more secret section of MI9, known as Room 900.

1
THE CREATION OF MI9

On 23 December 1939 a special meeting of the Joint Intelligence Committee was convened to discuss the fate of British servicemen in hiding in enemy-occupied countries or in prisoner of war camps.[1] Present at that meeting were the chiefs of MI5, MI6 and the Naval Intelligence Division.[2] It resulted in the issuing of a memo for the creation of MI9.[3] The objectives for this new organisation were clear: to facilitate the escape of British prisoners of war (known as escapers) from enemy territory and the return of those who had evaded capture behind enemy lines (evaders).[4] Within MI9's role was the collection and distribution of information to British prisoners and the denying of information to the enemy. MI9's modus operandi was divided into the following categories: preliminary training of personnel, issuing of information via a news bulletin, production and issue of escape aids (known as Q), the issue of 'Blood Chits' (to aid the helpers by promising them financial compensation) and preparation of maps and plans for escape and evasion in enemy territory.[5]

Underpinning MI9's philosophy was the belief that prisoners of war constituted one of the most valuable sources of intelligence.[6] They would have information that could prove useful for the Allies across a broad spectrum; for example: the enemy's military strategy, new technology and secret weapons, position of troops on the ground, battle plans, U-boat tactics and warfare, and new aircraft.

MI9 was divided into two branches. MI9(a) dealt with enemy prisoners of war being held in British prisoner of war (POW) camps,[7] and MI9(b) oversaw escape and evasion of British and Commonwealth prisoners of war from Germany and Nazi-occupied countries. By 1942, MI9 had become so large that it would be divided into two separate branches of military intelligence: MI9(a) became MI19 and MI9(b) remained simply MI9. The focus of this book is the history of the latter; for ease of narrative, the term MI9 will be used throughout the book.

MI9's role was clearly set out from the beginning as facilitating the escape from enemy territory of British prisoners of war and assisting the return of those who had evaded capture behind enemy lines.[8] The organisation's task included the collection and distribution of information to British and Allied prisoners in Axis POW camps via clandestine means such as coded messages, and smuggling escape and evasion devices into the camps.

The idea of a branch of military intelligence to deal with prisoners of war was not new. A rudimentary unit called MI1(a) had existed during the First World War and was responsible for the interrogation of enemy prisoners of war for intelligence purposes and matters relating to the escape and evasion of British prisoners. Much of its work had been carried out in France and involved devising secret codes to communicate with British officers held in German POW camps.[9] With the threat of another world war, British intelligence prepared to revive MI1(a).[10] Lieutenant Colonel Gerald Templer (later Field Marshal and a veteran of the First World War) was posted to the Directorate of Military Intelligence for the establishment of the Intelligence Corps to carry out this task. He appointed Major Arthur Richard (Dick) Rawlinson, who had served in MI1(a) in France from 1917 to 1918, to restore the operation. Rawlinson understood prisoners of war from an intelligence perspective.[11] In 1939, he was called up to an emergency commission by the War Office and within six months was appointed Deputy Director of Military Intelligence (Prisoners of War).[12] Rawlinson had barely had opportunity to explain the basic outline of a revived MI1(a) before Templer was despatched to France with the British Expeditionary Force.[13]

Rawlinson had a ready amount of research material to draw upon from the writings of escapers from the First World War. A number of them had published their memoirs, such as E.H. Jones who had written *The Road to Endor* recounting the escape of two British POWs at Yozgad in Turkey, and Johnny Evans' *The*

Escaping Club. These memoirs provided a basic grounding in the challenges that POWs faced when trying to escape from a prison camp, or hiding in enemy territory, and importantly the same routes out of those countries might be used again in the present war. The experiences of escape in the First World War were the closest parameters for the next generation to understand the spirit of escaping, what might be achievable and the correct mind-set, in other words the importance of believing that they really could escape. These elements could be built into an MI9 training programme for airmen and personnel prior to going into action to prepare them in case of capture.

The new MI9 originally operated from Room 424 of the Metropole Building in Northumberland Avenue, London. Its head was forty-five-year-old Brigadier Norman Crockatt of the Royal Scots, chosen because of his 'drive and initiative as a good judge of character and no respecter of red tape'.[14] He was unconventional and just the kind of man to lead MI9, as described by one colleague: 'His bonnet and tartan trews, and the panache with which he wore them, enhanced the originality, almost eccentricity, of his approach to war.'[15]

In the First World War, Crockatt had served as an infantry officer on the frontline in France, was wounded twice during the retreat from Mons, and awarded the DSO and MC. In 1927, he left the army to become a stockbroker. With the threat of another war, he was recalled to army service in 1939. Crockatt believed that 'A fighting man remains a fighting man, whether in enemy hands or not, and his duty to continue fighting overrides everything else'.[16]

This philosophy defined MI9's existence and was to be at the core of what Crockatt termed 'escape-mindedness'. Crockatt was the mastermind behind pushing the idea that all personnel had a mandate to escape or evade capture. Escape-mindedness was emphasised in all MI9 training lectures before airmen and soldiers went into action. It was a practical approach because if a pilot was lost in action, he could not be quickly replaced. It cost £15,000 to train a fighter pilot, £10,000 for a bomber pilot and took up to three months.[17] Britain could ill afford any reduction in the air force when it needed air supremacy over the Luftwaffe.

Crockatt knew that after capture a prisoner could feel quite desperate and demoralised. MI9 would therefore be tasked with communicating with prisoners in the camps to keep up their morale and encourage them to escape. Communication was achieved in a number of ways, primarily through coded messages, news bulletins, clandestine wireless contact and items hidden in objects that were smuggled into the camps. Crockatt recognised that escape and evasion may not come naturally to service personnel and they would benefit from special training before going into action. An active training programme was undertaken by MI9 throughout the war, later under the umbrella of its unit IS9 (Intelligence School 9). As directing chief of MI9, Crockatt 'attracted an immediate loyalty and devotion of all who served under him'.[18] He was assisted by his personal secretary Susan Broomhall.[19]

On 5 January 1940, preliminary lectures on escape and evasion were given by former escaper Johnny Evans to MI9's own staff.[20] The first lectures to airmen were given on 19 January 1940, and quickly expanded beyond RAF personnel to include the British Expeditionary Force, Fleet Air Arm and other officer Training Units.[21] Crockatt contacted the British Museum and asked for fifty books on escape stories of the First World War. These were despatched to his old school in Rugby where pupils were asked to summarise them and their synopses were used to create the escape and evasion training material.[22] The training was practical, providing tools for a better chance of survival in enemy territory. An airman could be disorientated after baling out of a plane or after capture and not think in a security conscious way. He was advised to hide his parachute and move as far away as possible from the landing place, lie low and wait for an opportunity to find help. If injured, and with no option but to give himself up, he was advised not to surrender to SS troops, but to hide until regular German army troops moved into the area as they were more likely to treat Allied personnel better. Training included advice on how to blend into enemy territory; so, not to march in a military fashion or use a cane or walking stick because these were distinctly British customs, but to acquire a beret as an effective disguise as a Frenchman.

Rawlinson, who had a background as a professional scriptwriter, was asked to produce a training film at studios in Walton-On-Thames in Surrey. Called 'Rank, Name and Number', the film was shown to airmen and soldiers to warn them about ruses the Germans might employ to gain intelligence.[23] It could include befriending a prisoner by offering him whisky, or hiding microphones in the prisoners' rooms to record their conversations. A stool-pigeon could be placed in his cell – masking as another prisoner – to gain his confidence, lead the conversations in a certain direction and extract information. Ironically, these same tricks were being used by MI9 on its German prisoners of war at Trent Park.[24]

Lieutenant H. de Bruyne interrogated returning escapers and evaders in one of the larger rooms on the second floor of the Grand Central Hotel, near Marylebone Station.[25] MI9 soon used female interrogators as the roles of women within MI9 began to expand beyond typing and translation work.[26] MI9 officers E. Hughes and M.S. Jackson were amongst a handful of women who interrogated returning escapers and evaders.[27] The only other women engaged as interrogators were in the Naval Intelligence team recruited by Ian Fleming and attached to MI9(a), interrogating German POWs at MI9's other sites.[28] They were the first and only known unit to use female interrogators in the Second World War. The use of women as interrogators underlined a principle within British intelligence of using the right person for the job, irrespective of gender in a role traditionally undertaken by men.[29]

Q Gadgets

Although MI9 might not appear to be as well known as MI5 or MI6, it has permeated our consciousness through the ingenious gadgets and spyware in Fleming's post-war novels. Exploding pens, fast cars adapted to fire weapons, poisonous hairpins and exotic cocktails – James Bond inhabits a fictional world that continues to fascinate the public. But many of Fleming's inventions originated from MI9 to which he was connected through his role as the personal assistant to the director of Naval Intelligence and head of the section for German prisoners of war within that department. He recruited the men and women of the Naval Intelligence section who were attached to MI9.[30] But he was not the brains behind the wartime gadgets. For this, two men stand out in the history of MI9 for inventing imaginative ways of hiding escape aids inside ordinary household objects. They were Christopher Clayton Hutton (affectionately known as Clutty) and Charles Fraser-Smith.[31] The wartime escape and evasion gadgets were called 'Q'. In the films based on Fleming's novels, Q has become the endearing eccentric English inventor of spy gadgets which were often bizarre, clever yet often funny.[32] It is widely believed that Charles Fraser-Smith was the inspiration behind the character of 'Q', though[33] in reality, it probably came from a combination of Clayton Hutton and Fraser-Smith.[34]

At the outset, the challenge facing MI9 was to find a suitable character to devise ways of smuggling escape devices into prisoner of war camps. Crockatt knew that it required someone who had a creative and unconventional approach to solving problems. At this time, Christopher Clayton Hutton had answered a call for an interview in Whitehall for unspecified war work. During the First World War he had served as an officer in the Yeomanry and Yorkshire Regiment and then the Royal Flying Corps. In the inter-war years he was a broadcaster and film producer. Aged forty-five in February 1940, he arrived for an interview with Major Russell, sitting opposite him in a smoke-filled office, not knowing that Russell worked for a branch of military intelligence.[35]

The major simply said: 'Tell me about yourself.'[36]

The open question gave Clayton Hutton opportunity to reply in whatever way he wished. He told Russell that he had wanted a career on the stage but his mother had opposed it. He had turned to journalism, then the film industry.

'Have you always been interested in show business?' Russell asked.

'All my life,' he replied. 'Magicians, illusionists, escapologists in particular. I expect it goes back to the night I tried to outwit Houdini.'

Now he had Russell's serious attention. Harry Houdini was the famous escapologist who had not yet failed to escape from a closed box. Clayton Hutton explained how he had challenged Houdini to escape from a wooden box built on stage in front of an audience so that no interference could occur. Houdini agreed. Clayton Hutton did not realise that Houdini had visited the carpenter and bribed him to modify the box. Houdini successfully escaped.[37] After the show, in what appeared to be a generous gesture, Houdini had given Clayton Hutton a silver watch, but even the watch turned out to be fake.

Clayton Hutton had been duped, but it did not lessen his fascination with Houdini or escapology.

Russell suddenly pushed back his chair, stood up and said: 'Come with me! I know just the person you should meet.'

As a result of this bizarre encounter with Houdini years earlier, Clayton Hutton found himself in front of Crockatt in the Metropole Building. Crockatt made an impression on him as being 'suave, well groomed and shrewd'.[38]

Crockatt explained how British prisoners during the Great War had been content to stay in the camps, but this was a very different war and prisoners were now given a directive to escape, even if they had made attempts before. Crockatt explained that he needed escape devices; however the difficulty was not the supply of escape gadgets but their size. Most items were too big to smuggle into POW camps. Crockatt needed tiny escape aids that could be concealed inside ordinary everyday items, like shaving kits and tubes of toothpaste. Clayton Hutton was ready for the challenge. As the interview drew to a close, Crockatt asked him if he had any questions.

'Just one question, sir,' said Clayton Hutton. 'Have you any suggestions as to how I set about my job?'[39]

'It's entirely up to you,' said Crockatt. 'There are no previous plans to work from and no official records . . . Put on your thinking cap, do as you like.'

Crockatt impressed upon him the need to work quietly out of sight of the Metropole Building and deliver items which MI9 could use. He had accurately assessed Clayton Hutton as being perfect for the job and, after meeting him, he commented to his colleagues: 'This officer is eccentric. He cannot be expected to comply with ordinary service discipline, but he is far too valuable for his services to be lost to this Department.'[40]

Clayton Hutton arrived that day as a civilian and left as an intelligence officer. The recruitment seemed odd to him because there were no British prisoners of war in early 1940 for escape and evasion, as he reflected:

I had to provide escape gadgets for non-existent prisoners. I was expected to keep away from the concern that was employing me. I had to buy a uniform that I was not expected to wear. And my passport to the whole curious business had been a casual reference to my thwarted efforts to get the better of Harry Houdini.[41]

Clayton Hutton took his role seriously and developed ingenious and weird gadgets for MI9. He was a man of 'tempestuous brilliance' who became the centre of 'a contemporary mythology'.[42] This was an accurate assessment of Clayton Hutton who preferred to be left alone, yet was determined that if he needed particular items, nothing would prevent him from acquiring them. As a result of this single-mindedness, he occasionally came into confrontation with bureaucracy; for example, when he needed to acquire a large quantity of an item urgently, it could take weeks for the relevant government department to authorise the funds. In these cases, Clayton Hutton used his own money and was often not compensated. Catherine Townshend, who worked for MI9, recalled:

> He was a maverick. In defiance of military procedures, he seized supplies (and sought permission afterwards) for the production of tiny maps and compasses to be used by servicemen for escape if captured . . . For those already in enemy prison camps, he devised ways to send wire cutters, spades, knives, flashlights, cameras and gadgets of all kinds. His infectious enthusiasm sparked the imagination of his helpers.[43]

The other person closely associated with Q gadgets was Charles Fraser-Smith. At the age of twenty-one, he had left England for life as a Christian missionary in Morocco where he bought land to farm. At the outbreak of war in September 1939, the Foreign Office advised him and his family to leave Morocco. They left Casablanca for England where Fraser-Smith found work for a while at the Avro aircraft factory in Leeds. His recruitment to MI9 was as unconventional as Clayton Hutton's. Fraser-Smith was delivering a sermon in church one Sunday evening and describing his recent work as a missionary. He mentioned how unorthodox and innovative methods were often required to keep various projects from collapsing. In the congregation listening to this were Ritchie

Rice (director of the Ministry of Supply in Leeds) and Sir George Oliver (director general of the Ministry of Supply in London).[44] They saw in Fraser-Smith a mind-set that they had been looking for.

The following day, Fraser-Smith was in Rice's office where he was asked about his background and whether he would be interested in doing something special and top secret as an assistant in the Ministry of Supply. For the next three weeks whilst background security checks were made, Fraser-Smith worked on supplies of clothes and textiles. He was then asked to sign the Official Secrets Act, although he still had no understanding of what the exact nature of his secret work would be. He was instructed to report to a head office in London, near St James's Park, which had become the main supplier of secret gadgets to MI5, MI6, MI9, SOE, the SAS and Naval Intelligence Division.[45] Fraser-Smith moved into an office on the first floor, furnished sparsely with a large oak desk and three telephones: one for local calls, one for long-distance, and the third red one for priority. His job in the Ministry of Supply was 'a cover to shield far less innocent activities', he later wrote, and he took orders from MI6 and MI9 as their 'floating production and procurement man'.[46]

Fraser-Smith rarely met the people behind the orders, they were just voices on the end of a telephone line, but he became the important interface to the military industrial complex, arranging manufacture, despatch and delivery of escape and evasion aids. His task was to despatch parcels to British POWs, mainly in camps in Germany. His range of procurements was vast, from shaving brushes to miniature cameras, gigli saws, compasses, radios and cigarette lighters. Popular items for escape and evasion included tiny compasses hidden in the back of buttons on uniforms or inside shaving brushes, silk maps, tissue maps hidden inside pencils, and foreign currency rolled in paper in a tube of toothpaste.[47]

Sending items into the POW camps relied on organisation at the other end too. The training lectures had underlined that if captured and in a POW camp, the senior British officer was to assume command of a secret Escape Committee. That committee was responsible for authorising escape plans and directed all activity connected to it. It liaised via coded messages with MI9 to inform them what escape and evasion devices were needed in that particular camp. MI9 despatched the devices, indicating by coded message which escape and evasion items to expect in the special parcels.

Care had to be taken not to supply items, particularly clothing for an escape, which could be betrayed by the way they were made. In Germany, the lining for clothes was sewn in a particular way, as was the stitching of buttonholes and the way buttons were sewn on a jacket. An escaper could be given away by simply having the wrong label in his shirt or buttons not sewn in the way of German manufacture. MI9 realised that German-Jewish refugees living in Britain could help such as Freddy Steiner, originally Fritz Steiner a Jew who had fled the Nazis, survived Dachau and been given refuge in England.[48] He received a visit from two plain-clothes men in the autumn of 1940 at his house in north-west London. He thought they were police officers in civilian clothes but later discovered it was a call from MI9 when, on occasional visits to the Grand Hotel in Marylebone Road, he seems to have assisted them. The men collected a number of items from him: shoes, laces, shirts, trousers, jackets – anything with German manufactured labels in them, and a German typewriter with dots and dashes on it.[49] The latter was used by MI9 to create authentic documents and was returned to the family at the end of the war. The items of clothing were taken away and replaced, so that MI9 could study how certain items were made or duplicate the labels to put in escape garments. Moreover, Steiner had been involved in menswear before his marriage in Germany and was able to show MI9 how items were made in Germany – vests, trousers, belts and shirts. Throughout the war, Steiner traded in wholesale fur in Upper Thames Street, City of London, selling furs to the military for lining for jackets and coats. He was therefore able to provide useful knowledge of the trade and relevant contacts to MI9. Steiner had a brilliant memory and could remember train timetables from his business travel in pre-war Germany. He was questioned by MI9 on German railways, routes and timetables that could be useful to escapers and a number of German trade magazines, books and encyclo-paedias that he had brought to England with him were also taken for the information in them. Whether MI9 ever copied the trade magazines for evaders to read on a train in enemy territory to authenticate their appearance is not known. Today, the family still has the typewriter and a single MI9 button compass.

Design and Despatch

Generally, it was Clayton Hutton who invented or designed escape and evasion gadgets and Fraser-Smith who procured them and despatched them. Small compasses were essential for escapers and evaders but the problem was to make them small enough to conceal. Clayton Hutton visited the unassuming shabby offices of Blunt's in Old Kent Road, behind which was a highly equipped scientific instrument laboratory with spacious workshops and around 1,000 employees.[50] He supplied them with 305 metres of trip steel (high strength steel), and within just a week it had been turned into 5,000 magnetised bars for use in miniature compasses. Blunt's experimented with making small compass cases that were as tiny as a quarter of an inch and soon succeeded in perfecting a miniature compass. Clayton Hutton was delighted with the results. It gave him the idea for the famous button compass which could be hidden inside the top button of a uniform. If the button was turned to the left, against the usual way of turning something (so it could not be discovered), the two halves separated and one part contained the compass. Clayton Hutton commented on the significance of this: 'Every soldier and every airman in future will carry his own passport to freedom on his uniform, in the shape of a compass button.'[51]

Operation Compass quickly expanded. Clayton Hutton developed various models and types and the tiny instruments were hidden inside a cap badge, pen, pipe or behind a button, and inside sweets.[52] Prisoners could carry a piece of magnetised bar metal, which could be hung on a piece of thread and would swing due north. This was known as the pendulum compass.[53] The pipe compass was inserted into the mouthpiece of a pipe and was protected by rubber so that the pipe could still be used for smoking. Later in the war, a bar compass was placed inside a wooden pencil. The pencil had to be broken in a particular spot, indicated by a certain letter in the maker's name. Razor blades in shaving kits were magnetised and 'north' indicated by the position of the name of the maker stamped on it; this meant that every British prisoner had a makeshift compass as long as he was allowed to keep his shaving kit. Another trick was to magnetise a paperclip that could be balanced on the lead of a pencil to become a compass. The

Royal Artillery, for example, was issued with a covert escape button and a replacement pen nib, magnetised, then dot punched at its point of balance, to allow it to be balanced on a pencil tip as an escape compass.[54] Another clever way of hiding a compass was in the hollow compartment of a fountain pen which contained a smaller cartridge of ink. This compartment could also contain a rolled up tiny tissue map. The achievements in miniature compasses were unprecedented:

> Ordinary bar compasses, tunic button compasses, fly compasses, collar stud compasses, 'three-penny-bit' compasses, every conceivable kind of miniature compass, first in thousands and later in millions, came in a steadily increasing stream from the Old Kent Road factory as the war progressed.[55]

During the war, MI9 was supplied with over 2 million of these essential items.[56]

Other improvised gadgets for MI9 included a saw that was edged on only one side, with a hole to thread string so they could be hung inside a trouser leg and hidden. 'Gigli' saws could cut through 1-inch steel bars and be hidden inside shoelaces. It was possible to hide a 9-centimetre double-edged saw, silk map and compass inside a brush, its contents revealed by removing the centre block of bristles.[57] Many shapes of ordinary-looking hairbrushes could be adapted by having a well-designed panel that could be removed to reveal a cavity containing tiny escape items. Saws and compasses were routinely disguised in uniforms with the help of Gieves Ltd in Bond Street who made uniforms for officers of the Royal Navy.[58] If it was known that the enemy had discovered a particular escape gadget, MI9 discarded its use in the particular POW camp and sent out items concealed in different ways.

One of the most ingenious conversions was the adaptation of an RAF boot that became known as an escape boot. Concealed in a cloth loop on the boot was a small knife which an airman could use to cut away the legging to leave only black shoes, thereby converting to civilian footwear. The boots would otherwise have given him away if he was on the run or travelling in a train incognito. The heel of the boot contained silk maps, a compass and a small file. The escape boot was one of the few gadgets that had to be abandoned by MI9 because they were not warm enough during winter flights and became waterlogged in heavy rain.[59] Prisoners were entitled to receive new uniforms in the camps, providing another opportunity for Clayton Hutton to find ways of hiding escape items. The uniforms could also be modified such that when the lining was removed it became a civilian suit – necessary if escaping through enemy territory.

MI9 arranged for grey woollen blankets to be sent to prisoners. These could be modified before despatch by printing the complete pattern of an item of clothing onto them with invisible ink.[60] To see the pattern, a prisoner had to put certain chemicals into a bucket of warm water and then dip the blanket in it. These special chemicals were smuggled into POW camps inside jam pots or dried milk tins. Depending on the chemical used, the blanket turned from grey to dark blue, field grey or brown and could be used to make a perfect copy of a German uniform.[61]

No escape items were ever sent by MI9 in Red Cross food parcels because discovery would jeopardise extra commodities being sent to prisoners.[62] A series of fictitious charities was therefore created to send parcels into the camps, including The Prisoners' Leisure House Fund, Brewers' Society of Great Britain, The Licensed Victuallers Sports Association and Welsh Provident Society.[63] Some parcels were genuine; others had escape and evasion devices in them. Board games were particularly useful for this: chess sets, Monopoly, Snakes and Ladders and Ludo.[64] The games could be sent into camps by the fake charities as 'innocent' leisure activities for the prisoners, but many were modified to hide Q items. A chess piece was adapted with a watertight compartment to hold special ink for forging documents and papers. A knight was the chosen chess piece for this; its head could be unscrewed in a counter-intuitive clockwise direction to reveal the ink. Dominoes could be hollowed out but this was considered too obvious to be used frequently.[65] Waddingtons, the manufacturer of games, was recruited to make special Monopoly sets with escape and evasion devices hidden inside, while maps were cleverly hidden inside their playing cards: 'The map would be made from a material impervious to water and sandwiched between the back and the pip side of the cards by water soluble glue. When dropped into a bucket of water the cards would come into three parts',[66] thus revealing the map. In May 1942, the Ministry of Supply ordered 224 packs of playing cards for use by MI9.[67]

MI9 Maps

Maps were essential in escape and evasion. Clayton Hutton arranged to meet the Managing Director of Bartholomew's, the famous mapmakers in Edinburgh, to secure all the designs of maps needed. Bartholomew's offered these free of copyright fees, thereby saving a fortune for the War Office. The company also gave Clayton Hutton the printing plates to enable the ongoing printing of maps. Over 300,000 copies of Bartholomew's maps would be reproduced for MI9.[68]

The range of different maps available to MI9 represented one of the most important escape aids of the war. It meant that wherever a prisoner was stranded in a Nazi-occupied country, or had just escaped from a POW camp, he had a better chance of crossing unknown territory to a border or a town or city where he could be hidden until smuggled out down an escape line.[69] MI9 escape maps were soon issued not only to airmen but to Special Forces and other units going into action. The difficulty was how to conceal them because the traditional paper maps rustled on movement and risked discovery by the enemy. Clayton Hutton needed to find a silent alternative and one that could be printed in small detail yet as clear as any Ordnance Survey map. His answer was to print silk maps because these would be durable and lightweight.[70] He contacted a friend in the textile world to supply the silk and also accessed it from a factory that made parachutes for the British forces.

MI9's silk maps were believed to have been printed by C.E. Layton of London.[71] Initial attempts at printing with ink were a disaster. The fine lines for the roads and railways were smudged and illegible. Clayton Hutton decided to experiment by adding pectin to the ink. Pectin was a naturally occurring gelatin obtained from seaweed and various fruits, and was already used in the food industry to thicken jam. By using pectin he discovered that it was possible to print a miniature map onto silk in clear, perfect detail. The maps could be printed single or double-sided, at a scale of 1:1,000,000 on a white background.

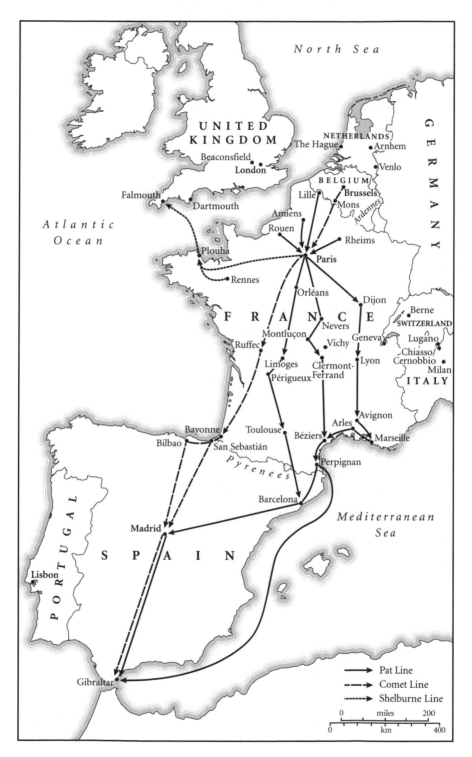

	Pat Line
	Comet Line
	Shelburne Line

```
0        miles        200
0         km          400
```

Major escape lines in Western Europe

Three colours were used: red for roads, green for frontiers and black for all other details.[72] Silk maps of Italy and North Africa were printed as early as the summer of 1940 and were issued to all airmen on operational duties.[73]

Maps could include useful intelligence on them, a prime example being an MI9 map of the port of Danzig.[74] Three versions of this map were produced with slightly different detail, showing for example where POWs could locate Swedish ships on which they could be smuggled aboard to reach neutral Sweden, or the position and extent of the arc of the port searchlights to avoid them. Maps of frontiers were especially useful: some prisoners, for example, tried to cross via the Schaffhausen Salient on the German-Swiss border where Switzerland protrudes into Germany.[75] Johnny Evans had used that crossing in the First World War and knew it could be used again. He took a holiday along the border to photograph the crossing points, noting key landmarks, and these photographs were used by MI9 to refine the escape maps. A special inset in the map of the Schaffhausen Salient indicated how to cross the border and where. Prisoners would already be familiar with Evans's photographs because they were printed in the MI9 bulletin with other relevant information. In 1942, this crossing point was used by Airey Neave, the first British officer to successfully escape from Colditz.[76]

Perhaps the least known and referenced MI9 maps were the tissue maps. With the threat of a German invasion of Britain in 1940, MI9 was concerned that Britain would be blockaded and the supply of silk would be impossible, leading to a cessation of the production of MI9's silk maps. Clayton Hutton contacted a friend at the RAF Club in Piccadilly to discuss the problem.[77] His friend alerted him to the possible use of Japanese mulberry leaves to make a type of 'wood' pulp; this could be used to produce incredibly durable and resilient tissue paper. Mulberry leaves had long been used in Japan for art and interior design in homes and, in many ways, argues historian Phil Froom, the tissue maps developed by Clayton Hutton were a bigger success than the silk maps:[78]

The tissue maps were gossamer thin. The new paper, if held up to the sky, was all but transparent, yet even when wet it proved to be incredibly strong. It could be soaked in water, screwed up and smoothed out to look almost new. A silk map the same size as a tissue map could be screwed up into the palm of a hand. But a tissue map could be folded to fit inside a gaming dice, domino or travelling chess set. The concealment value for MI9 shipping tissue maps into POW camps was invaluable.[79]

Tissue maps were even concealed inside imitation sweets and small fruit like dates.

The silk and tissue maps had slightly different advantages: silk maps were an excellent pre-capture item as they were much easier to handle in the field when evading. The tissue maps were an ideal post-capture escape aid that could be hidden inside different tiny, but seemingly innocent-looking, daily items and despatched to the Escape Committee of a POW camp.

In 1942, the Ministry of Supply in Leeds procured for MI9 the printing of maps by Waddingtons who had already proved their ability to print on silk. Contact with Waddingtons on this subject appears to have been as early as 1941[80] and now the company printed the maps as well as hiding them inside board games. However, the main sources of silk – China and Japan – became inaccessible once Japan entered the war with its bombing of Pearl Harbour on 7 December 1941. The other main sources, Italy and France, were under German occupation. The man tasked with procuring silk for MI9 from 1941 was Peter William Gaddum who worked for his family's silk business in Macclesfield. He was employed by the Ministry of Supply as chief assistant to source and control supplies of silk, travelling to Baghdad, Cairo, Tehran and India to secure silk for the war effort. With silk in increasingly short supply and not guaranteed from Gaddum's travels, any stock in England needed to be prioritised for the production of parachutes. Clayton Hutton sought an alternative material and found his source after the bombing of Pearl Harbour and America's entry into the war, following which MI9 was able to acquire a new synthetic material called rayon (nylon) that had been developed and manufactured in America, and on which the maps could be printed. Over a million of these were produced for MI9.[81] Barbara Bond, a former cartographer in the Ministry of Defence, commented in her study of MI9 maps that these man-made maps were 'multi-coloured and are layered, demonstrating a high level of technical competence in printing so many colours on fabric and maintaining the colour register . . . none appear to be printed on silk. All are irregular in size and coverage.'[82]

Maps were later produced on handkerchiefs to show escape routes and exits by land and sea.[83] By autumn 1942, aircrews were finding some maps too small for use and MI9 approved a series of new escape maps,[84] the printing plates being produced by the Kodak company. For the duration of the war, new designs of escape and evasion maps continued to be made. They were generally numbered and those with a prefix 43 were believed to have been made in 1943, all at a scale of 1:1,000,000 but with larger inserts at a scale between 1:250,000 to 1: 500,000.[85] These maps covered Europe from Spain to Holland and Portugal to Turkey. A new series of maps was produced for MI9 in 1943 and 1944 and in such large quantities to be issued routinely to operational personnel, especially ahead of D-Day.[86] Maps were essential for survival especially during the intense battles that would follow in Normandy after D-Day when fighting forces became trapped behind the lines, disorientated and tired from fierce fighting and probably unable to locate themselves accurately. With an escape map they could find their way back to their unit or to a safer area, hoping to be hidden.

Codes and Communication

Regular contact with the POW camps was essential for MI9's work in supporting the Escape Committee. The Geneva Convention allowed for prisoners of war to receive up to two letters and four postcards a month.[87] MI9 exploited this opportunity to the full and used code correspondence which became the principal means of communication between MI9 and the camps until radio sets could be smuggled in. Leslie Winterbottom devised secret codes and communication for MI9.[88] Prior to the war, he had been personal assistant to Gordon Selfridge, son of the founder of the London store.[89] A number of codes were eventually developed and examples of these and how they worked can be found in MI9 files.[90] The coded message was hidden inside an ordinary 'innocent' letter, as noted by Barbara Bond: 'This was a distinctly alternative way of employing cipher alphabets. In essence it did not matter if the general encryption method or algorithm was known; rather it was the specific key which identified the particular encryption which needed to remain secret.'[91] It was also the 'sheer cleverness of the codes' which were 'strikingly impressive'.[92] Essentially, a coded letter was identified by the date it was written.[93] If the date was written 22/3/42, rather than 22 March 1942, it was known to contain a coded message and MI9 knew to set to work on it. A signature at the end of the letter could also be underlined as an indication that it was coded. Even if intercepted by the Germans, the hidden message could only be read if the key was known: 'Since each code comprised three elements, two Arabic numbers and a letter of the alphabet, there were 2,600 possible permutations. This allowed for the existence of 2,600 coded letter writers, if each was to use a unique code. By December 1941 there were already 928 coded correspondents in operation.'[94]

Coded letters and cards became an important conduit for prisoners of war to request certain escape and evasion devices from MI9, which did its best to assist quickly, indicating in a return letter how POWs would recognise the parcels that were being despatched with escape aids. Winterbottom liaised with the families of British POWs, asking them to communicate occasionally with their relative in the camp to write a coded or fictitious letter for MI9. In order to recognise the letters, some personnel were trained in the use of codes before they went into action, and many prisoners undertook a considerable risk for MI9, especially in sending intelligence back in their coded messages. It is important not to underestimate their role as, if caught by the Germans, they would have been handed over to the Gestapo for espionage, whereas the penalty for a failed attempt to escape was thirty days in solitary confinement.[95]

As early as the end of April 1940 – within four months of its establishment – MI9 had already distributed 405 silk maps of Germany, 404 thin paper maps, 90 magnetised razor blades and 4,968 special compass needles to the British Expeditionary Force (BEF), RAF, Bomber Command, army formations in Rome, and the Advanced Air Striking Force (AASF).[96] The following month MI9 distributed 850 silk maps of Germany, 1,048 maps of frontier regions,

552 pencil points (magnetised), 5,160 needle compasses and 632 hacksaw blades. The continued volume of output, as listed each month in the official war diary, was surprising for an organisation that was still relatively small. But it demonstrates the foresight of MI9 to prepare Britain's fighting forces at a time when the situation in Europe was rapidly changing as the war progressed.

The story of Q gadgets and operations is one of 'breath-taking ingenuity and inventiveness engendered by necessity, initially by MI9, but the more so by the prisoners of war themselves'.[97] Although still a relatively small department of Military Intelligence in 1940, MI9 swiftly developed into a highly efficient organisation from necessity. Hitler had mobilised his armies and was heading for the occupation of Western Europe and after that, Britain was next on the invasion list.

2
EUROPE UNDER OCCUPATION

On 9 April 1940 Hitler's forces crossed the borders of Denmark and Norway and occupied them. The two countries had vital resources that could sustain the Third Reich: Denmark had food supplies and Norway a heavy water plant at Vemork. Germany had no means of producing her own heavy water, which was essential in the development of an atomic bomb – something Hitler's scientists were working on.[1] The Norwegian campaign was fought between 9 April 1940 and 10 June 1940, with British forces and Norwegian resistance fighters failing to hold back advancing German forces.[2]

Lieutenant Colonel E.J. King-Salter, the British military attaché to Norway, was one of the officials trapped in Norway after the occupation. He had only been appointed to his post in Helsinki a month earlier.[3] Two days after the German occupation, he received orders from the War Office in London to evacuate his office and find the Norwegian GHQ (general headquarters) which had moved into hiding,[4] and was instructed to keep the War Office informed of events on the ground. At 6.45 p.m. that same evening, 11 April, he left Helsinki on a special plane for Stockholm in neutral Sweden. The account of his escape to England from Norway via Sweden survives in MI9 files, not because he was directly helped out by MI9, but because as a returning escaper he was automatically interrogated by MI9.[5] In Stockholm, the British military attaché Lieutenant Colonel Sutton-Pratt obtained a car for him and the necessary papers to show that he had diplomatic status and protection. King-Salter travelled across Norway by road with personnel from the British Legation. Their journey was difficult, having to negotiate mountainous snow-covered roads and pass frequent roadblocks.[6]

On 17 April, King-Salter received a cypher message that British troops were coming to Norway's aid and would be landing at Narvik in the north, inside the Arctic Circle. Soldiers from 148 Infantry Brigade landed there the following day with other British troops. Alongside Norwegian troops they tried to protect various bridgeheads and roads from German occupation. By now, King-Salter and his colleagues were in the valley near the small village of Tretton, in the north of the country. As German troops advanced further, they hid in a forest; they watched as the German tanks and infantry went by, and found they were now behind German lines. King-Salter's MI9 debriefing report recalled how a German soldier crept up on them and aimed fire. He and two colleagues (Bradley and Barratt) decided to attempt an escape. They ran through the forest and up the mountain, ignoring the German orders to stop or be fired on. Bradley was killed. King-Salter and Barratt survived. On 24 April, they made it across the mountain ridge as the battle for Tretton took place below. They stumbled across a shed in which ten British soldiers and two officers were sheltering. Over the next two days, their numbers grew to ten officers and fifty other ranks. They had lost their rifles and were exhausted from lack of food and sleep.[7]

As the battle raged below, King-Salter and Barratt climbed further up the mountain and found an empty hotel they could use as billets. On 25/26 April, a young Norwegian man arrived there at night on skis, carrying despatches and offered to guide King-Salter and Barratt over the mountains. The following day, they reached a point above Ringabue, but would be seen if they advanced. The guide left them at this point. They waited until nightfall, acquiring food from various small farms. On 27 April 1940, King-Salter ran into German soldiers and was shot at eight times as he tried to escape, including in the foot. The Germans left, returning later to bandage his wounds. He was taken to a civilian hospital in Littlehammer where, due to the severity of his wounds, he was given an artificial leg and recuperated for six months. In November 1940, he was transferred to Germany. King-Salter eventually made it back to England and became secretary to the Joint Intelligence Committee.[8]

EUROPE UNDER OCCUPATION

Lightning War

On 10 May 1940 Hitler ordered his troops over the border into Holland, Belgium, Luxemburg and France in the blitzkrieg or 'lightning war'. For the second time in just twenty-one years, Germany occupied Belgium, France and Luxemburg. The MI9 war diary noted that the occupation caused 'considerable work for MI9', and all Whitsun leave was cancelled for its personnel.[9]

The RAF was soon flying sorties over enemy occupied territory and fighting in the Battle of Britain. MI9 told them that if shot down, 95 per cent of inhabitants in occupied Western Europe were believed to be sympathetic towards British escapers and evaders.[10] The German occupation was resented and the German aggression and occupation of the First World War were still well within living memory. Europe bore deep psychological and physical scars from a world war that had arguably been the bloodiest in European history thus far.

After Hitler's invasion of May 1940, MI9 escalated arrangements for the reception and special interrogation of enemy POWs at its facilities at Trent Park in north London. British forces sustained heavy casualties in the fighting around Le Paradis and Lestrem (the Pas-de-Calais region in northern France) as they tried to hold back German troops.[11] The German army advanced and the order was given for British forces to retreat and evacuate from the beaches of Dunkirk. Veteran Bill Howard was there at the time with the Auxiliary Military Pioneer Corps in support of the British Expeditionary Force. As his company evacuated from the beach at St Malo, the local French people spat at them in anger at being deserted but, as he recalled: 'We promised them that we live to fight another day and we will be back to liberate you.'[12]

At the time of the evacuation, Clayton Hutton entered one of the offices of an MI9 colleague to find him moving tiny Union Jack flags on a map on the wall. The flags were clustered in a small area near the coast around Dunkirk.

'It's as good as over,' the unnamed officer said to Clayton Hutton. 'The whole of the BEF is boxed in around Dunkirk. If we don't get them out, there will be more prisoners than you can cope with Clutty. All the maps and compasses in the world won't help now. These poor fellows want boats.'[13]

Clayton Hutton turned to the design of escape packs for airmen. These would prove essential alongside the miniature compasses, maps and saws as survival kits. He faced a number of difficulties in packing all the necessary items neatly into a single tin or box small enough to fit in the breast pocket of a uniform. He chose a 'flat fifty' cigarette tin, but acquiring thousands of these proved a challenge. He travelled to tobacco manufacturers W.D. & H.O. Wills of Bristol, finding from experience that a personal visit had a better success rate than a phone call. The firm was unable to supply the volume of around 20,000 empty tins that he needed. In a moment of quick thinking, Clayton Hutton purchased 20,000 full cigarette tins, knowing that he could easily shift the cigarettes and cover the cost of his acquisitions.[14] Back in London, he had to work out a way to pack the tins to maximum effect and use every millimetre of space. He sat at his desk with numerous items scattered across it, until each packed tin contained 24 tablets of malted milk sweets, a pack of chewing gum, a bar of peanut-blended food, 6 acid drops, a paper map of Germany and northern France, a bar of chocolate, a roll of adhesive tape, packet of matches, miniature saw, compass (a magnetised razor), a length of thread and 10 Benzedrine tablets to give energy.[15] It was Johnny Evans who noticed the absence of one essential item – a water bottle. Clayton Hutton tipped out the contents and started again. He set to the design of Ration Pack version 2, including in it a rubber bottle and 24 water purifying tablets. The escape box became one of the chief successes of the gadget department of MI9 and was issued to every airman, with £12 in cash in the relevant currency of a country over which they might be shot down. Cash enabled a pilot or aircrew to purchase items, bribe local people or buy train tickets.

Clayton Hutton was not satisfied with his early versions of the escape box. It needed to be sealed and watertight in case an airman bailed out over the sea, otherwise the escape pack would be ruined as seawater seeped in. He visited Halex Ltd, the firm that manufactured toothbrushes, and with their cooperation the escape tin itself was modified. Cigarette tins were changed in favour of a plastic cigar-case, manufactured by Halex Ltd, which could be carried in the outer pocket of battledress trousers. It was durable, transparent and watertight.

Clayton Hutton also foresaw that rubber would be in short supply as the war progressed and asked Halex Ltd to manufacture a plastic bottle with a shallow neck and screw stopper that did not require any sealant. It was possible to fit a tiny compass inside the transparent stopper. Clayton Hutton still struggled with the Treasury over the bills that he was submitting for reimbursement:

> There were days when the Treasury's cheese-paring attitude almost drove me to revolt. Time and again I had to abandon some vital project to answer letters from civil servants whose imbecile queries suggested that the writers had not yet realised that a state of emergency existed. During those dark days when German bombs and incendiaries were raining down on London, these blinkered pen-pushers were quibbling over pennies and halfpennies.[16]

His sense of frustration can be heard here and he had a valid point. It would have been more prudent for MI9 to allocate him a separate budget with a degree of freedom within that, but the official files do not elaborate on this kind of detail or discussion. Nor is it possible to tell how much of the work of MI9, if anything, was known to Treasury officials, while the urgency of his job was even less understood. Clayton Hutton has articulated a stereotypical bureaucratic view of the men in Whitehall who appeared to be divorced from the reality and urgency of war.

As he continued to improve his gadgets for MI9, news came on 10 June 1940 that Italy had entered the war on the side of Germany.[17] The MI9 war diary noted: 'The declaration of war by Italy has largely been anticipated.'[18] And Allied troops were still being evacuated from the beaches of Dunkirk as German forces marched on Paris and occupied it on 14 June. MI9's immediate priority was to keep up the flow of escape aids into POW camps and establish how many British personnel had been captured during the German advance. By the end of June 1940, an estimated 15 to 20 British personnel had success-fully managed to escape by their own means and arrived back in Britain where they were debriefed by MI9.[19]

One prominent army officer in France at this time was the Duke of Windsor, who as Edward VIII had abdicated the throne in 1936 to marry American divorcee Wallis Simpson. He was carrying out duties in northern France attached to No.1 Military Mission, in the rank of major general, and under the command of General Howard-Vyse.[20] He had been there, with the Duchess of Windsor, since his posting at the end of September 1939. The purpose of No.1 Military Mission was liaison between General Ironside (the Chief of Imperial General Staff in London) and General Gamelin (the French commander at Vincennes).[21] The Duke had undertaken three missions during 1939 and 1940 to inspect French troops in key areas; however, the British army was not permitted to inspect French defences against a German invasion although some reassurance about preparations was necessary. The French permitted the Duke of Windsor, as a prominent figure and one of the royal family, to honour them by inspecting French troops. It provided the Duke with an opportunity to note the situation of French defences in the region. He reported back to the British Military Mission that the defences would be totally insufficient against a German invasion.[22] When Hitler invaded France, the Windsors were at risk and escaped south to Nice where the British consul-general, Major Hugh Dodds, advised them to leave France urgently. Dodds accompanied them as far as Perpignan where they crossed the Spanish border at the same point where escapers and evaders would cross throughout the war. The following month, in June 1940, they were helped out of Spain to Lisbon by Arthur Dean, the British vice consul at Bilbao who soon became an instrumental figure for escape lines to that region.[23]

Dunkirk Evacuation

The mass evacuation from the beaches of northern France in late May and early June 1940 has been hailed historically as a triumph. The rescue of 300,000 Allied troops by British ships and small fishing vessels that sailed across the English Channel to Dunkirk has become legendary. However, mention is not often made of the fact that 2,000 wounded British and Commonwealth soldiers had to be left behind because there was no room for them on the evacuating vessels, and an estimated 50,000 British soldiers were taken prisoners of war by the Germans during the fighting in northern France, with another 5,000 in hiding or trapped behind enemy lines.[24]

Soldiers hiding in France or Belgium did try to escape, either by heading across France to the English Channel, or by going south to Vichy France (the unoccupied southern zone of France) and out via the port of Marseille. Although they could face arrest by the Vichy police, they were in fact less likely to be sent back over the border to the German authorities. Other escapers and evaders tried routes via neutral Switzerland where they were helped by the British military attaché at Berne, Lieutenant Colonel Henry Cartwright MC, himself an escaper. Cartwright questioned them on behalf of MI9 to establish how they had escaped and which routes they had used, and he liaised with his counterparts in Madrid and Lisbon to facilitate their repatriation via Spain, Portugal and Gibraltar.[25]

British personnel captured in France were usually transferred to POW camps in Germany and as the MI9 official history noted, 'We were in the unenviable position of having no secret means of communication arranged with any of them [POWs].'[26] That would soon change. From Germany, any attempted escapes would be trickier, but there were successes as immortalised and glamorized in famous films like *Escape from Colditz* (Colditz Castle, near Leipzig) and *The Great Escape* (Stalag Luft III, near Sagan). The British prisoners had a major advantage over POWs of European countries – Britain was not under occupation and therefore the Germans could not take out reprisals against their families and friends if the British POWs were disruptive in the camps or attempted escape. In Nazi-occupied Europe, those caught aiding Allied airmen and soldiers endangered not only their own lives but those of their entire family.

Neave summed up the situation aptly: 'The real risks were not taken in London, but in Marseille, Brussels and Paris.'[27] It was the people working for the MI9 escape lines in enemy-occupied countries whose lives were in most danger; they were working for an organisation that was supporting them with money, supplies and agents, but its name was unknown to them.[28] The preservation of this secret service for escape and evasion relied on the absolute secrecy of its identity.

Brigadier Dudley Clarke, a pioneer of various deceptions in the Second World War, had a high regard for the importance of this work when he wrote: 'In war it is given to few soldiers to be able to serve simultaneously the causes of humanity and country. All who work for MI9 have this special privilege, and few calls can have more appeal than that to rescue those whom the Fortunes of war have abandoned to the enemy.'[29]

As the British Expeditionary Force retreated, MI9 had no news of another key British official, Lieutenant Colonel F.A. Blake, the British military attaché at Brussels, who was trapped behind enemy lines in Belgium.[30] Like King-Salter, Blake eventually came out of occupied Europe on his own and without the aid of MI9 because escape lines had not yet been established. When he finally got back to Britain, he was interrogated by MI9, recounting his difficult escape amidst confusion as thousands of people tried to flee the occupying armies.[31]

When German forces overran Belgium on 10 May 1940, the Belgian government immediately removed to Ostend; six days later it headed for the French port of Le Havre, along with the British and French embassies. Amongst them were Lieutenant Colonel Blake and Sir Lancelot Oliphant (the British ambassador to Belgium). The journey to Le Havre failed because the Germans held all the Somme bridgeheads. They turned back and arrived at Fort Mahon on the coast of the English Channel in the Somme region. Blake and Oliphant obtained provisions from a farmhouse and hid for three days in the sand hills around Fort Mahon, helped by a Belgian man known only as Gerard. When Blake decided to try an escape Gerard brought him papers and civilian clothes (a peasant's blue cotton jacket and brown corduroy trousers) and then sheltered him in an empty house.

On 26 May 1940, the Germans arrived at the house and arrested Blake, who claimed he was a fifty-one-year-old peasant from Dunkirk who had lost his papers in the chaos of the German advance. Although the Germans believed his story, they escorted him 30 miles to a POW camp.[32] At dawn on 28 May, the British prisoners were formed into a long column and marched to Frévent.

Blake later recalled: 'The German escorts behaved like bullies. When French civilians came out with pails of water and milk to drink, the Germans threatened to shoot any person helping the British prisoners.'[33]

On reaching the town of Cambrai, Blake was unexpectedly set free with no explanation. He crossed enemy territory, evading recapture and travelled via Paris, then south to reach Marseille in January 1941. In March 1941, he arrived in Oran, then Tangier where he stayed until October 1941, and finally to Gibraltar. From Gibraltar, he was flown back to England. Blake brought useful intelligence back to MI9 about the port of Oran, ships, armed trawlers and destroyers and how the Germans quite openly talked about burning French towns. He was able to report that the Germans had ordered the construction of a thousand barges (of iron and concrete) at Nantes for a future invasion of England. He told MI9:

> Anti-German by tradition, they [the French] know that their salvation lies in a British victory . . . They look forward to the day when the British army returns to the continent, and large numbers of Frenchmen are busily secreting war material for the day when they hope to assist in the annihilation of the common enemy.[34]

This information proved valuable because it indicated to MI9 that the French people were willing to help the Allies from within enemy territory. MI9 could not smuggle escapers and evaders out of Europe without the aid of French, Dutch and Belgian helpers, guides and couriers. The major escape lines would all cross France, often across hundreds of miles. German patrols were on alert for people trying to leave their territory by short routes and the ports. Contrary to logical thinking, it was safer to bring evaders right across enemy territory, with multiple ways of hiding them and possible variations in that route, than over the shorter distances to a port or border.

These were dark days for the people of occupied Europe who waited on London as they tuned in their radios every evening at 2100 hours to listen to the BBC news. The channel had been banned by the Nazis and people risked being arrested if discovered. They waited for the familiar Beethoven's Fifth Symphony and the notes that represented the Morse code 'V for Victory', which preceded 'Ici Londres' (This is London), followed by personal messages. These messages appeared meaningless but they were coded with phrases for the Resistance movement about the arrival of fresh supplies by parachute, an agent drop or other instructions. These BBC broadcasts lifted morale during occupation.

British Naval Liaison

Diplomatic staff and the British Naval Liaison team were trapped behind enemy lines and had to evacuate too. Amongst them was Lieutenant Commander S.M. Mackenzie, who would become instrumental in helping MI9 with sea evacuations later in the war. He had volunteered for the Royal Navy and undergone training at various land bases from the spring of 1939.[35] In October 1939, he was interviewed by Naval Intelligence Division and sent to France, attached to the British Naval Liaison staff. German U-boats were already targeting British shipping and supplies, and it was believed the best way to combat this was through close liaison between the British and French navies. In November 1939 the French commander in chief, Admiral Darlan, moved his headquarters from Paris to the village of Maintenon, a few miles from Chartres. The British Naval Liaison staff who had been based at the British embassy in Paris moved to Maintenon too, where Mackenzie joined them, along with Lieutenant Patrick (Pat) Whinney (RNVR), two retired Royal Marine colour sergeants (Stapleton and Miller) and Charles Morgan (a bestselling English author during the 1930s and '40s). They were billeted in a villa a short distance from Admiral Darlan's headquarters. Mackenzie and Whinney would go on to play a central role in setting up the sea evacuations of escapers and evaders for MI9.

Pat Whinney and Mackenzie became good friends during the Second World War through their naval intelligence service.[36] Their work consisted of deciphering daily messages, sent from the Admiralty by teleprinter, which were then passed on to the French naval section to which they were attached at

Maintenon. An occasional visitor there was Ian Fleming of Naval Intelligence who, according to Mackenzie, 'had a very lively mind'.[37]

After the German invasion, the office at Maintenon held out until 9 June 1940. Three days later the Germans reached Mantes where the bridge over the river Seine was still undamaged. The British Naval Liaison office closed its doors and its personnel joined the queues of refugees trying to flee to the south of France. They arrived at the port of Bordeaux on 16 June where Mackenzie and diplomatic staff helped with the evacuation of British refugees onto ships. The following day, on 17 June, Ian Fleming arrived;[38] a concern that the French fleet might fall into German hands and be used against Britain may have been the reason for his presence. On 18 June, HMS *Berkeley* docked at Bordeaux with A.V. Alexander (the First Lord of the Admiralty) and Admiral Sir Dudley Pound (First Sea Lord) aboard. They made a final attempt to persuade the French fleet to surrender and sail for England. Their mission failed and this led to the decision by the new British Prime Minister Winston Churchill to order the sinking of the French fleet and with it the loss of lives of the sailors on board. Such decisions in a time of war can be controversial by modern day analysis, but it was a necessary strategic decision because without it the French fleet would have been used by the German navy against Britain.

Mackenzie and Whinney moved with consulate staff to Bayonne and then Saint-Jean-de-Luz. They spent three days trying to evacuate streams of people using sardine boats to take them out to larger ships waiting in the bay, having bribed the commander of the sardine fleet. The evacuation included King Zog of Albania who could be seen standing on the tiny quayside with his body-guards and £10 million in gold bars in boxes piled up on the jetty. The boxes of gold bars were guarded by his six sisters in battledress and armed with submachine guns.

Mackenzie and Whinney evacuated on 25 June aboard a Canadian destroyer, HMS *Restigouche*, and landed at Plymouth in Devon the following day. They took the night train to London; on board were King Zog and his entourage.

On their return to England, the two men were debriefed by Admiral Godfrey, head of Naval Intelligence, and were then promptly passed back to

Fleming. They would soon be in charge of new flotillas for the first sea evacuations, discussed in a later chapter.

Crockatt's nascent organisation was facing its first major challenge. With so many British soldiers behind enemy lines or in German POW camps, how were they to evade capture and be smuggled out of Nazi-occupied Europe?

The scale of MI9's role was about to accelerate and provide much of the ethos, help and encouragement for Allied escapers and evaders to make it back to Britain. By the end of July 1940, Crockatt was given authority by the Director of Military Intelligence to draw up to £5,000 worth of various foreign currencies 'for the use by air crews engaged in operations which may render them liable to capture'.[39] Now he had the resources but no formal escape networks across Europe. Creating escape lines by land and sea became the immediate priority for MI9.

3
GATEWAY TO FREEDOM

Neutral Spain and Portugal were to be key to freedom for many escapers and evaders with the establishment of the first formal MI9 escape line via Gibraltar in the summer of 1940. Claude Dansey offered to help MI9 on the escape lines in a gesture that was motivated by his need to control them. In 1940, MI9 was ill equipped to coordinate and manage escape lines on its own. Dansey's offer to take charge ensured that MI6 ultimately controlled all the escape lines out of Western Europe, whether those of MI9 or MI6. He was determined to avoid any interference from MI9 or SOE in the Secret Intelligence Service (SIS) (MI6) networks in Europe. This inevitably led to tensions between MI6 and SOE. It was said that Dansey had disliked SOE since its inception because 'it was not responsible to MI6 and he considered its personnel to be rank amateurs in cloak and dagger work'.[1] It was said that he 'recoiled in horror' when Churchill sanctioned the formation of SOE.[2]

Indeed, Dansey made no secret of his hatred of SOE, an independent organisation over which neither he nor MI6 had any control. The use of the word hatred is correct in the context here. Given that Dansey ran the MI9 and MI6 escape lines, it was within his power to keep both of these organisations of military intelligence away from SOE to allow for the survival of the others if one was compromised. It was a prudent decision for the organisations not to mix given that many of the SOE agents dropped into France were compromised, tortured and met their deaths.

Dansey also made his dislike of engaging female agents very clear. From his personal view 'they simply are not trustworthy'.[3] These strong prejudices did not ultimately deter MI9 from engaging female agents, with Dansey's reluctant agreement.

In mid-July 1940, Dansey met Donald Darling in a small sitting room at St James's Street and came straight to the point. He wanted him to set up an escape route between Marseille and the Iberian Peninsula that could also be used to send intelligence back to England.[4] Darling was himself an escaper and fluent in French and Spanish. He had been in Spain during the Spanish Civil War (1936–1939) and had knowledge of the Franco-Spanish frontier from Andorra to Port Bou. Dansey explained that after the fall of France and the Dunkirk evacuation, England had lost all communication with Western Europe, with no links by sea, radio, air or land. Darling could not be based in Spain because the Spanish authorities were suspicious of foreigners and their motives for being in the country, nor could he risk being on a constant watch-list of the local police, so Dansey sent him to Portugal, basing him in Lisbon where he had the support of the British ambassador, Sir Walford Selby. Darling arrived in Lisbon under cover of being the vice consul and was given the codename 'Sunday'. His handler was '4Z', whose real identity still remains a mystery.[5]

Darling initially contacted local properties and farms along the foothills of the Spanish Pyrenees to gain support for his secret route, as well as refugees living there having fled from the Spanish Fascist leader Franco. He also worked with a group of scouts who had formed mountain patrols to hold expeditionary competitions and whose knowledge of the region was invaluable.[6]

News began to reach MI9 that British escapers were trapped on the Franco-Spanish frontier, while some had been interned by the Spanish authorities in a camp at Miranda del Ebro, 50 miles from the British Consulate in Bilbao,[7] and others were at ports in the south of France, unable to leave because of the lack of space on the ships. On 6 August 1940, Crockatt met Stewart Menzies (the new head of MI6) in London to address the problem, with a view to gaining Menzies' cooperation in 'effecting the exit from France of a number of escaped British personnel known to be on the Franco-Spanish frontier'.[8] They discussed mutual help for an escape route from Marseille to Spain, run by Darling, whose first task was to make contact with an escaper based in Marseille called Captain Ian Garrow.

Ian Garrow

Ian Garrow of the Seaforth Highlanders became the first chief of the escape organisation in the south of France. His decision to stay in France in 1940 rather than escape was later described as 'in itself heroic'.[9] This is true – Garrow could have taken a selfish approach of self-preservation and secured his own safety, but he did not. He chose to stay and set up an escape line to help others, which he knew would place him at personal risk of arrest by the authorities.

Aged in his early twenties, Garrow had survived action at St Valery and evaded capture after Dunkirk. He headed south to Vichy France and arrived in Marseille to find many other British evaders in hiding. Garrow established safe houses for soldiers as they awaited evacuation: one such safe house was established at the home of Louis and Renée Nouveau at Vieux Port;[10] another was the apartment of Dr Georges Rodocanachi and his wife. Of Greek parentage, born in Liverpool, England,[11] Rodocanachi recruited his nephew, Georges Zariffi, as a trusted courier and escort to take evaders from Toulouse and Marseille to the crossing points of the Pyrenees. Donkey routes were often used, which necessitated paying shepherds and guides to take groups across the mountains, for they were not prepared to undertake risks for the Allies without payment. MI9 would source funds for them and arrange for payment via Darling. Other guides took escapers and agents in groups of six to twelve over the Pyrenees. Hundreds trekked on foot through the difficult terrain across the Pyrenees to Bilboa or Barcelona.[12] Once in Spain, escapers took a train to the British Consulate in Barcelona or Madrid where they were interrogated and a file created for MI9 about their escape or evasion.[13]

At Madrid, the interrogation was held by 'Monday', whose real name was Sir Michael Creswell.[14] In the 1930s, Creswell had worked as head of the Passport Office in London and MI9 now appointed him to ferry escapers, evaders and refugees after their escape over the Pyrenees and to Gibraltar.

Brigitte d'Oultremont, whose father Georges worked for the Comet Line, recalls how Creswell 'loved cars and would drive to the border to meet escapers and evaders, then take them from Madrid to Gibraltar'.[15]

Garrow set in place an industry of local people forging identity cards and papers, and issuing civilian clothing for escapers and evaders. He worked with Presbyterian pastor Revd Donald Caskie on getting men out of Vichy France. Caskie had been forced to flee his church in the Rue Bayard, Paris as German forces entered the city on 14 June 1940.[16] He arrived in Marseille and settled in the old Seamen's Mission at 46 Rue de Forbin and aided Garrow by hiding British soldiers in the cellar of the mission. Caskie believed it was his responsibility to help them and he frequently found himself trying to outmanoeuvre the Vichy police or Gestapo by moving the evaders: 'Detectives used to raid the Mission in Marseille every day in search of soldiers, sailors and airmen who might be in hiding there. Sometimes the raids were perfunctory; but at other times they were made in force.'[17]

When the Vichy authorities began to round up British personnel and intern them in Fort St Jean (Marseille), Caskie ensured they had an evening meal at the mission during the hours that they were allowed out of the fort and provided fresh clothes for them. He was also aware that their relatives would have received notification that the men were 'missing'. He sent a telegram to the Church of Scotland requesting that the Church notify the relatives and the War Office that the men were safe.

Garrow had no radio communication with MI9 back in England, which proved a major challenge. He had to rely on couriers from Barcelona and Gibraltar and it could take a fortnight to receive answers to his questions.

Helping Garrow and Caskie for a short time was Reg West, one of only six survivors of the Wormhoud Massacre.[18] The massacre occurred on 28 May 1940 when eighty British soldiers from the 2nd Battalion Royal Warwickshire Regiment, Cheshire Regiment and Royal Artillery were shot in cold blood after surrendering near the French village of Wormhoud.[19] The orders had been given by SS commander General Sepp Dietrich and constituted a war crime, for which he later faced justice.[20] Having survived, West evaded capture and headed for Marseille from where he was eventually evacuated and returned to England.

By the end of August 1940, the total number of British POWs in enemy hands was estimated at 34,000.[21] Around 5,000 personnel were still believed to be trapped in the south of France, awaiting evacuation and with no obvious means of swiftly getting them out of the country.[22] But Darling was about to cross paths with an American who would help him.

Varian Fry

Aged thirty-two, Varian Fry was a Harvard-educated, American editor for Headline Books who had been sent to Marseille by Eleanor Roosevelt, wife of the US president, on a temporary four-week mission to rescue two hundred Jews on her Special List.[23] The Special List was compiled of Jewish intellectuals, artists and anti-fascists whose lives were in danger under the Nazi regime. Fry had visited Nazi Germany in 1935 and witnessed the Stormtroopers beating Jews on the streets of Berlin. It had affected him deeply. On return to America he wrote articles for the *New York Times* on the fate of Europe's Jews and the impending Holocaust. When Eleanor Roosevelt was looking for someone to undertake her special mission, Fry volunteered to go under the auspices of the American Rescue Committee, New York. With cash to finance his mission, hidden by strapping $3,000 to his leg, Fry flew via Lisbon and arrived in Marseille on 15 August 1940. He discovered that there were thousands of Jews in the area who were not on Eleanor Roosevelt's Special List – all had fled the Nazi regime and were seeking ways to escape to Britain, America, Cuba, Canada or Mexico.[24]

With insufficient resources to help them, but profoundly moved by their plight, Fry explored secret escape routes across the Pyrenees. He also opened a refugee crisis centre under the guise of helping people with food, clothing and water;[25] in reality, he was embarking on a mission to smuggle them out of Vichy France by coordinating papers and rescue plans and by enlisting the help of local people who could forge papers and passes. Instead of a four-week mission, his work turned into a major humanitarian effort that would last over twelve months. Despite continued appeals to the American Consulate in Marseille, his own country refused to hand over visas for the Jewish refugees.[26] The American government had refused to support activities that evaded the laws of the country (Vichy France) with which the United States had friendly relations.[27]

By the end of August 1940, Fry was running out of money and cabled the American Rescue Committee in New York for more. He received a small sum, but the exchange rate was so poor that he turned to trading on the black market.

The following month, he discovered that 30,000 German-speaking refugees were hiding in the south of France. The Vichy government had already rounded up many of them and begun to intern them in camps. Amongst those in hiding were a refugee anti-Fascist couple, Heinrich and Claire Ehrmann, who were on Eleanor Roosevelt's original list, but the Nazi authorities had forbidden the Vichy government to issue visas for them. Fry explored a route over the Pyrenees as the only way to get them out of danger. On the border town of Banyul-sur-Mer, the local mayor was sympathetic to the plight of refugees and alerted Fry to an unknown hiking route through the Pyrenees. This discovery was to prove crucial for his future rescue work. The Ehrmanns succeeded in getting across the Pyrenees into Spain and on to Lisbon, from where they took a flight to America. They despatched a copy of their hiking map to Fry so he could help others.

On 16 September 1940, another group of refugees made the difficult trek by foot through the Pyrenees with one of Fry's hired guides. Amongst them were the novelist and poet Franz Werfel and his wife, and novelist Heinrich Mann and his wife Nellie.[28] Fry travelled into Spain separately with their luggage and was reunited with them once they were over the border. From there, he accompanied them to safety in Lisbon where they took flights back to America. This particular journey was to prove a turning point for Fry because he travelled on to the British embassy in Madrid. He reasoned that if his own country would not help him with the refugees who were not on Eleanor Roosevelt's Special List, then maybe the British would. In Madrid he met Major Torr, little realising that he was MI6's man in Madrid,[29] only to find Torr was not convinced by his rescue plans and he left empty-handed.

Not one to give up, Fry returned to the embassy two days later and this time was ushered in to see the British ambassador, Sir Samuel Hoare.[30] Hoare had been trying to work through a crisis of his own – the estimated 5,000 British soldiers who were trapped in France after failing to evacuate at Dunkirk. He had been unable to secure fishing vessels to get them out.[31] Hoare realised that Fry had all the contacts MI6 needed in the south of France, with a ready network of forgers, helpers, secret escape routes and connections with local fishermen. He proposed a deal to Fry: if Fry could help British soldiers by becoming a temporary agent of MI6, he would be paid $10,000 for his Jewish relief fund thus solving his funding shortage.[32] The work would require Fry to use his black market contacts to secure routes out of France for the British soldiers. Fry agreed, but on the understanding that his activities for MI6 were not made known to the US government. Now Fry had unexpectedly entered the world of espionage: 'I had come to the embassy to try to get the British to send ships from Barcelona to pick up men and take them to Gibraltar. I hadn't anticipated becoming a British agent myself.'[33]

The personal risks were high – he was not only smuggling Jews and anti-fascists out of Vichy France, but working for British intelligence as an agent.

Wilton Park

On 13 September 1940 an enemy bomb fell on the Metropole Building in London and set a corner of the building on fire.[34] Although the damage was small and there was no loss of life, it was a reminder to Crockatt that another direct hit on the building could kill his entire staff. He took the decision to move MI9's headquarters into the countryside and searched for a suitable site. By October 1940 he was able to requisition the estate of Wilton Park at Beaconsfield in Buckinghamshire.[35] The new headquarters became known as Camp 20 and was requisitioned from Colonel William Baring Du Pre.

Wilton Park dated from the thirteenth century and once belonged to the Whelton family. During the Georgian era, it had been purchased by the Du Pre family after the success of Josias Du Pre's profitable trading from the East India

Company. He commissioned the building of a large Palladian house, dubbed the White House for the colour of the stone. Located approximately 20 miles from London, the site was still within easy reach of the capital for meetings, and convenient for Crockatt who lived at Ashley Green a few miles away. The new location gave Crockatt an opportunity to operate his secret organisation away from interference by Whitehall and somewhere his staff could try out new unorthodox methods.[36] This was particularly relevant for Clayton Hutton whose experimental work with strange devices was best kept out of view so he could quietly develop them without questions or restrictions from Whitehall. He moved to a hideout bunker in a field at Wilton Park and developed his escape aids uninterrupted:

> He found a private hideout not far away on the edge of a disused graveyard, where he supposed – correctly – that none of the locals would care to come and find out what he was experimenting with late at night. He pursued various hobbies of his own, designing anti-tank grenades and a modern version of the lethal jungle blowpipe, as well as improving the escape kits he provided for MI9.[37]

Major L. Walton was appointed camp commandant at Wilton Park.[38] Crockatt's expanding staff soon outgrew the accommodation at the White House and construction began at the far end of the site of a purpose-built complex known as Shean Block.[39] For the duration of the war, Camp 20 at Wilton Park became MI9's administrative hub for clandestine operations, coordinating and dispatching the special parcels and escape gadgets to Allied personnel, wherever these items were needed in POW camps.

Liaison continued with MI6 and was reported to be 'producing satisfactory results, even if hampered sometimes by red tape. Success achieved in communicating in code with POWs in Germany.'[40] Letters received from POWs in Germany showed high morale and mentioned attempted escapes.[41]

Twenty-one-year-old Catherine Townshend (later Jestin) worked at Wilton Park and recalled meeting many of the escapers after their arrival there for debriefing.[42] Their escapades often circulated around the staff at Camp 20 before their arrival, giving MI9's staff an insight into the intensity of a prisoner's escape: from the detailed planning in a German POW camp, to the difficulties of excavating an escape tunnel and removal of the earth in pockets or trousers, to scaling a high wall, making German uniforms and forging identity cards and documents, or having to kill a guard with a knife to get out of the camp. Townshend recalled one escape story which highlighted for her the sheer ingenuity of the British prisoners:

> [The escapers] painted a white line down the centre of the road in the encampment, and when the main gates were reached, calmly continued past the German sentries who jeered at the British on their hands and knees. Without being challenged, the prisoners carried on slowly and painstakingly painting for hours along a straight stretch until round a bend, out of sight, they were able to drop their brushes and run.[43]

Richard Broad, a subaltern in the 51st Highland Division, evaded capture after his regiment surrendered at St Valery in June 1940. He took seven soldiers, all privates, and successfully got them all back to Scotland – after which he was playfully nicknamed 'Snow White and the Seven Dwarfs'.[44]

Some escapers found their own routes out without the help of MI9. Townshend wrote: 'Many of the bravest escapees were not tall, handsome and swashbuckling, but unassuming soldiers and airmen who insisted that they had done no more than their duty. In fact, they represented the best of courage, resourcefulness and humility.'[45] For many of these men it was about quiet courage and an unquestioned commitment to duty rather than a romantic view of themselves as heroes.

In December 1940, MI9 received its first official coded letter from an RAF prisoner of war, establishing a secret means of communication with Stalag Luft III in Upper Silesia – the camp where several attempts would be made to dig escape tunnels, and later immortalised in the film *The Great Escape*.[46] That same month saw the repatriation of fifty-five escapers via Gibraltar, including the first British prisoner of war to escape from a POW camp in Germany, Private Coe of the Army Dental Corps. Escapers and evaders were sometimes interviewed by representatives of three branches of military intelligence – MI5, MI6 and MI9 – because these interrogations could provide intelligence from enemy territory as well as helpful escape information.[47] They gave British intelligence information on enemy troop movements, airfields, weapons and other details about daily life behind enemy lines, all of which was useful in gaining a picture of the enemy's fighting capability and morale.[48]

Marseille

By October 1940 Varian Fry's funds had dwindled. He cabled New York for more money but it was not forthcoming. The Vichy government was beginning to get suspicious of him and increasingly his network faced restrictions. Fry sought to establish sea routes for escapes at night and to bribe trawler men to help him. It was a tricky business because they took his money in advance but did not help his refugees. Fry was lucky to gain some temporary financial support from an American heiress who was travelling in the region, but that is another story.[49] His hopes for another $10,000 rested largely on the British who still had servicemen to evacuate from France, but on 23 November 1940, Sir Samuel Hoare sent a telegram to London stating that Fry had not received any money: 'A secret messenger tells me that he [Fry] has had several opportunities for evacuating more than 200 British officers by sea but that he has no money at his disposal. I believe that we have lost, and are losing, many excellent chances of evacuating British personnel.'[50] This was followed by another cypher to Sir Alexander Cadogan at the Foreign Office:

Varian Fry has come with an urgent message from 120 British officers interned in Marseille, imploring us to help their escape. He has already succeeded in getting many Jews and intellectuals out of German hands. He has now offered his immediate help in getting our officers out.[51]

These cyphers appear to have gone astray in London.[52] Hoare sent another message on 9 December and implored Cadogan 'unless funds are immediately forthcoming, the organisation will break down'. Fry had been travelling back and forth to Madrid, but had to return to Marseille. Hoare wrote in his cypher: 'as there may be no further means of communicating with him [Fry] for some time, I have taken upon myself the responsibility of saying that we will back him up to this amount'.[53]

Without authorisation from London, Hoare proceeded to guarantee the sum of $10,000 for Fry. A week later, Hoare received formal confirmation that the War Office and C (head of MI6) wished him to proceed with Fry's scheme to evacuate British personnel.[54] Crockatt of MI9 was even prepared to advance $50,000 in cash, but the War Office was not prepared to release that amount until they had seen the results of Fry's work. After a number of delays, the sum of $10,000 was sent for his rescue work as confirmed by the Foreign Office.[55] There was another problem emerging for Fry and his British handlers. The United States Consul General at Marseille, Mr Hurley, on instruction from the US government, refused to renew Fry's visa, and the US State Department was showing 'persistent interest in payments being made to Revd Caskie and Fry'.[56]

The mission was in danger of collapse, this time due to US government policy: 'We learn that United States Consulate at Marseille and United States Embassy at Vichy have refused to renew Mr Fry's passport and Mr Fry has asked that we should intervene on his behalf. We should like to do so if you have no objection.'[57]

A cypher message sent on 4 March 1941 to Sir Samuel Hoare (Madrid) from the Foreign Office recognised that Fry was being 'extremely useful in difficult circumstances and he should not be left short of funds'.[58] Fry estimated that there were approximately 1,200 British military personnel in France and he could get all of them out. Hoare's estimate was higher, at 5,000 men.[59] A further $10,000 was authorised for Fry, along with 2.5 million francs for smuggling them out.[60]

Fry never knew that he was helping MI9 but these cypher communications demonstrate the difficulties facing the early escape line and also the commitment and lengths to which Military Intelligence and the British government were prepared to go to get British servicemen out of France.

By the spring of 1941, British military personnel were crossing into Spain at a faster rate than previously realised by MI9 or the War Office. And yet the whole scheme was in danger of collapse due to lack of funds at the Barcelona end.[61] Sir Harold Farquhar (Consul-General in Barcelona) reported that British soldiers were being brought to Spain by smugglers against promises that the smugglers would be paid but Farquhar was without any means to pay them. The escape line was 'in grave danger of breaking down at the Pyrenees end owing to lack of funds'.[62] Crockatt wrote to the Foreign Office:

> You will see that there is now a definite plan in operation for passing men from Occupied France into Unoccupied France, and for passing men from France into Spain. The former is being carried out by Fry, the latter by two British officers in conjunction with the Consul General in Barcelona.[63]

A discussion ensued about which department should fund the expenses of the Spanish end of the escape network. Peter Loxley, a senior official at the Foreign Office, discussed matters with Dansey and Crockatt;[64] the latter preferred the money be acquired on the black market at Lisbon and sent to Madrid and Barcelona. He impressed on the Foreign Office the importance of advancing 5 million francs, financed by MI6,[65] for the Consul-General in Barcelona.

In June 1941, the Vichy government threatened to expel Fry from the country. He was summoned to the American Consulate and told he must leave France. His government was refusing to renew his passport. The Vichy authorities were beginning to crack down on all attempts to help British personnel out of France and Fry was not the only casualty of this clampdown. The authorities then turned to Caskie and his work at the mission. That same month, Caskie was arrested by the Vichy police on charges of clandestine work and helping escapers. He appeared before a French Military Tribunal, was ordered to close the mission within ten days and leave the area.[66] Before he left for Grenoble in south-eastern France, he assisted all the men staying in the mission to success-fully escape over the Pyrenees. Once in Grenoble, he continued his work in helping British escapers. The university there, which proved to be pro-British, gave him an appointment as Professor of English providing a respectable cover for his ongoing activities with escapers.[67] Caskie acted as unofficial vice consul in the area and opened an office daily to give information and advice to British subjects. He continued to visit British prisoners in internment camps and was able to smuggle in identity passes for their escape.

Shortly after his arrival at Grenoble, Caskie was warned through the British Secret Intelligence Service that he was likely to be arrested: 'A woman came from Marseille and informed him that on the following Tuesday a party of detectives would be sent to fetch him. She advised him to cross the Swiss fron-tier at once.'[68] Caskie did not leave France. The unnamed woman was correct and he was arrested the following week and questioned by the police, but released with no charges made.

A few months later, in spite of all attempts to stay on in Marseille, Varian Fry flew back to the US and arrived on 2 November 1941. Deeply frustrated that Jews were still at risk in Europe, he threw himself into work to educate the American public about what was happening.[69] He remains the only US citizen to be honoured as a Righteous Gentile at Yad Vashem in Jerusalem.

With Fry's departure, Darling had lost a vital link in his escape line. Meanwhile, Caskie was permitted to visit British personnel interned at Saint-Hippolyte-du-Fort, near Nîmes where he took winter clothing and extra food given by the local French peasants and farmers. When the men were moved again, this time to Fort de la Revère above Monte Carlo, Caskie was able to use his pastoral role as a cleric to visit them, a role that enabled him to smuggle forged documents and passes to the men to aid escape.[70]

On 16 April 1943 in collusion with the Nazi regime, Italian forces moved over the border into Vichy France. Caskie was betrayed by one of his Italian guides and imprisoned in a villa near Nice where selected prisoners were regu-larly tortured.[71] He was subjected to months of solitary confinement and star-vation. On 5 June, he was transferred, in chains, to the fort at San Remo where he remained until the fall of Mussolini the following month.[72] Caskie was transferred to the 'house of torture' at Nice again, then handed to the Gestapo and transferred to Fresnes prison near Paris. On 26 November, he was brought to trial on charges of 'aiding and abetting in the escape of British soldiers and also with being in contact with the British Intelligence Service'.[73] Testimony was given against him by a Frenchman whom he had engaged as a guide across the Pyrenees. The unnamed witness claimed that Caskie worked for SIS and he had received an offer via the British ambassador, Sir Hoare, to contact Caskie if he ever wanted to work for SIS.

Caskie was sentenced to death at the trial and his life was only saved by the intervention of a German Lutheran chaplain, Pastor Peters, who pleaded for a pardon on Caskie's behalf. On 7 January 1944, Caskie was transferred from Fresnes prison to a civilian internment camp at St Denis until its liberation in the summer of 1944. Two months before the end of the war, the Foreign Office wrote to Colonel Rait at MI9 and recommended Caskie for an award for his work with escapers;[74] in June 1945 he was awarded an OBE.[75]

Jimmy Langley

One escaper who arrived in Marseille in early 1941 was Jimmy Langley.[76] He had joined the Coldstream Guards and in 1940 his regiment was posted to France, along the Brussels–Louvain road. On 28 May, it began to retreat back to Dunkirk for evacuation to England after the German occupation. Langley had witnessed the fierce dogfights over Dunkirk between the RAF and Luftwaffe, and been badly injured when a shell hit the roof of a cottage where his battalion was sheltering. They evacuated to the outskirts of Dunkirk and it was there that he was taken prisoner by the Germans. Having sustained wounds to the leg, left arm and head, Langley was soon moved to Zuydcoote, between Dunkirk and La Panne but when gangrene set in a British surgeon operated on Langley and amputated his left arm. In spite of everything Langley did not let these severe injuries affect his morale or the hope of an eventual escape. For him, the psychology was important – that a determined and healthy mind-set was more important for escape than strength of body.[77] A few days later, he was moved to a French convent near Roubaix that had been adapted by the German occupying forces to be a prison.

A week later, Langley was transferred to the University of Lille, which the Germans were using as a collecting centre for British POWs until they were well enough for transfer to POW camps in Germany. It was here that he met Airey Neave before Neave was transferred to the famous Colditz Castle in Germany. Both Langley and Neave would soon be central to MI9's history.

Just prior to Langley being moved from Lille to Germany, the German soldiers and guards had a cocktail party to drink all the alcohol, rather than leave it behind. Whilst the party was underway, Langley managed to escape via an unguarded porter's lodge. Once out of the camp, he was helped by Madame Caron of the Faculté Catholique who gave him a map of Lille and the address of a nearby safe house. Madame Caron had already sheltered a number of British escapers, including Captain Griffiths (South Wales Borderers) and Captain Robertson (Argyll and Sutherland Highlanders) the previous night. With the constant danger of discovery by German patrols and the difficulty of hiding three servicemen at one property, Langley was moved to a presbytery and sheltered by the village priest of Ascq. He remained in hiding there until he could take a train to Paris.

Langley was helped on the next stage of his escape by another French woman, Madame Veuve Samiez, who arranged false French identity papers. He eventually arrived in Marseille where he met Ian Garrow who engaged him as a courier to collect money from a rich source on the Riviera. It was now January 1941. During the hard winter conditions that made a crossing over the Pyrenees too difficult, time was spent planning Langley's exit from France and finally, with Garrow's help, he succeeded in returning to England in March 1941.[78]

As an escaper, the first priority for MI9 was to interrogate him and he was interviewed by Major de Bruyne at the Grand Central Hotel. With little communication between Garrow and London, Langley was able to update de Bruyne on the success and challenges for Garrow and the escape line in

Marseille. After the debriefing, he reported back to his regimental headquarters, only to be told that he was no longer fit for military service. It was perhaps not wholly unexpected. His commanding officer instructed him to report to the Savoy Hotel that afternoon for a meeting with a man with a red carnation. Langley had some inkling that it might be for some kind of intelligence work and indeed this first meeting with Claude Dansey was his introduction to MI6.

Langley was given the codename P15 and replaced the mysterious 4Z who had been Donald Darling's handler.[79] It was not immediately obvious to Langley why he had been sent to MI6, as he later commented: 'Major de Bruyne had said MI9 was responsible for helping POWs to escape and yet I was on loan from that organisation to Uncle Claude who seemed to be taking a very direct interest in evasion.'[80]

A few days later he met Crockatt, and as Langley recalled: 'His cheerful greeting, words of congratulations on getting back home, and his enquiry as to how I had got on with the old buzzard [Dansey] in London warmed my heart.'[81] Langley became 'the point of junction between MI6 and MI9 and was nominally on Crockatt's staff, but paid and commanded by MI6'.[82] Dansey made the position clear when he told him 'Whilst you will liaise with Colonel Crockatt on routine matters, you will not give him any detailed report of your activities without my agreement.'[83]

Langley arrived at MI9 at a time when the Pat Line had been penetrated by a traitor and betrayed. Dansey warned him to work slowly and methodically and not rush because it was going to be a long war and 'mistakes made now will not be easy to rectify'.[84] Working out of Broadway Buildings, Langley soon learned that MI6 wanted nothing to interfere with its own intelligence gathering in Europe and consequently MI9's evaders were a low priority, in spite of Dansey heading the MI9 and MI6 escape lines.[85] It raises the question, what were Dansey's real motivations? And was he acting on the wider instructions of MI6? Without access to MI6 files by historians today, these questions are difficult to answer.

Dansey despatched Langley to meet Donald Darling in Gibraltar.[86] On the meeting's agenda was discussion of pressing matters: the lack of funds to support men in hiding, setting up wireless communications, organising sea evacuations, and possible expansion of escape lines into northern France. With the ongoing threat of the Gestapo, even networks in Vichy France were contemplated.

Langley returned to England, having achieved nothing for Garrow's escape line in Lisbon, nor had he secured real support from Sir Samuel Hoare in Madrid. Dansey was not surprised. He had taken a bet with his colleagues that Langley would return empty-handed within five days.

As Dansey was playing his own games back in London, the war was changing direction. With much of Western Europe occupied by German troops, Hitler's expansionist policies turned towards Russia and in June 1941 the German invasion, code named Operation Barbarossa, took place. MI9's work in bringing escapers and evaders out of Europe obtained an increased urgency. That work was about to receive an unexpected boost with the arrival of two new figures on the scene who would lead two principal escape lines for MI9. They were Patrick O'Leary and Andrée De Jongh.[87]

4
THE PAT LINE

A few weeks after Langley's return from Lisbon he received a request from
Garrow asking if he could enrol a new man into the network.[1] He was Patrick
Albert O'Leary, a Belgian whose real name was Albert-Marie Guérisse. O'Leary
had been picked up by the Vichy authorities and had told them that he was an
evading Canadian airman. They believed his cover story and had him transferred to Saint-Hippolyte-du-Fort, near Nîmes. Garrow went to visit him there
and immediately picked up on O'Leary's sense of adventure and thought him
ideal for MI9; he described O'Leary as 'formidable . . . with bold, clear eyes'.[2]

When Langley raised the subject of O'Leary with Dansey (the only one
with the authority to admit a new person to the network), Dansey was forceful.
He did not trust O'Leary because nothing was known about his background –
a valid objection on grounds of security. Garrow enquired into O'Leary's background and learnt that as Albert-Marie Guérisse he had served as a doctor in a
cavalry regiment in 1940. He then escaped to England after Dunkirk and had
been permitted to serve on the armed merchant cruiser HMS *Fidelity* which
had been engaged in the clandestine dropping of SOE agents near Collioure on
the south coast of France.[3] In April 1941 O'Leary was accidentally left behind
after a night landing mission near Étang de Canet.[4] Eventually Dansey accepted
Garrow's judgement as O'Leary's immediate history was verifiable from his
service record and the ship's crew lists, but his pre-service history remained of
some security concern. In the end Dansey was reassured by the fact that, given
the extent of his knowledge, O'Leary could have worked as a German agent

had he wished but chose not to. Dansey impressed on Langley the importance of the Belgians never finding out that O'Leary was working for British intelligence. Langley described O'Leary later as 'a man of immense drive and energy who would never admit defeat . . . His modesty, shyness and delightful sense of humour effectively masked a first-class calculating brain and the indomitable courage he was to show in the future.'

Langley protected O'Leary's real identity even from staff at Beaconsfield, but now that his appointment had been approved, MI9 needed to get that message to Garrow. A pre-agreed coded message went out over French BBC news which said 'Adolphe doit rester' [Adolphe must remain] – an indication to Garrow that he could now organise O'Leary's escape from Saint-Hippolyte-du-Fort. Langley later commented: 'It was the beginning of his [O'Leary's] glittering service to the Allied cause which won him the George Cross, the DSO, and over twenty other decorations.'[5]

The Pat Line ran from Paris down to Marseille via Lyons, Amiens, Lille or Limoges, then from Marseille across the Pyrenees to Barcelona and Gibraltar.

The Pat Line relied on a complex network of helpers, many of whose names have not been released into the National Archives. One helper who is known was Dr Rodocanachi, an American representative of the Medical Board of the Vichy Armistice Commission, an official role that enabled him to work for the Pat Line undetected by the regime. He also issued medical documents to enable Allied soldiers to be repatriated on 'health grounds'. Another named helper was Michel Pareyre (aka 'Parker').[6] Parker secured a garage at Perpignan, right on the border of the Pyrenees. From here he collected parties of escapers and evaders for which MI9 agreed to pay him £40 per officer and £20 per man he succeeded in getting into Spain. The Vichy authorities were watching him closely so he engaged a network of local smugglers and guides to escort people over the border.

MI9 required an agent who could operate in the underworld within Vichy France. That man was Nubar Gulbenkian who worked as an official at the neutral Iranian Legation. In the 1930s Gulbenkian had worked as an agent for Dansey's secret Z Organisation which was collecting industrial intelligence.[7] Its independence from MI6 is questionable and it may have been intended as a substitute if MI6 was ever totally compromised. Nubar Gulbenkian, the son of an immensely rich and powerful oil magnate, Calouste Gulbenkian, had left Paris after the German occupation and was living in Vichy France.[8] Darling and Gulbenkian met in Lisbon where he was instructed to travel via Barcelona, cross the Pyrenees and to Perpignan on the French side of the border, to establish some useful contacts in the region for MI9. A few weeks later, having flown on to England, Gulbenkian received his mission: he was instructed to make contact with Parker at the garage in Perpignan to arrange the payment for MI9 to the guides crossing the Pyrenees. It became known as the Gulbenkian mission.

Gulbenkian met Parker in Perpignan, identifying him at a café by the fact that Parker was reading a French newspaper upside down.[9] There they struck a deal that all payments for smuggling servicemen over the border would be made into a UK bank account, where the funds would accumulate until the end of the war, when Parker could collect the money. Once in Spain, the servicemen were passed to the British embassy for arrangements to return to England.

Direct contact with London remained weak at this time because O'Leary had no wireless operators or communication. Messages were hidden in tubes of toothpaste and carried out via a courier who smuggled them over the Pyrenees. The escape line soon included American evaders from the American 8th Army Air Force. Although no help was received from the American consulate in Marseille, the Pat Line did receive support from the American vice consul in Lyons.

Room 900

During the summer of 1941, Crockatt authorised the establishment of the most secret part of MI9 called Room 900, known also as Intelligence School 9 (IS9). He realised that it was necessary to professionally coordinate the escape lines, otherwise they would continue to be run by amateurs who took pity on airmen, sheltered them, but who lacked proper security, thus putting other intelligence networks at risk. The role of Room 900 was to keep in contact with the leaders of the escape lines, to train airmen and soldiers in escape and evasion techniques, bring Allied servicemen back from enemy-occupied Western Europe and return them to their fighting unit.[10] This definition was surely the role of MI9. Historically, it has been difficult to understand the work and relationship of MI9 and Room 900, even as regards MI6. A declassified MI9 file defined Room 900 as 'Controlled in its activities by the overriding authority of SIS [MI6], and was in fact started as MI6(D), with an office in Broadway and a staff of one junior officer and two clerks'.[11] It was not to conduct espionage or undertake acts of sabotage.[12] The former was the domain of MI6, the latter of the Special Operations Executive (SOE). However, the situation and the relationships became complex. Langley ensured that all communication with O'Leary went out from Room 900.[13] However, messages back to MI9 and Room 900 from the escape networks and evaders came via the War Office's Room 055A which dealt with counter-espionage and the 'turning' of enemy spies as double agents.[14]

IS9/Room 900 ran an intelligence school from a secret location in north London called Caen Wood Towers, covered in a later chapter. The work of Room 900 was segregated from the rest of MI9 and was practically unknown to MI9 staff at Beaconsfield.[15] Eventually, with the support of the Belgian government-in-exile from its temporary headquarters in London at 38 Belgrave Square, Room 900 was able to recruit a number of Belgian agents. Indeed, Langley ran Room 900 as its sole member until the appearance of Neave in June 1942.

The output at Wilton Park had gathered pace, especially in escape and evasion items. By the end of March 1941, MI9 had successfully distributed 14,875 maps, 9,562 compass studs, 7,658 other compasses, 2,253 pouches for money and 4,092 hacksaws. It was reported that the Escape Committee of Colditz Castle consisted of officers of all three services, which highlighted 'the necessity for the closest collaboration and unified control from this end', and official codes were operational now at a number of POW camps.[16] MI9 soon had an increasing base of British officers with whom secret communication could be established to start Escape Committees within the POW camps.

In July 1941, 100 newsletters were sent into 13 POW camps. It was reported in the official MI9 war diary written at the time that morale of Allied prisoners in German camps remained high, in contrast to the guards who were becoming increasingly frustrated with the prisoners who continually wasted their time on trivial requests.[17] That same month, the postal censor received 4,279 letters from British POWs for distribution; the following month Wilton Park received 76 coded messages and sent out 67.

In October, MI9 learned that Garrow had been arrested and sentenced to ten years in Fort Meauzac for aiding escapers and evaders. O'Leary took over as leader of the escape line, now renamed the Pat Line after him. Within a year, he had helped 600 airmen, soldiers, Belgians and Free French, and recruited over 250 people as helpers, couriers, passeurs, and forgers.[18]

MI9 was struggling to keep abreast of its workload, as the diary noted: 'the volume of work in every sphere is increasing steadily and rapidly and the staff shortage is becoming daily more and more serious'.[19]

Traitor Harold Cole

British agent Harold (Paul) Cole started working for MI9 in 1940 and brought airmen and couriers to Spain and Vichy France from Lille and Paris. The story of Cole began to unravel when Pat O'Leary discovered that Cole was partying in Marseille when he should have been in Lille. Cole genuinely helped escapers and evaders to safety in the early days and had a reputation for his work.[20] It was hard for helpers of the escape line to believe that he could be a traitor. Scotland Yard already had a file on Cole because he had been convicted of minor offences, including burglary and fraud, so he was a known con man, but even a con man could be useful to British intelligence.[21]

Once O'Leary became suspicious, he arranged to meet Cole, accompanied by Bruce Dowding (an Australian in MI9). The situation came to a climax when O'Leary confronted Cole about spending MI9's funds on women and loose living, and not having paid agent François Dupré.[22] Cole denied it. O'Leary then opened a door and there stood Dupré. A fight ensued and O'Leary punched Cole in the face, after which he confessed to having behaved badly in a moment of weakness. Dowding and O'Leary locked Cole in the bathroom while they discussed the options: Dowding suggested that they should kill him but O'Leary was not convinced that embezzlement of MI9 funds justified death. As they discussed his fate, Cole evaded them and escaped out the bathroom window into the centre of Marseille.

O'Leary and Dowding reacted quickly and warned Abbé Carpentier who was their chief agent in Abbeville and supplied all the necessary false documents. MI9 sent out an alert to warn every branch of intelligence, including SOE, to change all cover names, post boxes and safe houses that were known to Cole. A message also went out to the resistance groups that Cole was a traitor and was to be shot on sight. Cole fled Marseille and hid in Lille for a few weeks.

Although O'Leary suspected Cole of denouncing Garrow to the Germans, no evidence emerged to prove his betrayal. A few months later, on 6 December 1941, Cole was arrested by the German authorities. It was thought by MI9 that Cole was loyal to the organisation and escape network until this arrest; however, it has not been possible to verify from official sources whether that was true. What is known from contemporaneous accounts and Cole's personal MI5 file was that during the subsequent interrogation by the Germans, he did collaborate; the transcript of his interrogation by a Dutch agent, Cornelius Verloop, of the German military intelligence service, the Abwehr, allegedly ran to 30 pages in which he gave away everything about the escape lines. The Germans finally released Cole from custody on condition that he worked for the Abwehr and sent bogus airmen to the escape lines to penetrate them.

His first treacherous act for the Abwehr was to escort five evaders to Abbé Carpentier in Abbeville: two Belgian pilots, an RAF officer, an English soldier and a Polish pilot. The Polish officer was in fact not an evader but the head of the Lille branch of a police unit being used by the Abwehr. On 8 December 1941 Abbé Carpentier was arrested and taken to prison, but a few weeks later managed to smuggle a letter out to MI9 with the information that he had been betrayed by Cole.

After Abbé Carpentier's arrest, O'Leary wrote to Donald Darling and told him that he was personally going to kill Cole. He had already discussed the best method to kill Cole – one that would not compromise the Pat Line – with Dr Rodocanachi. He had to avoid a public police inquiry, so Dr Rodocanachi proposed that an overdose of insulin be used to induce a coma, a method that would be difficult to trace if a police inquiry did happen, and O'Leary could then push Cole's body into the water at a discreet spot by the port basins. When Darling heard of these plans, he felt duty bound to inform Dansey that O'Leary was going to 'dispose' of Cole. Dansey was not keen on the idea.[23]

Questions have been raised about why Dansey would object to the assassination of traitor Cole. It is believed by some historians that Cole was being run as a double agent by Dansey to double cross the Abwehr.[24] If true, it would mean that Dansey had risked part of the MI9 network for his greater goal of running Cole for MI6 and the personal risks were in fact being taken, not by Dansey, but Cole. Without new archival material or access to MI6 files, it is not possible to assess whether Dansey did indeed sacrifice MI9's work for MI6's own agenda.

In spite of Dansey's reservations about an assassination of Cole, Darling took control of the situation and, without Dansey's knowledge, sent a message to O'Leary to travel urgently to Gibraltar for a face-to-face meeting. In April 1942, O'Leary travelled on false papers to Gibraltar. He was brought over the Pyrenees with a group of evaders and met by 'Monday' who hid him in the boot of his car as he drove over the border from Spain into Gibraltar. O'Leary met both Darling and Langley in Gibraltar. They discussed their growing concern about Cole, whom Langley now believed to be a traitor.[25] For Langley, Cole was 'very attractive to women, with mistresses all over France. He also loves money and this may be a clue to his actions.'[26]

MI9 in London was not convinced by Langley's concerns and in response merely downgraded Cole's duties. Before Langley left England for the meeting, he was contacted by Scotland Yard who had Cole on a wanted list. Langley was convinced that London should reverse its decision about Cole. O'Leary agreed too that Cole had to be eliminated. But their opportunity passed because Cole was arrested by the Abwehr for double-crossing them, tried for espionage and imprisoned in France.

It is hard to know the exact number of helpers and couriers who were betrayed by Cole because the figure is not given in the official files. Neave placed it as high as 150 people.[27] It is known that Cole was responsible for denouncing, and the subsequent death of, Abbé Carpentier, Bruce Dowding and Dupré. Cole even betrayed his own French wife, her elderly relatives, and his mistresses for money. Langley described Cole as 'a con man, thief and utter shit who betrayed his country to the highest bidder for money'.[28] Cole was seen a few days before the liberation of Paris in August 1944 in a German staff car and in the uniform of a German officer.[29] Nothing further was heard of him until spring 1945 when he gave himself up to the American unit in southern Germany. He managed to persuade them that he was a British intelligence officer who had lost his way and promptly betrayed Abwehr figures to save his own skin:

> It was presumably with the idea of returning to France that he sent a post-card to a girlfriend in Paris. She, convinced that he was a genuine British agent working on evasion, showed it to Donald Darling at the Awards Bureaux. Cole was arrested and brought to Paris under guard where he succeeded in escaping from the SHAEF [Supreme Headquarters Allied Expeditionary Force] military prison wearing a stolen American sergeant's uniform jacket.[30]

The landlady at the rooms where Cole was hiding reported him to the Allies because she suspected that he was a deserter. Two French police officers came to arrest him and Cole was killed in a shoot-out. Pat O'Leary went to the morgue in Paris to formally identify his body.[31]

There were other problems for the Pat Line. By mid-1942, it was desper-ately short of money and had almost run out; it needed at least 100,000 francs a month to operate. Getting money to O'Leary was sporadic and he now relied on the generosity of a number of helpers, including M. Fiocca (a Marseille businessman) who gave £6,000, and Louis Nouveau who donated £5,000.

In June 1942, Langley despatched Belgian fighter pilot Jean (Alex) Nitelet to the Pat Line. He had been shot down in occupied territory and wounded, losing an eye. MI9 had helped him escape to Spain and now he returned to work for them as a wireless operator.[32] To avoid detection by German patrols he never transmitted more than three messages from any one address, was constantly on the move, and disguised his 'fist' print in messages by sending them sometimes with his left hand, thumb or another finger.

As a measure of the extent of the network at the time, the Pat Line was estimated to have around 250 helpers, men and women. It included Jean de Olla who operated in the north, the Fillerin family in the Pas de Calais region and Jacques Wattebled in Normandy. Madame Arnaud helped evaders cross into Vichy France from her farm at Les Tuyères. The line was aided by the Morel sisters, also in Vichy France, who carried messages for the Pat Line sewn into the hems of their dresses. In Monte Carlo a teahouse run by two elderly sisters, Grace and Susie Trenchard, provided shelter for evaders before they were passed down the escape line to Marseille. At Nîmes, between Avignon and Montpellier in southern France, Gaston Nègre operated in the black market for MI9. The Spanish guides lived in the French city of Toulouse near the Spanish border. The audacity of the helpers and risks taken for the escape line were sometimes surprising; for example one of the safe houses for sheltering evaders (the apartment of Françoise Dissart) was located directly opposite the local Gestapo headquarters.[33] Françoise would never have been suspected by the Gestapo because she was a grey-haired Frenchwoman aged sixty and somewhat eccentric: 'She smoked all day long with a black holder permanently in her mouth. She seemed never to go to bed and attired in a black petticoat lived entirely on black coffee.'[34] She escorted some servicemen to the Swiss border 'with great ingenuity and indomitable spirit'.[35] She would become O'Leary's successor after he too was turned in to the Gestapo in March 1943.

THE PAT LINE

America Enters the War

The bombing of Pearl Harbour on 7 December 1941 brought America into the war and within just two weeks, American intelligence officers began to arrive in England to work with MI9.[36] Approximately six weeks later, in February 1942, Major General Carl Spaatz of the United States Army Air Force travelled to England to meet with Crockatt, discuss the work of MI9 and plan an American equivalent. In March, Charles Medhurst (British Air-Vice Marshal) flew to Washington to brief General George Marshall (chairman of the US Chiefs of Staff) and Henry Stimson (US Secretary of War) about escape and evasion matters. This meeting led to the foundation of MIS-X (Military Intelligence Service-X), the equivalent of MI9.[37] Although the foundations for MIS-X were there in early 1942, its formal establishment was delayed until 6 October that year because Henry Stimson was sceptical of its merits and needed persuasion. MIS-X became part of the US Military Intelligence Division.[38] It was as top secret as MI9, with the main headquarters located at Fort Hunt in Virginia, 20 miles south of Washington. It operated with the postal address of PO Box 1142 and was commanded by Colonel Catesby ap C. Jones (commander of POWs).[39]

There was much travelling and exchange of intelligence officers across the Atlantic as part of the ongoing Anglo-American intelligence cooperation. MI9's code expert Leslie Winterbottom flew to America to help select suitable officers for MIS-X. Captain Robley Evans Winfrey, an American officer and engineer by trade, arrived in England in February 1942, attached to MI9 for five months of intense learning with Clayton Hutton on escape aids.[40] Lieutenant Colonel J. Edward Johnston, a wealthy American businessman and heir to the Lucky Strike tobacco fortune, was assigned as the Pentagon's commanding officer for MIS-X.[41] He became the primary liaison between MIS-X and MI9, and was based at the newly opened Pentagon building in Washington.[42] Lieutenant Colonel W. Stull Holt was appointed to form a unit called P/W&X which was independent of MIS-X and liaised directly with Crockatt in England on escape and evasion for US personnel operating in the European theatres of war from their bases in the UK.[43] The orders were to 'study and perfect the escape and evasion techniques into a program to be used by the American briefers . . . how to behave if captured, what to say during interrogation, how to escape from a POW camp, and the selection of certain individuals in combat units who would be taught a secret letter code'.[44]

MIS-X went one step further than MI9 and issued a mandate that it was the duty of escapers and evaders not only to escape, but to obey instructions from the escape lines as if the orders had come from their own unit commander.[45] In camps that held both British and American POWs, the POWs worked together in escape efforts. The charter for MIS-X mirrored that of MI9 and was divided into five sections: interrogation; codes and communication; training and briefing; technical skills; and POW locations.[46] American escapers and evaders were interrogated for information and intelligence from enemy territory that could be useful to the Allies. An example of information from escapers was the discovery of special German interrogation centres which held prisoners in solitary confinement in conditions that made them susceptible to giving away too much information. The training and briefing section gave training to Army Air Force crew and Marine Corps in techniques of escape and evasion, codes and communications. The technical section was tasked with the design, procurement and despatch of gadgets and escape kits. In this respect, it worked particularly closely with MI9. The gadgets were despatched in parcels from phoney charities and, like MI9, were never sent in Red Cross parcels to avoid compromising the work of that organisation.[47]

The section for 'POW locations' was responsible for locating prison camps in enemy territory so Allied bombers did not bomb the sites holding prisoners. It also issued reports about the camps to disseminate information to personnel. The section for codes liaised with POWs known to have been trained in coded letters, and also worked with their relatives and fictitious next-of-kin to send out further coded correspondence. Altogether the US trained 7,724 code users (CUs) from the armed forces personnel.[48] The correspondence section at Fort Hunt, codenamed The Creamery, received coded letters via the Censor Office in

New York where all POW mail was initially sorted. Each censor had a list of CUs who were in enemy hands and watched out for their letters which were then sealed in a pouch and sent via the military air shuttle to the MIS-X 'Creamery' at Fort Hunt. A letter or parcel was known to be coded if the envelope or packaging bore a return address of a POW camp in Europe or the name of a CU. The first coded letter from an American POW came via MI9, sent from Lieutenant Colonel Albert Clark who had been trained in codes by MI9 whilst based in England. His coded message was sent from Stalag Luft III at Sagan (later the scene of the 'great escape' of March 1944),[49] and informed MI9 that he was the most senior officer of 87 American officers being held in Stalag Luft III.

In the POW camps, the highest-ranking officer was selected as the liaison officer for escape and evasion. Another officer would volunteer to work in the mail room of the camp in order to discreetly intercept coded messages or important parcels. Another officer distributed the food contained, and a third ran the escape and evasion committee to 'harass, confuse and disrupt their captors, and make every effort to escape'.[50] The identity of the Escape Committee was kept secret so that if the Germans interrogated personnel in the camp, the prisoners quite genuinely could not give away information about escape plans. Their point of reference for the escape personnel was an officer appointed by the chairman of the committee, who was in charge of all main escape sections within the camp; this officer appointed the head of each section, but to guarantee the utmost security, other prisoners did not know whom he had selected. The sections were responsible for tunnels, forgery, codes, gadgets, tailoring (making uniforms or clothes for escape), intelligence gathering, parcels, copying and updating escape maps, and security.

A finance officer intercepted money smuggled into the camps for use after escape. A nuisance group created diversionary tactics to distract the guards during an escape. Clandestine radios (receivers rather than transmitters as the latter were too risky and easy to detect) were built from parts smuggled into the camps.[51] One prisoner was responsible for disseminating news received via the radio contact to the other prisoners in his hut. When coded letters were being deciphered, other prisoners ensured no guards would enter the hut, but when there was a risk of a guard coming, the decoder could swallow the paper he was working on and get rid of the evidence of his translation. All that was left was the original 'innocent' letter.

MIS-X smuggled escape gadgets into the POW camps. A new building was completed at Fort Hunt in 1943 to house the gadget department and was kitted out with the necessary machinery and technical equipment. Captain Winfrey, who had learned much about Q aids from Clayton Hutton in England, was now back at Fort Hunt sourcing games and household items to hide escape and evasion maps and aids. These included counterfeit passes hidden inside a chessboard and tiny compasses inside chess pieces, while other items were secreted in ping pong sets, shoes and hairbrushes. Tissue paper maps were hidden inside table tennis bats, or part of a map might be printed inside a deck of cards. A number of American companies made escape gadgets for MIS-X[52] and parcels containing them were sent by false charities created for the purpose, such as the War Prisoners' Benefit Foundation and The Servicemen's Relief Organisation. Three types of parcel could be sent: food parcels with items to supplement POW camp rations, clothing parcels which contained many hidden escape and evasion gadgets, and recreational parcels in which sports equipment like baseballs could conceal various tools.[53]

MIS-Y was formed in the United States in 1942 for the interrogation of Axis prisoners and mirrored the MI9/MI19 interrogation of prisoners in the United Kingdom.[54] It worked alongside MIS-X and was commanded by Colonel Russell Sweet. The primary MIS-Y interrogation centre was located at Fort Hunt, completed in April 1942 with covert listening equipment installed to listen into the conversations of German prisoners:

MIS-Y installed sophisticated listening devices into various rooms in which prisoners of war were accommodated. This enabled them to meticulously record and transcribe the indiscretions of their occupants, which included U-boat officers and crews, Wernher von Braun [rocket scientist] and General Reinhard Gehlen [spymaster].[55]

The largest section of MIS-X operated in the theatre of war in the Pacific and the Far East, and in the course of the war MIS-X orchestrated the escape and evasion of 12,000 US personnel, bringing them out of enemy territory to fight another day.[56] The close working relationship between the two trans-Atlantic units of military intelligence, MI9 and MIS-X, was described by British Prime Minister Churchill as one of 'absolute brotherhood'.[57] MI9 provided support to American intelligence in the setting up of MIS-X and thereafter the two organisations shared escape lines and intelligence. It meant that escapers and evaders from the forces of the British Empire and America 'had one enormous advantage over the rest: effective government help, supplied through secret channels'.[58] Germany did not have an equivalent organisation or formal network to facilitate the escape of its own prisoners from Allied POW camps, nor training in an escape-minded philosophy.[59]

Escape from Colditz

One of the camps best known for escapes was Colditz Castle, the imposing fortress near Leipzig in Germany. Colditz, officially named Oflag IV-C, was reserved for 'special prisoners' – captured Allied officers and those who had already escaped from other German POW camps and been recaptured. The official MI9 history of the camp described it as 'a camp for Ausbrecher, or escapers. There were also Jews and political prisoners there. The total number was over 550 and it is very strongly guarded by a complete battalion. General morale was very high and everything was done by escapes, demonstrations etc., to keep guards occupied.'[60]

Colditz was an eleventh-century fortress built on a rocky ridge overlooking the river Mulde with defences the Germans believed could not be breached. The old fortress had an inner and outer courtyard completely enclosed by high buildings. The castle was surrounded by an outer wall 9 metres high, with a terraced garden below, built on another high wall that reached down to a dry moat. The roofs of the buildings inside the outer walls were covered in thick barbed wire. The larger outer courtyard had only two exits and housed a

German battalion. The castle had eighteen sentry towers, each with a search-light and machine guns.[61] Guards permanently manned each tower, two guards patrolled between the towers, and two were stationed in the courtyard of the prisoners' quarters. In total, 200 German army guards were stationed there, and this later increased to around 500.[62]

The escape from Colditz by Lieutenant Airey Neave of the Royal Artillery and Anthony (Abraham Pierre) Luteyn of the Dutch East Indies Army was arguably one of the most audacious escapes of the war. On 5 January 1942 they escaped from the castle dressed as German officers. Neave became the first British officer to successfully escape from Colditz Castle and return to England – one of only eleven British prisoners to do so.[63]

Neave had been taken prisoner because his unit had been instructed to fight to the last man to create time for the British Expeditionary Force to retreat and evacuate from Dunkirk in May 1940. He was serving as a troop commander in France with 1st Searchlight Battalion, the Royal Artillery. During the retreat, he ordered the men to take up position 2 kilometres south of Calais, but on 24 May, he sustained minor wounds and was transferred to a French hospital. Whilst lying wounded on a stretcher he was taken prisoner by the Germans but soon began to harbour ideas of escaping. The following month he received a visit from a Frenchman, Pierre d'Harcourt, who entered the hospital wearing a Red Cross armband. Neave had no reason to suspect that d'Harcourt was anything other than a member of the Red Cross, but for months after Dunkirk, d'Harcourt had been aiding British soldiers to escape and acting as their guide in unoccupied France. He suggested to Neave that he could smuggle him out of hospital in a coffin in the place of a corpse, though in the end the plan was not implemented. The Gestapo eventually caught up with d'Harcourt in Paris where he was arrested and sent first to Fresnes prison and then to Buchenwald concentration camp, which he survived.[64] But Neave's discussions with him on various methods of possible escape stayed with him and Neave later carried these ideas into MI9.

Neave was transferred from hospital to a number of different German pris-oner of war camps. The first was Oflag IXA at Spargenberg near Kassel and then Stalag XXA, at Thorn in Poland.[65] Conditions in Stalag XXA were terrible: underground rooms with no daylight and guards who threatened the prisoners with rubber truncheons. Neave attempted to escape to Russia on 16 April 1941 but was captured near Warsaw and handed over to the Gestapo. That saw him transferred to Colditz.

In January 1942, the Escape Committee in Colditz believed that with heavy snow on the ground the Germans would never suspect an escape. Neave and Luteyn were paired together and a plan was made to break them out in early 1942, dressed as German officers. In the weeks preceding their escape, every care had been taken to duplicate German overcoats and caps. The MI9 camp history of Colditz notes that Neave made his own German uniform for the escape:

> He obtained a Dutch Army greatcoat from the Dutch Escape officer and painted the buttons with grey paint obtained from the canteen. The collar was covered with dark green material. The epaulettes and regimental numbers were carved out of linoleum and painted gilt. The cap proved difficult and finally was made by covering a Service dress cap with green material and sewing in the peak, which was covered with varnished black paper, at a sharper angle. The cap badges were carved from linoleum and painted silver.[66]

It took six weeks to make the uniform.

After roll call at 9 p.m. on 5 January 1942, Neave and Luteyn were led by Pat Reid and Howard Wardle (a Canadian) to a position above the guardhouse that adjoined the prisoners' quarters, down a spiral stone staircase and out onto the drawbridge.[67] The sentries thought Neave and Luteyn were German officers and saluted them accordingly. The plan had worked. Neave and Luteyn calmly walked out of Colditz.

Once over a high bank, they cast off their overcoats. Underneath, they were dressed as Dutch electrical workers, a disguise chosen because they had the right as foreign workers to travel from Leipzig to Ulm. Neave and Luteyn paid for their tickets by selling chocolate from the Red Cross in Colditz. Two days later on 7 January 1942 they reached Ulm then travelling on various trains towards the frontier town of Singen on the German-Swiss border. The Germans had already alerted border guards that two British prisoners were on the run and might try to cross at any border point. Neave and Luteyn sheltered overnight in a beekeeper's hut and, taking shovels and white coats they found there to look like local workers, they made their way towards Singen. They passed a patrol of the Hitler Youth who stopped them and said they were searching for two escaped POWs. Neave replied that they were workmen from Westphalia and they were allowed to carry on. By now they were exhausted and hungry and could have accidentally given themselves away if they had not been quick thinking. There were stressful moments, as Neave recalled:

We could hear the voices of the Frontier Police and the tramp of sentries, dangerously close to us. Then the wind rose, and choosing our moment, we crowded across the road towards Switzerland. It took us an hour to struggle through snowdrifts till we reached a road that led to the town of Ramsen in Swiss territory.[68]

They crossed the border via the Schaffhausen Salient where Switzerland protrudes into Germany, a crossing that had been used by escapers in the First World War.[69] Within eighty-four hours of their escape from Colditz, Neave and Luteyn were in Berne with the British attaché, Colonel Henry Cartwright.[70] It was a great achievement.

Cartwright understood the plight of escapers and evaders having himself escaped in the First World War after being taken prisoner by the Germans in 1914.[71] It could take months for an opportunity to arise to get them safely from Switzerland to Spain and on to England. In the interim, escapers and evaders had time on their hands and this could be a dangerous period because the Gestapo had their spies in Switzerland who tried to surreptitiously gain information from evaders about the escape lines. The most common technique was the use of attractive girls to seduce the men and trap them in bars and bedrooms. Cartwright gave cautionary instructions to Luteyn and Neave not to keep the company of unreliable characters and certain women and in the meantime he waited for instructions for repatriation.

Cartwright played 'an indispensable role in the wartime escape organisation of MI9'.[72] Without warning on 15 April 1942, he called for Neave and told him: 'We're sending you back first. MI9 has asked for you.'[73] Neave had never heard of MI9. Cartwright then raised his glass and said: 'Here's to your safe journey to Spain tomorrow! We are sending you out before the others, even though they escaped from Germany before you. MI9 have sent orders for you and Hugh Woollatt to cross the Swiss frontier as soon as possible.' Captain Woollatt of the Lancashire Fusiliers had escaped from Oflag VC in southern Germany.

Neave was instructed to travel to Geneva and meet Woollatt by a particular bookstall; the two men were smuggled across the border by Salvador Augustus 'Don' Gomez-Beare, assistant naval attaché at the British embassy and were then brought out of occupied France down the Pat Line by a whole chain of helpers who escorted them on each stage of the journey. The risks were high for the helpers who could face torture or a concentration camp if caught aiding them, but also for Neave and Woollatt who could be arrested and handed back to the Gestapo. A young (unnamed) girl who looked less than eighteen, led the two men through the back streets of Annemasse, a town on the Swiss/French frontier, until they came to a scruffy door of a safe house. Neave never knew her name but later recalled:

> In her eyes there was a strange light. Nothing could have expressed more powerfully the spirit of resistance to Hitler . . . I never forgot this first revelation of the courage of ordinary French men and women in helping us escape.[74]

Until then, Neave had been in control of his own destiny through his various escape attempts since Dunkirk. Now he had to place his life in the hands of a chain of helpers and trust them, as he said: 'Now, I felt myself to be entirely in the hands of a secret organisation over which I had no control.'[75]

In May 1942, they successfully crossed the Pyrenees on foot with their Spanish guide Francis Blanchain whom they met at Port Vendres.[76] They were escorted to the British Consulate in Barcelona and on to Gibraltar where Donald Darling interrogated them.[77]

Neave and Woollatt left Gibraltar on a troopship bound for the Clyde in Scotland and travelled from there to England. There was jubilation at HQ at Wilton Park as a staff officer rushed in to the main office, having received a radio message that Neave and Woollatt were back in the country.[78] Out came the glasses of pink gin in celebration in the mess before lunchtime.

Neave arrived at the Grand Central Hotel in London where he and Woollatt were interrogated by MI9 on the second floor.[79] He recalled:

I climbed the wide stairs, with my cheap suitcase, still feeling I was a prisoner arriving at a new camp. The corridors were stripped and bleak. Everywhere I could hear the sound of typewriters and the bustle of troops in transit. I entered what had been a large double bedroom, which now served as an office for the interrogation of returned escapers of MI9. In place of the brass bedsteads were trestle tables and wire baskets.[80]

That day, Neave and Woollatt parted. They never saw each other again. Woollatt went back into action and died in July 1944.

Parts of the network were still being compromised. In August 1942 the Pat Line suffered another disaster when Jean Nitelet and Gaston Nègre were arrested by Vichy authorities. Pitched against this, though, were incredible achievements: it was now possible for an airman shot down over northern France to be returned to his unit via Spain and Gibraltar within just twelve days. Neave's own escape marked a significant milestone in MI9's history. He had demonstrated that it was possible to escape from the impenetrable fortress, evade recapture across 1,500 miles of Nazi-occupied Europe and return to England.

Neave Joins Room 900

MI9 posted Neave to its most secret section, Room 900, to help Langley in the training of new agents and establish other escape routes through Spain. The experience of Cole's treason had shaken the organisation and its escape lines and it was now understood that the Pat Line from Marseille could soon be compromised and betrayed. New escape networks had to be established and Langley intended to set them up in Belgium and Holland. He took Neave for lunch at Rules Restaurant in Maiden Lane, Covent Garden. Brigadier Norman Crockatt was waiting for them, wearing his uniform of the Royal Scots with his medals. Neave later commented: 'This man was a real soldier and I liked him immediately.'[81]

Crockatt told Neave: 'You will look after secret communications with occupied Europe and training of agents. It won't be a bed of roses.'

Neave was given the codename 'Saturday' and joined Room 900 (IS9) with a hero's reputation. From his own experience, he believed that escape was open to anyone and 'what one needs is confidence, plenty of luck and a powerful motive'.[82] The staff of Room 900 remained small and consisted of Langley and Neave, two secretaries and a handful of agents at any one time. Langley and Neave 'ran' Darling ('Sunday') and Creswell ('Monday'). They carried out their work with no interference from Crockatt or Dansey and it was not until later that the full impact of their work was realised.

Neave rented a flat near Langley's and later reminisced: 'Langley and I would sit in the masculine armchairs, drinking whiskey in the evening, and discuss the state of our two-man organisation. We were always on duty . . . Sometimes, I felt thinking of those I left behind in Colditz, that I had no right to this luxury.'[83]

When Neave met agents or evaders he used one of a number of different pseudonyms: one was 'Anthony Newton', another was 'Albert Hall'. The latter he occasionally signed on micro-photographed messages which travelled via a courier to Brussels. The name could lead to some humorous incidents such as the evading airman who told Donald Darling that he was to report to the Albert Hall. Neave commented that MI9 'was not amazed' by this.

An increasing number of evaders on the continent were unintentionally getting too near to secret SIS lines and endangering SIS agents.[84] This restricted the work of Room 900 but even so they were able to obtain a high standard of agents without the assistance of SIS or Allied intelligence services. SIS had 'an ignorance of and lack of interest in the rapidly increasing evader problem'.[85]

Room 900 achieved considerable success in both air landings and sea operations because it had the cooperation and support of the Royal Navy, and after 1942, the Air Ministry. Prior to 1942, the Air Ministry did not support escape and evasion as a priority as the MI9 rescue missions also involved the loss of pilots who could not be trained and replaced in less than three months. Cooperation from the Air Ministry was to transform the work of Room 900 and MI9 and became essential for dropping agents and equipment, including wireless transmitters, behind enemy lines to aid the escape routes.

Room 900 and Intelligence

One question that has remained unanswered until now has been whether Room 900 was involved in intelligence gathering. A declassified file now reveals the answer to that question: Room 900 was indeed involved in collecting intelligence in much the same way as other branches of military intelligence, and most specifically MI6.[86] The sources of that intelligence were agents and contacts behind enemy lines. This strand of work was different from the other type of intelligence being collected from Allied POWs and can further illuminate MI9 as an organisation and place it firmly within intelligence history. It is also possible to be more specific on its relationship to MI6.

A series of intelligence briefings was sent out by Room 900 to G-2 Section (Intelligence) Allied Force Headquarters a month before the Anglo-American invasion of North Africa in Operation Torch (8–10 November 1942).[87] This file, the contents of which relate to North Africa, Algeria, Tunis and French Morocco, had not been declassified when Foot and Langley wrote their history of MI9. The results of Room 900's work were shared with American intelligence.

Amongst the reports was information from an (unnamed) Basque guide about the appointment of a new Commissioner of Mobile Police in Setif, Algeria. A list was given of anti-Axis personalities, such as the chief of the

Mobile Police force in Bordier (Oran), and details of Mr Flandin, owner of the *Oran Republicain* (sic) newspaper.[88] There is also geographical intelligence, information on personalities who could help the Allies or become agents after the invasion of North Africa, providing details of political allegiances of people in civic positions who could be approached to join a clandestine Allied network. An eleven-page report on French Morocco gives a list of agents and suspects, for example, that Commissaire Angeletti, described as the worst police official at Oujda, had installed torture chambers.[89]

The same report gives details of Louis Henry, an inspector employed in Marrakesh who previously ran a 'letter-box' at Tangiers for the French Military Intelligence Service and was stated to be anti-German. Captain Jacquot, naval attaché in Casablanca, was noted to be very anti-British. Meanwhile, indications had been received that Friedrich Mueller, a representative of the Skoda Works, was being sent to French Morocco as an enemy agent in September 1942. It was said that the French authorities were aware of his activities and were planning to arrest him.[90] A list of pro-Axis sympathisers included the director of the garage and motor works Auto Hall at Casablanca, who was a collaborator and Anglophobe. Mr de Solminihac, a resident of Casablanca, had a library that was patronised by the Germans and said to be a centre for Nazi activities. Military intelligence to understand which local personalities were working for Axis forces and who would help the Allies was needed ahead of the capture of Casablanca in November 1942 after a short siege.

A separate list provides names of pro-Allied sympathisers, like Israel Behar, a forty-five-year-old Jewish industrialist in the cereal business, who was 'in a position to give useful shipping information; has Persian nationality and is married to a Bulgarian Jewess; a report of September 1941 declares him to be entirely pro-Ally'.[91]

Pilot Maleverne, living at Rabat, had knowledge of the Oued Sebou river valley which 'would be most valuable to a landing force'.[92] Useful too was Alexandros Vardas, a forty-seven-year-old Greek electrical engineer who was employed in repairing ships at the port of Casablanca. He was reported as very pro-Ally and 'could give much information regarding the port installations'.[93]

Noted to be strongly anti-German and anti-Vichy was Jean Vogel, an agent of the Mobile Police force at Casablanca, who had fled Alsace before the Germans occupied Europe.

The collection of such detailed information demonstrates that Room 900 was tracking enemy agents as an intelligence agency would, a tactic classified as counter-intelligence work. This places Room 900 in a completely different light than previously understood, not only running agents and aiding escapers and evaders, but as an intelligence-gathering organisation.

Italy was part of the Axis forces until her surrender in autumn 1943 and prior to this Italians were known to be operating in North Africa. Room 900 had intelligence that Italian vice consul Tortorici at Bone (Algeria) was known to be engaged in intelligence work, and was described as a social success, boasting of mistresses belonging to all the local prominent families.[94] Tortorici was clearly under surveillance by a British agent (who remains unnamed) because a longer report written from Room 900 on 9 October 1943 noted that Tortorici had visited a scent shop and left with two small parcels, and subsequently met a resident by the name of Aliprandi in Bougil. Mr Aliprandi was responsible for reporting aspects of military intelligence along the coastline from Bougil to Djedjelli. Another Italian by the surname of Sartage, quite affluent, was noted to be in daily contact with the Italian Armistice Commission and had a secret wireless transmitter in his cellar.[95] In the Algiers and Tunis regions, Poirier Hesse was suspected of being an important German agent who had recently left for France.[96] A certain Dr Badaroux was believed to have arms hidden in his house and was pro-German, while a Mr Begue was reported to be a German agent who was regularly visited by four men from the Gestapo or German intelligence service. He was also a Vichy spy through links with a Madame Devilelle who resided at the Hotel Albert Premier.

These are definitively different from other MI9 reports and have nothing to do with matters of escape and evasion, but rather espionage and counter-espionage. However, occasionally information was picked up about Allied escape lines. A Mr Slosse was said to be responsible for the Italians discovering a Belgian escape organisation (not named), but it was noted by Room 900 that it was not clear whether this was due to carelessness or a deliberate betrayal.[97]

In the Oran province, the report gave the names of new suspected agents, including Lieutenant Castel who was in charge of French Naval Security Control at the port of Oran. He was pro-German and worked in collaboration with the harbourmaster, Mr Despres. The latter was defined as being a possible agent and suspect personality who was involved in an active naval intelligence service (known as Service Special de Documentation).[98]

Colonel Morell was named as a former officer of the Spanish Red Army, living in Oran and an active agent of the German consul at Cartagena.[99] A separate report dealt with information obtained from a French officer from a branch of the French intelligence service in Algiers, pertaining to personalities involved with the Italian intelligence service or who had contacts with Italians who were spreading propaganda.[100] Another dealt with naming the board members of a Society for Collaboration in Bone which had around fifty active members.[101]

Intelligence was received by Room 900 in November 1942 about a special telephone line from Rabat to Tangier. This line went to a well-known Vichy agent, Mr Neuville (consul at Gibraltar) who was trying to supply Rabat with intelligence about the fortress at Gibraltar.[102] Financial transactions by Germany in the region were being monitored, for example that the German Consulate in Tangier had exchanged all its gold for pesetas, indicating perhaps that it expected an imminent evacuation.[103]

Darling ('Sunday'), MI9's representative in Gibraltar, sent intelligence back to London, including to Room 900, notifying them of a POW camp outside the village of El Kef in Tunisia which was holding 110 British POWs, a Canadian and 100 Spanish refugees.[104] This was important to ensure that the invading armies did not attack the camp. Intelligence was also being shared about the movement of foreign diplomats, secured by Room 900 from (unnamed) secret channels.

A cypher sent from Africa HQ to General Dwight Eisenhower (chief of US forces) and British Brigadier Mockler-Ferryman (serving in the intelligence branch of Eisenhower's Anglo-American Army) read: 'Military Intelligence Nine

[MI9] report that microphones are installed in all rooms, Poggio Quarantine camp near Rome.' This cypher confirmed that MI9 had not only learned about the use of microphones in prisoners' cells at Poggio, but was engaged in collecting intelligence and sharing it with the relevant counterparts of the Allied forces.

Kim Philby and Room 900

In November 1942, the intelligence notifications from Room 900 were being sent out, and personally signed, by Kim Philby – the MI6 officer and deputy head of Section Five (counter-intelligence) at MI6, later the British Cold War traitor who defected to Moscow in 1963. This fact provides hitherto unknown information about both Philby and Room 900. Philby was therefore working for the secret branch of MI9 and Room 900 but for how long is currently unclear.[105]

In 1942–43, Philby was overseeing offensive counter-intelligence for North Africa and Italy for MI6. On 14 November 1942, he sent out a 'Most Secret' notification from Room 900 that read: 'It is reported that there may be an enemy wireless station in buildings opposite ferry in Tunis port.'[106] He sent another the same day that a French national by the name of Challiol was buying a hotel in Casablanca from a French man named Parrain: 'Challiol is said to be a German agent and intends to use the hotel for espionage on German behalf.'[107]

Another intelligence brief read: 'The task of reconstructing an espionage network in French Morocco is being considered by Gibhardt, former head of German espionage in Casablanca, who is now in Tangier. An attempt to keep in touch with his agents presumably left behind in French Morocco, is being made via Tangier.'[108] Another from Philby noted:

One of the mobile intelligence units which, as was reported yesterday, had reached a point south of Limoges, advanced to within 100 miles of the French Mediterranean coast. The SS Division to which the unit was attached, is being withdrawn to a North Westerly direction towards Cognac, but the unit itself is to proceed forthwith to the Franco-Spanish border in the central Pyrenees.[109]

These examples are clearly within the boundaries of what is traditionally understood as MI6 work and counter-intelligence. From Room 900, Philby was tracking enemy agents, their movements and activities, thus undertaking conventional counter-intelligence work.

The above provides reliable evidence that Room 900 was unmistakably engaged in intelligence gathering, intelligence sharing and counter-intelligence work. This sheds a different angle on MI9 and firmly places it as an intelligence-gathering organisation on a par with MI6. However, the situation is more complex because it obscures further the boundaries between MI9, MI6 and Room 900. The same file also has intelligence briefings signed by Major Felix Cowgill (Philby's boss, who had been seconded to MI6). It appears that two major figures, Philby and Cowgill who worked for Section V of MI6 (counter-intelligence) were also operating from MI9's Room 900. Langley and Neave were in charge of Room 900 and both had been engaged by MI9 and MI6, and were overseen by MI6's deputy chief, Dansey. In essence, all the key figures in Room 900 at the War Office were MI6 officers. Over the decades, much has remained unclear about the extent to which MI6 controlled MI9 or the escape lines, even though it was known that Dansey headed both. Keith Jeffery, the MI6 official historian, wrote that much of the comment on the MI6/MI9 relationship has come from Foot and Langley who were 'unable to reveal the true extent of SIS involvement with the organisation [MI9]'.[110] With the benefit of the new research here, it is possible to draw the conclusion that Room 900 was in fact part of MI6. Room 900 was not limited to gaining intelligence for escape and evasion, but had wider functions of espionage, counter-espionage and military intelligence akin to the brief of MI6. This sheds a new light on the traditional history of MI9 and MI6.

5

THE COMET LINE

An effective MI9 escape line had already been operating since the summer of 1941 from Belgium, across France to Spain, that was later named the Comet Line. In June 1941, Belgian businessman Arnold Deppé, who had a residence in Spain and knew the Pyrenees well, visited the region with a twenty-five-year-old Belgian woman, Andrée De Jongh.[1] The purpose was to set up safe houses along the Pyrenees to bring Allied airmen and soldiers out of Europe and form an escape line. De Jongh was the daughter of a Brussels schoolmaster Frédéric De Jongh and part of a tight-knit family. Her father had nicknamed her 'Little Cyclone' because she swept through life in a whirlwind of energy. She was trained in first aid and drew her inspiration from Edith Cavell, the British nurse who had been shot by the Germans in the First World War for helping Allied soldiers and airmen in Belgium.[2] Now it was another war and De Jongh's country was under occupation for the second time. In 1940 in a hospital in Bruges (Belgium) she had nursed British soldiers who had not been evacuated at Dunkirk and were trapped by the German occupation. They spoke to her about wanting to go home and she decided to help.

During the visit of June 1941, Deppé and De Jongh stayed with the de Greef family at Villa Voisin in Anglet, between Biarritz and Bayonne, on the French side of the Pyrenees. The family had fled there the previous year after the German occupation of Belgium. Madame Elvire de Greef (known as 'Tante Go'), her husband Fernand, her mother Bobonne, seventeen-year-old son Freddie and fifteen-year-old daughter Janine left Brussels in a convoy of four cars with members of *L'Indépendance Belge*, a daily newspaper.[3] Members of *L'Indépendance Belge* eventually left France for the United States. The de Greefs would become central to the foundation, and success, of the Comet Line from its beginnings in 1941 until the end of the war, working with De Jongh and Deppé.[4] Basque runners would be hired to smuggle the 'parcels' (airmen and others) over the Pyrenees.

Tante Go arranged for airmen and others to be hidden near the fishing town of Saint-Jean-de-Luz before guides and smugglers could escort them over the mountains into Spain. Her husband was a friend of the French mayor of Anglet. Aware that Fernand spoke German, the mayor asked him to work at the Town Hall to represent French interests against the Germans who were requisitioning local houses for their occupying troops. The Germans had taken over part of the department of Basses-Pyrénées in the occupied zone where special passes were needed to cross the frontier between France and Spain. Fernand became the regular liaison with the Germans in the region, a position that enabled him to smuggle out blank identity cards, official stamps and travel passes for the evaders as well as provide extra supply coupons for the houses which were sheltering them. Freddie, Fernand's son, acted as a courier and forger. Daughter Janine escorted evaders from Paris to the railway station at Biarritz and to the safe houses.

Living with the de Greefs was an Englishman, known simply as 'Be', who may have been an MI9 agent.[5] 'Be' was Albert Edward Johnson who had been a chauffeur to Belgian aristocrat Count Henri de Baillet-Latour, owner of *L'Indépendance Belge* in Brussels before the war. For reasons not given in surviving documents, he had been unable to take the last boat to Britain in June 1940. Fernand offered him hospitality and Johnson stayed with the family for the duration of the war.[6] Being a British subject, and therefore of enemy nationality in the German occupied zone, it became dangerous for Johnson and he was given false papers as a nephew of the de Greefs whose 'Belgian brother' was missing in the Congo.

De Jongh Arrives at Bilbao

In early September 1941, De Jongh arrived at the British embassy in Bilbao in Spain and asked to see the consul-general. With her were two Belgians who wanted to fight for the Allies and a Scottish soldier of the 1st Gordons, Private J. Cromar, who had survived the fighting at Saint-Valéry-en-Caux the previous year and escaped as a POW.[7] His MI9 interrogation report does not mention the names of De Jongh or the other two Belgians. He said that they crossed the Somme on 23 August 1941 and headed for Paris, taking a train to Bordeaux and on to Saint-Jean-de-Luz. In his account, they crossed the frontier in September 1941 from Anglet to San Sebastian, helped across the Pyrenees by smugglers. They headed for the British Consulate in Bilbao. De Jongh had trekked hundreds of miles across Nazi-occupied France with them, arriving at the consulate without any official help and no links at that time to MI9.[8] Vice Consul Arthur Dean agreed to see her; she explained that she had escorted the three men across enemy countries (Belgium and France) on a journey that had taken approximately a week and her companions were waiting in a room downstairs. Dean was struck by how petite and young she was, and physically strong to have endured the challenging trek over the Pyrenees, but he remained cautious because she might be a Nazi agent who had been planted to infiltrate the area.

'There are many British soldiers and airmen hidden in Brussels,' she explained, 'most of them survivors of Dunkirk.'[9] His initial scepticism changed to surprise as he learned that an escape line had already been established from Brussels to Saint-Jean-de-Luz. De Jongh underlined how she and her father were dedicated to bringing out as many trained fighting men as possible, but money was needed to feed them and pay the escape line guides.

'How much?' asked Vice Consul Dean.

'Six thousand Belgian francs to bring a man from Brussels across France and 1,400 Spanish pesetas to pay the mountain guides to take them over the border,' she replied. She offered to hand over details of the safe houses if she could receive money to pay off the debts she had already incurred.

Vice Consul Dean soon believed that this young woman had risked her life to set up the escape line. He heard how a few months earlier she had accompanied a party of ten Belgians, wanted by the Gestapo, and an Englishwoman out of Belgium and down to the Pyrenees. It was a challenging and dangerous journey as the large party trekked across Nazi-occupied countryside. They had travelled with false identity papers via Quiévrain in Belgium on the border to Valenciennes in northern France where they changed trains for Corbie on the river Somme (tracing the Demarcation Line). Here De Jongh and her companions were to cross the river Somme by boat. Unable to retrieve a boat that was hidden for them, they had to swim in relays across the river with the danger of discovery never far away.[10] Patrols were visible a few hundred metres away and campers were in tents along the river, yet they succeeded in crossing. When De Jongh and her party arrived in Spain some of them were arrested and interned by the Spanish authorities, then released.

Vice Consul Dean listened, then told her he had to consult his superiors. As he deliberated with London on the course of action, De Jongh waited almost a fortnight in a local hotel visiting the vice consul every day for good news whilst the ciphers flew back and forth between Bilbao, Madrid and MI9 in London.[11] Dansey, the man given final authority over the escape lines, did not trust her, initially believing her to be a German agent. He believed it was folly for a woman to run a network, even though he had made one exception to that rule himself and had one clandestine SIS network headed by a woman in France, codenamed Noah's Ark.[12] Dansey would be proved wrong and women could run a network as well and efficiently as men, with the advantage of not necessarily being suspected by the Germans. De Jongh is an example of this – she avoided capture until 1943 because the Germans did not believe such a young woman could be head of a network.

The consular team at the embassy in Bilbao were ahead of Dansey in realising that De Jongh must not only be tough, but deeply loyal to be risking her own life in Nazi-occupied countries and in crossing the most difficult parts of the Pyrenees. Dean wrote to London:

Crossing the frontier is an arduous and tricky business. The Postmistress [as Dean called De Jongh] with her own haversack on her shoulders literally drives the men through this eight-hour struggle. They all speak of her wonderful endurance and unerring direction finding. I have the impression that no one [the evaders] could have got through unguided.[13]

While De Jongh waited for Vice Consul Dean's response, MI9 contacted its representative in Madrid, Michael Creswell ('Monday') and asked him to visit De Jongh in Bilbao. Following his visit he reported back to London that he had confidence in De Jongh and believed her offer was genuine. Dansey agreed to MI9 working with her after hearing the testimony of three men she had brought out of occupied Europe who spoke of her 'incomparable courage'.[14] Only Crockatt back at Wilton Park remained cautious.[15] Any lingering concerns which MI9 may have had soon waned as she arrived in Spain with more evading airmen. To MI9 she was known as Dédée, the name used for her hereafter.

On 14 October 1941 Sergeant Alan Cowan, who had survived the fighting at St Valéry-en-Caux (with Private Cromar), was escorted from Brussels with another escaper, Private Bobby Conville, 'by a Belgian girl [Dédée] who acted as our guide all the way to Bilbao'.[16] They crossed the Somme by boat, then travelled on to Amiens, Paris and Bayonne. From Bayonne they travelled by bus to Saint-Jean-de-Luz and, according to their interrogation reports, arrived at San Sebastian on 16 October. On 20 October Dédée took them by train to Bilbao where they reported to the British Consulate. She stayed with them there for four days. It is believed that at this point she first met her handler 'Monday'. He made a verbal contract with her on a monetary amount for each soldier or airman brought to Spain and on that day the escape line was formally established in Bilbao.[17]

While Dédée was in Bilbao on that visit her father received a visit from the Gestapo at their home at 73 Avenue Emile Verhaeren in Brussels and narrowly avoided arrest. The Gestapo gave him a description of a woman they were searching for whose details matched those of his own daughter. It was clear that they did not suspect his daughter but were looking for a woman whom they believed to be a courier for an escape line. Frédéric gave nothing away but it was a tense moment. Hidden at the school where he worked at Place Gaucheret was a stash of false papers and identity cards for the escape line. The Gestapo did not search the school but promised to return. Clearly, it was no longer safe for Dédée to work from their home and she moved temporarily to Valenciennes before eventually relocating to Paris.

'Dédée was a lady of action,' says Brigitte d'Oultremont who knew Dédée after the war and whose father, Georges d'Oultremont, was a member of the Comet Line.[18]

Comet Line Begins

The Comet Line was initially named the Dédé Line (the male spelling).[19] One aspect of the relationship between this escape line and MI9 differed from that of other escape lines. The Comet Line insisted on retaining its independence from MI9 in its decision-making. The Belgians maintained that they knew the dangers on the ground at any given time, and if a crisis arose where a swift decision had to be made, they did not want to wait hours or days for instructions from London: such delays could jeopardise the network.

Dédée had her non-negotiable terms for MI9 and insisted that the escape line remain under control of the Belgians chiefs. She selected girls for the network who were known to be discreet and could pass unnoticed through railway stations and public places. The male guides were chosen for their ability to merge into the background and not arouse suspicion. Dédée refused a radio operator at her end. Consequently, the only contact between her and London was via the consulate in Bilbao and mostly via Creswell in Madrid. This caused much angst at Wilton Park and in London because the Comet Line had to rely on couriers to pass messages along the escape line. The fiercely independent figure of Dédée became a symbol of 'courage and defiance . . . and to the last she made her own decisions'.[20] Elsie Maréchal recalls:

> The helpers were working for 'the line' and did not know it was called the Comet Line. They discovered the name once the war was over. They were just obeying instructions from their particular chief in the chain. They did not need to know anything else. All they knew was they were helping the Allies to succeed in the war.[21]

After Dédée's arrest in 1943, the Dédé Line was renamed the Comet, or Comète, Line in Belgium. The change derived from the speed with which airmen arrived back in England after being shot down – around fifteen days – and the remark of an MI9 member that it was faster than a comet.

Dédée's father, Frédéric, took charge of the escape line in Brussels by organising the collection of evaders, their accommodation in hiding and despatch to the French frontier where they were met by Dédée and escorted to Spain. The Comet Line ran Brussels – Paris – San Sebastian – Madrid – Gibraltar. It became so efficient that in one instance, the whole crew of a bomber were brought safely over the Pyrenees from the Belgian capital just seven days after they had been shot down.[22]

On the French side of the Pyrenees, Tante Go built up her own network of smugglers and agents in Bayonne and Saint-Jean-de-Luz, often herself participating in the shadowy black market. The latter was her biggest asset because if she had any difficulties with German officers and patrols, she could blackmail them and threaten to reveal their involvement in the black market: 'She was a match for the Gestapo over three years of continuous underground activity. She bribed, cajoled and threatened the Germans and deceived them to the end. Her contribution to victory was tremendous.'[23]

Her work demonstrated a total fearlessness of the occupying forces and resourcefulness for the Allied cause. Between June 1941 and August 1944, the de Greef family helped 337 Allied airmen and soldiers through the Comet Line. This is known because Tante Go kept the Little Black Books with the accounts, names of the 'packages' (evaders) and the dates they were given shelter.[24]

One of the safe houses in Saint-Jean-de-Luz was denounced during 1942 and new accommodation was found for the evaders. It prompted a visit one day to the villa by the Gestapo. Johnson was working in the garden and feigned being the deaf and dumb nephew, but a second visit by the Gestapo followed and each family member was interrogated. The denunciation was believed to have been local people's jealousy of Fernand's influence at the Town Hall rather than any knowledge of their involvement in the Comet Line. Nevertheless, it underlines the difficult circumstances under which families operated in running the escape lines. Johnson's role in the organisation was the interrogation of evaders to ensure that they were genuine. Between July and December 1942, he himself made many journeys into Spain with evading airmen.[25]

'Monday' travelled frequently between his station in Madrid and Bilbao or San Sebastian in his Bentley to collect airmen and soldiers every time a party was brought over the Pyrenees. He provided a supply of money to keep the network running, which was reimbursed to the British after the war.[26]

Tante Go and Fernand were able to smuggle intelligence to MI9 via the couriers. Examples of this were information relating to the airfield at Palme, as well as a gunpowder factory at Blancpigeon, details about the port of Bayonne and the 12-kilometre stretch of the coastline of Anglet.[27] The discovery of this work alongside the escape and evasion roles will add to our increasing awareness that MI9 was also engaged in intelligence work.

Florentino – The Basque Guide

The terrain over the Pyrenees was steep and difficult to cross even with a mountain guide. The Franco-Spanish frontier, on a north flank of the mountainous end of the Pyrenees which peak at over 3,800ft, descends for 4 or 5 miles to the Perpignan Plain and is characterised by steep slopes and narrow ravines. Only a few footpaths led into Spanish territory over the Pyrenees, and with the exception of two villages in the higher valleys, all settlements were coastal villages and towns. One of the Basque guides working for the Comet Line was Florentino Goicoechea. Reliable and trustworthy, he was described as 'a great, powerful man of the mountains whose knowledge of the region was unrivalled'.[28] It was said that, because of his physical strength, if necessary he could carry a person over the powerful currents of the Bidassoa river and find his way across the mountains 'even when under the influence of copious quantities of cognac'.[29] Florentino knew the Pyrenees better than any other guide and could find small tracks across the mountains in thick fog or the dead of night.

A well-tested route was used to bring evaders to Florentino. First a train to Saint-Jean-de-Luz or Bayonne, then the evaders were escorted to various safe houses to rest and from there they could walk to a house at Urrugne where Florentino collected them.[30] The farmer's wife, Francia Usandizaga, gave them hot milk and soup. The rescue mission became an almost weekly occurrence in the final weeks of 1942. Ahead of the parties was an arduous twenty-hour trek over the Pyrenees, much of it during the night to avoid detection. Florentino issued strict instructions that the group was to walk in single file and in total silence until they reached the foothills where they could drop down into the valley and cross the Bidassoa river on the Franco-Spanish border. Using the main bridge was too risky with patrols, so they waded into waist-high water and were led by Dédée and Florentino, one by one. If the current was strong, they joined hands and crossed together to avoid being swept away. Florentino gave a signal to Dédée, who quietly ordered everyone to remove their rope sandals, typical Basque sandals furnished by Florentino, and trousers, and tie them in a bundle round their necks. Even in mid winter they crossed the strong torrent of the Bidassoa river in which another experienced agent, Count Antoine d'Ursel, drowned.[31] The danger inherent in these missions was described by Neave:

> Florentino climbed down first to test the depth. If the river was formidable, he would take the first airman by the hand and lead him across with the water up to his waist . . . Dédée would come last, often helping the airmen herself. Her strength and vitality amazed them . . . The sternest test was yet to come. They must climb a rocky embankment, cross the railway line and then the frontier road, followed by a steep slope on the far side.[32]

Florentino watched for any movement of the guards who stood just a hundred metres away. On one occasion, Florentino and Dédée were ambushed by two German soldiers but managed to escape back to their starting point and crossed two days later. But there were still dangers once they were across the border because the party could be discovered by Spanish border controls, arrested and interned or sent back over the border into France again. If they avoided arrest, immediately ahead of them was the steep ascent towards the mountain peaks of 'Les Trois Couronnes' before they could take a short rest and food. Dédée gave the evaders physical assistance if they needed it – many were weak and exhausted from their escape journeys or time in POW camps.[33]

The party would then arrive at a farmhouse where they were given a potato omelette to eat, clean clothes and time to sleep. There was no time for Dédée to rest: she changed from her fisherman's trousers into a skirt and blouse, and walked 5 kilometres to Renteria where she could take a tram to San Sebastian. In San Sebastian she slept for the day at a friend's flat before returning in her friend's car to the farmhouse to collect the evaders. The evaders were driven along the main road to San Sebastian until the driver, Bernardo, spotted Creswell's Bentley parked at the side of the road. They were taken in Creswell's car to the consulate in Madrid to be repatriated to Britain via Gibraltar. Dédée then returned to Florentino to be guided back over the frontier.

The stories told by returning airmen about the Comet Line were a huge morale boost to the Allied air personnel flying dangerous missions over enemy territory. They could leave on their missions knowing that if they were shot down, they had a 50–50 chance of making it back to England.[34]

Nemo

The loss of several guides, lodgers and helpers in 1941 was catastrophic for the Comet Line because 'The line had lost nearly as many of their own people as they had brought back airmen'.[35] After the arrests, Dédée and her father fled to Paris where they were hidden by friends and funded by MI9. They continued to run the escape line from the fourth floor of No.10 rue Oudinot.

Amidst the chaos at the Brussels end of the escape line a new leader emerged. He was thirty-six-year-old Baron Jean Greindl, a Belgian aristocrat who was running a soup kitchen in the capital on behalf of the Swedish Red Cross.[36] 'In the Greindl family, there were five brothers and lots of cousins and friends,' explains Brigitte d'Oultremont. 'They were all patriotic and wanted to help the Allies. They shared the same values and ethos and made a strong group in the Comet Line.'[37]

Jean Greindl had already been supplying food to Frédéric De Jongh for the airmen in hiding. He became the new chief and was given the codename 'Nemo' after the hero Captain Nemo in Jules Verne's books.[38] He divided Belgium into four regions to efficiently coordinate the escape of airmen: Liége, Namur, Gand and Hasselt. The route for escape was Brussels – a border crossing – Lille – Paris – (Bordeaux) – Bayonne – Saint-Jean-de-Luz – San Sebastian. Parties crossed the river Somme by boat (at the beginning of the line). Nemo's headquarters were in the middle of Brussels in a building occupied by an aid centre under the auspices of the Swedish embassy on Rue Ducale.[39] Under the auspices of a Swedish woman, Madame Scherling, the centre distributed clothes to poor children and provided them with food from a soup kitchen in the basement each day at midday.[40] The premises were known as 'the Swedish Canteen' and were located only two houses down from the German headquarters:

> [The office was] a long, rather narrow room, half panelled, half papered in a sombre design. To the left in a corner stood a large desk and armchair. At the other end of the room, a fireplace, a settee, two armchairs and a door opening onto a winding little staircase which led to attics. Worn out carpets. There was rather a lot of dust everywhere. Two windows looked out onto a derelict garden.[41]

The Germans suspected nothing at the 'Canteen' because Madame Scherling ensured that she was on good terms with General Alexander von Falkenhausen, the head of the German military government in occupied Belgium.[42] The clandestine escape work continued without suspicion.

Between July 1942 and November 1942, Nemo successfully sent fifty-four evaders down the Comet Line to Dédée in Paris. He recruited new guides to take airmen from Brussels to Paris, where others operated the route to the Spanish frontier and Florentino took them over the Pyrenees. Dédée and Florentino made nine journeys over the Pyrenees to bring these fifty-four men out.

On 2 July 1942, Dédée's married sister Suzanne (Madame Wittek) was arrested for helping the escape line. She had been the liaison figure between the old organisation under her father and the new leader Nemo. She was transferred from imprisonment in Belgium to Germany in 1943, then Ravensbrück and Mauthausen. She survived. Their aunt, Eugenie De Jongh, was arrested too but released within five months.[43] Dédée managed to meet Nemo in July 1942 on a brief clandestine return visit to Brussels from Paris. Room 900 had tried unsuccessfully to persuade Dédée and her father Frédéric to escape to England as the Gestapo was closing in on the network. Other members of the network were arrested, including Francia Usandizaga (the farmer's wife in Urrugne). She did not survive the war; she was transported to Ravensbrück concentration camp for helping the escape line and died there.

The following month, another helper, nineteen-year-old Andrée Dumont ('Nadine'), was arrested with her father; they and several other helpers were betrayed and the Gestapo invaded their house.[44] Nadine was transported to various prisons and ended up in Ravensbrück in 1945, then Mauthausen but she had already helped twenty airmen down the Comet Line.[45] In October 1940 she had begun working with her father in the 'Luc-Marc' resistance group for couriers, bringing soldiers and later airmen to safety in Brussels and then passing them on to the Comet Line. Almost a year before the Comet Line was established, Dédée's father, Frédéric De Jongh, was also active in the Resistance and worked with Eugène Dumont, father of 'Nadine'. Nadine returned from the camps but her father did not survive the war and died in a concentration camp.

Nadine's eldest sister, Aline Dumont (aka Micheline, Michou, or Lily), was working independently of her family on the escape line with Jean Ingels from as early as 1941, possibly earlier. She undertook responsibility for feeding and lodging airmen in Brussels and handled more than 250 evaders across Belgium for the Comet Line, where she was known as Michou; the airmen only knew her as Lily.[46] Michou played a crucial role in the connection between MI9 and the Comet Line, and the men she helped spoke very highly of her in debriefings in London.[47] Her work for the Comet Line was carried out whilst also training to be a nurse at St Pierre's hospital in Brussels.

After the arrest of her sister and father, Michou was asked to guide airmen to Valenciennes or Paris. She refused and instead transmitted messages to various people and carried on with coordination meetings between key sources, including the transfer of airmen and evaders to various lodgings. Within a year she was also issuing false identity cards.[48] She would go on to save the Comet Line at a critical stage in 1944.

Throughout 1942, Frédéric De Jongh's life remained in danger, but he refused to be smuggled to England by MI9. Money was sent to him in Paris from Room 900 via 'Monday'. Dédée continued to refuse a wireless operator, fearing it might compromise the escape line or that she would have to take direct orders from Room 900. She believed that the success of the escape line was only possible if she retained her independence. From her place of hiding in Paris and in defiant fashion, she reminded MI9 that her role was to escort Allied personnel over the Pyrenees, not to send messages to London.

The Maréchal Family

The Maréchal family was at the heart of the escape work from the early days. Georges Maréchal, his English-born wife Elsie and their teenage daughter (also called Elsie) had been involved since the occupation of Belgium. Daughter Elsie was interviewed for this book. Today in her late nineties, her inspiring spirit of resistance is still evident when asked why they risked their lives:

> Under German occupation things became worse each day. Trains were leaving every day from Brussels to Germany, packed with food and supplies. Our nation was being robbed of food and coal. We had a shortage of food. I saw the posters and the Germans every day. I saw all the Jews with yellow stars – children taken from my school class to Auschwitz. We thought 'out with the Germans!'[49]

From 1940, Georges Maréchal was part of an intelligence-gathering network in Belgium called Marc-Luc.[50] He had worked for a similar intelligence network for the Allies in the First World War, fought in the trenches and had been invalided out of the fighting forces.[51] Now middle-aged and extremely patriotic, he took up intelligence work again for the Allies. He worked in Flanders along the coast and in the Resistance movement. This German-occupied area was forbidden for most people, but because of his work in economic affairs, Georges was permitted to travel and could send intelligence back to the Allies at a crucial time after the Belgian government had gone into exile in England:

> The resurgence of Belgian patriotism in such quarters immediately after the German occupation [1940] generated many such activities and, as the occupation added the longing for liberty to simple patriotism, the pioneers of resistance such as Georges gained increasing numbers of recruits . . . Churchill, in his war memoirs, paid special tribute to Belgian intelligence gathering, which in 1942 had provided 80 per cent of all agent-gathered intelligence about radar, including the theft of a map of all German night-fighter control in western Belgium.[52]

The Maréchal family, including Georges's own parents, had a house each on Avenue Voltaire in Brussels. His daughter Elsie bought shopping for her grandparents because her grandfather was very ill. She was only sixteen at this time, had not yet finished school and was studying for her exams. One day she arrived at her grandparents to find her aunt there. Wanting to help to hide a British soldier from Dunkirk, she turned to Elsie: 'Ask your mother and father if you can shelter him.' Although Elsie's family discussed the situation, shelter was found elsewhere but the Maréchal family was evidently prepared to shelter British soldiers and airmen trapped behind enemy lines.

Dédée was already looking after wounded British soldiers in 1940, but Elsie did not yet know her. Their paths crossed after a priest disguised in civilian clothes called at the Maréchal house to discuss the hiding of British airmen, Belgians who wanted to escape to fight with the Allies, and members of the Resistance. He indicated that if he did not return, a young girl would come in his place. The priest was being hunted down by the Gestapo and had to go into hiding, so one day Dédée arrived in his place. She was 'very energetic and full of ideas,' said Elsie. 'The evading soldiers and airmen were known as parcels or children.'[53] Frenchman Charles Morelle was helped by Dédée and brought to the Maréchals' home for shelter. He was so grateful that he volunteered for the Comet Line. His sister Elvire had made a crossing over the Pyrenees with Dédée in February 1942; she too joined the line and hid airmen in a safe house at Saint-Maur, in the south-eastern suburbs of Paris.

The first prisoner sheltered by the Maréchals was a Polish airman who had escaped from a POW camp and walked his way into Belgium, as Elsie recalls: 'Dédée said to our family: "I am bringing you someone." And this was Gustav. We didn't have him very long because he had a wound to the head and had to leave us.' When Elsie had finally finished her exams, she became much more active at a time when the Germans were hunting for Dédée:

Once Dédée had fled to Paris with her father, we were cut off. Our family had been the only connection with Dédée. Dédée's mother and sister were still living in the family home, but no prisoners were being hidden there for security reasons. I went to see Dédée's mother and said: 'We are waiting. We have a man and want to get him out on the escape line.' But Dédée's house was being frequently watched and I had to run from the house, and make sure that I was not being followed. We waited at home, then I received a letter from Elvire Morelle. I was to take news to Dédée's family and that's when I expressed my wish to be more active in the escape line. Elvire gave me the name and address of Nemo who became my chief. The Comet Line had no name at the time. It was just called 'the line'. We all had to keep quiet and give no names to anyone – ever. And I never learned about MI9 until after the war.[54]

Elsie visited the Swedish Canteen at 11 a.m. at least twice a week to receive instructions from Nemo. He sent her north on the first mission, to a tiny place called Blauwberg (west of Antwerp) which had a small hotel. There she was to make contact with the owner because an airman was in hiding nearby, having been shot down. His aircraft on fire, he had bailed out and landed close to Arnhem (Holland). He had found an old bicycle, repaired it and cycled to

Blauwberg in an area that was mainly a forest of dense fir trees. She travelled by train and walked the final distance to the hotel. The owner explained that the airman was hiding somewhere in the woods:

> I found the Canadian air force officer and said to him 'You follow me. No smoking. No speaking until I do.' I walked ahead and he followed me for a long time. He was only 21. I brought him to our house in Brussels where he stayed with us for about a week. My father then took him to Brussels Midi station and there he met Georges d'Oultremont who took him to Paris. By this time, there was a small group of escapers, dressed as workmen who were allegedly working in France – hence their reason for crossing from Belgium into France. Nemo arranged for their false papers.[55]

In her diary, Elsie's mother recorded the names of the fourteen airmen whom they sheltered.[56] All returned to England safely with their own escape story for MI9. One of them, Flying Officer Ivan Davies, wrote a moving letter to the family: 'My brave Belgian friends, thanks to your kindness and courageous assistance I am now in a place of safety. If ever you are in my country, please write to me and give me the opportunity to repay you in part for all you have done for me.'[57]

Two female helpers of the line in Brussels were friends in their twenties, Elisabeth Warnon (codename Nounou) and Elisabeth Liégeois (codename Constance). The latter wrote an unpublished memoir in 1958 that recounted their experiences working for the Comet Line. In it Liégeois recalled the moment that Elsie Maréchal joined the escape line:

> The Chief (Nemo) sent us little Elsie, a new messenger with the Comète Line. Charming and so young, she carried out tasks entrusted to her with an uncommon mastery for her age. She was in charge of getting to know our wishes about the Pole (a Polish officer with a heroin habit). We did not hide the truth from her, nor our entirely understandable misgivings. That morning, he went out again, without even telling us . . . We sheltered him

for five days, which seemed to us much too long . . . we were living on tenterhooks, we were in a state of uncertainty . . . his comings and goings, even if not suspect, could compromise the accommodation we intended for the RAF airmen. Little Elsie gave us an address where we were free to take him.[58]

On 29 April 1942 an RAF Halifax bomber was shot down en route to Cologne. Two of its airmen were a twenty-two-year-old British navigator, Ronald Shoebridge, and a twenty-seven-year-old Canadian co-pilot.[59] The airmen were rescued and taken to a house in the Ardennes by a local teacher to be sheltered for the night. They were then disguised and escorted by train to Brussels to be hidden by Warnon and Liégeois, the 'two Bettys'. The airmen were soon passed to a series of safe houses organised by the Comet Line, but once it was infiltrated the two airmen were arrested and spent the rest of the war in POW camps.

The Spirit of Resistance

By early 1942, five Belgians were to be instrumental in running the Comet Line. They were Peggy van Lier, Count Georges d'Oultremont and his cousin Count Edouard d'Oultremont, Baron Albert Greindl (brother of Nemo) and Jean Ingels. Peggy van Lier was to become an important figure in the Comet Line after first meeting Nemo in 1941 during a period when he was then delivering bags of rice and flour to families sheltering airmen. He had gradually been drawn further into the network to become its leader after Dédée's departure.[60] Peggy van Lier wrote secret notes to him on how they could help young Belgians escape to England. Twenty-five years old, the daughter of a Belgian businessman and an Irish mother, she was 'a slight, fresh-faced girl with splendid bronze-red hair'.[61] She and Nemo forged papers, sent escapers down the Comet Line and organised hiding places. Their secret papers were hidden in a small winding staircase in the building of the Swedish Canteen. Members of the network frequently went out to meet airmen in hiding, as Peggy recalled:

One day I had to collect two airmen who were hiding in a pine forest. The pines were not more than five feet tall. I took clothing, [and a] shaving kit with me. These men had been hiding in the wood for three days, they had to shave and change. We knew that the woods were being searched by Gestapo police, and planes were circling about. We had to crawl out of the wood (sic), trying to escape the notice of the planes above and also endeavouring not to run into a search party.[62]

How did figures like Peggy cope emotionally with the dangers of rescuing Allied personnel? Of her own experience, she later wrote: 'Grace seemed to descend and one felt calm.'[63]

Jean Ingels was involved in the intelligence network Marc-Luc and collected information for the Allies travelling between Ghent and Brussels. If he came across airmen in hiding, he put them in touch with the Comet Line through his contact with Michou in Brussels.

During the spring of 1942, Belgian aristocrat Count Georges d'Oultremont met his friend Albert Greindl (Nemo's brother) and told him that he wanted to reach England. At the time, Nemo was about to take over the leadership of the Comet Line and Albert suggested it would be better for Georges to stay in Belgium and help the network. Georges agreed to work for Nemo who asked him to help expand the network and sent him to locations south of Brussels and Liège to find people who could help if safe houses were needed in the villages. Georges sought out teachers, doctors and priests (people who could be trusted in villages) and asked them to pass any airmen who needed to evade on to the Comet Line. If an airman had been shot down near Huy or in a nearby region, Georges was to bring him by train or foot to Brussels and ensure he was safe. Once in Brussels different people would furnish the airman with necessary items: false papers, food and civilian clothing.[64] Brigitte d'Oultremont comments about her father:

The war was a huge adventure for him. He was not married then. It was a great lesson in life. The war was something exciting and he never said he was

afraid or it was dangerous. He was a good, generous man, reliable and posi-
tive in spite of poor health. But I believe he hid a lot, especially his anxiety.
For a short time, my father worked (in autumn 1943) for the Possum Line
under Dominique Edgard Potier to learn the trade for MI9. This line organised and fed airmen in hiding before moving them to safe houses near Reims
in northern France (waiting for a pick-up by Lysander, sent from MI9
London).[65]

Between April 1942 and November 1942 Georges's main role in the Comet
Line was to guide the airmen from Brussels to Paris.[66] Georges's mother was
French and originally from Normandy, so it was easy for him to pass off as a
Frenchman and cross into France, but if a mission was too risky he knew not
to continue. Brigitte d'Oultremont recalls:

Guides of the Comet Line, like my father, often had two evading airmen
with them. He told us . . . that he never sat next to evading airmen on a
train – it was too dangerous. He told them to feign sleep or travel with a
lady to pretend she was their girlfriend if things became dangerous and they
could kiss on the train so the guards would not take any notice. In the train
one day from Brussels to Paris, at the frontier he heard the Gestapo come
on board. My father distracted the Gestapo with jokes. They were so
amused. It took their attention off the evading airmen and they soon left
the compartment.

Georges's cousin Edouard lived near Huy and carried out the same work.
He was a quieter character and also acted as a guide for airmen from Brussels
to Paris.

The Comet Line was achieving results and saving lives in spite of the
personal risks for those running it. It stretched from Belgium across Nazi-
occupied terrain for hundreds of kilometres, but could be penetrated at any
point. The Abwehr and Gestapo knew that the local population was sheltering
Allied personnel and launched a strong campaign to infiltrate and break up the

lines. Working for the line was so dangerous that Dédée believed Nemo would not survive half a year and from Paris she expressed her doubts to Peggy van Lier. Nemo did survive six months of the work and this coincided with the fortieth airman being passed down the escape line. In the Swedish Canteen headquarters, a celebration was called for with champagne, English cigarettes and glasses raised to Nemo.[67]

In spite of rebuilding the escape line and the successes under new leadership, the Comet Line was again about to be betrayed.

6

ESCAPE LINES UNDER ATTACK

The Comet Line met with disaster in November 1942 when members of the network, including the Maréchal family, were betrayed. Nemo was already concerned that the Maréchal family might be arrested and instructed that no more airmen should stay in their home. On 18 November, the family received a green envelope through their letterbox at an unusual time for a postal delivery.[1] The letter said to expect two evaders that same day, but the Maréchals had not been given advance warning to expect anyone. It was customary to have two or three days' notice of the arrival of airmen. This also came in an envelope rather than a postcard. There was insufficient time for Elsie to meet the airmen and guide at the usual rendezvous at St Joseph's Church in the Square Frère Orban. When she failed to turn up, the regular guide from Namur brought the two American airmen to the Maréchal house instead – in itself a security risk.[2]

Madame Maréchal invited them in. The circumstances were already odd and young Elsie wasted no time in questioning the airmen over supper. She asked them why they were wearing khaki shirts rather than blue ones. The airmen seemed subdued and spoke with an accent. They told her that they had flown over in a Halifax, which Elsie knew was not an American aircraft.[3] It all seemed rather odd. They then asked to go for a short walk for fresh air; an unusual request for Allied airmen in hiding, but the family had no way of keeping them indoors. Leaving her mother in the house, Elsie left immediately to alert Nemo at the Canteen that something was wrong. Nemo instructed her to return home, stop the men from leaving the house and try to interrogate them again. If something was still wrong, then to alert him.

During their brief walk the men used a telephone to alert their superiors. Back on Avenue Voltaire, Madame Maréchal answered the door to them and was confronted by one of them pulling out a revolver: 'Madame, the game is up!' he said. When Elsie arrived back home from the Canteen she walked straight into the trap, finding eight Geheime Feld Polizei (Secret Field Police of the German army) there, including the 'airmen'.[4] Now her interrogation and rough treatment began. They led her to believe that her mother was dead on the kitchen floor. Elsie stalled for time whilst thinking of a strategy of how to warn Nemo. She pretended that she had been to the black market and spent all her money. It was 4.30 p.m. and she told them that she had to meet her chief at 5 p.m. at the entrance to a large park. They swiftly bundled her out of the house and got on a tram. In the meantime, her captors had called for back-up and extra Secret Field Police were waiting in the shadows near the alleged meeting point but, as time passed and there was no sign of the chief, the men became restless. After nearly two hours of waiting, they took Elsie to Gestapo headquarters where she underwent interrogation and was badly beaten.[5] Neave learned about what had happened to Elsie at the many reunions after the war when personal stories were shared. Many of the personalities who had worked with MI9 formed a close-knit community and the ties which had bound them in the war continued in friendships afterwards. Neave wrote in his autobiography:

> Under the portrait of [the head of the German air force] Hermann Goering, the bastards beat eighteen-year-old Elsie until she was covered in bruises and unable to lie on her back for weeks. All night long the inmates of the prison of St Gilles could hear her heart-breaking sobs. I thought of her when, as an official at the Tribunal at Nuremberg, I met Goering in his cell three years afterwards.[6]

A few hours later her father was brought in. He had returned home from work in Flanders to find the Secret Field Police in his home. He and Elsie were taken to St Gilles prison where, at an opportune time, he whispered to her to say nothing and hold on. Those moments were written up later for Elsie:

A warder, heavy boots echoing, led them down a long, badly lit corridor, noisily trailing a huge key along the grilles they passed, to the central point from which the different wings stretched and there he separated them. When she clung to her father, he laughed loudly . . . She was thrust into an unlit cell and, feeling her way, tripped over a palliasse, on which she dropped exhausted. Alone at last, in spite of a blinding headache, she tried to calm down and collect her wits.[7]

Elsie took a box of matches from her handbag, which had not been confiscated, and struck a match to see her way around the cell. She took out her work permit for the Swedish Canteen, tore it up and swallowed it so the network would not be compromised.

In the interim, Nemo and Peggy van Lier had heard nothing more from Elsie or her family. Nemo sent a twenty-six-year-old lawyer Victor Michiels, a guide for the line, to check on them. He arrived at the Maréchal house to find all quiet with no movement or sound. He knocked on the door, only to be met by the Secret Field Police. Instead of talking his way out of the situation, he instinctively ran down the street. They chased after him and called for him to halt. When he failed to stop, they shot him dead.

The Maréchal Affair

The horrifying ordeal for the network was far from over. When Michiels failed to return to the Canteen, Peggy volunteered to visit Michiels's sister who was her friend, to ascertain what was wrong. She did not then know that Victor was already dead.

Peggy arrived at the Michiels's home to find the Secret Field Police there.[8] She was arrested and interrogated by a man she described as 'a fat, evil, rat-faced SS officer'.[9] She stuck rigidly to her cover story that she did not know Victor. She reached into her handbag and passed around photographs of herself relaxing with German officers to demonstrate that she was 'on their side' and they released her. It was a narrow escape. She returned home and swiftly gulped down three glasses of wine, surprising her brother who asked: 'What happened to you today?' Peggy replied: 'Oh, nothing. Just a little more work than usual.'[10]

Her interrogation at the hands of the secret police was etched in her mind.[11] She also knew that had she been interrogated by the Gestapo it may have been a very different ending. Peggy returned to Nemo with the news of the betrayals – but it was not yet over.

Elvire Morelle, one of Dédée's French guides, was travelling overnight as planned from France to see her brother Charles and stay with the Maréchal family. No one could get word to her of the events. She arrived at the Maréchal house, was arrested and taken to St Gilles prison. Under intense interrogation she also gave nothing away. The Maréchal affair had severe consequences. A hundred people suspected of being involved in the Comet Line were swiftly arrested in Belgium. Elsie's father Georges was sentence to death by the Nazis on 15 April 1943. He was shot on 20 October 1943 at the Tir National (military shooting range) in Brussels and 'died in simple, brave heroism with a pride and nobility which command admiration. His self-sacrifice and heroism are a perpetual lesson.'[12] Georges Maréchal was posthumously awarded the Order of Leopold with Palm.[13]

Elsie's mother had not been killed by the Secret Field Police and was also brought to St Gilles prison. In a spirit of continued resistance Madame Maréchal managed to smuggle messages out of the prison to her son Robert. These were written on cigarette paper and in miniature neat writing. Dirty washing was sent out in parcels and the clean washing returned, so letters could be hidden between the cardboard of the washing parcels. She also produced a number of sketches of conditions in the prison.

On New Year's Day 1944, young Elsie and her mother were transferred from St Gilles prison and subjected to three months of hard labour by the Germans.[14] They were then transported to Ravensbrück concentration camp – a journey which she described as a 'journey of night and fog'.[15] Seventy-five years later, Elsie only comments a little on the trauma of their experience in the concentration camps:

In Ravensbrück I saw the guards shovelling sick women who had been beaten and were still alive into the ovens, I still today have the howling in my ears. We did not know if we would survive this evil. We did not die. We survived. In 1945, as the Russians were marching towards the region of Ravensbrück, we were evacuated by the Germans to Mauthausen concentration camp. It took five days journey by train. The train was full. We vaguely knew where we were being taken.[16]

Comet Line helper Elisabeth Liégeois wrote about the moment she and Elisabeth Warnon learned of the Maréchal arrests. They had just returned from a visit to some relatives and were waiting for news of the arrival of two airmen they were to hide. Liegeois wrote about it in her unpublished memoir:

We returned laden with country foodstuffs and we were ready to welcome the expected 'parcels'. The whole day was spent waiting for the famous ring at the doorbell. Eventually at the end of the afternoon, it rang and it was Peggy (van Lier) devastated, to tell us of the arrest of little Elsie and her parents. Everything suddenly seemed to collapse in front of us . . . How had this happened?

'The so-called American airmen were Germans who have been sneaking through the entire network from the province of Namur to Brussels,' Peggy told us. 'I was arrested by the Gestapo and was able to get out of it, just . . . However, I am "burned" . . . I am leaving for England. Are you coming with me? I don't know how things will turn out at present. It's horrible.'

'We will return to Spontin [Ardennes],' declared Elisabeth. 'There we will find means of hiding ourselves.'

'Yes, you're right, it's better to lay low for some time . . . what a misfortune and what a bad thing, the line was working so well,' said Peggy, clasping our hands tightly.[17]

The two Elisabeths decided to pack and leave their apartment for an indefinite absence. They went to Spontin in disguise for a few days then returned to

Brussels, where it was easier to operate undetected than in a small village, and stayed with friends.

> After that, we met with Moustache [a go-between for the line], with whom we had made contact by telephone.
>
> 'Everything is fine,' he declared when we entered his office. 'The interrogations are almost finished, nothing has leaked. The Maréchals came through admirably. All the same, I think it's better if you wait a little longer before going home . . . Telephone me again in about ten days.'
>
> Before taking up the offer [of somewhere safe to stay], we decided to see Moustache again.
>
> 'You've come just at the right moment!' he cried happily. 'There's news for you. The Chief is looking for you . . . He wants you to bring back a British airman, shot down over France and hiding on the Belgian border. Here's the paper that he gave me for you. You will find the address and the password there, the people will then know who they are dealing with.'
>
> 'Under these circumstances, is it possible for us go back home? Otherwise, where can we shelter the airman once we're back?' we asked.
>
> 'Yes, yes certainly . . .' he replied. 'Unfortunately the Maréchals will not be leaving, because they were caught red-handed, so to speak . . . it seems that little Elsie handled it so well! She passed off the man shot by the Gestapo for the Chief! So the line can resume its activity.'
>
> A feeling of relief swept away all the setbacks of the past few days and we were overjoyed as we went back home. The masquerade was over! We became the 'two Bettys' again, happy to resume our activities and absolutely convinced that there was no longer any danger, since Moustache had assured us so.

Warnon and Liégeois worked for the Comet Line until their arrest on 20 February 1943. In May 1943, they were both sentenced to death by a Luftwaffe tribunal as political prisoners. Their sentences were never carried out. After terrible treatment by the Gestapo at a number of prisons, they were sent to Ravensbrück concentration camp. In March 1945 they were transferred to

Mauthausen. In both Ravensbrück and Mauthausen concentration camps, they met comrades from the Comet Line. Their first concern was to check who had survived. Elisabeth Liegeois wrote about how the women looked out for each other in the concentration camps:

> Word went round among the Belgian prisoners that little Elsie [Maréchal] could no longer walk, her frozen limbs refusing all efforts to move. Emotion woke us up from the semi-conscious state we had slipped into without noticing. Luckily we soon learnt that some companions were carrying our friend, thus getting her out of the way of the coup de grâce that our tormentors would not hesitate to administer if anyone fell out of line. Few of us felt robust, and at any moment we had to pull up a woman who staggered.[18]

The women of the Comet Line remained defiant in circumstances of absolute evil until their liberation by the Swiss Red Cross in April 1945. Elsie Maréchal and her mother survived to be liberated. Although her mother was desperately ill with pneumonia, they were both able to live in freedom again in Brussels – the freedom for which they, and others of the Comet Line, had sacrificed so much.

The Abwehr Closes In

After the Maréchal affair, the Abwehr was closing in on the network. MI9 sent an urgent message to smuggle Peggy van Lier out of Belgium along with Georges and Edouard d'Oultremont.[19] On 2 December 1942, Georges d'Oultremont left Brussels, his cousin Edouard and Peggy the following day. They travelled together and escaped down the same line they had been helping for so long.[20] They crossed the Bidassoa river and the Pyrenees in the middle of the night with Florentino. It was dead of winter; the river currents were rough and strong. Georges later wrote:

> We were given long sticks to fight against the current and followed our guide. The current is always very strong, even when the water is low . . . It

is dangerous because we had to cross a road which has a house on the Spanish frontier. We had to run across the road, then climb the steep mountain, in silence. After 15 minutes of running, we stopped in the bushes. The guide stopped us to rest. The big danger was gone but the road was still long and difficult. Often we had to walk along a steep ridge with precipice. We walked until the early hours of the morning. Sometimes we had some white wine from the guide. Exhausted, we arrived in the plain. We could see in the far distance the lights of the first village on the Spanish side of the border.[21]

'Monday' (Creswell) met Peggy, Georges and Edouard on the other side and drove them to the embassy. After an overnight stay, Peggy was escorted to the port of Seville from where she was smuggled out in a boat of Seville oranges to Gibraltar. It was thought that because of her red hair she might be too conspicuous travelling publicly across Spain and would have been picked up by the Spanish authorities if the embassy car was stopped. MI9 could not take that risk. Before leaving Europe, Peggy said she had a premonition that the first Englishman she met on English soil would become her husband. She was correct. When she arrived at Hendon aerodrome in north London on 3 January 1943, a young officer named Jimmy Langley was waiting to meet her on behalf of MI9,[22] deputising for Neave who was on his honeymoon.[23] Peggy's personal evasion file in the Belgium Military Archives summarised her significant contribution to the line: 'She has displayed high qualities of courage and has been an inspiration to very many civilians who through her direction have contributed enormously to the war effort as a whole by the evacuation of Allied military personnel.'[24]

Georges and Edouard d'Oultremont were driven to Gibraltar by Creswell where Donald Darling was waiting. They stayed in his apartment, then left on the ship *Llangibby Castle* bound for Greenock in Scotland.[25] They arrived on 13 January 1943 and took a train to London where they were interrogated by Jimmy Langley at the Royal Patriotic School (RPS) where all civilians entering Britain during the war were interrogated and screened.[26] It was headed by SIS and Intelligence Corps officer Bertie Acton Burnell and located in the

Royal Patriotic Building in Wandsworth. The primary purpose was to intercept German spies arriving in Britain who were masking as refugees or civilians. Belgian helpers and guides who had escaped down the Comet Line were
treated by MI9 as civilians rather than personnel in uniform. The interrogation
of people like Georges and Edouard could last for several days and was an
opportunity for MI9 to gather information from behind the lines in occupied
Europe. Georges commented in his unpublished memoirs that MI9 particularly wanted to learn where RAF planes had been shot down to locate pilots
in hiding, and about particular areas where German army training exercises
were held.

Edouard d'Oultremont went on to join the Allied forces and served
throughout the war. Later in 1943, and at great personal risk, Georges d'Oultremont would return to Paris for MI9 to strengthen the Comet Line in the
period prior to D-Day.

Dédée's Arrest: January 1943

After the Maréchal arrests and the departure of Peggy, Georges and Edouard from
Europe, Dédée was finally persuaded to leave Paris in early January 1943. Even as
she was fleeing down the Comet Line towards the Pyrenees, she took three Allied
airmen with her. Bad winter weather prevented the party from crossing the mountains on the first evening. Dédée left her father in a safe house and took the
airmen to the farmhouse near Urrugne. He evaded arrest, but Dédée and the
airmen were taken on 15 January 1943, just before crossing into Spain. She
believed that they were betrayed by a Spanish farm labourer for money.[27]

Dédée was taken to Villa Angele on Rue Cepe at Saint-Jean-de-Luz near
the Pyrenees. The Germans were using the villa as a prison and here Dédée was
tortured in the basement. The Gestapo did not discover her true identity
because she gave her name as 'de Tonga'.[28] She was interrogated no fewer than
19 times by the Luftwaffe Secret Police who were known to be less brutal than
the Gestapo. Dédée told the truth to save her father, but neither the Gestapo
nor the Secret Police believed that such a young woman could be the real

architect of the escape line. They thought it was her father and she was a decoy. Frédéric became a priority on the Gestapo's wanted list. At Room 900, Neave received a coded message from 'Monday' (Creswell) in Spain:

> Saturday from Monday. Deeply regret Florentino reports Dédée arrested with three pilots at Urrugne. Imprisoned Villa Chagrin at Bayonne. Attempts being organised for her escape.[29]

Neave found it difficult to remain at his desk in London as members of the network were being denounced. He resolved to go to France as soon as he could, but it would be several months before he could do so. Dédée was taken from Bayonne to Fort-du-Ha prison in Bordeaux. Robert and Yvonne Lapeyre, two loyal agents of the Comet Line, were saved and smuggled out; during their debriefing in London they were able to tell Neave of her fate. She was soon transferred to Fresnes prison in Paris. After Dédée's arrest, Madame de Greef cycled around the countryside to warn the helpers and guides of the dangers to the network. She and her husband continued their rescue efforts helping airmen to cross over the Pyrenees into Spain until the end of the war.[30]

It was estimated that Dédée had conveyed 112 British and American personnel in different groups across the Pyrenees, as well as Belgian officers, in all weathers, including heavy snow and ice.[31] The Director of Military Intelligence wrote in Dédée's citation for a George Medal that the Comet Line was 'responsible for the evacuation of more Allied service personnel than any other organisation. It was due to her, and her alone, that the organised evacuation of Allied evaders and escapers took shape.'[32]

It was true that Dédée had shaped and led the escape line until her arrest in January 1943, but the legacy and success of the Comet Line were due also to the tight-knit network around her. After she had gone, others took on the leadership or continued to save Allied personnel as they had done since the start of the escape route. Between July and October 1943, the Comet Line was bringing twelve men a month over the Pyrenees with Nothomb, Michou and Johnson meeting 'Monday' at the other side.

Frédéric De Jongh remained in Paris after Dédée's arrest and continued his work under the pseudonym Monsieur Moreau. He recruited a promising new Belgian guide called Jean Masson but disaster followed again when he turned out to be a traitor. Masson told Frédéric that a very large party of evaders was expected on 7 June and Frédéric must ensure that as many helpers as possible were present to help them.

On 7 June 1943, Masson delivered seven airmen and one American to the Gare du Nord railway station in Paris where Frédéric's helpers and guides were waiting.[33] He did not attend the rendezvous that day. The group was arrested by the Secret Police and taken to Gestapo headquarters at Rue des Saussaies; Frédéric De Jongh was arrested at his flat the same day. He survived less than a year and was shot by the Germans on 28 March 1944.

René Coache and wife Raymonde, who lived in a second floor flat in a northern suburb of Paris, also worked for the Comet Line. Madame Coache organised food and civilian clothing for escapees and evaders. In 1943 she was arrested whilst in Lille and survived two years in a concentration camp. Her husband René escaped to England, but only a short time after MI9 had informed him of his wife's arrest he bravely agreed to be sent to Brussels as a radio operator for MI9. In 1944 he returned to occupied Europe as a radio operator for the Comet Line under the codename 'Dover'. A few weeks before the liberation of Brussels, he was arrested by the Gestapo but survived.[34] For his treacherous actions Jean Masson was arrested after the war, tried for treason and executed at Lille.[35]

MI9's declassified files provide insights into the work of other individuals for the Comet Line. Their specific roles are now known because they were recommended for awards at the end of the war by MI9 and thus their citations survive in the files. One woman who received an award was Madame Olympe Biernaux who headed the escape organisation from Hasselt (Belgium) in 1943. She sheltered at least 50 evaders in her house in the centre of the town and most of them returned to Britain safely, having been escorted personally by Biernaux to Brussels or Liège.[36] She was arrested in 1944, deported to Germany where she spent time in a number of prisons and concentration camps, yet she survived the war. Of her work the Director of Military Intelligence (DMI), John Sinclair, wrote in the citation for an MBE: 'It is entirely due to Madame Biernaux's courage and initiative that some fifty Allied evaders were able to regain freedom; her work for the Allied cause is outstanding and merits the highest praise.'[37]

Another example was Sophie Grandjean who worked for the escape line as early as 1941 with her brother, the Abbé Grandjean, sheltering several evaders. They were both arrested in 1942 and she spent six months in St Gilles prison before being released. In 1944 she resumed her work for the escape line and helped at least seven evaders in her district. Her citation by the DMI said that she 'showed, at all times, a complete disregard for personal danger; she was courageous, loyal and a patriotic helper'.[38] At the time she was recommended for an award by MI9 her brother had still not been released from a camp in Germany. Baroness de Ruyter and her husband collected, sheltered and evacuated a number of Allied personnel until the end of 1943 when they were both arrested. She survived to be released on 1 May 1944 but the Baron was shot.[39]

Rescuing the Comet Line

After the betrayal of the Maréchal family and arrest of Dédée, Neave and Colonel Cecil Rait (MI9) flew out of Bideford in North Devon to Lisbon. It was Neave's first return to Europe since his escape from Colditz. He recalled: 'The aircraft with its blacked out windows, rose into the night. The heat inside was stifling and it was difficult to sleep.'[40] He and Rait were wearing civilian clothes and posing as barristers in case they were tracked in Portugal by Abwehr spies.[41] They arrived in Lisbon at dawn and travelled to Gibraltar where they met 'Sunday' (Darling), 'Monday' (Creswell) and twenty-three-year-old Jean-François Nothomb (aka Franco) who had succeeded Dédée as leader of the Comet Line. Franco was 'dark, rather Latin looking, and though pale and strained, very sure of himself. Like others, he had an unshakable faith in his mission and he would see it through to the bitter end.'[42] A recurring trait in the heads of the escape lines was the absolute commitment with which they led the networks, with their own quiet confidence and as an example to those working under and alongside them, for the entire war or until they were betrayed.

Franco had been smuggled into Spain for the meeting, collected by 'Monday' in his car and driven to Madrid, then on to the fortress at Gibraltar. At key points in the journey, he travelled in the boot of the car to avoid being picked up by authorities at a Spanish checkpoint. Guards would certainly have questioned why a man of military age was not on active service and travelling in a neutral country.

The aim of the meeting was to re-establish the Comet Line. The Governor of Gibraltar at the time was Lieutenant General Sir Noel Mason-MacFarlane who had originally been involved with Major Rawlinson in setting up MI9. A short ceremony took place in Government House, hosted by Mason-MacFarlane and attended by Neave and Rait. Mason-MacFarlane gave a rallying message for Nothomb to take back to members of the Comet Line:

> On behalf of His Majesty the King and the Belgian Government I am asked to convey our gratitude for your magnificent work. Please give this message to all members of the Comet Line and with it the sincere thanks of the Allies. Tell them that the day of liberation will soon come.[43]

The occasion was not lost on Franco who responded in his speech: 'It is wonderful to be here in this great fortress, if only for a day. It has given me great hope. I feel for the first time that the forces of evil will not prevail.'

He and others tried to break Dédée out of the prison, but all attempts failed. One scheme involved trying to get her out of a camp in a large soup container but was unsuccessful because the Gestapo moved Dédée overnight without warning and she ended up in two concentration camps.

Franco made 20 crossings over the Pyrenees and saved 67 Allied personnel, leading the Comet Line until his own arrest by the Germans in Paris on 18 January 1944. He was transported to Germany and condemned to death but survived.

Neave was preparing to drop Henri Decat (aka 'Sergeant Drew') into Belgium as Nemo's first radio operator. Decat was to be accompanied by another

Belgian, only known at the time as 'Lieutenant Boeuf'.[44] Boeuf has since been identified as Armand Vigneron.[45] Boeuf and Decat were to be dropped near Waterloo in Belgium in the third week of January 1943, but Dédée's arrest on 15 January escalated matters and Room 900 decided to parachute them in immediately. It was a risky mission because they were to be dropped blind with no reception committee. The men were accompanied by Neave to a rest house for agents at Farm Hall, Godmanchester near Cambridge. This house would be used by British intelligence from May 1945 to hold Hitler's top atomic bomb scientists where their conversations would be bugged.[46] Neave accompanied the agents to see them off:

> At ten, on the night of departure, I drove with the two agents to the special duties aerodrome at Tempsford, ten miles east of Bedford. I sat with them and the crew of the Halifax from 161 squadron RAF which was to take them on their mission, drinking coffee until midnight. After helping them equip with parachute, revolver, money and identity cards, I saw them into the Halifax. Then, standing back from the roar of the engines, I saluted as they took off into the night.[47]

Decat and Boeuf were successfully parachuted into occupied territory near Braine-L'Alleud.[48] Shortly after their landing Nemo made the mistake of going back to the Canteen in Brussels and was arrested there on 6 February 1943. News of his arrest came to Room 900 over the wireless set from Decat, now in Brussels. The message simply said: 'Nemo arrested sixth of February.' For the next few weeks there was only silence from Brussels.

Peggy van Lier believed that Nemo always knew deep down that he would be captured.[49] After the arrests of others in the network, he had remained outwardly calm, with no display of emotion or panic. Unruffled, he had continued to issue instructions for routine tasks, in this giving a sense of security to those around him. The precise details of Nemo's arrest were given to Neave a month later when Nemo's younger brother Albert Greindl escaped to England. Albert Greindl, 'a dark young man, polite and apparently unruffled by his narrow escape', had acted as a guide for the Comet Line.[50] On 14 February 1943, he was escorted over the Pyrenees by Florentino to safety with three American pilots. But not only had Nemo been arrested, it was the last that either MI9 or Room 900 ever heard from their wireless operator, Decat. MI9 eventually discovered that in April 1943 he had been murdered near Rouge Cloître in Belgium, although it was never discovered by whom.[51]

It was a sombre time: 'In a few weeks, the Gestapo struck savagely not only in Brussels, but all way to the South. It was a concerted attack on all the lines.'[52] All the great leaders of the Comet Line were gone – Dédée, Louis Nouveau and Nemo. Although morale was shaken, it did not prevent other figures coming forward to continue the escape line. The idea that the work should cease was never contemplated. Elsie Maréchal explained in an interview that Belgians who resisted Nazi occupation did so because they wanted to be rid of the Nazis and there was never any question of collaboration. Belgians knew that their acts of resistance could lead to torture and death if caught but they were still prepared to help the Allies. The traitors who betrayed them were fully aware of what would happen to those who were arrested, and clearly exhibited the worst of human traits.

In June 1943, Dédée was temporarily transferred from Fresnes prison to Brussels to testify against her French helper, Elvire Morelle who had been arrested at the Maréchal house. The trial took place at the Palace Hotel in Brussels. Dédée was fearless in interrogation, described by Neave as indifferent to fear.[53] Elvire Morelle was eventually released, but it was at this trial that Dédée saw Nemo for the last time: 'He was thin and pale, and months of imprisonment and torture had aged him.'[54] Dédée's own future was precarious. The Germans transferred her to Ravensbrück concentration camp, then Mauthausen but she would survive the war.

Nemo was condemned to death and held at artillery barracks at Etterbeek, a suburb of Brussels. On 7 September the barracks were hit by Allied bombing and Nemo was killed. His colleagues, who had been arrested at the same time, were executed at the Tir National, the military rifle range in Brussels where nurse Edith Cavell had been shot by the Germans in the First World War for helping Allied airmen and soldiers.[55]

In the latter months of 1943, seven other (unnamed) Belgians were betrayed and executed for saving Allied personnel. One of the men wrote a last letter to his family on the eve of his execution. A transcript of the letter survives in MI9 files. Originally written in French, it expressed why he had given his life for others:

> My dear uncle, I write to you to ask you to do one last and great favour, and that is to go with all speed to H---- in order to announce the news contained in this letter. Tomorrow at dawn I shall be shot for Belgium, for the King and for Freedom. I die conscious of having done my duty as a soldier and I am proud to die for my country . . . I greatly desire that you shall be the first to announce the news to my dear parents for you will, I am sure, help them to bear it bravely . . . I desire you to insist my family do not wear mourning for me . . .[56]

The man's name did not appear in the official files because MI9 had a policy of protecting the identity of the helpers as a security measure for their families and friends who may also have been helping the escape line.

The Rescue of Garrow

Amidst the attacks on the Comet Line, MI9 was handling the challenges that it faced from the Pat Line. Towards the end of 1942, MI9 received rumours via contacts of Pat O'Leary that Ian Garrow (the Pat Line's founding leader) was about to be moved from Fort Meauzac, where he was imprisoned, to Dachau concentration camp from where there would be no opportunity to break him out. MI9 weighed up the risks of mounting a rescue mission as O'Leary asked MI9 whether he should take the necessary actions to save Garrow.

MI9 faced a dilemma – did one prisoner merit more risk by O'Leary and his escape line than other prisoners or evaders? Would key members of the line go down too if the rescue failed? Norman Crockatt made the final decision that a prisoner was given special priority for rescue if, first, he was of exceptional value to the war effort because of his training and record of service, and second, he had already shown initiative and resource in evading capture or had worked for one of the escape lines. These guidelines became policy for Room 900.[57]

Crockatt exerted pressure on Room 900 to get Garrow out. Langley and Neave attended a meeting with him at Beaconsfield to discuss how O'Leary could mastermind Garrow's escape. MI9 sanctioned the rescue, but decided that O'Leary was to be responsible for deciding the lengths to which he would go to break out Garrow.

It was as difficult to mount an escape at Fort Meauzac as it was at Colditz Castle: it was surrounded by three barbed wire fences and heavily guarded. It came under the Vichy authorities and held only two kinds of prisoners: those sentenced to death or those in long-term imprisonment. O'Leary sent his best guide, Francis Blanchain, to undertake a reconnaissance of the fort. Blanchain was caught and detained by French police, but managed to escape and cross the frontier into Spain, eventually arriving in London in early 1943. It was not a good start to the mission.

It was known that Garrow had been placed under special guard, so the challenge was how to break him out. And once out, where to hide him in a region heavily patrolled by French police and Gestapo. It was decided that the best plan was for Garrow to walk out of the camp in a French uniform. O'Leary engaged Paul Ullman, a Jewish tailor in Toulouse, to make a perfect uniform: it took Ullman and his wife just forty-eight hours to complete the job. The uniform was smuggled into the prison via a guard who was bribed. Known only as 'Pierre', the guard was earning 3,000 francs a month, so a bribe of 100,000 francs immediately, and further payment once Garrow was safely out, was enough to turn him; altogether he was paid a total of 216,000 francs for Garrow's successful escape and O'Leary also received help from a young Frenchman, Fabien de Cortes.

On 6 December 1942, Garrow walked out of Fort Meauzac and went into hiding. Now he was high on the list of the Gestapo's most wanted men and the order went out that anyone found to be sheltering him would be executed. Three weeks after his escape, Garrow was brought over the Pyrenees into Spain:

O'Leary accompanied him to a shepherd's hut on the Spanish side of the mountain, and the last Garrow saw of him was a figure disappearing against the skyline, before the guide took him to Barcelona and freedom. O'Leary's final words were: 'Can this go on much longer?'[58]

Garrow was accompanied to Barcelona, from where he was flown to London. It was an important success story for MI9 and Room 900, albeit with moments of extreme tension. Back in London, Neave chatted with Garrow late into the night, with Harold Cole one of their main concerns. Garrow suggested that totally new networks should be established in a different part of France with new agents.

As a result, after Harold Cole's treachery and threat to the Marseille end of the line, Pat O'Leary moved his headquarters from Marseille to Toulouse. From there he continued to send parties over the border to Barcelona.[59] But that did not save him. At a meeting in a café on 2 March 1943 he was betrayed by Roger Le Neven (aka Roger Le Legionnaire), one of Cole's accomplices. O'Leary was arrested with Fabien de Cortes, who had taken part in Garrow's escape, and tortured by the Gestapo in Toulouse, but did not break down. He and Fabien were transferred by train to Paris. Every time the train passed into a tunnel, they planned Fabien's escape. O'Leary was prepared to take sole responsibility for the escape line and the consequences to protect his own people. Just as the train pulled into Paris, Fabien vanished through the window. Room 900 first received news of O'Leary's arrest via a telegram sent on 20 March from 'Victor' (an unnamed MI9 agent in Geneva). It read 'Fabien requests orders to be sent to all organisations to shoot on sight Roger Le Neven or Roger Le Legionnaire.' Fabien had managed to get a message to Victor from his place of hiding.

O'Leary's arrest was catastrophic. Langley and Neave began to question whether they as central figures within MI9 were solely responsible as the department was 'slow to understand the menace of Cole and other agent provocateurs'.[60] Neave concluded that the real blame lay with those who 'despite the efforts of "Monday" and Darling, for so long refused to allow sufficient recruits and wireless communications to Room 900 to create new lines'.[61] It was believed that new escape lines and agents should have been established in early 1943 to relieve the older escape lines and replace them swiftly if compromised.

Nothing was known of O'Leary's fate. Then in the summer of 1944, a woman walked into Brooks's Club in St James's Street and asked to speak to Jimmy Langley. She was carrying a message for Langley that O'Leary was alive in Germany. Her son, a POW in Germany and responsible for secret communication from the camp, had sent a coded message to her on O'Leary's instructions, having crossed paths with O'Leary when on a work detachment with SS guards from Dachau, unloading waggons at Bad-Tölz. For the remainder of the war, O'Leary spent time in Mauthausen, Natzweiler and Dachau concentration camps. He survived and was liberated from Dachau in 1945. He went on to serve in the Belgium Army as Major-General Médecin Albert-Marie Guérisse. He was awarded the George Cross and DSO. Neave wrote that O'Leary had 'performed feats of daring unrivalled by any of his successors'.[62]

The Comet Line Continues

Tensions arose between MI9 and the War Office when Neave and Langley were criticised for placing other missions in jeopardy, like those of MI6. In response Neave and Langley argued that the saving of a bomber pilot's life could be as important as blowing up a bridge.

In spite of the catastrophic betrayals in 1942 and 1943, the Abwehr and Gestapo failed to completely dismantle the escape lines. The Comet and Pat Lines resumed again because of the bravery of the people who stayed on, including Madame de Greef and her family, Jean-François Nothomb (Franco) and Françoise Dissart of Toulouse (successor to Pat O'Leary). The local occupying Germans in the area, who had respect for Fernand de Greef, did not suspect the family involvement in the line and warned him of dangers. After Dédée's arrest, a new route had to be found across the Pyrenees during 1943. On 14 February, Franco crossed the mountains with Johnson ('Be'), three Americans and Albert Greindl (Nemo's brother). But the new route was not safe, and only Johnson, Greindl and Ellissondo (a guide) escaped. The three Americans and Franco were arrested and Creswell told Johnson to secure Franco's release.

Johnson travelled to Paris to meet with Dédée's father. On his return, he took a new route towards Saint-Jean-Pied-de-Port in the Pyrenees, accompanied by Tante Go and Madame Lapeyre. He was arrested on the train but through Fernand's influence with the Commandant of Biarritz, Tante Go managed to secure his release. Meanwhile, the Dassié family who had sheltered Dédée's father in Paris were arrested, placing Madame Lapeyre and her husband in danger because they were related. Johnson accompanied the Lapeyres into Spain on 13 March 1943.[63] During 1943, two paths had to be found over the Pyrenees in the direction of Larressorre: 'In this period the crossings took three days with a routine minimum of four aviators. This period of work increased the necessity of using bicycles in good condition.'[64]

Arnold Deppé did not witness the full success of his work at Saint-Jean-de-Luz. He was arrested at Lille, interrogated, tortured but gave away no information and was transferred to concentration camps. He survived three camps and was liberated from Dachau by American forces in 1945. After Deppé's arrest, Charles Morelle from Valenciennes took over from him, but he too was eventually arrested and died of tuberculosis in Dachau ten days before the liberation of the camp.[65]

Throughout the war several thousand Belgians worked for the Comet Line; precise numbers are hard to define because a full list of the helpers was never made.[66] There were other escape lines operating in Belgium, some of which worked with Comet but not necessarily linked to MI9.[67] Some used a route to Switzerland;[68] another escape route between France and Spain was led by Belgian pilot Charles de Hepcée.[69] Monique Hanotte, who was interviewed for this book, recounts how she and her family helped soldiers and airmen prior to Dunkirk in 1940 and before it became known as the Comet Line. Like so many helpers, her father had fought in the First World War and had been involved in the resistance for British intelligence behind enemy lines. Monique recalls:

Between the two world wars, my father was President of the Veterans. He was already well known by MI6 from when the British were stationed in France during the Phoney War, preceding Dunkirk. My parents were Custom Agents, living on the border in Rumes and they were also running a little hotel and restaurant. They were well known to those soldiers and officers wanting to cross the border to enjoy life in Belgium. Our family was already helping everybody to cross that border in 1940. Jimmy Langley even came to our house one day and this was before Dunkirk.[70]

On another occasion, Monique arrived in Paris escorting two airmen to the house of Madame Stassart and her daughter Mouchka (aka 'Diane'). They did not answer the door and when Monique asked the concierge about them he alerted her to leave as quickly as possible because the Gestapo had come for them, and the patrols were probably still around. Not daring to walk too long with the airmen, Monique hid them in the courtyard behind which there was a small narrow toilet room: 'I shut the door and ordered them not to move under any circumstances. And I went to a neighbour I knew, but no answer either. Coming back, I thought of going to visit an uncle living in the outskirts of Paris who I had not seen very much.'[71]

Monique and the airmen arrived at her uncle's home with no advance warning. He was astonished to see her with the two men and knew nothing about her dangerous rescue work for the escape line. But he quickly welcomed them and let them in, giving them shelter for at least one night.

The Germans knew that ordinary inhabitants were hiding Allied airmen. Hermann Goering, Supreme Commander of the German air force, issued an order that anyone caught hiding or assisting Allied airmen was to be executed. Those working for the Comet Line were aware of this risk and yet they continued their work. Their fighting spirit became an inspiration to the airmen and soldiers they saved, and who returned to England with tales of quiet heroism from across Europe.

7
GREAT ESCAPES

The Germans regularly searched prisoner of war camps for any signs of escape plans or subversive activities. Indicators of escape preparations could include a stash of hidden tools and radio sets, diaries and notes, or the discovery of entrances to secret tunnels. Bribing the guards was useful for gaining warning of impending searches of the prisoners' quarters, but the Abwehr department soon discovered that prisoners seemed to be aware of searches and changed their policy, giving guards only a few minutes notice. Even this could be circumnavigated. At Colditz, one of the guards still had a few minutes to hang up a pair of socks at the window in the German quarters so it was visible to the prisoners as a sign that a search was imminent. This went undiscovered until the summer of 1944.[1]

Escaping from a POW camp involved a number of challenges which did not deter prisoners, rather it kept up their morale as they thought of new ways to escape. Colditz was, arguably, the hardest camp to escape from because of its heavy fortifications and being built on hard rock. In spite of this, at least fifteen tunnels were attempted by the British officers at Colditz.[2] Any tunnelling had to begin with breaking through a floor or wall and camouflaging the entrance. The first major tunnel was attempted in January 1941; it took four months to build and ran from the canteen cellar to the outer ramparts of the castle. The work could only be carried out at night because staff worked in the canteen by day. Access to the cellar was possible because keys had been made by Flight Lieutenant Parker. The biggest challenge was how to dispose of the rock and earth. This was achieved by filling ash-cans, buckets and sacks, carrying them up to the attic where they were stored under floorboards. Old tunnels were also useful for storing the rubble. Instruments used to tunnel through rock were either stolen or made from iron taken from the doorways. The tunnels were lit using tins filled with margarine with pyjama cords for wicks.[3] This idea was soon abandoned in favour of stealing electrical equipment from the Germans.

All escapes from Colditz during 1941 failed. This included an attempt by nine prisoners on 30 May that year in which they had bribed a guard to help the escape but he had given them away.[4] Lieutenant Colonel German (RASC), a senior British officer in Colditz, appointed Pat Reid to approve any plans for an escape; Reid would himself escape from there in October 1942.[5] An Escape Committee, headed by Lieutenant Colonel G. Young of the Royal Engineers, was formed in August 1941 to plan and execute methods, tactics and routes.[6] Airey Neave and Captain R. Howe were responsible for acquiring maps for the escapes.

Neave successfully escaped from Colditz in 1942. Nine months later, Pat Reid also succeeded with three other officers.[7] On 15 October 1942, Reid, Major R. Littledale, Lieutenant Commander W. Stephens and Flight Lieutenant H. Wardle escaped at night through the German kitchen, each carrying his civilian clothes, food and false papers. Bars on the windows were removed and they were able to escape onto flat roofs over a boiler house in the courtyard. Reid and Wardle went first onto the flat roof, dropped to the ground and waited in the shadows for the all-clear sign. They made their way along the foot of the Kommandantur buildings and waited in a cellar until joined by Stephens and Littledale. They then exited via a flue, and descended three levels of terraces each 3 metres high using a sheet. The top terrace was only a few steps away from sleeping Germans. The bottom terrace was only 10 metres from the dog kennels. Twice a guard dog barked but did not raise the alarms.

At the bottom terrace the four escapers walked along a road through the German married quarters, then scaled the gate in the wall that was covered in barbed wire. They split into pairs for the rest of their escape. The full reports of their escape can be read in the official Colditz file.[8]

Littledale and Stephens walked to Rochlitz and took a train to Chemnitz, then another destined for Stuttgart via Nuremberg. From Stuttgart they travelled to Tuttlingen, then continued the journey partly by foot and train to

Singen, hoping to use the same crossing as Neave earlier that year. They travelled the Helsingen to Singen road to the frontier, crossed over and gave themselves up to Swiss police at daybreak. They made it back to England to be
debriefed by MI9.

Reid and Wardle walked for two days, crossed the Mülde river and hid in
the woods. They took a train from Penig to Zwickau, then on to Munich where
they purchased tickets to Rothwell and on to Tuttlingen, leaving on 17 October
1942. From there they made for Singen and walked to Ramsen where they gave
themselves up to Swiss authorities at 8 p.m. on 18 October. Their journey may
have seemed straightforward, but there were constant dangers and during their
escape they were stopped, their papers checked and found to be in order.

Escaping from a German POW camp was always high risk, but Neave's
successful escape in 1942 provided inspiration to other prisoners, demonstrating it was possible. Lieutenant A.M Sinclair made two attempts to escape
from Colditz. The first was on 3 September 1943 and on that occasion he was
shot at point blank range, even though he had his hands up, and was taken to
hospital where he recovered from his injury. He made a second attempt the
following year on 26 September, and was shot dead whilst trying to escape over
the fence in broad daylight. After several attempted escapes by prisoners
at Colditz, the Germans planted informers amongst the prisoners to try and
uncover escape plans and identify those who were organising them. They also
implemented a number of physical security measures, such as attaching deto-
nators to trip wires at the base of the castle between two barbed wire fences and
doubling the number of guards.[9]

In spite of these measures, prisoners continued to think of new and more
inventive ways of escape. Cavities were dug in floors and walls and their
entrances camouflaged.[10] Window ledges, beams and parts of furniture were
hollowed out and escape material hidden, even in the bellows of the organ in
the chapel – any potentially secret space could be part of the plan. The prisoners
developed a fascination for creating secret rooms and cavities and the work
involved kept them occupied, as well as physically and mentally stable during
months or years of incarceration. When prisoners escaped or were engaged in

clandestine work in a secret workshop, colleagues would make a dummy and put it in the bed, in case a guard peered into the sleeping quarters. These were made from pillows used for the body, while the head was made from pumpkins painted to look like a human head. Hair was obtained from the barber's room and glued onto the head of the dummy, making it incredibly realistic.[11]

The British officers at Colditz communicated with MI9 and even sent a secret message to Wilton Park for King George VI, which read: 'All officers send respectful best wishes to [the] King for Christmas and New Year. Dutch officers same to their Queen [Queen Wilhelmina].'[12] They received a reply just a few days later from King George VI:

> The King was touched at receiving the message from our Officer Prisoners in Oflag IVC, and will be glad if you will convey to them, by whatever Secret means are available, the following reply: The King sends his best wishes to all at Oflag IVC, and thanks them warmly for their New Year message. He earnestly hopes that they will all be safe home again before very long.[13]

The Dutch officers in Colditz received a boost when HRH Prince Bernhard called at the War Office in London with a message from the Queen of the Netherlands. It was secretly transmitted to Colditz. The message said: 'The Queen thanks the officers for their loyal message and sends her best wishes to them. She assures them that their patience and their endurance will be rewarded.'[14]

This two-way communication significantly raised the morale and defiance of the British and Dutch officers in Colditz.

Prisoner Initiatives

MI9's training lectures encouraged prisoners to make a polite nuisance of themselves in captivity to waste time, resources and make the life of their captors a misery. The official history noted: 'Prisoners are always escaping, and although the majority are eventually recaptured, they are doing great work by being such a nuisance and keeping so many troops occupied in looking after them.'[15]

MI9 had been sending parcels to prisoners since its early days. The German censor intercepted many of them in the post room of the camps containing items such as pens, paper, needles, maps, compasses, German worker's caps, false identity papers and a small radio receiver. In some POW camps, prisoners tried to volunteer to work in the post room to intercept parcels with devices hidden in them. The Germans began to x-ray parcels and examine them from the summer of 1941 and as a result discovered the escape and evasion devices. Only those parcels intercepted by the prisoners got through. The first of MI9's special parcels arrived at Colditz in autumn 1941, but in spite of the interceptions by the Germans, it was believed that thirty parcels successfully got through to the prisoners in Colditz.[16]

Radios were smuggled into the camps, often in various parts and needing to be constructed by the prisoners. A radio receiver was hidden in the attic at Colditz in a small cabin hollowed out of the wall by the prisoners. To get to it, POWs had to enter a camouflaged trapdoor which led to the eaves of the castle. There was a drop between the outer wall of the castle and the inner wall of the attic; the latter was a false wall built by the prisoners and the outer wall concealed the hidden cabin with the radio in it, the location only known to the radio operators. The official file notes: 'Although the Germans were aware of its existence [the radio] and spent a great deal of time searching for it, they were unsuccessful.'[17]

The first radio set to be smuggled into Stalag Luft III at Sagan came from British officer POWs who were transferred from Oflag VIB at Dössel in northwestern Germany to Sagan in spring 1942. A group of RAF prisoners were being transferred to Stalag Luft III and were given a homemade two-valve set by British army officers to smuggle into their new camp. When tested at Stalag Luft III, it was not working and was put into storage by the Escape Committee. The Germans discovered it when a tunnel was being built and confiscated it, after which the Escape Committee decided to keep all radio activity separate from escape activities. The prisoners tried to secure another radio set and succeeded in December 1942 when a German guard with sympathies for the Allies brought them a 1933 German People's three-valve set with one broken valve. The prisoners decided to modify it because they could not secure a replacement valve and succeeded in getting the radio to work. In Oflag XXIB at Szubin in Poland, the prisoners managed to secure enough materials to build their own radio set with paper, tinfoil, razor blades, fine wire and cigarette tins.[18] The condensers were made from used cocoa tins. These radio sets provided a daily news service which raised the morale of the prisoners. A report on the use of radios in POW camps concluded:

> It had taken approximately 3 years to collect sufficient radio parts to produce any sort of daily service . . . with the use of chewing gum, matches, etc it was kept serviceable until the day of release . . . The need for so much improvisation in the making of parts such as condensers, smoothing chokes, headphones, etc. called for ingenuity on the part of the technicians.[19]

Duplicate copies of the MI9 maps were needed for each escaper. This is where prisoner imagination came to the fore, finding ways to copy the maps by using the limited resources at their disposal. At Colditz, the MI9 maps were hand-traced using toilet paper.[20] Maps were sometimes enlarged using a pantograph (an instrument for altering the scale of an outline being traced), which was acquired from the camp canteen.[21] Maps could be reproduced using a jelly process whereby jelly crystals sent in Red Cross food parcels and ink from indelible pencil leads were boiled down.[22] It was a slow process and took several prisoners working every day for a month to reproduce a single large-scale detailed map.

The motto, 'If it moves, keep it!' enabled prisoners to make escape items out of everyday things like dough taken from the kitchen, paper and even the wooden boxes in which Red Cross parcels arrived could be used for something. The prisoners were arguably as ingenious as MI9 in creating gadgets and useful utensils to do a job that needed to be done. Colditz even had a forgery department where metal items were made: buttons, buckles and insignia for German uniforms. This was done by pouring molten tin-foil, obtained from lead paper taken from cheese and cigarette packets, into casts made with plaster of Paris obtained from the sick quarters. Leather from flying boots was used to make pistol holsters; leather belts were altered to turn them into German uniform issue.

Any tools left around by German workmen were stolen at every opportunity, though some were smuggled in by MI9. Items that could not be smuggled into Colditz were made inside the camp. For example, wire cutters were made from bed iron and gramophone springs, dummy rifles from bed-boards and floorboards, and electrical fittings removed for lighting in the escape tunnels.[23] Other examples of homemade equipment included a camera made from a pair of field glasses and wood taken from a cigar box. The camera was said to be better than the original one that had been confiscated by the guards. Flight Lieutenant V. Parker, a Colditz prisoner, could make any shape or size of key required. He made a complete set of keys which enabled the Escape Committee to access any part of the castle, an achievement that was instrumental in aiding escapes from Colditz.

Stalag Luft III

Escapes could be from any POW camp at any time. However, the other famous camp most associated with escape and evasion is Stalag Luft III, as immortalised in the two films *The Wooden Horse* (1950) and *The Great Escape* (1963).[24] It was from here that Lieutenant Richard Codner (Royal Artillery) and two colleagues succeeded in escaping in July 1943.

Stalag Luft III was a camp for captured non-commissioned air force officers, located near Sagan in Silesia (now Zagan in western Poland). Like Colditz, it was considered a difficult place from which to escape, surrounded by two 3-metre-high barbed wire fences around the perimeter with 70 centimetres of tangled barbed wire between them. There were sentry towers at each corner of the fence and in the middle of the long stretches, with machine guns and searchlights. The camp had 500 to 600 German guards and regular checks by special Luftwaffe personnel were made for any sign of escape.[25] They conducted daily searches from 8.30 a.m. until 6 p.m. and were nicknamed 'the ferrets' by the prisoners: 'They crawled under huts looking for tunnels, dug spikes into the ground to uncover sand, peered through windows, eavesdropped and entered rooms . . . All vehicles leaving the compound were searched and any loads prodded with a spike.'[26]

After a successful daylight escape through the perimeter fence in September 1942, sentries were placed on patrol outside the fence between the watch-towers and specially trained patrols with dogs were positioned in the woods during the night. The official history reported:

> Ground microphones were installed shortly after the Compound was built, at depths of 3 yards below the ground, and at intervals of 32½ yards along the perimeter fence. These contained a highly sensitive swinging pen which was set in motion by the slightest disturbance in the ground. The noise was registered through the microphone and transmitted by a cable to the central listening post in the Kommandantur.[27]

The purpose of this apparatus was to pick up the sound of any tunnelling below ground. As an MI9 report stated: 'Escape from Sagan is exceedingly difficult. No one has got home direct from Sagan or succeeded in making a break from the East Compound where Lieutenant Codner was imprisoned for over a year.'[28]

The prisoners in Stalag Luft III showed as much resourcefulness as officers in Colditz. They made clothing for escape and hid it in secret cupboards concealed in walls, and in the beds which they slept on. The list of items made by them is impressive.[29] They made forty overalls of the type worn by the 'ferrets' and by camp workmen, faked from sheets and unstriped pyjamas which were dyed dark blue. Thirty German uniforms were made from tunics and trousers and the lapel badges from yellow dusters; seventy German caps from field service caps of the ordinary ranks with the embroidery added, and two hundred other caps from blankets; a hundred overcoats from officers' great coats with shoulder straps removed and civilian buttons exchanged for gilt ones; and ninety German uniform buckles, buttons and badges by pouring molten silver paper into plaster casts made from plaster of Paris stolen from the infirmary. 'Contacts' could be bribed to lend buckles, badges and buttons so an impression could be taken for a mould, or borrowed if a guard left his jacket over a chair. German uniform belts were made from black paper from hut walls or leather. The list extended to civilian clothes: sixty civilian jackets were made from ordinary rank tunics, dyed after the removal of pockets and rounding off corners to make them less formal; and thirty pairs of civilian trousers from ordinary rank trousers or blankets.

The forgery department was codenamed 'Dean & Dawsons'.[30] Linoleum and rubber could be used to make stamps for forging passes, while identity papers, gate passes, railway travel tickets, German pay books and headed note-paper from German firms were all copied. High-nutrient food was made by mixing together milk powder, Horlicks powder, raisins, chocolate, glucose and crushed biscuits into a fudge-like substance which hardened as it cooled. Items found lying around the camp were all taken: nails, screws, wood, putty, concrete, glue and coal shovels. Replica rifles were carved from wood, stained with brown polish and 'metal' parts created by filling in with lead from pencils and polishing until they shone.[31]

A hollow gymnastic vaulting horse, light but strong, was constructed at Stalag Luft III under the direction of Wing Commander Maw. The team used pieces of wood and three-ply from boxes of goods sent to prisoners by the Canadian Red Cross, creating a vaulting horse used by the prisoners for exercising.[32] On the surface there was nothing to alert the German guards to anything suspicious and indeed they suspected nothing – but it was placed near the barbed wire perimeter fence. Whilst the prisoners exercised, the vault concealed the entrance to an escape tunnel that was being excavated by prisoners who were hidden inside the vault. It was a clever ruse and the vaulting horse was soon nicknamed 'the Trojan Horse'. After exercise, the prisoners covered the entrance to the tunnel with wood and soil and moved the vault back inside. Disposing of the soil and sand was the most challenging aspect:

> When the horse was taken out for a vaulting session, one of us would be inside in its belly. This person would then open up the trap, work at the tunnel, fill 12 sand bags (consisting of trouser legs cut-off below the knee) and hang these bags inside the horse.[33]

The sacks of soil were then hidden in the roof space above the camp canteen and beneath the barber's shop.

The prisoners began the scheme on 8 July 1943. It was a very slow process, ultimately requiring the excavation of a 30.5-metre-long tunnel with two small air holes. On 29 October 1943 at 1800 hours, Lieutenant Richard Michael Codner finally broke through and came out almost 5 metres outside the wire.[34] He was followed by Flight Lieutenant Oliver Philpot and Flight Lieutenant E. Williams.[35] They parted on the other side of the fence and went their separate ways. Codner's escape was narrated in his MI9 escape and evasion report which told of his travels through Germany, partly by train, partly by foot, to Danzig.[36] When he reached the Baltic port, it was still early, so he sheltered in a pine forest adjoining the open sea. He told MI9: 'Whether the whole of this wood is empty of Germans I do not know, but it seems a possible lying up place for escapers, and it might even form a rendezvous for sea-borne commandos. The dock supervision by police all round Danzig seems poor.'[37]

Codner smuggled himself onto a Swedish ship and after fifteen hours by sea, the ship docked at the port of Södertälje in Sweden. On 4 November he arrived at the British legation in Stockholm.

The other two escapers took longer to reach Stockholm, taking a different route. They travelled by train to Frankfurt-an-der-Oder and then to Stettin, another major seaport on the Baltic (now in Poland). On 1 November they entered the dockyard hoping to board a Swedish ship; initially they were unsuccessful. Then on 6 November they were put in touch with a Danish sailor who smuggled them aboard a Swedish ship bound for Denmark, which docked at Copenhagen on the 7th. Occupied by the Nazis, Denmark was not safe, so after being secreted in an apartment by the Danish sailor on 10 November the men again boarded a ship bound for Sweden, concealed this time in the chain locker for twenty-four hours. On 11 November, the ship docked at Strömstad and the escapers arrived at the British Legation in Stockholm the following day.

'The Great Escape'

Prisoners in Stalag Luft III had learned that if a large-scale escape was to be successful they needed to make a tunnel at a much greater depth than previously.[38] They decided to build two tunnels from Barracks 67 at two levels – a false one and a real one. The dummy tunnel was built at a depth of just over 1 metre with a trap door made in its floor to a shaft down to the proper tunnel, which was constructed another 6 metres below. Workers were divided into three shifts of seventeen men each and dug all day and all night. The dummy tunnel and trap door were discovered. Prisoners built another tunnel and trap door but this was found to be structurally unsafe, so they constructed another. The final stretch received oxygen flow via a chamber under the floor of the kitchen and extended beyond the perimeter fence. The tunnel ran 92 metres at a depth of over 6 metres. It was finally discovered in October 1942, as was the dummy 30.5-metre tunnel. A total of 122 metres of tunnelling was found by the Germans.

Prisoners were undeterred in spite of this major setback and tunnelling began on a new set of tunnels nicknamed 'Tom', 'Dick' and 'Harry'. These allowed a much larger and far riskier escape to be orchestrated. 'Harry' was a square tunnel measuring just over half a metre wide, and could be described as a masterpiece of engineering: it was an impressive 111 metres in length, 6 metres below ground, and kitted out with electricity, a roped trolley and primitive air conditioning. On 25 March 1944 German guards discovered the entrance to the tunnel and the alarm was raised. Commandant Friedrich von Lindeiner ordered an immediate roll call and was incandescent with rage when he discovered that a total of eighty Allied airmen had escaped. The prisoners had fled into the woods.[39] Four were swiftly recaptured, leaving seventy-six on the run, but over the next few days, fifty airmen were recaptured and shot in secret locations. These events became known as the Sagan Case and at the end of the war were the subject of a successful war crimes investigation and prosecution.[40]

The pattern of killing the airmen was the same: instructions were issued to the local Gestapo chief to carry out Hitler's order to shoot the airmen once caught. A squad was assembled to carry out the killings and sworn to secrecy.[41] The bodies were swiftly cremated. The names of the murdered airmen were pinned to a noticeboard at Stalag Luft III as a warning to other would-be escapers. Amidst the shock of what had happened, the prisoners in the camp held a memorial service for the dead airmen. In spite of the killings and warnings about the consequences of escape, the Escape Committee at Stalag Luft III continued to make plans. By September 1944, the North Compound Escape Committee had built a secret underground chamber for the radio department to operate undisturbed. Here the team worked in complete safety all day without ever being discovered by the German guards. By January 1945, the radio operators were able to listen into enemy radio transmissions for sixteen hours a day. They then reported the progress of the fighting and Allied advances to the senior British officer in the camp who could disseminate this information to the other POWs to raise morale. The risks of operating the radio sets were well known and consequently the importance of discipline and total security was drummed into the prisoners, including not discussing what they had heard through the news service.

A 'German General' Escapes

Lieutenant General William ('Tubby') Broomhall was the most senior British officer in Colditz towards the end of the war. He was captured near Rouen on 8 June 1940, escaped for a short time but was recaptured. He was in charge of the Escape Committee in Oflag VII-B (Eichstatt), Oflag VI-B (Dössel) and Oflag IX-A/H (Spangenburg Castle). In 1943, he was transferred from a POW camp where he had been held with captured officers from the Indian army, one of whom had betrayed Britain and was working for the Germans.[42] When Broomhall discovered this betrayal, he promised the officer that he would be shot for treason at the end of the war. When the officer complained to the camp commandant, Broomhall was woken in the middle of the night and transferred to an unknown destination by train. He arrived at Oflag VII-B at Eichstatt in Bavaria and here was interrogated by, in his words, 'a very stupid German lieutenant' who appeared concerned about such a high-ranking British officer being in a camp reserved for young British officers. Broomhall said to his German interrogator: 'This camp contains only young officers who, naturally, are not very good at tunnelling. I am a Colonel of Engineers and a great expert on tunnelling and no doubt the German War Office, in their wisdom, have sent me here to give these young officers the necessary instruction.'[43]

This comment swiftly ended the interrogation and Broomhall found himself in solitary confinement for insolence; he was released into the main camp a few days later. Morale in the camp was high and Broomhall observed how the young officers spent their time educating themselves, annoying the Germans or trying to escape. Tongue-in-cheek Broomhall later wrote: 'I kept my word to the Germans, as a few months later over 40 officers got out through a tunnel which started from the passage just outside my room.'

The escape could be successful because Broomhall's room was in the only part of the camp where the Germans had not installed listening equipment by the perimeter fence because the ground was too rocky and thought impossible to dig and escape in that area. But forty officers did escape down the tunnel, though unfortunately all were swiftly recaptured. Broomhall wrote: 'We heard afterwards that when the escape was discovered the Germans deployed over 40,000 troops, boy scouts and forest guards to recapture them, and even little paths through the forests were watched.'[44] This was the last mass escape from any POW camp before 'the great escape' from Stalag Luft III in March 1944, after which Hitler ordered escaping prisoners to be shot as a deterrent.

Broomhall was a burly figure who could not easily escape down a tunnel.[45] Over the months preceding June 1943, a bold plan was hatched that almost succeeded. If they could dress Broomhall as a German general, a small group of prisoners could simply walk out of the camp gates 'under escort' by Broomhall and no camp guard would dare challenge a German general. The officers set to work to produce the uniform, using gold paint for the gold cords on the general's cap – acquired for scenery in theatrical activities which the Germans permitted to keep prisoners occupied and, ironically, to prevent them from thinking about escape. The general's uniform was complete with medals and decorations:

The Germans took away all our khaki shorts in which we played games and had them dyed bright red to prevent us using them for escaping. Cut into strips, these made the most convincing red stripes down my General's trousers. The uniform was based largely on blankets, coloured German field grey with various amateur dyes.[46]

If questions were asked, Broomhall was to be the German Director of Works from Berlin who had inspected the camp with a view to improving security against escape attempts. He was to be accompanied by a 'Staff-Captain' (a British officer who spoke fluent German), a corporal and two civilian contractors. One of the prisoners chosen to be a 'civilian contractor' was the British racing driver Tony Rolt who had trained at Sandhurst prior to 1939 and been commissioned into the Rifle Brigade. He and his unit defended Calais just before the evacuation of Dunkirk and he was awarded the Military Cross for valour. He was taken prisoner on 26 May 1940 at Calais and force-marched with other prisoners to Stalag VII C (Laufen) in Germany.[47]

Rolt was knowledgeable on collected medals and so advised the Escape Committee that the 'Director of Works' would not have a decoration higher than the rank of Iron Cross 3rd Class. The medals for Broomhall's disguise as a German general and Director of Works were made in the camp from cardboard, carefully painted and covered with celluloid.

Two days after discovery of the escape of the forty officers, Broomhall learned that Oflag VII-B was to be split and the inmates moved within twenty-four hours. He had to implement his own escape plan immediately. On 30 June 1943, he and his small escape party dressed in secret and, with the Iron Cross around his neck, he accompanied his 'prisoners' towards the back gate. It was customary for the presence of German senior officers and visitors to be reported to the commandant. This had to be avoided. At an opportune moment when the hospital telephone in the camp was vacant, a fluent German-speaking POW telephoned to the back gate and reported that a senior general was just leaving the premises and no further action was required.

In a prearranged scenario just as the party reached the gates, two British inmates rushed passed them without saluting. Broomhall bellowed at them in his best German and asked if that was how they behaved in the British army.

They replied that it was a typical response from a German general. The guard came running, his hands shaking, and fumbled to unlock the gates. Now Broomhall made a fatal mistake and overacted his part: just outside the gate, the two civil contractors spread out a plan of the camp as the 'Staff Captain' explained it to Broomhall. The plan was then rolled up and the corporal saluted Broomhall. The 'Staff Captain' said loudly: 'The General does not wish to be reported.' In full view of the camp, they walked down the road and out of sight, with Rolt struggling to keep up the pace because he was carrying packs of food and supplies under his uniform.

Broomhall's pistol and holster had been made from chocolate sent to the prisoners in Red Cross parcels. By the time they were a mile from the camp, the chocolate had started to melt down the red stripes of his trousers. From behind them a German sergeant major and corporal on bicycles called them to stop and show their passes. Broomhall produced his false identity papers but they did not pass scrutiny. At gunpoint they were all marched back to the camp and held in solitary confinement in a cell the size of a large desk.

The commander of the guard during the period of solitary confinement was the same corporal who had originally let them out of the back gates. He was bemused by the whole story and thereafter called Broomhall 'Herr General'. He stated that Broomhall had overacted the part, had frightened him and he (the corporal) had warned his colleagues that a grumpy general might well come back into the camp and to watch out. He also reported to the commandant that he had seen his important guest out of the camp, to which the commandant replied that he had had no visitors that day. But for this, the escape could have succeeded. Broomhall and the other escapers were removed from the camp, as he recalled in a previously unpublished account of the episode:

After many days of solitary confinement we were removed under heavy guard to an unknown destination. On arrival we were delighted to find it was the celebrated Colditz, so we had graduated to what we always described to our captors, much to their annoyance, as the 'strafe college'.[48]

From July 1943 until liberation in the spring of 1945, Broomhall and Rolt were held in Colditz. For a short time, Broomhall was the most senior British officer in Colditz.[49] Rolt was the mastermind behind the construction of the wooden glider for another daring escape plan.[50] The glider was built between January and October 1944 in a secret room that had been constructed by the prisoners. They had built a small workshop under the eaves above the chapel; a false wall rose up to a trap door in the ceiling leading into the hideaway. Designed by Flight Lieutenant L. Goldfinch (RAF) and a small team including Rolt, they intended to launch the glider from the roof and land in the valley below the castle.[51] It was never used for an escape and was abandoned in the latter stages of the war when prisoners were awaiting liberation by the Allies. Rolt went on to become a famous racing driver and participated in three Formula One World Championship Grand Prix.[52] Broomhall was mentioned in despatches for his escape work and being in secret communication with the War Office.[53]

Escapers, Evaders and Intelligence

Foot and Langley acknowledged that they were not able to assess whether prisoners of war provided any valuable intelligence for MI9.[54] With the benefit of declassified files, it is now possible to answer this question. MI9 collected a significant body of intelligence from a number of sources: prisoners of war in POW camps, escapers and evaders who returned to Britain, helpers of the escape lines and agents behind enemy lines. Much was learned from these debriefing interrogations because experiences in enemy territory could be used to shape the advice in future training and be printed in the regular MI9 bulletins. This was an entirely new development: there had been no precedent for escape work combined with intelligence in the First World War. The official declassified history of MI9 states that 'Clandestine escape work as a specialist form of intelligence was an entirely new development'.[55]

The kind of information that was useful to MI9 from escapers and evaders included information such as the particular route an escaper had taken out of a country, and whether he had come out on his own or via an established escape line. A returning escaper could provide eye witness observations about a town, city or port to provide fairly current intelligence, for example, on where the Germans had mounted their searchlights and range across a port, how to avoid the searchlights and move undetected towards a neutral ship to be smuggled aboard. It was helpful to know if a town had imposed a new curfew – knowledge of this was important because to move around during a curfew risked recapture by German patrols. The debriefings provided snippets of information which might seem insignificant but when collated together helped to build a bigger picture and thus aid escape and evasion.

Thousands of interrogation reports of escapers, evaders and helpers exist from throughout the war. These provided lots of information which could be collated into the MI9 bulletins updating Allied personnel on aspects of escape and evasion.[56] The bulletins gave details of the changing situation in enemy-occupied countries, information on Swedish and German shipping routes, identifying military and naval uniforms of other countries (including colour sketches of Spanish and Swedish uniforms), printed maps of Poland and the German ports of Stettin and Danzig, details of living conditions in European countries, the state of partisan groups and their organisation, and danger areas for evaders to avoid. A series of appendices gave very detailed information for survival including what kind of food could be found in the wild in a particular country, what could be eaten by way of vegetation, animals, insects and fish, and how to cook them. This sort of comprehensive information was provided in a separate section of the bulletin for each country: Norway, Italy, Poland, Sweden, Spain, Holland, Germany, Australia and the South Pacific.[57]

Throughout the war, a huge volume of information was collected from the interrogations of civilians coming into Britain from occupied Europe. They provided details of a military nature, such as defences, troop movements and reinforcements in a particular town. Information was secured, for example, about the number of troops stationed at Liège, where they were quartered in the city, the regiment, identification badges on uniforms and the existence of underground tunnels in the region.[58] Interrogations also provided details about the German coastal defences, particularly important in advance of planning D-Day to minimise casualties on the beaches of Normandy.[59]

One MI9 file noted that intelligence from returning prisoners of war was not difficult to obtain. Every POW camp had personnel who had made an attempted escape.[60] Prisoners who had attempted escape from any enemy POW camp and been recaptured were interrogated by the Escape Intelligence Officer in the camp, who also briefed prisoners about the kind of information he needed if they were taken outside the camp for a hospital visit or court martial hearing. Prisoners were known to have provided details about European frontiers, countries, names and addresses of people who could be relied on, and knowledge was gained from other nationals (Dutch, French and Polish POWs) in the camp who had attempted escapes. Prisoners tried to gain information from German guards and civilian workmen by bribing them with chocolate, food and cigarettes to befriend them.[61] They succeeded in gaining details of travel conditions in Germany, positions of guards and the times of their shifts, the names of nearby towns, and imposition of new curfews. All this was invaluable for planning escapes and having knowledge of the area outside the camp. The intelligence gathering was so efficient that by the time the Americans liberated Colditz Castle on 16 April 1945, the intelligence section in the camp was able to furnish the US forces with a complete list of all Nazis and non-Nazis in the area.[62]

This analysis of prisoners of war and the information gained from them will add to the growing evidence that MI9 was not only a secret service for escape and evasion, but was also an intelligence unit. It makes for a fascinating new understanding of the nature of MI9, especially when considered alongside an even more secret section – known as Room 900 and Intelligence School 9.

8

INTELLIGENCE SCHOOL 9 (IS9)

Whilst MI9 coordinated escape lines across occupied Europe, Norman Crockatt understood the importance of training Allied personnel in escape and evasion before they went into action. This would ultimately aid MI9's work in getting them out of enemy territory. Training was especially important for RAF pilots whose chances of being shot down over enemy country were high. Training a pilot was not only costly but could take three months to complete. Britain did not have sufficient time to do that if pilots were lost in action or shot down and captured. Without air superiority over the Luftwaffe, Britain would be defeated, therefore airmen had a mandate to escape and evade to return to England to fight another day.

The first course in escape and evasion was given just three weeks into the war in Hibbert Road in Harrow.[1] The courses transferred temporarily to 14 Ryder Street, St James's, London and later became established within MI9 as Intelligence School 9, otherwise known as IS9.[2] Underpinning the training programme was the belief that escaping or evading in enemy territory was primarily a state of mind. Michael Bentine, later of the radio comedy programme *The Goon Show*, went through IS9 training during the war and commented: 'If you are determined to do so, your chances of escape are greatly increased.'[3]

By April 1940, lectures in escape and evasion were extended to the British Expeditionary Force, Fleet Air Arm and Officer Training Units before personnel went on their first missions. The following year, the courses were run from a school in Fisher Road in Harrow, known as Station X or 'RAF Intelligence

School Harrow'.[4] MI9 ran an advanced three-week intelligence course which was given to senior RAF officers, and army and naval intelligence officers.[5]

Crockatt was an open-minded and practical commander who adjusted the training programme according to the experiences of returning escapers and evaders. His rallying motto remained constant throughout the war and was instilled into all the training lectures: 'Keep in mind this point – if you are cut off or captured – you are not forgotten – go on – never give up!'[6]

A part of MI9's success lay in the fact that it never abandoned the airmen and soldiers trapped in enemy territory, whether in prisoner of war camps or in hiding. The rigorous training programme at its Intelligence School 9 was fundamental to that success. Documents captured from the Germans at the end of the war revealed that so successful was the escape and evasion training that British army prisoners became known by German interrogators as 'the silent service'.[7] The documents said that 'As a prisoner the Englishman is arrogant, proud, cautious and absolutely secure'.[8]

Training in Escape and Evasion

The IS9 training was designed to prepare personnel in escape and evasion matters which were based on common sense but would help men focus and react in the first disorientating moments after being shot down or captured. One of the first instructions given to each new intake on a course at RAF Highgate was: 'Do not be captured!' But if capture could not be avoided, then:

> Only as a last resort should you be in a position of being captured. Your job is to fight – and only through wounds, lack of ammunition or food should you ever allow yourself to be captured. Should you be captured, it must be your firm and constant determination to escape at the earliest opportunity – to bring back information to our people.[9]

The above instructions were at the heart of the 'escape-mindedness' which Crockatt understood to be so fundamental to success. If taken prisoner, personnel were encouraged to actively make a nuisance of themselves in POW camps to distract the enemy because 'every German soldier occupied in guarding you – every German soldier occupied in searching the countryside for you – is one less in Germany's war machine'.[10]

It was known that after capture every prisoner would be interrogated. IS9 covered training in what to expect during interrogation, including German methods.[11] It advised personnel that a prisoner had certain rights under the Geneva Convention (1929) and that included during interrogation, when they were only required to give their name, rank and number. MI9 provided as much preparation as possible on ways to resist interrogation and warned about Dulag Luft, a notorious German interrogation centre for RAF prisoners at Oberursel near Frankfurt. It was known for its brutality and torture. At Dulag Luft and Dulag Nord (for interrogation of naval prisoners), subtle interrogation techniques were also used, such as hidden microphones to record prisoners' conversations and alcohol to loosen the tongue.[12] MI9's training guidance warned: 'Watch out for microphones – they are concealed and because you find one or more it does not mean you are safe. Even in the open be careful – trees no less than walls have ears.' The escape and evasion handbook said: 'Don't jump to the conclusion that your room is free from microphones because you cannot find one. The enemy has years of experience.'[13]

All personnel were to be on the alert for bogus prisoner of war forms and a phoney medical officer who was actually an interrogator.[14] They were told how the Germans might use 'stool pigeons' – enemy personnel masked as prisoners of wars to befriend them for information. The IS9 lectures warned about Major Binder, a particularly unpleasant German interrogator from Dulag Luft who disguised himself as a medical officer. His job was to arrive at the hospital in the port of Wilhelmshaven to subtly gain intelligence from injured POWs whilst they were disorientated and confused. General security advice was to 'avoid conversation with apparently harmless enemy officers'.[15]

Training courses included discussions on baling out over enemy territory; conditions in France, Belgium and Holland; making first contact with helpers and the escape lines if evading capture; travelling by train in enemy territory; and evasion and exit from Germany.[16]

The Geneva Convention allowed for escape and the escape and evasion handbook was encouraging: 'Don't be downhearted if captured, opportunities for escape will present themselves.'[17] The lectures impressed on the soldiers and airmen that the first moments after capture might provide the best chance of escape, especially when the enemy's attention was still drawn to fighting a battle. For airmen shot down over enemy territory, MI9's standard advice was to get away as far as possible from the wreckage of the aircraft and hide. Escapers were to make sure they were well into a country before seeking help, otherwise they might be picked up and sent back into enemy territory.

A key aspect to successful escape and evasion was how to blend into the background and become 'invisible', often right under the noses of the Nazis. The simplest of errors could give an escaper away, as in the case of the escaper who acquired a bicycle, cycled 400 miles across enemy territory and remembered to keep to the right-hand side of the road (instead of the British left-hand), until he came to a roundabout. He cycled the wrong way which alerted a nearby policeman, and was promptly arrested and sent back to a POW camp.[18] Personnel were taught not to march in a military fashion, but to adopt a slouch, to wear a beret (like the French), not to use a walking stick because it was a British custom, and sling a haversack to look more like a local.[19]

Training lectures had a section about MI9's helpers in occupied territories, the largest concentration of whom were to be found in Belgium. Allied personnel were taught to think about the security of those helping them and reminded:

For no reward they risk their lives and those of their families to help you. The only repayment they ask is that you do not tell anyone they helped you. Do not talk – write nothing – remember everything. Remember that anyone who helps you risks death. If caught, you face nothing worse than a German prison camp. They face certain death for themselves and their families. You must protect them with the greatest care.[20]

IS9 issued instructions that all information about helpers and their locations had to be kept totally secret.[21] An evader must never contact an escape line or organisation direct – they would find him and contact him. This latter point was borne out by the first-hand testimony of Elsie Maréchal who was sent north in Belgium by the line to find an airman known to be hiding in the woods.[22] Nor were airmen and soldiers ever to mention the names of previous helpers who had aided them or their methods. The names and addresses of helpers were never to be written down. The real example was given in lectures of an RAF evader who gave details of a helper to his closest comrade in case he ever needed help behind enemy lines. The details were written down, slipped into a wallet and forgotten until the comrade was shot down and the paper found by the Germans. The helpers – a French farmer and his wife – were arrested as a result and shot.

Service personnel were told that they must obey all instructions from helpers without question, as if they had come from their own commanding officer. MI9 reckoned that 95 per cent of the population in Holland and Belgium would be friendly towards an escaper and evader because their country was under enemy occupation. The helpers could be relied upon to link them to an escape line to try to reach the British consulates at Bilbao, San Sebastian or Barcelona. Personnel were not to give themselves up to Spanish authorities just inside the Franco-Spanish frontier because they risked being sent back over the border and handed to the Germans.

In Denmark, fishing harbours were found to be less guarded by sentries than ports in other Nazi-occupied countries and the fishermen (who resented the occupation) were more likely to help evaders and ferry them to Sweden or direct to Britain. MI9 noted that 'Danes are all extremely anti-German and pro-British and very keen to help anyone escape'.[23] In Spain, an escaper had to take care not to give away information in overheard casual conversations or comments that the Spanish police could pass on to the Germans. One training lecture cautioned that 'through thoughtlessness the lives of brave men and women are endangered and efficient escape organisations have to close down'.[24] Courses included identification of enemy aircraft, technical intelligence, economic warfare, and identification of merchant shipping.

Special instruction in codes was given to a small number of staff on the training course – usually no more than ten personnel at a time and only those officers capable of grasping the details easily were selected to learn about codes. Training remained current and was constantly reviewed and updated. In March 1942, diagrams, maps and escape and evasion lectures were prepared by MI9 specifically for the commandos and special forces embarking on the St Nazaire Raid and two future (unnamed) operations.[25]

RAF Highgate

On 1 September 1942 the RAF Intelligence School moved to Caen Wood Towers in Highgate, north London, today called Athlone House.[26] Publicly, Caen Wood Towers appeared to be a convalescent home for injured pilots, but this was a cover for its real activities as the intelligence training centre 'RAF Highgate'. The comedian Michael Bentine served in the RAF in the war and trained there in 1943. He described the site as 'a large Victorian mansion, set in extensive grounds, and surrounded by high, barbed wire topped walls, patrolled day and night by armed guards and RAF police dogs'.[27] The new location provided more facilities than at Harrow and had 'first class lecture rooms, sleeping quarters and recreation grounds in ideal surroundings'.[28]

Requisitioned from Sir Robert Waley-Cohen in 1942, the 12-acre estate bordered Kenwood House, the former home of Lord Mansfield, which he bequeathed to the nation on his death and today is managed by English Heritage. Both estates border Hampstead Heath and provided opportunities for practical exercises in evasion techniques there.

A week after the move to Caen Wood Towers, the strength of the centre was six RAF officers, one WAAF officer, thirty-four other ranks and thirty-six women auxiliaries.[29] The main house provided mess accommodation for permanent staff and between sixty-five and seventy officers attending courses.[30] Offices and three lecture rooms were situated on the ground floor. Additional premises were requisitioned from nearby private houses at Nos 7, 13 and 19 Sheldon Avenue.[31] No. 7 provided accommodation for seventy other ranks of RAF and WAAF (a mess and canteen), No. 13 was used as an RAF hostel for thirty-five to forty airmen as RAF Quarters, and No. 19 was a hostel for thirty-five to forty-five WAAF.

Three courses – A, B and C – were run from Caen Wood Towers. Course A provided a broad, general background of Air Force intelligence and lasted seventeen days.[32] Course B dealt with prisoners of war and evaders and lasted for five days, running almost continuously until September 1944.[33] Course C was aimed at training cadets who had been earmarked for some kind of intelligence work. Course B had started for RAF officers only, but soon expanded for the training of inter-service personnel.[34]

As courses expanded it was necessary to use the adjacent Kenwood House, which was codenamed 'Melbourne' during the war as part of RAF Highgate. Lectures were held in Lord Mansfield's former dining room on the ground floor; a poolroom was set up in his former dressing room, and his breakfast room became a dining room.[35] The rooms on the first floor provided additional sleeping quarters for those attending the courses.[36]

There was also an American presence at RAF Highgate, including US Navy Commander Bill Casey of the Office of Strategic Services (OSS) who later became a director of Central Intelligence (DCI). From April 1943, the first course was given for selected USAAF Operational Air Crew because captured US personnel could be held in different camps from British POWs, necessitating their own special training in escape and evasion. The American version of the course at RAF Highgate included learning American POW codes, propaganda and sabotage. The course ended with a visit to Scotland Yard where personnel were given instruction in lock picking, forgery and trades useful to a prisoner of war.

Michael Bentine had fond memories of his training at RAF Highgate: 'We all felt the same way about the war. We all realised that we were fighting an archetypal demonic force within man.'[37]

MI9 Bulletins

MI9 issued regular monthly bulletins to update personnel on aspects of escape and evasion. It gave new advice, for example that prisoners in occupied Europe were usually transported to Germany by railway in small goods wagons or boxed cars, with a guard placed in every second car. This afforded an ideal opportunity to escape from the unguarded carriages and it was estimated that, thanks to this knowledge, hundreds of prisoners escaped from trains.[38] They were able to remove ventilators or windows, make holes in the floors, and even remove door runners with hidden escape aids. When the train slowed down, it had been known for whole cars of prisoners to escape.[39]

More advice pointed out that if pilots were shot down in the vicinity of Munich, it was better for them to head to Lichtenstein or Switzerland and escape. They were alerted to the well-guarded border between Germany and Switzerland, and how the shape of the border zigzagged such that it was possible to accidentally re-cross into Germany via one of the narrow salients (pieces of land jutting out). Another valuable piece of information in the bulletins included advice to cross the river Rhine between Lichtenstein and Lake Constance, and to carry out a reconnaissance of the border patrols and the use of dogs. This was essential because, as MI9 warned, 'many evaders had been caught within sight of safety because they rushed the last few miles'.[40]

The only way to escape from southern Germany was deemed to be via the Klagenfurt region, to make contact with partisans there and in the hills west of Graz, where they would provide help to cross the border. Evaders from Hungary were to make their way south and contact partisans in Yugoslavia. As a general rule, if injured and escape was impossible, personnel were advised to surrender to regular German troops, and not SS or police units, as they would have a better chance of being treated according to the Geneva Convention.[41]

Returning prisoners could give information and intelligence to MI9 on the situation behind enemy lines, on German military installations, defences, German morale, food shortages and German patrols. Updated information coming out of France and occupied Europe was as important for evading capture as any other part of IS9 training. One example given in training and included in a regular MI9 bulletin was how undercover Gestapo officers in Paris and Marseille had started to wear soft brown felt hats and this could be used to distinguish them from the local French people.

After D-Day, the number of courses at RAF Highgate declined as the final stages of the war approached.[42] Between November 1939 and November 1945, an average of a thousand personnel a year passed through RAF Highgate, including WAAF and naval officers. The first peacetime courses were held there from January 1946 until it was disbanded in October 1948 and moved to the Air Ministry in Monck Street in Westminster.

IS9, Escape and Evasion

Each section within IS9 corresponded with the equivalent escape and evasion section of MI9. IS9(X) equated to MI9(X) and dealt with location of POW camps and despatch of escape material, escape and evasion planning, collection of material for the MI9 bulletin and the preparation of maps. IS9(W) was formed on 25 February 1943 and was responsible for the interrogation of escapers and evaders; at its peak the staff numbered 157.[43]

The MI9 files noted: 'The right type of woman is as good an interrogator as a man.'[44] Staff Officer E.A. Hughes (WAAF) and second Subaltern M.S. Jackson (ATS) were two of the very few known female interrogators of the Second World War, while others worked for the Naval Intelligence section attached to MI9's sites at Latimer House and Wilton Park.[45] Hughes's signature appears on many of the interrogations of escapers and evaders. The file noted that 'besides being responsible for the whole of office routine, [she] carried out occasional interrogations very efficiently'.[46] Interrogating returning personnel provided useful information for IS9(X) in planning escape routes. It also kept track of the names of helpers who could be recommended for awards at the end of the war. Information obtained from the debriefings described current conditions in enemy occupied countries and kept MI5 informed of any matters of security interest. Originally debriefings were based simply on a questionnaire, but as escapes became more complex after the Dunkirk evacuation, interrogation was conducted by a specially trained officer. It was deemed better to have a few trained interrogators than a large number of untrained ones.

IS9(Y) dealt with codes and communications, undertook the preparation and despatch of coded messages to POW camps, organised correspondence with the camps and liaised with relatives of the prisoners. Underpinning the use of codes was the belief that 'Prisoners of war are of great value to their country as code users. They are still in the war and doing a most important job for the war effort.'[47] The letters to the camps often gave information and news that would boost the morale of the prisoners by updating them on the campaigns, the situation at home regarding the high spirits of the British people and the belief in ultimate victory. These were read by the German censors and, surprisingly, allowed to go through. The Germans never suspected code messages in any of them.

Code users in the camps were encouraged to send back information of military and economic value: 'It is probably the most reliable source available for keeping the country informed of what is going on inside Germany.'[48] An example of this was a decoded message from a flight lieutenant held in Stalag Luft II who wrote, 'Germany much impressed Kiel raid. Two intelligent sources say German people will not stand intense bombing.'[49] Another example was a message sent from an officer at Colditz: 'We are all fit and well here and have enough clothes to have no dread of winter. The biggest joke is that the sentries now have to keep people from breaking in to the camp which is so well supplied.'[50] This was important because it affirmed that food supplies in Colditz were adequate and officers were not starving.

The most important communication was by wireless, which had a great effect on morale in the camps. Every Wednesday, just after 9 p.m. on the BBC radio service, an army padre, Ronald Selby-Wright, addressed the forces by wireless, broadcasting coded messages to British POWs. M.K. Howat of the ATS encoded the messages for use in his broadcasts. Communication was also conducted via Morse code, in cooperation with the Admiralty and SOE, transmitting messages regularly, all of which were picked up and correctly decoded. As an example, in 1941, 581 coded messages were sent to Germany and Italy, and 799 were received back.[51] The highest number was in 1943 with 924 messages sent and 3,527 received. The official files noted: 'Our code work proved that prisoners of war can be utilised with advantage as suppliers of intelligence.'[52]

Miss M.K. Howat, who served in the ATS from 1938 until 1945 and had joined MI9 at Wilton Park in May 1941, was attached to IS9(W) in 1943.[53] In her unpublished memoirs she also mentions a number of Americans at Wilton Park under the command of Lieutenant Colonel Holt. She recalls how she was sent to Aldford House in Mayfair one day where the diplomatic section of the Government Code and Cypher School (GC&CS) was based until it moved to Bletchley Park in 1942. The Americans had staff stationed there on the upper floors:

> I remember being sent to Hooker's HQ in Aldford House by Crockatt to be present when he was imparting some of our intelligence information to Winston Churchill – with instructions to kick Hooker on the shin if he started to say more than Crockatt wanted him to! I could only hope my aim under the table was correct and I didn't kick the wrong leg.[54]

Howat had worked initially at MI9 for Brinsley Ford who was also overseeing a team of WAAF officers working with Code 1, which was formulated on the basis of a dictionary.

IS9(Z) was the technical section responsible for the production and despatch of escape and evasion devices.[55] It was assessed that 90 per cent of the 1,200 special parcels that were despatched reached POWs intact. The prisoners knew by coded message what was being sent to them and where to look for the material. Books written by escapers from the First World War were used in escape and evasion training, but there was a down side: Germany studied the books too and issued details of how British POWs might escape or how escape gadgets might be hidden, so IS9 had to come up with new ways of concealing them.

Like its counterpart at MI9, IS9(Z) never despatched escape aids inside Red Cross parcels, and used fictitious charities, clubs and organisations. An example of an early invented charity was The Prisoners' Leisure House Fund which had allegedly collected money to buy games, books and extra comforts for the prisoners. Other phoney institutions included the British Local Ladies Comforts Society, Empire Service League, Jigsaw Puzzle Club, Lancashire Penny Fund, League of Helpers, Welsh Provident Society and The Wilberforce Foundation. In 1943 the ingenuity of the prisoners themselves made it possible for them to intercept the escape and evasion aids (known as 'contraband') before they were examined by camp censors, making it possible for them to be sent out without concealing them. From Christmas 1943, money and escape maps were hidden inside Christmas crackers and sent into POW camps with a letter to the German camp commandant asking him to pass on the Christmas crackers to the POW leader to help brighten up their Christmas. Fifty per cent of these got through to the British prisoners.

From 1941 until March 1945, a total of 12,808 parcels were despatched to POWs by IS9(Z). They included 9,283 parcels with extra cigarettes and tobacco to bribe the guards and 3,525 special parcels with hidden aids. To give an idea of the sheer scale of operations, it despatched 9,247 maps, 1,119 hacksaws and 942 passes.[56] IS9(Z) prepared and despatched special containers for dropping supplies to IS9 agents on the continent. A special clothing store in Regent Street was available for agents to be fitted out. During 1944, IS9(Z) helped to obtain special boating equipment for Holland in connection with the evasion activities of IS9(WEA – Western European Area). The following items were included and despatched: special food packs, first aid equipment, flasks of rum and whisky, silent Sten guns, 'Q' type dinghies, razor blades, needles, hacksaws, wireless equipment, soap, and infra-red equipment. In addition, special equipment was sent out: S-Phones, canoes and certain explosives.

IS9, MI9 and MI6

IS9 became a cover for MI9's field units and was coordinated from Room 900.[57] From 1943, IS9/Room 900 sent trained agents into Belgium and established radio links. The official file noted: 'During 1943 and 1944, IS9(Z) clothed and equipped many agents selected by IS9(D) for work in connection with our clandestine organisation in Western Europe.'[58] One of those operations at the end of 1943 was Operation Cornet to send in 30 parachutists to destroy the dam at Mohnetal in Germany, some 26 miles east of Dortmund and the largest in Europe.[59] IS9(X) provided clothing under the uniforms, special food packs, compasses, maps and routes in and out for the clandestine mission. An increasing number of evaders on the continent were coming too close to MI6 operations and endangering MI6 agents and operations like Cornet; something which Dansey had always tried to avoid.[60]

However, the boundaries between MI9, IS9 and MI6 did become particularly obscure. It was noted in an official MI9 file that section IS9(D) was responsible for 'carrying out escape and evasion plans in Europe and training agents under MI6'.[61] IS9(D) officially came under the direct auspices of MI6, and was engaged in the employment and training of agents. Those agents were sent into enemy-occupied Western Europe to assist escapers and evaders, and also communicate with IS9 agents in those countries. IS9(D) was formerly section MI6(D) and was still within the overriding authority of MI6.[62]

Given the fact that IS9(D) could not be openly acknowledged as being part of MI6, it seems to have operated as an out wing of MI6 and largely secret from other personnel within MI9 and MI6. The official history further said that 'for IS9(D) to survive it had to work on its own, consequently few people in England knew of its existence, or even within MI6/SIS itself or other branches of the intelligence services'.[63] As a result of this complete secrecy, it has taken a long time to understand the real relationship between MI9, IS9 and MI6.

It was also noted that 'It took MI6 more than two years to realise that it needed more than merely nominal support of IS9(D). This was because an increasing number of evaders were coming close to MI6 areas of operation and its agents.'[64] IS9(D) believed that it was looked on with suspicion by its parent organisation, MI6, though whether that was in fact true is hard to verify without documentation from MI6 archives.

During 1944, IS9(D) handled effective sea evacuations to Brittany with cooperation from the Royal Navy.[65] It had no support from the Air Ministry by way of air evacuations and parachute drops, in spite of the numbers of airmen being saved. The Air Ministry had good reasons for keeping out of the evacuations. Escapers and evaders were seen as a low priority because of the risk of losing aircraft and personnel in the rescue operations

Once they found themselves trapped behind enemy lines many Allied personnel directly benefited from the help of IS9 – whether from their original training at RAF Highgate or using the escape equipment and gadgets. Crockatt was proved correct in his foresight to create a psychology of escape mindedness in Allied personnel. The formation of IS9 as the more secret branch of MI9 marked a significant moment in MI9's history because it gave a formalised structure to this particular type of training for airmen and Allied personnel.

9
SEA EVACUATIONS

The first escape line by sea was established in June 1940 by Frank Slocum, a veteran of the First World War and now in his forties. Slocum worked out of MI6 headquarters at Broadway Buildings on opening up communications in occupied Europe for evacuation by sea: 'Starting on his own in June 1940, with no visible assets other than a lively imagination and great strength of character, Frank Slocum built up a system of clandestine transport which successfully carried many hundreds of agents to occupied Europe in the next four years, ranging from Norway to the Mediterranean.'[1]

Slocum was directly responsible for air and sea operations, including drop offs and pick-ups of agents by Lysander liaison aircraft into Europe until 1942. He secured a good working relationship and cooperation with the Air Ministry. He also oversaw the use of motor gun boats (MGBs) and motor torpedo boats (MTBs) for clandestine operations between England and the French and Dutch coasts. Instrumental in Slocum's successful sea evacuations were Lieutenant Commander S.M. Mackenzie and Pat Whinney of the British Naval Liaison office in France, who had been evacuated after the German invasion. On their return to England in June 1940, Godfrey, the head of Naval Intelligence had sent them to Ian Fleming who instructed them to report to Slocum. At the time, new flotillas of motor torpedo boats were being built in Southampton and Slocum posted Mackenzie and Whinney there, putting them in charge of the preparation for cross-Channel operations to the Normandy coast. Mackenzie and Whinney were transferred to Portsmouth to make two MTBs ready for use.[2] Two newly trained navigators, Milner-Gibson and Golding, successfully landed two agents at the mouth of the river Orne in France at the end of July 1940.

In the autumn of 1940, the armed services sent out an appeal for bilingual French, Belgian or Dutch volunteers for special missions behind the lines. Pilot Officer Philip Schneidau of the RAF was one of those who came forward.[3] Schneidau was born in the Channel Islands, but had grown up in Paris. He enlisted in the RAF in Paris in 1939 and worked as a driver to the air attaché. He evacuated with the RAF after the fall of France but his wife and son had remained in Paris. Schneidau was quite open about his reason for volunteering – he wanted to return to France to check his family was safe. Mackenzie and Whinney interviewed him and deemed him suitable to become an agent. Schneidau was trained for reconnaissance missions and basic wireless transmissions and was then sent on a mission to set up a network of informers within Paris, which he believed he could successfully achieve. It was not without risk because he, his wife and son were Jewish.

On 9 October 1940, Schneidau was dropped back into France from Tangmere airfield in Sussex as an agent for SIS to link up with his family and establish the new Felix network. He was dropped from a plane into a large sandpit in the middle of Fontainbleau Forest. The only form of communication was two homing pigeons that would carry a message back to London to confirm his safe arrival. One of the pigeons successfully made it back to the rooftop of MI6 head-quarters at Broadway Buildings. Schneidau spent two weeks in the area establishing the foundations of the network before being picked up, again by Lysander. Mackenzie commented that it 'was not spectacular, but ran successfully'.[4] It is not to be confused with a Felix network that later operated briefly out of Holland.

Slocum handed over the Felix network to another section in Broadway Buildings under Bill (Wilfred) Dunderdale (former head of the SIS section in Paris). Schneidau joined Dunderdale's staff, operating under the name Phillipson. He subsequently made two further drops into France, one in December 1940 and the other in late January 1941. The latter mission went cold for six weeks, with no radio contact between Schneidau and London. London suspected the worst, but in fact Schneidau's wireless set had been damaged on landing and he eventually made contact in March as he continued to build a network of informers behind enemy lines. At the French end, it was run for the next two years by Schneidau's father-in-law until he was transported to a concentration camp as a Jew, not as a spy. He survived, returning to Paris at the end of the war.

From May 1941, Slocum's unit officially came under Naval Intelligence and aided MI9, SOE and SIS in the rescue of Allied POWs.

Clandestine Sea Operations

During 1941, MI9 worked to expand its escape routes to include sea operations. To achieve this required the development of suitable naval equipment and an increase in personnel. Slocum's office moved from Broadway Buildings to Palace Street and his staff increased, still operating within the Naval Intelligence Division. He tasked Mackenzie and Whinney with investigating the technical side of operations to oversee the development of scientific aids for navigation and surf boats that could land in choppy waters to drop agents into occupied Europe and pick up evading airmen. Work had already begun to design a boat that could carry three or four people, managed by two oars and a steersman, capable of landing through strong surf. He now found himself occasionally cooperating with SIS and SOE.

Areas of clandestine operations during 1941 involved Norway, submarine missions in the Bay of Biscay and cross-Channel operations to France. Much of the sea operations continued to involve dropping agents in and out of occupied territories and reporting on German naval movements. Fishing boats regularly arrived via the Shetland Islands from Norway, packed with young escapers from the Nazi occupied country.[5] Although one or two boats were captured, the flow of operations between Norway and Britain continued unhindered right up to 1944.

Mackenzie continued to organise future sea operations for Slocum and worked closely with nineteen-year-old Daniel Lomenech who carried them out. Lomenech, whose parents had a fish-canning factory in Brittany, was well versed in the fishing industry and sea life. His parents were already helping Dunderdale with SIS operations within Brittany, though they were later compromised and shot. Lomenech suggested to Mackenzie that a suitable fishing vessel should be used between England and the west coast of France. A French trawler was taken over, restored at Shoreham and renamed N.51. Operations to the French coast were fraught with danger, even after the Luftwaffe bombing threat had subsided. The Germans had constructed heavy defences and installed a number of radar stations along the coast. MI6 scientist Professor R.V. Jones was consulted for up to date information on radar capability and new German technology.[6]

The covert naval operations during 1941, which increased in 1942, were concerned with dropping agents for SIS and SOE, and picking up evaders for MI9. Much like MI9's escape gadgets, new items needed to be developed to help with the operations since the coast was heavily patrolled by the Germans and torch signals could not be used. Experiments were made with infrared signals, in their infancy then, and primitive walkie-talkie sets.

During 1942, Pat Whinney was loaned to SOE for undisclosed work, then was detached to Gibraltar to organise a flotilla for irregular operations in the western Mediterranean.[7] After a brief return to England, he visited Spain to organise the clandestine purchase of Spanish feluccas for aiding the Mediterranean flotilla, then to North Africa for Operation Torch (Allied landings in North Africa) to locate suitable bases and craft in the region in readiness for the Allied landings in Sicily and Italy the following summer.[8]

Mackenzie spent most of his time in 1942 working out of Dartmouth and Falmouth on cross-Channel operations that ran to Normandy and Brittany on the French coast. The use of fishing craft as part of the secret flotillas was increased in 1942 to sail between Devon, Cornwall and Brittany on clandestine missions. These particular sea routes were to prove indispensable for a new escape line (the Shelburne Line) the following year.[9]

Operation Marie Louise

Operation Marie Louise took place between April and June 1942 and involved the use of N.51, the French trawler that had been converted on the instruction of Slocum.[10] In April 1942, N.51 sailed from Dartmouth to the Isles of Scilly to be painted up for wartime. She was given a blue hull, brown upper body-work and a French name and number. When completed, N.51 sailed across the English Channel to the French coast to observe fishing activity and assess the results of RAF bombing of the coast. It made several trips across to a point just south of Brest where, at a particular location at sea, French fishing boats with people hidden on board could come alongside. On one of these sea missions, Madame Rémy with her three young children and a six-month-old baby, as well as an unnamed man described as having several suitcases, were evacuated.[11] They were hidden in a fishing boat and had not been discovered during a search by a German patrol boat. The rescue of the Rémy family was important as Colonel Rémy (the unnamed passenger) was an outstanding personality in the French Resistance and a principal secret agent for the Allies.

Mackenzie had first met Rémy in London just a couple of days before Rémy returned to France where he was operating with the French network, Confrérie de Notre Dame (CND). This was an important network, made up of a whole series of resistance groups with such tight security that if one was betrayed, the others could still function. Mackenzie described Rémy as 'a man of middle height, apparently of middle age, with a tendency to stoutness, a tendency to baldness with the softest and yet brightest brown eyes . . . a man with the courage of a lion, the determination of a bulldog, and the charm of a royal ambassador'.[12]

Rémy was already known to the Gestapo and was being actively hunted down in Paris. His family were at risk and so on 17 June 1942, Mackenzie arranged their secret evacuation from Brittany aboard N.51. It was an emotional moment, as he later wrote, 'I felt deeply moved by the sight we had seen; four young chil-dren and their mother helped to safety, their smile of thanks, their obvious confi-dence of security in our hands.'[13] The mission was hugely risky because of the constant threat of German patrols and destroyers. N.51 landed back at the Scillies where an MTB took them to the mainland. N.51 made numerous trips across the Channel. 'How many times N.51 changed colours during the coming months and years I would not like to guess,' wrote Mackenzie. 'Suffice it to say that the link had been forged; it endured for more than two years.'[14]

In Operation Marie Louise, Rémy successfully smuggled documents out of the German headquarters of a section that employed slave labour to construct the coastal defences of France.[15] On this mission, 'Rémy brought with him a blueprint of the entire German fortifications which were being built along the north coast of France'.[16] Documents continued to be smuggled out of France for the Allies. For his extraordinary sacrifice and bravery for the Allies, Rémy was awarded De Gaulle's highest medal – the Croix de La Libération – and a military OBE from the British government.

The Coastal Watching Flotilla

By 1942, MI9 had a backlog of evaders awaiting repatriation from Spain to England. Donald Darling looked at ways to bring them swiftly out via new sea routes. Evacuation by sea was always going to be an important route. In April that year Darling met Jimmy Langley and Pat O'Leary in Gibraltar to deal with the problem. Slocum authorised a special unit to be formed in the south of France called the Coastal Watching Flotilla (CWF); its main role was to drop MI9 agents into the region and pick up evaders from the Pat Line. The hulls of the vessels were painted the colours of fishing boats of neutral Spain or Portugal so they would not be intercepted. The Coastal Watching Flotilla carried out seven clandestine rescues for the Pat Line, aided by the British trawler *Tarana*, a vessel that had been secretly armed and had a British crew.[17]

The first mission dropped Pat O'Leary ashore near Port-Vendres with the help of the *Tarana*. Flying the flag of a neutral country, alternating between the flags of Portugal and Morocco, she ran between Gibraltar and Canet-Plage, a secluded beach near Perpignan, on the coast near the Pyrenees.[18] Just off Canet-Plage she picked up escapers and evaders from small boats that rowed out to her. The second mission took place on the night of 14/15 June 1942 and saw the successful evacuation of evaders from Port-Miou, some 20 kilometres south-east of Marseille.

The third took place a month later and was codenamed Operation Bluebottle.[19] It was the largest of the Coastal Watching Flotilla operations and involved the rescue of 35 evaders, one of whom was Squadron Leader Whitney Straight. An

American by birth, Whitney Straight was an extremely charismatic personality, and an international racing driver who had joined the RAF during the war. He was shot down on 31 July 1941 whilst attacking German E-boats near Le Havre,[20] his Hurricane landing in a field, wheels up. He failed to blow it up and headed off as far from the wreckage as possible. Straight had received training in escape and evasion from MI9 prior to his first mission. He also spoke fluent French which meant that he could pass through occupied France relatively easily.

The Germans had seen the plane come down and were on the search for the crew. Straight headed for Bolbec, took a train to Rouen where he changed trains to Paris. In Paris he made for the American embassy but, finding it had closed down, he telephoned instead and a man answered. The man had heard over the radio that Straight had been shot down. He came to a nearby café, met Straight and gave him 10,000 francs. Straight stayed overnight in a hotel, bought a map the following morning and took a bus 100 kilometres to Chateauroux where he boarded a train to Pau, and then walked towards the border. He was betrayed as he sat in a local café, arrested by French police and transferred to Saint-Hippolyte-du-Fort in Vichy France under the name of Captain Whitney of RASC. The French failed to recognise that he was the top pilot who was on the Germans' wanted list.

Back at Wilton Park in Beaconsfield, Norman Crockatt issued a direct order that all measures were to be taken to prevent Whitney Straight and his colleagues from falling into German hands. He phoned Room 900 on a daily basis to ask whether Straight had escaped from the fort.

When news reached O'Leary that Straight was imprisoned in Saint-Hippolyte-du-Fort he arranged for Dr Rodocanachi to certify he was unfit for service because of a 'fractured skull and wound to the back'. Both serious injuries were complete fabrication. Rodocanachi, who was covertly working in Marseille for O'Leary and Revd Caskie, was already issuing documentation for Allied airmen and soldiers to say that they had to be repatriated on 'health grounds'.[21] The precise number of men helped by Dr Rodocanachi in this way is not known. He did not survive the war, was betrayed by Harold Cole and died in a concentration camp in 1944.[22]

Whitney Straight and 43 other POWs were passed down the Pat Line to Perpignan. The medical evidence from Dr Rodocanachi had been accepted by French Admiral Darlan, who authorised temporary passports, valid for one month, to leave Vichy France. Even with this paperwork, and with confusion as people were being turned back from the Pyrenees area, their luck ran out at Perpignan and they were taken to Fort de la Revère in Nice.[23] Whitney Straight feigned illness and was transferred to the nearby Pasteur hospital under heavy guard. O'Leary used his inside contacts in the hospital and a sympathetic nurse gave Straight some drugs to slip into the drink of two guards. As the guards slept, Straight escaped from the hospital on 22 June. A short distance away, helper Francis Blanchain was waiting to escort him via the Pat Line and sea evacuation aboard the *Tarana*. Straight arrived in Gibraltar where Donald Darling received him. On 24 July 1942, Room 900 received a telegram from Darling which began as usual: 'Gibraltar: Room 900 from Sunday'. It confirmed that Whitney Straight had been rescued and the telegram continued: 'Sending by air and should arrive Hendon tomorrow 25 July.'[24]

Neave wrote that 'the rescue of Whitney Straight and other airmen from the beach at Canet-Page was a landmark in the history of Room 900. It showed we could mount such sea operations with success.'[25]

In August 1942, the *Tarana* rescued seven evaders and an unnamed woman, probably an MI9 courier, from St Pierre a small village north of Nice. That same month another operation was underway in which MI9/IS9 sought to break out Flight Lieutenant Higginson who was being held at Fort de la Revère. O'Leary gave Room 900 advance notice that they intended to break him out on 23 August.[26] Higginson had been in enemy occupied territory for over a year; on 17 June 1941 he had been escorting bombers on targets near Lille and experienced flak. He had to bail out of his Hurricane near Dunkirk, landed in a forest and managed to walk only a short distance before being taken prisoner by two Germans on motorbikes. As the Germans looked up at a passing enemy plane, Higginson knocked them unconscious into a ditch and was quickly helped to evade capture by a Frenchman. By the following day he had walked to Fauquembergues, in the Pas de Calais region, and was put in touch with

Abbé Carpentier who was working for the Pat Line. He was given false documents and passed down the line to Marseille where he stayed for two days at the home of a Greek doctor. In his escape report Higginson told MI9: 'I met the following people – Captain Ian Garrow, Patrick O'Leary, Lalonde (sic), Mr Kenny and Mrs Elizabeth Hayden-Guest.'[27]

On 4 July 1941, Higginson had been passed down the line to Perpignan where, while he waited for a guide to take him over the Pyrenees, he was arrested by French police. He was taken to Port-Vendres prison where conditions were described as bad, then to Perpignan prison where conditions were worse. On 5 September he was transferred to a military prison at Montpellier, and the following month on 25 October to Saint-Hippolyte-du-Fort. In March 1942 the Consulate secured his release and arranged exit visas, but his release was cancelled at the last minute in reprisal for the Allied bombing of the Renault works near Paris. On 17 March he was moved to Fort de la Revère, from where O'Leary and Room 900 planned to break him out.[28] In his escape report Higginson mentioned three people who helped him whilst in the Fort: a Polish padre called Midar, a Russian called Val (Val Williams), and a Frenchwoman. Preparations for the escape were planned and discussed with Val.

> From our room there was a coal shute down into the kitchen which we locked, barred and wired. Sergeant Dalphond made a key for the lock and at 22:15 hrs we crawled through the wire. After breaking three bars across the windows we let ourselves down into the moat from the kitchen, which we knew to be empty, by means of a rope which we had made ourselves. From the moat we got through the sewer which led us beyond the bounds of the Fort, having cut another bar at the far end. In order to cover the noise that we made, a concert had been organised.[29]

Val arranged that guides would meet the escapers outside the fort. Higginson was never told the actual name of the escape line. Within ten minutes of the escape, the breakout had been discovered and the guides caught by the guards.

Higginson and Dalphond ran without the guides to a safe house in Monte Carlo. On 2 September, dressed as a priest he and another evader, Sergeant Hickton, went to Marseille where Higginson was sheltered in Madame Nouveau's flat on the waterfront. On 17 September, under the cover name of Captain Bennett, RASC, Higginson was taken down the escape line with Hickton to Perpignan and Canet-Plage: 'We were picked up by a Polish fishing smack (sic) on 20 September, from which we were transferred to HMS Minna in the region of the Balearic Islands and taken to Gibraltar.'[30] He arrived in the UK from Gibraltar on 5 October.

Clandestine sea operations continued throughout September 1942 using the vessel *Seawolf* from an excluded location not far from Canet-Plage.[31] O'Leary planned another operation with *Seawolf*, scheduled for 5/6 October. He was sheltering 34 British servicemen at a safe house at Canet Plage and arranged for them to be brought to the rendezvous, a walk that involved them crossing the river Têt up to their necks in the water. However, contact with *Seawolf* had failed just before the operation and the men had to return to the safe house. O'Leary rearranged the evacuation for 11/12 October. By now the evaders were filled with a mixture of fear, excitement and pent-up boredom. In the dinghy on the way out to the *Seawolf*, they were rather boisterous and risked being discovered by French patrols. This particular journey by *Seawolf* was rough and resulted in the vessel breaking her radio silence to seek aid not far from Majorca yet, in spite of the challenges, it proved another successful operation and all 34 evaders made it back to England.

Between 13 September 1942 and 12 October 1942, O'Leary's sea operations rescued over 100 servicemen.[32] The final operation by the Coastal Watching Flotilla for the Pat Line took place on 3/4 November when an MI9 agent was landed at Port Miou.

15th Motor Gun Boat Flotilla

During 1942 Mackenzie laid the foundation for the Inshore Patrol Flotilla and commanded the first three operations to the French Biscay coast.[33] He trained and recruited volunteer officers and men, disguised as French fishermen, for the rapidly expanding flotilla. They achieved

a long, unbroken series of successful operations, unarmed and unescorted to the enemy's doorstep by daylight . . . The capture of one vessel of the flotilla would have wrecked the whole enterprise, since although outwardly identical to a French fishing vessel, the interiors were fitted out with navigational aids, living quarters and armouries of hand weapons.[34]

The 15th Motor Gun Boat Flotilla operated between Brittany and Cornwall, bringing SIS agents into France one way and returning with escaping Allied servicemen to Falmouth in Cornwall.[35] One agent who was landed by the flotilla was François Mitterand, later French president.[36] The naval base at Dartmouth became the focus for these clandestine operations in support of MI9, SIS and SOE. In 1943 American troops and personnel of the United States Secret Service began to arrive in England; amongst them was US commander Ray Guest, one of the wealthy Guest brothers and a polo player. He headed a flotilla based in Dartmouth that was to aid operations in Europe. The 15th Motor Gun Boat Flotilla became the principal means of maintaining communications with enemy-occupied France, particularly during the six months preceding D-Day.[37] It also ran in support of Colonel Reéy who continued to smuggle intelligence out of France for the Allies at a time when to send it over wireless transmission was too risky.

The fleet of flotillas moved from Dartmouth to a new, even more discreet base, at the Helford river in Cornwall. One of the fleet was the *Angèle Rouge*, named after Slocum's red-haired secretary Angela Sykes Wright, who later married Commander Mackenzie. She had been made at the Isle of Wight to a new design with two powerful motor torpedo boat (MTB) engines that gave her a cruising speed of over 20 knots.[38] The advantage of her speed meant that she could carry out clandestine operations over two days instead of three.

Operations became increasingly difficult after the Germans imposed a 20-mile exclusion zone around the coast of France, but this did not prevent the daring cross-Channel missions and they continued unabated. The flotilla soon operated in conjunction with a new line, the Shelburne Line, which ran overland from Paris–Rennes–Brittany, then across the English Channel to Falmouth and Dartmouth.

The Shelburne Line

Air operations over Europe intensified in 1943 and with them the number of airmen being shot down over enemy territory increased. Many had evaded capture and were in hiding. Other evaders were in hiding in France after raids on French ports, including Brest and Cherbourg. Smuggling them 900 kilometres down to Spain was considered difficult after the betrayal of the escape lines by Harold Cole and the number of other evaders whom MI9 was trying to evacuate. The escape routes over land could be complex and criss-crossed hundreds of miles across the heart of Nazi-occupied countries. The shortest routes across occupied Europe could not necessarily be used because they were too obvious to Nazi patrols. MI9 and Room 900 considered the possibility of establishing a new escape line by sea from the coast of Brittany in northern France. The naval base at Dartmouth in Devon and port of Falmouth in Cornwall became the focus for clandestine operations in support of MI9, SOE and SIS. SOE had a base at the Helford river in Cornwall and there were inevitably tensions between SOE and MI9 over this.

The setting up of the operation at the Brittany end was codenamed Oaktree. Françoise Le Cornec, a local Frenchman, formed a resistance group of Breton farmers and fishermen from along the coast near Plouha, 15 kilometres from the port of Paimpol and 25 kilometres from the railway station at Guingamp.[39] They would become an integral part of the whole sea operations and had already been hiding Allied airmen. A leader emerged in the person of a White Russian called Vladimir Bouryschkine who had already worked with O'Leary. Bouryschkine was born in Moscow in 1913, had grown up in America, and in 1940 was working with the American Red Cross when the Nazis occupied Paris. He escaped south to Marseille and was evacuated on the

Tarana to Gibraltar on 13 September 1942. He was met by Donald Darling in Gibraltar.

Back in England, Langley asked Val Williams if he was prepared to return to France on behalf of Room 900 to run the escape routes from Brittany to Dartmouth. Williams agreed and was trained in air and sea night landings, evacuations and parachuting. Mackenzie and his colleague Collie Barclay (Sir Colville Barclay) trained Williams on naval matters at the St Ermin's Hotel in London.[40] By the time he had completed his training, the Pat Line had been blown.

The other agent who was essential in the sea operations was a French Canadian called Ray Labrosse, described as 'an excellent man of courage', and who became Williams's wireless operator.[41] On 28 February 1943, Williams and Le Cornec were dropped at night near Rambouillet. They were given two folding bicycles, the first time these had been used by MI9 in an operation.[42] The two men set about founding the Shelburne Line – a route that ran from Paris or Rennes to Plouha, then by sea evacuation to Falmouth (Cornwall) or Dartmouth (Devon).

MGBs sailed from Falmouth or Dartmouth to Brittany on a moonless night with a crew of 36, a six-pounder gun aft (back of the vessel) and twin turrets. Their relatively small size meant it was difficult for E-boats to target them. The MGBs dropped the MI9 agents at 'Bonaparte' – the codename for the pick-up point at Anse Cochat beach at Plouha in Brittany which had never been used by Val Williams and therefore had not been compromised. The MGBs waited about a mile from the coast as the agents were ferried to the French shore in smaller boats and then returned to Cornwall and Devon with escapers and evaders.

Williams arranged for the hiding of evaders in Paris, before bringing them by train to Guingamp, then to Plouha where Le Cornec had established a safe house. François Campinchi, a French lawyer, was recruited to collect the airmen from hiding and issue them with false identity documents and passes. Campinchi was seen as one of Room 900's best agents in France. Williams and Le Cornec undertook considerable risks for the network, and their success was remarkable given that they operated in such close proximity to Nazi coastal patrols, heavy defences and searchlights. Williams discovered that ninety British and American airmen were hiding in Brittany, thirty-nine of them in the Château de Bourblanc near Paimpol which belonged to Comte de Mauduit and his American wife, Comtesse Betty.[43] Labrosse's wireless transmitter had been damaged during the drop which meant that no secure message could be sent to London to arrange a sea evacuation for the ninety airmen. Williams then inadvertently compromised an important layer of security when he allowed Labrosse to transmit a radio message via another network. After this breach of security, Room 900 could not risk sending MGBs to the Brittany coast. Williams decided to move thirty-nine of the airmen himself by train to Spain. All but Williams and four airmen made it out safely. Val and four airmen were arrested on a train on 4 June 1943 near Pau on the Franco-Spanish border and taken to Fresnes prison in Paris for interrogation.

Le Cornec, who was running the safe house at Plouha, had already become suspicious of Roger le Legionnaire (real name Roger Le Neveu) when he had been asked to send airmen to him in Paris: the scenario looked too similar to the methods used by traitor Harold Cole. Roger le Legionnaire had indeed moved to denounce the network in Brittany. Comtesse de Mauduit, who had hidden the ninety airmen in her chateau, was betrayed by him, arrested by the Gestapo on 12 June 1943 and taken to Ravensbrück concentration camp. A short time after this treachery, Roger le Legionnaire was liquidated by the Resistance.

During interrogation at Fresnes prison, Williams kept to a cover story that he was a member of an RAF ground crew and the Gestapo could not prove otherwise. He was held there for a month before being transferred to Rennes prison for further detailed interrogation. As a fluent Russian speaker, he befriended fellow Russian prisoners and with one of them, known as 'Ivan' (real name Bougaiev), hatched an escape plan that succeeded on 20 December 1943.[44] They waited for the next air raid alarm, when Ivan took the opportunity to steal the key to the punishment cell and climbed out via ladders that had been left by workmen. They reached the outer wall and jumped, but Williams fractured his leg on landing on the ground. Their escape was discovered and search parties with dogs were sent out to comb the area. Williams used a trick that he had learned in training – to urinate which caused the dogs to do the same, resulting in the scent being thrown off. He hobbled to a farm at Bain de Bretagne and was taken in by a French woman, Madame Dubois. As he recovered from his fracture, plans were made to smuggle him back to England via Paris.

Eventually, under the pretence of being 'arrested', Williams was escorted back to Paris by two sympathetic French police officers who were in the pay of the Resistance movement. He remained in hiding in the capital until he could be evacuated on the first sea operation ('Bonaparte') in January 1944. A new leader took over the Shelburne escape line – Sergeant Major P.S. Lucien Dumais of the 1st Battalion Fusiliers Mont Royal, Royal Canadian Forces, himself an escaper from the famous Dieppe Raid who had been evacuated to England by O'Leary from the south of France on the *Seawolf* in October 1942. Dumais had left the UK with his platoon during the night and crossed the Channel for the early morning raid, but had been captured on 19 August 1942.[45] His platoon had arrived at 5 a.m. with a mission to cover the withdrawal of the raid. Even before they landed they were visible from 600 metres and were caught in the crossfire from German patrols on the cliffs. The Dieppe Raid was considered a disaster because it failed in its intention to destroy German coastal defences and gather intelligence. In addition, the Allies sustained huge losses – 3,623 killed from 6,086 forces who landed ashore. Just before 1300 hours some officers decided to surrender, raised a white flag and gave themselves up, including Dumais. The Germans marched them about 15 miles inland to a large building and later that afternoon put them on a train for Germany. In measuring the disaster at Dieppe, little attention has been given to the fact that some of the Allied personnel succeeded in evacuating from the raid, taking German prisoners with them. These prisoners were taken to one of MI9's special interrogation and bugging sites and unwittingly provided intelligence to the Allies.[46] Perhaps this is an example where a nuanced reassessment of the Dieppe Raid would be helpful in understanding whether there were some benefits from the raid in spite of the losses.

After his capture, Dumais remembered his training at Intelligence School 9 that 'even if taken a prisoner, the war is not over for you'.[47] He immediately looked for opportunities to escape and succeeded in jumping off the train, as he recalled to MI9 in his interrogation:

> We pulled a bar off the window. I got out first when the moon was clouded and got in between the freight cars. When the train slowed down on a gradient I jumped off. The guard shot at me and missed. The train did not stop, and I heard shots about every 30 seconds till the train had disappeared. I took this to mean that others were jumping off all the time.[48]

Dumais walked along the railway track for about 4 miles, and then about 8 miles along a path. He came to the small town of Thuit where he slept in a barn, then approached a woman with a child; she took him to a male helper who gave him civilian clothes and hid him in the woods. 'In the morning (22 Aug) my helper brought me more food and clothes, some money and a small map of France torn from a school geography book.'[49] He guided Dumais on the best route to take, via train to Le Mans, Tours and Poitiers. At Poitiers he was given a lift by a lorry driver who happened to be part of the Free French organisation and took him to Limoges. During the night of 25 August he crossed the demarcation line, walking across countryside for about 3 kilometres south of Flores.[50] He was picked up by a taxi and taken to the Hotel de La Gare (Lussac-Les-Châteaux) and sheltered there for five weeks by the Vayer family who had already helped RAF men nine months previously. From Limoges Dumais was sent to Marseille and sheltered for three days in the US Consulate, then passed to O'Leary. O'Leary sent him to Canet-Plage, from where he was evacuated to Gibraltar by boat a week later. Dumais arrived in St Ives, Cornwall on 21 October 1942.

Once in England, Dumais was trained by Room 900 along with Raymond Labrosse ('Claude') who became his radio operator and second-in-command. Neave described Labrosse as 'quiet and unflappable', in contrast to Dumais who was 'a forceful personality'.[51] Dumais and Labrosse were both dropped back into France, some 60 miles north-east of Paris during the night of 19 November 1943 in a mission codenamed Magdalen II.[52]

'Bonaparte'

The first sea operation for the Shelburne Line was scheduled for December 1943 but postponed until January because of bad weather. On 29 January 1944, sixteen airmen, travelling in peasant clothing and escorted by guides, were moved by train from Paris towards Brittany. At St Brieuc they were handed over to the local Resistance, given forged passes to enter the usually forbidden heavily defended coastal areas of Brittany, and escorted on to Plouha. They were sheltered at Maison d'Alphonse, a small two-room dwelling, just 1,500 metres from the cliff above Anse Cochat, belonging to local French sailor Jean Giquel and his wife.[53] If a German patrol arrived at Maison d'Alphonse, the men could be hidden behind the hay in the loft. Dumais and Le Cornec were not far away and armed, so they could come across swiftly and defend the property if necessary. Both were prepared to kill a German patrol to protect the airmen.

Ahead of the operation, when an MGB was en route to France across the Channel, the BBC was to send out a message any time between 7.30 p.m. and 9 p.m. with the words: 'Bonjour tout le monde à la Maison d'Alphonse [Good day to everyone at the Alphonse house]'. At Plouha every evening, the signal was eagerly awaited. Pat Windham-Wright sailed from Dartmouth with the crew of MGB 503, a spare wireless set, money and whisky for bribes. At 11.30 p.m. the occupants of Maison d'Alphonse prepared to move down to the pick-up point on the 'Bonaparte' beach. The guides that night were Le Cornec, Mainguy, Huet, Francis Baudet, Jean Trehiou and eighteen-year-old Marie-Therese Le Calvez.[54] Val William's fractured leg meant that he could not walk down the cliff and had to be carried on a stretcher. A signal was flashed to the MGB waiting off shore:

The morse letter B was flashed every two minutes from a point on the cliff, with a masked torch with a blue shining light on the beach below. The engines of the MGB made no sound as it stood about one and a half miles out at sea out of range of German searchlights.[55]

After the signal, four small rubber boats rowed from the MGB with muffled oars to the shore, always made on a rising tide to ensure no footprints were left on the beach. Time was of the essence. Its crew of commandos with blackened faces stepped ashore and rescued the escapers and evaders. The whole mission took only twenty-five minutes, including unloading supplies for the Resistance movement.

Back at Room 900 in London, Neave telephoned daily to Dartmouth for news of the operation. At 9 a.m. the following morning, 30 January, he received the good news he had been waiting for. Thirteen Americans, three RAF airmen, two Frenchmen (the latter were enlisting in the Allied forces), Val Williams and the Russian 'Ivan' had been brought to England. They were all interrogated at MI9 headquarters at Beaconsfield and the airmen were able to give MI9 details of what they had observed on the ground: one had observed the results of successful Allied bombing raids over Paris which had destroyed a Renault factory and damaged a ball-bearing plant. Ivan was detained at Beaconsfield for a while until he was handed to the Russians.

Before each of the sea operations a guide, known only as Huet, carried out dangerous preparation work. The Germans had laid mines along the coast and on the beaches to prevent any commando landings and Huet undertook to mark the mines with a piece of white cloth and remove them again as soon as the evacuation was complete. MI9 arranged for a mine detector to be parachuted into the area.[56]

Dumais organised a second evacuation on 28 February which saw the rescue of twenty men, sixteen of whom were American airmen. The third evacuation took place on 18 March and, although men were rescued, it had become riskier after MGB 503 was fired on from the direction of Paimpol. It avoided detection and finally at 3 a.m. the coast was clear to continue the operation which succeeded in rescuing twenty-four airmen, mainly Americans. Six days later, a further thirty airmen were evacuated, eighteen of whom were from the United States Air Force. They were mainly pilots and crew shot down whilst on bombing missions of German military installations at Kiel on 13 December 1943 and Bremen on 20 December. The airmen went into hiding and eventually made it out down the escape lines three months later. Soon, it was possible for Neave to write to the command of the USAF about the extraordinary success of the Shelburne Line: 'A substantial proportion of those who bailed out of their aircraft on these raids [across Germany] were being returned by Shelburne within a month, or few days, of being shot down.'[57]

The operation on 30 March rescued ten men from Brittany but it was to be the last for a while. Neave gave instructions to Windham-Wright to halt sea evacuations; the excuse he gave was the short nights going into the summer. The real reason was that the invasion of Normandy was imminent within a matter of weeks and, if the Germans discovered MI9's coastal operations, they may have strengthened the coastal defences even further, posing an even greater problem for the Allied landings.

Numbers vary in sources, but an estimated one hundred Allied airmen were evacuated from a beach in occupied France between January and March 1944 by the Shelburne Line working with the 15th Motor Gun Boat Flotilla.[58] They carried out two final missions after D-Day, on 13 and 14 July 1944 that saw the rescue of eight American and two RAF airmen, as well as seven agents. In the short time of its existence, the Shelburne Line saved a total of 135 airmen.[59] In addition, Shelburne guides also escorted ninety-eight men to the Spanish border, thus into neutral territory. Val Williams was awarded the BEM, but was not permitted to return to France for further missions, which marked the end of his work in France for MI9.

There were other escape lines by sea.[60] The VAR Line operated from winter 1943 until April 1944 using the north Breton beaches for evacuation,[61] working alongside and occasionally with the Shelburne Line. It was estimated that 150 people worked for the VAR Line at the French end, led by Erwin Deman, a 39-year-old Viennese Jew who had escaped the Nazis. Trained by SOE, in August 1943, Deman was secretly flown to Paris to link up with a Madame Jestin in Rennes whose two daughters, both in their forties, ran safe houses and recruited guides and couriers.

Another line, the Burgundy Line was operated, not by MI9, but the French intelligence service Bureau Central de Renseignements et d'Action (BCRA) whose wartime headquarters was located at 10 Duke Street, near Green Park in London.[62] Close links and some cooperation existed between BCRA and MI9. The Burgundy Line was headed by a Frenchman, Georges Broussine ('Burgundy') who had originally been recruited by Airey Neave and trained for clandestine wireless work.[63] In December 1942 he was parachuted into France from Britain to establish an escape line from Paris to the port of Douarnenez, between Brest and Quimper. The risk was greater for Broussine because he was Jewish and if caught by the Germans they would have had no hesitation in killing him immediately. Key figures in the Burgundy Line were given the codenames of alcoholic spirits: Simon Martel ('Brandy') who operated out of Paris from 1942 to 1943, Yves de Henaff ('Curaçao') active from May 1943 to February 1944, and Pierre Guillot ('Pernod') in charge of the Lysander pick-ups round Tours from November 1943 to April 1944. In spite of the arrests of Comtesse de Mauduit and others of the Shelburne Line, Roger le Legionnaire failed to penetrate the Burgundy Line and it remained intact.

Intelligence for MI9 and the Allies was brought out via the flotilla operations from various locations on the French coast until Brittany was finally liberated in August 1944. This included detailed intelligence about Germany's V-I and V-2 secret weapon sites.[64]

At the end of the war, Mackenzie was awarded the Croix de Guerre for planning over 200 irregular operations, and post-war joined the SIS staff. Seven officers and fifteen men of the flotilla were decorated for their work.[65] They received awards for 'outstanding courage, skill and devotion to duty shown in the planning and execution of many hazardous operations'.[66]

10
SECRET INTELLIGENCE SERVICE (SIS) ESCAPE LINES

The Secret Intelligence Service (SIS/MI6) ran its own escape lines under the direction and control of Claude Dansey, the controversial and often unpopular figure who became deputy head of the service in 1939. There were occasions when the boundaries of the SIS escape lines became blurred with those of MI9 or SOE and that rendered more than one organisation vulnerable to infiltration on various occasions. Reconstructing the MI6/SIS escape networks across Western Europe poses its own challenge because very little material is available and MI6 does not release its files into the National Archives. However, it is possible to glean some information from published works and from MI9 files where their escape lines occasionally crossed with those of MI6 in spite of trying to keep them separate. This was true for two female agents: British born Mary Lindell (aka Comtesse de Milleville, Marie-Claire) and Dutch born Beatrice Terwindt (aka Trix, working on the Felix line). Dansey had already declared his opposition to women becoming agents for SIS and MI9, but even he had to concede. And so, Mary Lindell became the first woman to be trained by Room 900 and dropped back into France to establish an escape line and run agents for IS9.

MI9 had successfully established escape routes across Western Europe – from Belgium to France to the Pyrenees, from Paris to Marseille, from Brittany to Cornwall. However, the situation in Holland was very different. Establishing escape routes prior to 1943 had been a challenge because of a lack of trust. That had arisen because, although Holland – like Belgium and France – was occupied by the Nazi regime, the Abwehr had already penetrated Dutch intelligence networks in 1939 in the Venlo incident.[1] This disaster occurred on 9 November

1939 in which two SIS/MI6 officers, Captain Payne Best and Major Richard Stevens, were captured close to the German border in the Dutch town of Venlo and were abducted on the orders of Heinrich Himmler, one of the most powerful men in Hitler's government and the incident helped Germany to justify its invasion of the Netherlands, previously a neutral country. Thereafter British intelligence experienced difficulties getting agents into Holland because of Dutch mistrust.

Confidence with the Dutch had to be restored and that took time. In addition to these factors, few other Allied countries had people who could speak fluent Dutch and therefore British intelligence found it difficult to recruit any Dutch-speaking agents. The Dutch themselves had provided little resistance to the German occupation until around February 1941, by which time they had established their own network for hiding and moving Jews and Onderduikers (those who did not want to work with the Germans). In the winter of 1940/41 it is believed the Dutch helped hundreds of French POWs to escape through Limburg province. MI9 was determined to succeed in Holland and its mission would do so, particularly in 1944 and 1945. Against this backdrop, Beatrice Terwindt became the first and only known woman to be dropped into Holland for IS9.

Mary Lindell (aka Marie-Claire)

Marie Madeleine (aka Marie-Claire), whose real name was Mary Lindell, headed an SIS network called Noah's Ark, so named because its agents were given code-names of animals.[2] Its boundaries inevitably became blurred with MI9 as Lindell, working for both MI6 and MI9, embarked on the rescue of British airmen and soldiers.[3] Forty-five-year-old Lindell was a woman of steely nerve who enjoyed dangerous adventures. Although she may not be a household name today, she went on to save the only two survivors of Operation Frankton. Lindell had married a French aristocrat, becoming the Comtesse de Milleville, and enjoyed a pre-war life mixing in Parisian high society. In the First World War she was decorated for her work as a nurse. With France under occupation again in 1940, she volunteered as a nurse for the Red Cross. When the occupying German

1. Colditz Castle, Leipzig, Germany. It was an impenetrable eleventh-century fortress used by the Germans in the Second World War for Allied officer prisoners of war, heavily guarded, and from which the Germans believed it impossible to escape. Built on bedrock, its high outer and inner walls were fortified with thick barbed wire. Eight British officers succeeded in escaping before the end of the war.

2. Christopher Clayton Hutton, MI9's gadget man who invented many of the ingenious escape devices that were hidden in ordinary objects and smuggled into POW camps. He is pictured here with his escape boot. An airman's boots could be converted into civilian shoes to blend into enemy territory when evading capture.

3. (a) A shaving brush and (b) an escape pipe with concealed compasses. One of Clayton Hutton's many inventions was to conceal compasses inside ordinary objects to smuggle into POW camps. A shaving brush proved ideal because it could be found in every POW's kit. The bottom of the brush unscrewed to reveal the miniature compass. MI9's compasses were among the most valuable escape aids for escapers and evaders.

4. Prisoners in German camps were permitted to receive parcels and letters from Britain. They were allowed to receive games like this Monopoly set to relieve boredom in the camp. MI9 recruited Waddingtons to make special Monopoly sets to hide escape and evasion devices inside the pieces.

5. Brigadier Norman Crockatt, the head of MI9, c.1942, here in his office at MI9 headquarters at Wilton Park, Buckinghamshire. Crockatt was responsible for developing MI9's philosophy of 'escape-mindedness' which gave a directive to Allied personnel that it was their duty to evade capture and escape if behind enemy lines or in a POW camp.

6. A rare wartime photograph of MI9 headquarters at Wilton Park, c.1942. It was known as Camp 20 and used from October 1940 when MI9 moved out of the War Office building in London. This purpose-built complex was constructed after Crockatt's expanding staff outgrew accommodation at the White House at the other end of the site.

7. Wedding of Jimmy Langley and Peggy van Lier, November 1942. An escaper himself, Langley was recruited into MI9 and its highly secretive Room 900 in 1941. He coordinated the escape lines and agents for Claude Dansey. Peggy van Lier worked for the Comet Line in Brussels with its leader Nemo until the network was betrayed in 1942 and MI9 had to smuggle her to England.

14. The Vatican, Rome, from where Monsignor Hugh O'Flaherty ran the Rome Escape Organisation with escaper Sam Derry. Outside the Vatican precincts O'Flaherty wore a number of disguises and smuggled Derry in dressed as a priest. When the Germans discovered O'Flaherty's identity the SS tried to assassinate him, but the German ambassador warned O'Flaherty and he met his contacts on the steps of St Peter's Basilica.

15. Sam Derry, head of the Rome Escape Organisation from 1943. As a POW he had jumped off a moving train on its way to a concentration camp in Germany. He hid in the precincts of the Vatican and with Monsignor Hugh O'Flaherty ('the Scarlet Pimpernel') saved nearly 4,000 Allied personnel via their escape line in Italy. Derry went on to become the head of MI9 in 1945.

16. Wartime photograph of Renata Faccincani della Torre. From an Italian aristocratic family, she was just twenty-one when she first headed Stazione Goldoni, an escape network and intelligence headquarters. It was run from the family home at Via Carlo Goldoni 19 in Milan and, with her friend Nam de Beaufort and the Austrian Resistance in Italy, they smuggled intelligence for the Allies and Allied POWs from northern Italy into Switzerland.

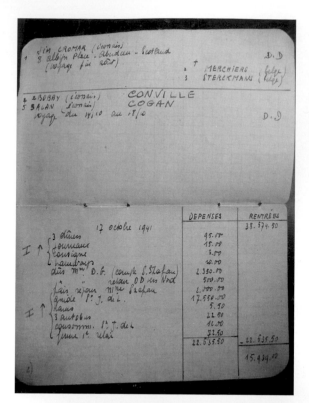

17. The opening entry in the first of the Little Black Books. A number of tiny Black Books were kept by Elvire de Greef in which she entered the accounts, names of the 'packages' (evaders) and the dates they were given shelter before being escorted by guides over the Pyrenees into Spain. This first entry is for evaders in August and October 1941.

18. Some of the airmen saved by the Comet Line. The de Greef family and the network organised photographs to create false identity cards if the evaders were stopped by patrols before they escaped over the Pyrenees. Their names correspond with entries in the Little Black Books.

19. Airmen about to be repatriated back to Britain. Michael Creswell is seen here standing second from the right. Creswell was MI9's representative in Madrid and codenamed 'Monday'. Once the airmen had been escorted over the Pyrenees by guides he met them on the other side with his Bentley car.

20. Airmen being repatriated to Britain by Michael Creswell for MI9. After D-Day, Creswell continued to organise the escape of Allied airmen and other POWs from the Spanish frontier. Without these escape lines through Spain, MI9 estimated that less than 1 per cent of airmen would have reached the Pyrenees and escaped.

21. Georges d'Oultremont, the Belgian aristocrat who escorted evaders from Brussels to Paris for the Comet Line. MI9 twice had to smuggle him out of Europe when he was at risk. Prior to D-Day he returned to France for MI9 to set up Operation Marathon, an operation to rescue escapers and evaders after the D-Day landings. He went on to serve in the Belgian SAS.

22. Lieutenant Airey Neave, who became the first British POW to successfully escape from Colditz in January 1942. He returned to Britain and became a pivotal figure in MI9 with Jimmy Langley. He joined Room 900 and ran agents into occupied Europe, and masterminded Operation Marathon to rescue escapers and evaders after D-Day, June 1944.

23. The tented camp at Forêt de Fréteval, established as part of Operation Marathon to hide escapers and evaders after the D-Day landings. It was located between Châteaudun and Vendôme, 100 miles south of Paris, where the dense woodland was ideal to ensure its inhabitants' safety. The camp was nicknamed 'Sherwood' after Robin Hood and Sherwood Forest.

24. Kim Philby, who worked in counter-espionage for MI6 during the war. Philby's involvement in Room 900, as per the below transcript, raises new questions over the true relationship and boundaries between MI9, Room 900 and MI6. It suggests the possibility that Room 900 was part of MI6 or intended as a replacement should MI6 be compromised.

25. A transcript from Room 900, the top secret side of MI9. It is signed by MI6 spy (later traitor) Kim Philby and reveals that he worked for Room 900. The transcript reveals that Room 900 was engaged in counter-espionage and tracking enemy agents. This new research firmly places Room 900/MI9 as an intelligence gathering organisation like MI6.

Room 900,

War Office.

November 14, 1942.

British: MOST SECRET
American: SECRET

D.O.67

Dear Major Eyre Huxt.

We have suggested to your Brigadier that the following be passed Most Secret and Personal to Captain PARK.

"It is reported from Geneva that a French national, CHALLIOL, is buying the Hotel des Princes or possibly the Bar de Lorraine in CASABLANCA from a Frenchman named PARRAIN. CHALLIOL is said to be a German agent and intends to use the hotel for espionage on German behalf."

Yours sincerely

H.A.R.Philby.

authorities placed restrictions on movement around the country unless issued with a special permit, Lindell's work was severely hampered as she needed to move freely around the countryside. She decided that as a French aristocrat her name would provide an entrée into German high military circles and sought an interview in Paris with General von Stülpnagel, the supreme commander of German-occupied France. He was more than willing to receive her. She beguiled him with tales of needing to reunite children and babies with their parents on the Riviera. He succumbed to her charm and worthwhile charitable work, issuing her with travel permits and petrol coupons. Her new freedom meant that she could secretly smuggle escapers and evaders to Marseille.

In 1941, Lindell was caught and arrested by the Gestapo while aiding the escape of British officers. She spent nine months in solitary confinement in Fresnes prison, south of Paris. Her sentence could have been longer but for her award of the prestigious Croix de Guerre in 1916.[4] Lindell was released but did not give up her work. She visited the American vice consul in Lyons claiming to have lost all her money and documents and was issued with papers providing a disguise as a governess which enabled her to cross the Pyrenees in late July 1942. She arrived unannounced at the British embassy in Barcelona. The embassy sent a telegram to Neave and Langley via the War Office that Lindell wanted to restart her network for MI9. She was flown to London and interviewed by Neave and Langley in a flat above Overton's restaurant in St James's Street. Neave commented on their first meeting:

Standing in the sunshine, dressed in the royal blue uniform of the French Red Cross, with a row of French and British decorations . . . She had dark brown eyes and chestnut hair and her face was finely proportioned. Her figure was slight, and her uniform well cut. She seemed very feminine but in her expression was an intensity, a stubbornness which somehow did not fit her smart appearance.[5]

Neave's description highlights how female agents and helpers, although feminine on the exterior, could be anything but soft and vulnerable. Their outer appearance did not necessarily match their character as forthright, strong women with judgements of their own and views that they were ready to express in what was still a largely male-dominated world.

Neave and Langley were cautious with Lindell. They had to assess whether or not she was a Nazi agent or had been 'turned' to work for the Germans because her story initially seemed unreal and too simple. When she left, Neave turned to Langley and asked him what he thought of her.

Knowing that the major challenge would be to persuade Dansey to allow Lindell back into France, Langley replied: 'I've nothing to say at the moment, except I want a very large whisky and soda.'[6] Dansey did concede and Lindell was trained for several weeks by Room 900.

Showing the same independence of spirit and tenacious leadership as Dédée of the Comet Line, Lindell refused to work with the wireless operator suggested by Room 900. She set about re-establishing her network and, against the advice of MI9, without any wireless operator.[7] The dangers were enormous because the Gestapo regretted her freedom, had subsequently rounded up her network and promptly issued a death warrant for her. She was once again high on the Gestapo's wanted list and had Dansey known that the Gestapo were after her, he would probably not have agreed to send her back. Undeterred by the personal risk of being caught, Lindell was ready to go back to France and Room 900 discussed with her a location for her new headquarters to run an escape route into Spain, eventually deciding on Ruffec near Angoulême where a number of RAF and American pilots had been shot down.

On 21 October 1942, Lindell was dropped at night near Limoges in south-eastern France, with identity papers as Ghita Mary Lindell. Neave wished to accompany her on the flight but was refused because of his position within Room 900 and his knowledge of all the agents and operations. Room 900 could not risk him being shot down over enemy territory, captured and interrogated. Instead he settled with accompanying Lindell to RAF Tangmere and said goodbye to her there.

'I did not doubt that Mary had the boldness and capacity to lead a réseau,' he wrote, but 'the thought of sending a woman on such a dangerous task was unpleasant . . . There was the possibility that they [women] would be subjected to the most degrading methods of torture, if captured, which distressed many intelligence officers of my generation.'[8]

Occasionally MI9/IS9 needed to work with SOE, as in the case of Lindell's return mission. It was SOE who organised the reception committee that met her at the drop zone 60 miles south-east of Limoges. Room 900 received confirmation from 138 Squadron and SOE that the drop had been successful. Nothing was heard of Lindell for several weeks, except a message from the American vice consul in Lyons that she had visited him and requested funds for her work. On her way back to Ruffec with her French guide, they were accidentally struck by a car. Lindell was left with life-threatening wounds: serious head trauma, five fractured ribs and injuries to her arms and legs. With the help of the local French people she was smuggled to a farmhouse though there was little hope of her survival. She was given medical treatment and, after slight improvement, was secretly moved to the hospital at Loches, in the Loire valley.

The Gestapo had heard rumours of an injured agent in a hospital and began to search all in the area. They arrived at Loches hospital, but did not find Lindell who had been moved into the hospital cellar and hidden behind a stack of wood. By Christmas she was still gravely ill and a message was smuggled to her son, Maurice de Milleville who managed to visit her. She remained ill for a long time, but in spite of this, she would soon carry out her greatest mission – saving the only two surviving commandos of Operation Frankton – the 'Cockleshell Heroes'.

Operation Frankton

At the end of 1942, IS9(X) briefed a party of twelve Royal Marine Commandos in escape and evasion ahead of a clandestine night mission. It was to be Operation Frankton, a night operation against German cargo ships in the port of Bordeaux, authorised as part of Combined Operations under Vice Admiral Lord Louis Mountbatten. The men were to canoe down the mouth of the river to the German cargo ships and place limpet mines on their hulls, timed to explode after the commandos had made it back to safer territory.

Under cover of darkness on 1 December 1942, the men and their equipment were loaded into submarine *Tuna* and sailed down the Irish Channel towards the French coast. It was not possible for them to return on the submarine, so they were instructed to make their way across land to Ruffec after the mission and link up with helpers by entering one of the cafés. Ruffec was 70 miles north of Bordeaux and the escape line was being run by Mary Lindell.

The submarine arrived at the mouth of the river on 6 December. Splitting off into six two-man canoes, it took the twelve men five days and nights to canoe down the river in two groups, each taking their own route to avoid detection by patrols. Only two canoes managed to reach the Gironde estuary; they attacked and damaged six German ships, one being successfully sunk. The four men escaped the scene using escape maps, compasses and kit issued by MI9 but became separated, and one of the teams was never heard of again. Major Herbert Hasler and William Sparks were the sole survivors of Operation Frankton.[9] Of the eight men who did not make it to the port of Bordeaux, four were presumed drowned, and the other four were captured and shot under Hitler's Commando Order of 18 October 1942 which stated that 'No Quarter' [no clemency] was to be given to captured members of the Allied Special Forces. Hitler had become so enraged by successful raids and acts of sabotage by Allied commandos that he issued the order:

All men operating against German troops in so-called Commando raids in Europe or in Africa are to be annihilated to the last man. This is to be carried out whether they be soldiers in uniform, or saboteurs, with or without arms, and whether fighting or seeking to escape . . . I will hold all Commanders and Officers responsible under Military Law for any omission to carry out this order.

The order was a direct breach of the laws of war and was intended to remain a secret from the Allies. The deaths of the commandos on Operation Frankton were discovered and deemed a war crime.

As instructed during training, Hasler and Marine Sparks obeyed instructions and headed for Ruffec. They received civilian clothes from a farmhouse and were safely passed through a number of farmhouses, where they were sheltered as 'French peasants'. On 18 December they finally arrived at Ruffec and entered the Hotel des Toques Blanches where they ordered a bowl of potato soup and two glasses of red wine.[10] Hasler slipped a five-franc note to the woman to pay the bill. Inside was a hand scribbled note: 'We are escaping English soldiers and beg for help.'

She returned with their change and a note: 'Stay at your table until I have closed the restaurant.' She was wary and thought they could be deserters from the German army. She questioned them, still suspicious about their identity, but then agreed to try and find a helper (Lindell), and gave them a bed for the night. Hasler's escape report says: 'She sheltered us for twenty-four hours and got in touch with two of MARIE CLAIRE'S contacts in Ruffec. They visited us in our room.'[11]

In the meantime, after visiting his mother in the Loche hospital, Maurice de Milleville returned to Lyons to find a message for her: 'Two important parcels of food waiting.' Realising the significance of the coded message, he returned to his mother. From her hospital bed, Lindell instructed her son to contact a guide, Armand Debreuil, to prepare to evacuate Hasler and Sparks:

> About 1400 hrs on 19 December we were taken in the back of a [closed] baker's van to a wood just S.E. of Benest. At dusk a guide took us about three-quarters of a mile across the Line of Demarcation [into Vichy France] to a farm owned by another member of MARIE CLAIRE'S organisation.[12]

The farm belonged to Debreuil who hid them there for weeks. Sparks wrote that he felt uncomfortable about leaving his fate in the hands of a woman, but in time came to realise that she was the best person to help them. Although still not well, Lindell had discharged herself from hospital and on 7 January 1943, she met Hasler and Sparks.[13] Back in London it was weeks before confirmation was received about any survivors from Operation Frankton. Colonel Henry

Cartwright, British military attaché in Berne, sent a telegram to Room 900 on 23 February 1943 that confirmed the survival of only two Cockleshell Heroes who were hiding in Lyons and that Lindell needed urgent hospital treatment. At MI9 headquarters at Beaconsfield there were celebrations at the news of the survivors who had yet to be brought out of France.

Lindell had failed to establish a route through the Pyrenees and told Hasler and Sparks that they would be evacuated via a contact in Switzerland. She then smuggled herself across the border at Annemasse into Switzerland and, at a party, met a trusted ally of the Swiss Intelligence Service whom she asked to help take Hasler and Sparks out of France. She returned to give them the good news that she had secured their escape route, then returned to Switzerland for urgent medical treatment. She passed them to the Pat Line, and they were smuggled to Marseille. At the end of March 1943 the only two survivors of Operation Frankton were escorted over the Spanish border to Perpignan by their mountain guide, called Martineau, with three other escapers.[14]

The escape story back to England of Hasler and Sparks – the Cockleshell Heroes – became legendry in the history of MI9 and Room 900. As for Mary Lindell, her tenacity and determination to help airmen and soldiers remained unabated. After further hospital treatment in Switzerland, she chose to return to France to concentrate her efforts on an escape line from Ruffec. She operated with a new identity as 'Comtesse de Moncy' and successfully established a frontier crossing point for evaders at Andorra. Between October and December 1943 her escape line rescued ten servicemen and brought them safely into Spain. But Lindell was still wanted by the Gestapo and she was finally caught on 23 November 1943.[15] A large sum of money could not bribe them to release her. She attempted an escape from the train that was transferring her to Paris and was shot in the head and back as she tried to flee. A German surgeon in the hospital at Tours saved her life.

For the remainder of the war, Lindell was tortured at the hands of the Nazis.[16] In February 1944 she was taken to the SS section of Dijon prison where she was chained by the hands and feet for three of her eight-month imprisonment there. Three times she was taken out to be shot, then sent back to her cell where she was cut off from the world and with no food for twen-ty-two to twenty-six hours at a time. On 26 July she was taken to Saarbrucken concentration camp, Neue Bremme, then to Ravensbrück on 3 September 1944 where she was subjected to hard labour.[17] Then because of her medical training, the commandant put her to work in the camp hospital. Again, she suffered from food deprivation and bouts of serious pneumonia. When she was liberated at the end of the war she weighed just 33 kilograms.[18] She was released due to the work of Swedish diplomat Count Bernadotte who negoti-ated the release of Jews and Allied prisoners in exchanges that saw 11,000 prisoners repatriated via Sweden in 1943–4. His work continued in 1945 when he negotiated further releases with Heinrich Himmler before Himmler was arrested by the British in May 1945.

Lindell survived. Neave later wrote: 'Her career, as an Englishwoman defying the Germans by sheer pertinacity and daring, was almost without precedent . . . one of the most colourful agents in the history of Room 900.'[19] Lindell was awarded the Croix de Guerre by the French and was mentioned in despatches by the British. In 1966 she was granted compensation from the German government for her disablement as a result of Nazi persecution.[20] Nigel Morgan, whose father was an interrogator for MI9, commented: 'We owe so much to these people who took on the SS and Nazis at mortal risk. For them it was at a terrible cost.'[21]

The Felix Line

Another woman, Dutch-born Beatrice Terwindt, was to be dropped into Holland by MI9 to start a new escape line. Terwindt was born in Arnhem in 1911 and in the late 1930s, until December 1939,[22] she worked as a stewardess with the airline KLM for its European routes. Because of the war, she then undertook secretarial work for the airline at Schipol, then moved to their offices in the Hague. From November 1940, she worked for a bureau there, assisting refugees from Rotterdam. On 20 February 1942 she left Holland, aided by a number of Catholic priests, evaded arrest at various German checkpoints and crossed into Switzerland at

Collonges with the help of local people. Because she had no papers, the Swiss authorities interned her in Bellechasse Prison but, with no explanation, she was released on 30 April 1942, taken to Geneva with other Dutch refugees and given a replacement Dutch passport. On 2 July 1942, she left by train to Barcelona and from there to Bilbao. She experienced visa problems at Bilbao and travelled on to Madrid where she obtained the correct exit visas to fly to Lisbon. Airey Neave was offered her services by Donald Darling because she had expressed a willingness to evacuate RAF personnel from Holland. Neave wrote 'I found her quiet and thoughtful and eager to return to Holland.'[23]

Terwindt became an agent and liaison officer for MI9/IS9 under a number of aliases: Trix, Felix, Beatrice Thompson and Johanna Maria van der Velden.[24] Beatrice Thompson was the name she used whilst training and the name Johanna Maria van der Velden in the field, operating under the codenames Felix and Trix. The escape network was known as the Felix Line and only operated for a short time.[25] During training she was described as 'very intelligent, capable, practical and most discreet. She is hardworking, serious-minded . . . a very pleasant personality, quiet but forceful.'[26] Her slim file at the National Archives in London provides scant detail of her life or mission. She spoke several languages, including Dutch, English, French, German and Italian.

MI9 had a strict policy of not overlapping with SOE, however Holland proved to be the exception because an escape line from Holland through Belgium could not be set up without their help.[27] Room 900 had no radio contact with Holland and could not verify or contact its helpers, so the Dutch section of SOE agreed to train Terwindt and drop her into Holland for IS9. Plans to parachute her into Holland in December 1942 were postponed because of the betrayal of the Maréchal family and subsequent swift departure of Peggy van Lier, Georges d'Oultremont and Edouard d'Oultremont.[28] Neave feared that Terwindt might be recognised in Holland and he considered whether she should undergo surgery to change her appearance, but decided against such drastic measures.[29]

News had just arrived of Nemo's arrest and consequently Neave forbade Terwindt to contact anyone in the Comet Line for risk of being compromised.

She was despatched into the field as Trix by Room 900 on 13/14 February 1943 in an SOE mission, Operation Chicory.[30] Terwindt's mission was cleared by SIS/MI6, but little is revealed about the operation in its slim declassified file.[31] Neave accompanied her to Tempsford aerodrome in Bedfordshire and reflected: 'Those journeys sitting beside an agent on the way to unknown dangers are unforgettable.'[32]

Once parachuted in, nothing could have alerted Trix to the fact that the reception committee was not the Dutch Resistance: Abwehr agents were waiting and they prevented her from taking a suicide pill. She was escorted to headquarters at Dreibergen and came before Lieutenant Colonel Hermann Giskes, the head of the Abwehr in occupied Holland. Giskes caused problems for the Dutch Section of SOE, one of whose agents had been picked up by the Abwehr and made to transmit under German orders. Although he adopted the agreed 'mistakes' in his radio transmissions to alert SOE that he had been compromised, those receiving the messages believed it to be human error and continued to send in agents.[33] Of the fifty Dutch agents parachuted into Holland, forty-seven were caught and executed by the Germans. Giskes operated fourteen SOE agents who passed messages with disinformation back to the British. Two escaped and returned to England to alert the authorities but were immediately imprisoned in Brixton because it was thought that they had been 'turned'.[34] Giskes was not the only problem for MI9 in Holland: Harold Cole's associate, double agent Christiaan Lindemans (aka King Kong) betrayed another escape line from Holland to Spain and passed back information to Giskes.[35]

After capture, Trix was interrogated across three months and subjected to sleep deprivation. Her interrogators believed she was working for SOE, which in fact was not true and she revealed nothing about SOE or Room 900. News of her incarceration in Haaren concentration camp came to Neave and Langley four months later via two SOE agents who had successfully escaped from the camp. Neave poignantly wrote: 'The first attempt to set up an organisation in Holland had been a tragic failure and I never sent a woman on a similar mission from England during the rest of the war.'[36] Trix was taken to Ravensbrück concentration camp and was then transferred to Mauthausen in January 1945. Before the final surrender of Germany in May 1945, she was transferred by the Red Cross to Switzerland where she received medical treatment.[37]

Although missions in Holland in 1942 and 1943 had been a widespread disaster, in the final two years of the war, Room 900 would achieve successes in the country, especially with operations under a newly formed section called IS9(WEA).

IS9 Agents

When originally writing *Saturday at MI9*, Neave commented that Mary Lindell and Beatrice Terwindt were the only women to be sent behind enemy lines by Room 900.[38] Declassified files now reveal this not to be the case and other women, such as Antonia Maria Hamilton who was dropped behind enemy lines on 9/10 August 1944, were despatched into enemy territory for IS9/Room 900. Again, scant details are given of their missions in files at the National Archives.

The rescue of Jews by field officers of IS9(ME – Middle East) was attempted at the Black Sea region in an operation codenamed Chicken I, but its primary files remain classified.[39] Hannah (Anna) Szennes was deemed to have been part of it. She was a Hungarian Jew who had escaped to Palestine where she was recruited by Zionist leaders to join MI9/IS9.[40] She enlisted in the WAAF and was parachuted into Yugoslavia with two other agents on 14 June 1944 in Operation Chicken I. Her codename was Minnie. She was arrested on the Hungarian border and taken to Budapest. Whilst in prison, she passed information to a colleague who managed to escape and pass it on to Cairo by radio transmission. She underwent intense interrogation, then torture by the Gestapo and was shot on 6 November 1944. Her official file records that she was 'killed by enemy action, whilst in the course of her duties'.[41] Notification of her death was sent to Teddy Kollek, then head of The Jewish Agency for Palestine and himself a refugee from Vienna who later became mayor of Jerusalem. She was described in her file as 'aircraftwoman' and one memo states: 'By special agreement this agent is paid on a salaried basis of £30 per month. Payment drawn via the RAF and passed to Jewish Agency to pay part of it, with balance paid by IS9(ME).' Clearly she was part of IS9 in the Middle East.

Martha Martinovic from Czechoslovakia enlisted in the WAAF on 4 April 1944 and also worked for IS9 in the Middle East. According to her file, IS9 paid £500 to the Jewish Agency in settlement of her death and corresponded with Teddy Kollek. She had been missing for a considerable period and was believed killed as all attempts to trace her had failed. IS9(ME) decided to place her death on 1 September 1945.[42] Another of MI9's agents, Miss Poumboura, was arrested in Athens whilst engaged on MI9/IS9 work and was imprisoned in Greece and Italy.[43]

There are around twenty declassified personal files for Jewish émigré women and men. All were Europeans who fled Hitler and worked for MI9/IS9 in liaison with Teddy Kollek. The files give no details of their work as agents, except that they all died in the service of MI9 /IS9. It is hoped that further files may be declassified to provide an understanding of their missions. If their work had overlapped with, or involved, SIS this could explain why the files remain classified. Although mention has already been made of how MI9 and SIS networks were kept separate, escape and evasion operations, especially in northern Italy, would prove trickier without not only SIS, but also the American intelligence equivalent, OSS (Office of Strategic Services, forerunner of the CIA). The central figures here would include an Austrian émigré, Fritz Molden, and several Italian women, about whom very little has previously been written. Given the inherited negative portrayals of Pope Pius XII in relation to the Second World War, it had not been expected to find that the Vatican also became involved in MI9's clandestine operations in Italy.

11

ITALY

Escape and evasion in Italy were initially very limited and more informal than other escape lines in Western Europe. The primary problem was one of communication. MI9 had great difficulty establishing contact with prisoner of war camps there as the inefficiency of the Italian administration meant that any coded messages, letters and equipment were either lost or destroyed, or could take up to a year to reach Italian POW camps. Escape attempts were difficult because the Italian camps were surprisingly better guarded than those in Germany. Good communication was eventually established with a POW camp in Florence which was reserved primarily for captured British generals. The training of British paratroops in codes and communication before going into action meant that, after the paratroop raid on Italy in January 1941 in which some were taken prisoner, they could begin to communicate in code with MI9 as well as teaching the codes to other POWs in the Italian camps.[1]

According to Fritz Molden, an agent on the ground in Italy, the Italian population was generally not Fascist or anti-Nazi, nor did they appear to be pro-German or pro-Allies. They wanted peace and many were prepared to secretly help the Allies.[2] However, in contradiction to this view, an official MI9 report concludes that there were problems for MI9 in Italy because the population was hostile.[3] Prior to the invasion of Italy, MI9 could not easily infiltrate agents into the country and unless they could be given perfect cover, they were soon detected and arrested. An attempt was planned to penetrate agents into Italy via submarines from Malta but this did not materialise because no submarine was available at the time this was needed.[4]

The role of the Italian resistance groups and the Vatican in helping MI9 would reach far beyond Italy's borders. Italy would become the only viable base from which the Allies could also penetrate Austria. After annexation of the country by Hitler in March 1938, Austria remained largely isolated until 1943. The only contact with the Allies was from Italy via Switzerland and France – for reasons that will soon become apparent, and even then, it was often through neutral Vatican channels or isolated individuals.[5]

Establishing escape lines out of Italy posed its own challenges for MI9. The Scheideck and Brenner Passes over the Alps between Italy and Switzerland were so well guarded that it was almost impossible for evaders to cross there.[6] Any achievements in escape and evasion relied on expert guides, one of whom in northern Italy was Guerrino Tasinato. He escorted between 150 and 200 POWs from Padova to Milan and then to the border into Switzerland, although it is not known where they crossed the frontier.[7]

Captain Peter Barshall was one British soldier who escaped via Como into Switzerland. Serving with the Royal Artillery, he had been captured in Tunisia on Christmas Day 1942 and transferred to a POW camp in Italy, from which he twice escaped.[8] His unpublished memoirs provide an eyewitness account into the difficulties of crossing the border in early November 1943:

> In the evening we travelled by car to the north side of lake Como. At night we rowed across and started walking up the mountain, led by our new smuggler friends. After many hours of climbing, we reached somewhere near the summit of Monte Generoso and could see below us the Swiss valley and the town of Chiasso. By now it was snowing quite heavily, which turned out to be a blessing in disguise, because we could hear dogs barking. We knew that they were the dogs used by the frontier guards trying to trap smugglers, but by now the snow was thick on the ground which covered the scent of our tracks.[9]

Once in Switzerland, Barshall was engaged at the British Legation in Berne, attached to the British military attaché, and helped with escape and evasion.

The main figure operating for MI9 from the British Legation in Berne was diplomat Sir David Kelly MC. Kelly had served in the First World War, after which he joined the Diplomatic Service and saw postings to Buenos Aires, Lisbon, Mexico, Brussels and Cairo. In 1940, he was posted to Berne where staff at the British Legation, including Barshall, were also aiding Allen Dulles in bringing American airmen out of Switzerland. Allen Dulles, a US attorney and former diplomat, had been posted to Berne in November 1942 and was the OSS representative there.[10] It was not his first posting to Berne: during the First World War, when America declared war on Germany in 1917, he had been transferred from Vienna to Berne. In the Second World War, he returned to Berne as US president Roosevelt's special emissary and was stationed at the office of the OSS there. Aiding him in OSS headquarters on the classified work was a German-American named Gero von Gaevernitz.[11]

Dulles discovered a group of Austrian émigrés living in Zurich and made contact with their leader Dr Kurt Grimm who had left Vienna in May 1938 after the annexation by Germany and had good contacts in Switzerland. Dulles was able to secure high-level intelligence from German and Austrian covert contacts, including Grimm's contacts amongst German industrialists and the Wehrmacht.

As Dulles increased his OSS networks and agents, Barshall's role was extended to include liaison officer with the Foreign Office at the Palais Fédérale, making daily visits to sort out problems relating to the number of internees in the country.[12] Barshall subsequently moved to Annecy between Geneva and Chambery in south-eastern France, from where he organised the evacuation of escapers, evaders, scientists, undercover agents and some refugees by train to Marseille.[13] The Swiss authorities sent trains to a station near Geneva to pick up refugees and the escapers and evaders who had been hidden in a nearby cellar were secretly smuggled onto these trains. Barshall commented 'quite a few Americans escaped this way'.[14] The work was not without its personal risks. Barshall was thanked at the end of the war in a personal letter from Brigadier General Barnwell Legge, military attaché of the United States for 'the most valuable services which you rendered my office in aiding the escape of a considerable number of American aviators who were interned in Switzerland . . . you succeeded in effecting the escape of valuable aviators whose presence in England and elsewhere was extremely valuable to the American Cause.'[15] Barshall was mentioned in despatches 'for distinguished service'.[16]

Fritz Molden

Dulles and Kelly concentrated efforts in establishing links across the countries that were isolated and difficult to penetrate, primarily Italy, Germany and Austria. They succeeded through a young Austrian student called Fritz Molden, first introduced to them by Kurt Grimm.[17] Molden had been studying at the gymnasium in Vienna and had already been arrested on several occasions by the Gestapo for anti-Nazi activities. In 1942 he joined the Wehrmacht and was stationed for two years in Italy where he was wounded.

Molden described his first impressions of the wiry grey-haired Dulles with trim moustache: 'Behind his steel-rimmed glasses his clear, grey-blue eyes were alive with interest.'[18] The two men instantly connected and discussed Allied support for the Austrian Resistance movement in Italy. Between Hitler's annexation of Austria in 1938 and 1945, over a million Austrians were conscripted into the German army. Many were anti-Nazis and once they found themselves serving in Italy, they deserted their units and formed into resistance groups, uniting with the local Italian Resistance to establish communication centres in central and northern Italy. It was a perfect opportunity for Molden to use these groups to gather intelligence for the Allies as well as supporting their acts of sabotage.[19]

Whilst still serving in the German army, he made contact with a group of disaffected German officers who had joined the Resistance movement. The movement needed leadership and Molden seemed the ideal man. During his active service in Italy, the German army never discovered that Molden was part of the underground resistance and a spy for the Allies. He successfully conducted missions within Italy and ran agents who smuggled Allied POWs into Switzerland by working closely with British intelligence (MI6 and MI9) and the American Secret Service (the OSS) in Berne. In the course of his work in Italy, Molden had to create new identities, each with a different parentage and background. His aliases included that of Luigi Brentini, Pietro de Lago, Hans Steindler, Jerry Wieser and Peter Stummer.[20] Each change of name also required a slight change to his physical appearance: dyed hair, false teeth, maybe a moustache – they were almost standard textbook spy disguises. The brief from his mysterious handler, Alfons Stillfried whose real name was never known, was to travel to Milan from where he was to attempt to get into Switzerland with the help of a military administrative group called Kriegsverwaltungsrat. Three main figures in this organisation would go on to help Molden in this respect: Dr Kurt Baumgartner (a senior administrative advisor to the German military), Corporal Count Franz Otting (a Bavarian aristocrat) and Lieutenant Franz Schromm (a Viennese journalist by profession).[21] They were already working with several operational figures in Milan including Renata Faccincani (della Torre), Nam de Beaufort, Lily (Lori) Possanner (Molden's cousin), Canon Michael Gamper and Erich Amon.[22] These figures worked closely with the Austrian Resistance in Italy and were part of the line smuggling Allied POWs from Italy into Switzerland. Underground resistance cells had already been established in Turin, Bologna and Milan, but later too in Trieste, Alessandria and Verona.[23] Molden's cousin, Lily Possanner ran a small business in Milan and entertained on a lavish scale.[24] Within her circle of friends were Baumgartner, Schromm and Faccincani.[25] She used her own home as a safe house. Molden recounted the period when he was in hiding in his cousin's home 'in a room immediately adjoining the big drawing room where she used to hold court every evening and receive her many friends, including German officers of all ranks'.[26] During the times when Molden had to hide, Lily could use her influence with her German acquaintances and surreptitiously find out if Molden was still on the wanted list. She procured a new identity card for him at great expense.

It the autumn of 1943 in Milan, Molden first met Renata Faccincani and her brother Gianfranco; later he owed his life to Renata whom he described as 'a real beauty'. Whilst stationed in Milan, Molden worked for a short time as interpreter to the German brothel patrol.[27] Sexual activities by German officers needed to be strictly regulated by special police patrols to avoid the officers contracting sexual diseases from prostitutes. Three permitted brothels in the city were monitored by these special patrols to ensure that army regulations were observed. Molden recalled:

> The work was far from disagreeable, since the madams of the various establishments overwhelmed us with hospitality, serving up champagne and excellent food in order to concentrate our attention on culinary matters and prevent us from keeping a careful check on the visitors of the establishment. Each brothel was equipped with an intriguing device in the form of small peep-holes through which ladies could be observed at work in their rooms.[28]

As Molden himself admitted, it was an education for him as a naïve eighteen-year-old.

New instructions arrived one day from Stillfried for Molden to ask the Wehrmacht for a transfer near the frontline where he was to link up with the 356th Infantry Division.[29] Molden succeeded and the Wehrmacht transferred him to the Economic Administration Centre HQ in Treviso, northern Italy. Here one evening, over a glass of wine with the officers of the division, he discovered their links to the Resistance movement and realised he had successfully penetrated a division within the Wehrmacht that had turned anti-Nazi. This division would later aid Count Stauffenberg in the failed assassination attempt on Hitler's life in July 1944.[30] Molden established important links with the underground movement in this part of northern Italy.

'A Handful of Flour'

New accounts of small acts of bravery are emerging from the period of Italy's struggle with Fascism and Nazism. In the autumn of 1943, a group of Italians went into hiding in the mountainous region of Abruzzo, surrounding lake Scanno in the south of the country.[31] The Germans had already placed garrisons in the villages and issued orders that anyone found sheltering Allied POWs would have their houses burned to the ground. One local shepherd had already been executed for sharing bread and cheese with a prisoner in his hut.[32]

Prisoners liberated from the camp at Sulmona on 8 September used the mountain paths on their way south, stopping overnight in local houses. The local partisans and peasants knew the risks they were taking for the Allies, but did not want compensation, preferring to remain anonymous. The author of a report to the Allied Screening Commission wrote:

> Above all, this was the great, unconcerned Homeric sense of the sacred right of the guest, of the stranger, who has things against him, and must be protected. In this sense, the humble people of shepherds and Italian peasants gave then to the world a proof of civilization which should not be forgotten . . . This moral revolt was anonymous . . . neither will we tell the name of the small part of the country of the Abruzzo where the number of prisoners was so vast, sheltered in farmhouses and in huts, and in grottoes in the mountains, that the intervention of a single person could no longer be sufficient to sustain them.[33]

The local women who went to the mill to grind wheat have remained unsung heroes for over seventy-five years. They made a conscious decision to leave behind from their own bags a handful of flour to make bread for the escaped prisoners, and the region introduced an extra tax to provide food for Allied prisoners. Occasionally, they were lucky and the Allies managed to parachute supplies into the region. However, the parachutists often ended up in the hands of the Germans, who had no idea of the humanitarian work of the local helpers – if they had, the local villages would have been burned to the ground. If arrested and interrogated the women knew nothing, but their simple 'handful of flour' was their form of resistance to the Nazis and unspoken help to the Allies:

> The period of German occupation has taught us what our women are capable of doing, also only for a spontaneous sense of defence of life, and of human dignity against any abuse of power.[34]

A prisoner could be in the villa of a wealthy count one night, and the next sleeping on straw in a peasant's stable. The headquarters of local operations was the house of Nunziata. She cared little about the Fascist squads who patrolled the area and when she faced a difficult situation, she charmed and befriended them. She also personally nursed and cared for an Italian agent who fell ill with typhus and could not be evacuated from Italy by sailing boat.

The mother of one particular peasant family oversaw the comings and goings of English generals, officers and non-commissioned officers in her home. She always ensured that a certain number of beds were available in the house in readiness for prisoners and a plentiful supply of food. The tales of help to the Allies were numerous: from the peasant women, to the countess with snow white hair who indulged seven English generals with cups of tea as they waited to escape, and the dressmaker of Sulmona who organised assistance to prisoners liberated from the camp of Badia. These women were part of a powerful hidden resistance to occupation and their quiet determination was later remembered by the evaders they saved.

Volumia Ugolotti and her family, who lived in Parma, gave shelter to Lieutenant Beasley and others.[35] She was discovered by the German authorities and taken to Parma prison with her husband, daughter and son-in-law. She was released with her daughter after five months, but her husband was transferred to a camp in Germany. Her son-in-law's whereabouts were unknown, but the Allies eventually traced him to a POW camp in Egypt.

Britsh Generals in Florence

One of the successes achieved for MI9 in Italy was the escape of senior British officers from a POW camp at Florence. Known as Camp 12, it was in the Castello di Vincigliata, an eleventh-century castle on a rocky hill in the Tuscan countryside, 8 kilometres north-east of Florence. The castle had been requisitioned by the Italian government in 1941 as a prisoner of war camp for high-ranking military personnel. The Escape Committee, under camp leader Lieutenant General Neame, spent several months in the preparation of maps, collection of provisions, making and dying of clothes, and reconnaissance of the prison camp security.[36] In the camp was Brigadier James Hargest, DSO of the New Zealand Army, captured in North Africa on 27 November 1941, having been wounded in action. After receiving medical treatment he was transferred to Italy aboard an Italian submarine with twenty-nine other officers and his batman. They were held first at Sulmona in the Abruzzo region of Italy for four months before being transferred to Camp 12. Over a period of twelve months, the British officers made plans for an escape:

> In August 1942, we decided to tunnel out from the Castello chapel by first sinking a shaft 10 feet deep in the chapel porch, then tunnelling for about 30 feet under the castle walls, under the driveway and the outer battlements . . . We used the Chapel as a spoilage dump, and by taking a lead from the lights there, were able to have a chain of electric lamps in the tunnel.[37]

To fool the inspection guards whilst they were carrying out the tunnelling work, they made dummy figures for their beds, which were so convincing that the men were not reported missing until twenty-four hours after the escape. By mid-March 1943, the tunnel came within 5 inches of the surface.

The senior British officers broke the surface at 9.30 p.m. on 30 March 1943. The escapers were Lieutenant General O'Connor, Air Vice Marshal Boyd, Major General Carton de Wiart, Brigadier Combe, Brigadier James Hargest and Brigadier Miles. They successfully came out to the surface immediately under shelter of the outer walls. Generals O'Connor and de Wiart headed straight for the frontier. The remaining four officers walked into Florence and took a train for Milan via Bologna, reaching Milan at 8.30 a.m. the following morning. Philip Neame wrote about the escape in his book *Playing with Strife* which, apart from the last chapter, he wrote whilst a POW in Italy. During the Italian Armistice in September 1943, his manuscript was concealed in a tomb in a monastery, and later retrieved by MI9 agent Cagnazzo in November 1944. On arrival in Milan, Boyd and Combe took a tram but were subsequently recaptured.

Hargest and Miles took a train at 10.30 a.m. from Stazione Nord to Como from where they walked towards Chiasso, leaving the roads and heading into the mountains, where the shadow of trees would help avoid discovery. They came to the frontier after stalking a patrol in the darkness, succeeded in cutting a hole with wire cutters and entered Switzerland at 10.30 p.m. In their attempt to cross Italy, they had been aided by Ruggero Cagnazzo, an engineer in civilian life.[38] Cagnazzo spent a good part of his own private funds providing food, shelter and clothes for British generals and senior officers.

Hargest and Miles surrendered to Swiss police the next morning, were freed after three days and handed over to the British military attaché in Berne. They were repatriated back to England and debriefed by MI9. Tragically, Hargest's son was killed in Italy in March 1944 and Hargest himself was killed in action in Normandy in 1944.[39]

Operation Simcol

The Italian Armistice in September 1943 resulted in immediate freedom for Allied POWs who walked out of their camps after the guards had deserted their posts. In the Pescara-Ancona area on the Adriatic coast, POWs fled into the neighbouring hills and countryside. There were concerns that the Germans would take steps to round them up and transfer them to Germany where their chances of escape were more challenging. An operation to rescue them was requested in mid-September 1943 by 15 Army Group and to MI9 it was evident that an operation should be mounted as soon as possible to bring them back to Britain. Detailed planning for Operation Simcol began at the end of September 1943, headed by Lieutenant Colonel Simmons at Bari.[40] To have any chance of success, it was decided that five detachments should be parachuted into different areas of Italy.[41] The earliest date by which this could be achieved was 2 October 1943. Each detachment comprised one officer, an interpreter and eight other ranks. The Americans provided one of the detachments, another came from the 2nd Special Air Service Battalion, and three from the 1st Parachute Brigade.[42] Each detachment was to seek out escaped

POWs and bring them to designated safety locations where British armed guards would evacuate them by sea from Termoli. The detachments were dropped into the region with just two days of rations and supplies; further supplies were to be parachuted in by Dakotas. The duration of Operation Simcol was planned to be fourteen days. Major John Timothy was in charge of No. 2 Parachute Brigade which was to be dropped into the Fermo region to find Allied POWs between Tolentino, Macerata and the coast. His account of the operation can be read in detail in his memoirs and an appendix to the official war diary.[43] Major Timothy and his detachment took off from Bari aerodrome in the late afternoon of 2 October 1943. Unfortunately they were dropped at a point near the river Tenna, some 32 kilometres from their intended drop zone, but proceeded to move south to Civitanova where they began to search for POWs. At first they made no contacts and moved to the river Chienti. A week later, they still had no success and were now in the region of Servigliano where the first nine POWs were discovered in hiding near Falerone. The following day they came across between sixty and seventy POWs, including Americans. The search continued over the next few days and they picked up small numbers of POWs in isolated places. The aim was to evacuate the prisoners from designated beaches with the help of the SAS. The operation had extended beyond the original intended fourteen days. In his diary for 23 October, Timothy wrote:

> The control point overlooked the riverbed and was manned by CSM Marshall of the SAS. He told me that two days previously a German patrol had picked up 2 of his men and 6 POWs near the river. He (CSM Marshall) had killed two Germans and one of his men had been able to escape, but had apparently been picked up again later the same day. Because of this shooting, the locals were extremely jumpy.

On 24 October 1943 the detachment reached a point on the coast and collected some two to three hundred POWs. CSM Marshall allocated his men as a beach protection party in the attempt to evacuate as many POWs as possible:

0205 hours: we could see black shapes out to sea, and within half an hour rubber dinghies began to appear. We had a final round up but without luck. The final result was 5 officer POWs and 17 Other Rank POWs. We were all taken off by 0250 hours.[44]

The mission was high risk as Hitler's order that all captured parachutists were to be shot had already led to the execution of SAS soldiers captured in Italy. Operation Simcol finally concluded in November 1943. In spite of the difficulties, it resulted in the safe coastal evacuation of at least 500 Allied POWs. Timothy was transferred with the others to Termoli where he spent a few days at an SAS base and wrote his account of the mission.[45]

There were other MI9 sea evacuations from Italy, including 'Plan Gooseberry' and 'Strawberry' which entailed running a fast motor boat to an (unnamed) beach at the mouth of a river to evacuate Allied personnel after 2300 hours on 17 and 23 April 1944.[46] The success of these operations was dependent on the rendezvous pick-ups and collecting points being known to escapers and evaders beforehand, rather than seaborne rescues being undertaken on the off-chance of picking up evaders.

Italian Military Figures and IS9

Some Italian military figures were prepared to help the Allies and a number of them were attached as agents to IS9(CMF – Central Mediterranean Force). Italian parachutist Lieutenant Alberto Orlandi, who had already served on active duties with the Allies in France, Croatia and Sicily, was one of them.[47] In January 1944, he joined 5 Field Section of IS9, having trained with the Italian Intelligence Service, and was posted to the Adriatic region, operating agents just a few miles from the front line. He often accompanied the agents into no-man's-land before their despatch and received agents back. He coordinated the evacuation of escapers and evaders whom he also interrogated on behalf of MI9 for debriefing and gathering intelligence. Several hundred escapers and evaders owed their freedom to his mission to get them out of Italy.

On three occasions, he successfully penetrated enemy lines. In February 1944, Orlandi took a patrol deep into occupied territory in the search for fifty POWs who had been dispersed due to enemy fighting. That same month, Italian Captain Giacomo Benello of the 3rd Grenadier Regiment landed in northern Italy and set up headquarters at Milan where he carried out work in assisting Allied POWs for MI9/IS9.[48] He was responsible for evacuating 109 POWs to Switzerland, in spite of losing radio contact with IS9 headquarters in Florence and losing some of his agents to Fascists and German arrests.

Operating at this time, too, was Attilio Parma who came to IS9 from 2 SAS Regiment with whom he had already carried out three missions.[49] In March 1944, he accompanied Major McKee to the Tenna river valley as a radio operator and served there until the end of May 1944. The Germans suspected him of being an Allied agent, captured him and he was tortured for ten days. He gave nothing away and managed to escape and return to Major McKee who then organised a secret IS9 mission which left from Corsica and involved Parma. In June 1944, Parma landed from Corsica by boat in an IS9 mission to help POWs until October 1944, when he acted as a guide to a party of evaders, bringing them to Allied lines.[50] His work with IS9 proved him to be totally loyal even in the most testing of times. Another Italian helping Major McKee in the Tenna river valley was Aristide Silenzi who acted as a guide and carried out reconnaissance missions. Silenzi gathered POWs together and led eight parties of them down to a beach on the coast of the Marche for their evacuation.[51]

Giuseppe de Eise, an NCO of the Italian army, served with IS9 for eleven months during which time he completed four missions behind enemy lines and was instrumental in the rescue of Allied POWs. He and his team organised an escape route, down which over 300 POWs successfully escaped.[52] For this particular escape route to succeed, IS9 sent an Italian lieutenant, Nanni Giovanetta, deep undercover behind enemy lines for over six months.[53] Giovanetta sported a distinctive red beard, was strict and bold and gained a reputation with Allied POWs for his fearlessness. So too with the Germans, who issued a reward for his arrest, but he was never caught.

Another Italian lieutenant working for IS9 was Hugh Raniere Bourbon del Monte who operated behind enemy lines from November 1943 until June 1944, organising escapes for POWs. When the land escape routes were disrupted by enemy patrols, he arranged the evacuation of evaders by sea, always mindful of the atrocities committed against them by the Germans and Fascists. The citation for a recommended award after the war, noted: 'through the partisans he pursued the originators of these atrocities and saw to it that a number met their proper fate.'[54]

These stories of heroism are just the tip of the iceberg but they provide a glimpse into how much the Allies owed to the Italians who were prepared to risk their lives for freedom and democracy.

Stazione Goldoni, Milan

The centre of clandestine operations for northern Italy was run from headquarters in the centre of Milan at Via Carlo Goldoni 19, the home of the aristocratic family Faccincani della Torre. At the centre of the clandestine operations was the twenty-one-year-old daughter Renata, stunningly attractive and with a university education. She was born in April 1921 to a family that had once ruled the area for centuries. Her father was credited with being one of the first people to bring frozen food into Italy and had farms in Bulgaria and Hungary – all lost during the Second World War. He was a colonel in the Alpine regiment and was sent home from the Russian front because he was dying of cancer. His wife Ida was known for being tough, resilient and an ardent anti-Fascist. She spoke numerous languages, ensuring that her children, Renata and Gianfranco, were fluent in German, French, English and Spanish. During the war, Gianfranco was taken away and his whereabouts remained unknown; it was later discovered that he had been killed by the Germans in Piedmont in northern Italy.

Between 1942 and 1943, Renata was an Italian resistance worker, risking her life to aid the Allies. She became the head of the Milan station, known in clandestine circles as the Stazione Goldoni. She was perhaps the person least expected to head operations, and had not appeared to her family to be someone to take risks. 'She was shy and very academic, destined to become a lawyer had the war not intervened,' her daughter Vanessa Clewes recalled in conversation with the author. 'But in fact, she was perfect because her youth and innocence meant the Nazis never suspected her until they arrested her towards the end of the war.'[55] From Stazione Goldoni, she operated a safe house for couriers, agents and anyone who needed immediate shelter from the Nazis. Years later, after the war, her daughter asked her: Why did she do it? Renata shrugged her shoulders and replied: 'It was the right thing to do.'[56] Vanessa Clewes comments:

> My mother had an incredibly strong sense of what was right and wrong that came from her strict upbringing. But I still find it astonishing that at the age of only 21 she took on such enormous risks. My family knew that she helped anyone who needed to escape from Italy, including Italian anti-Fascists and Jewish refugees. Just how deeply she was involved as the actual head of the station, I was not aware until the research for this book. It places my mother's bravery in a whole new light for us.[57]

Renata was working with the Resistance long before Molden arrived in Italy. This helped Molden when he needed to link with the partisans operating in northern Italy on the Swiss border as Renata was able to contact them in just two days.

Molden's own life was in danger. He was soon on the SS and Abwehr's wanted list and a hunt was on for his arrest. He arrived unannounced at Via Goldoni one day, operating under the alias of Luigi Brentini, with just 5 lire in his pocket. Renata gave him money and forged papers. Molden had contacts too in the German Armaments and War production department who gave him 50,000 German marks for future operations.[58] The Stazione Goldoni held a special place in his heart and he wrote about it with affection:

> The Via Goldoni with the Faccincanis and their friends, Lori Possanner and her little world, Franz Otting and many others in Milan – these were to

provide the firm stanchion for the nerve-racking wire I had to walk between the Allied and German camps, between Switzerland and Vienna . . . The Via Goldoni spelt home, security, warmth and affection . . . I had established bonds of sympathy and esteem which nothing could now sever. The Goldoni station had about it a permanence that would outlast war.[59]

With Renata's help, the partisans smuggled Molden across the border near Mendrisio. Renata accompanied him on his escape as they first took a train to Varese, then a branch line towards Porto Ceresio on Lake Lugano. They alighted two stops before Porto Ceresio and walked into a small inn where they waited for their rendezvous – two partisans who would take Molden over the frontier. Renata and Molden parted, and she took the train back to Milan. Molden narrowly avoided Italian police patrols and succeeded in getting over the barbed wire fence of the border.

From the HQ at Via Carlo Goldoni 19, Renata continued to help British troops who had been captured by Italian Fascists and subsequently escaped. Hidden behind huge cupboards and curtains in her mother's large dressing room was a secret printing press, forged passports and papers for Allied POWs. She charmed her way through society – discreet and quiet, whilst still running dangerous missions for Molden. As an expert skier and ski jumper, she personally guided groups of Allied POWs over the border into Switzerland via remote parts of the mountain ranges. On her way back from one such escort, she was kidnapped by angry and frightened deserters hiding in the mountains. Her daughter recalls:

Held in a remote hut in the Alps, Renata feared being raped and for her life. She kept the men talking about their female relatives: wives, sisters and children to remind them of home. It worked and she survived. Her work for the Allies went further because, being somewhat exotic in her youthfulness and a stunning beautiful blond, she could pass off as an Aryan German. She was bilingual and could quietly charm her way into the centre of German operations with her fluency in perfect German. She arrived at German headquarters in Milan one day, pretending to be a German and gained access to photograph documents; intelligence which she passed to the OSS.[60]

Renata also photographed electricity installations and passed them to the Resistance to blow up in night operations.[61]

Whilst there was generally a reluctance to discuss details of her wartime work, Renata did share some stories. Until now, these have remained largely within the family, unpublished for over seventy years, with the exception of an obituary for Renata in *The Times* and the *Observer*. Her friend Nam de Beaufort corroborated these stories to the family, for Nam had worked with Renata in some clandestine activities for the Allies.

Nam de Beaufort

Renata first met Nam de Beaufort, who became a close friend and accomplice, in the summer of 1944. Nam arrived in Milan after the failed assassination attempt on Hitler's life in July 1944. Her real identity is still shrouded in mystery and it is not known whether she operated under her real or an assumed name. Nor is her original nationality certain, even though she was known to have lived in Berlin as a young girl. Nam, who was thought to have been married to a French aristocrat for a short time.[62] She was a strong self-confident woman and could easily pass off as a 'lady of high society' in any of Europe's salons with her aristocratic elegance, compelling bright green eyes, dyed red hair and smart clothes. Vanessa Clewes recalls:

Nam was very beautifully dressed, always with a pillbox hat and feather. Although she could speak many languages, none of them very well, it meant that she could not really pass off as a native of another country. She and my mother were a double act.

Nam joined the cosmopolitan social life in Berlin as a young woman in the 1920s but was firmly an anti-Nazi from the time Hitler came to power in

January 1933. The Nazis never found out about her political views and she secured a job with Admiral Canaris, head of the Abwehr [German Secret Service] in Berlin.[63] At this point she may well have already been working undercover. In early 1944, she left Berlin for Vienna where she linked up with Rudolf von Marogna-Redwitz, a Colonel in the Wehrmacht and member of the Resistance movement in Austria. With Count Stauffenberg, whom Nam knew, he was a leading figure in the attempted assassination on Hitler's life on 20 July 1944. They were closely connected to Austrian anti-Nazi officers like Lieutenant Colonel Robert Bernadis who aided in the implementation of the July plot. The plan failed and Bernadis and others were executed on Hitler's orders.[64] With the help of Colonel Erwin von Lahousen, a high-ranking Abwehr official also in the German resistance and a key player in the July assassination plot, Nam was transferred to 'Station Zeno'. She was now placed at the heart of Abwehr headquarters in Milan. Molden already knew Nam from pre-war days, although the exact connection is not known, and he called on her in her Milan apartment in the Albergo Milano:

> I found an elegant and extremely entertaining woman, full of witty and original ideas and speaking the language of a Germany about which my generation only knew by hearsay – the Germany of the pre-Hitler period. Nam was entirely fearless and declared herself ready to attempt things that would have been too hazardous for anyone else. She would try to obtain the Abwehr's minutes for us and even try to get their code.[65]

At this point, Molden and his network knew nothing about the cracking of the Abwehr Enigma code by Bletchley Park because of the secrecy surrounding their operations.

Nam's fearlessness extended beyond codes and minutes as Vanessa Clewes comments: 'When I was a young child, Nam told me tales of how she had suffocated a German officer with a pillow and drowned another in the bath in one of the waterholes frequented by the SS and Nazis. Nam lured them upstairs to their deaths.'[66] Meanwhile, downstairs in the bar area, Renata surreptitiously stole guns from the other German officers and smuggled them out to the resistance to dismantle.

Renata and Nam were extraordinary women: they were well educated, intelligent, unusually courageous and not frightened to lead double lives for Allied intelligence.

Italy and Allied Intelligence 1944

In January 1944, Fritz Molden was posted south near Monte Cassino, again on a secret mission that involved agents and partisans. One of his contact men was an Italian called Franco Baldi who had been trained by the British and was dropped into Italy as a liaison officer, working out of Bari.[67] Molden was transferred to central Italy, covering substantial geographical areas within the country, which would aid his spying work for the Allies. He was then posted to Florence where he procured supplies and food from Italian depots for the German army, during which time he could conceal his true mission to make contact with Italian partisans. At that time, he frequently passed through the Stazione Goldoni and occasionally, fearing he might be picked up by the SS or Italian Fascist patrols, went into hiding at his cousin Lori's address. It was here that he received a message one day from his handler Alfons Stillfried. It was for a new mission, one that came directly from Allen Dulles in Switzerland, and he was informed that a courier would contact him within a couple of days. Renata forwarded the message to Molden, but realising the potential hazards, she arranged for the courier, an unnamed German officer of Austrian origins, to meet Molden in a small café not far from Lori's home. He and Molden identified each other by code words rather than an exchange of names.

Molden's primary mission was to make contact with the Allies via the British Consulate in Lugano in southern Switzerland to establish 'a smoothly functioning intelligence and courier service between Austria and German-occupied Italy, and Austria and our station in Switzerland [Berne]'.[68] He was also to unify all resistance groups under a central committee to ensure coordination of action against the Germans; a task in which he succeeded. He established secure and efficient courier services with liaison centres across as many routes and borders as possible. The Austro-Swiss border posed the greatest challenge because of vigilant SS patrols stationed there. He discovered that the only secure route into northern Italy was through the Chiasso and Cernobbio border zone, just south of Ticino in the Monte Bisbino district and into South Tyrol via Engadine.[69]

In June 1944, Molden arrived in Ticino, an Italian-speaking region in southern Switzerland.[70] He was arrested straightaway by Swiss police and before he could make contact with the Allies. He struck an agreement with the head of Swiss Military Intelligence that allowed Austrian resistance groups to use illegal routes between Switzerland and Italy without interference. In return, Molden and his Austrian network promised to supply intelligence to the Swiss on any Wehrmacht plans that might affect Switzerland. Molden signed an agreement, to which both sides held for the remainder of the war, at the head-quarters of the Swiss Military Intelligence in Lucerne.[71]

In liaison with Swiss Military Intelligence a detailed reconnoitre of the region was undertaken and it was decided to set up a small base in the Zentral Hotel at Sagno. The frontier was crossed by members of Molden's network at Tre Croci, on the south-eastern slope of Monte Bisbino. From there it was possible to walk a route used by smugglers and descend into Cernobbio, a small village on Lake Como. The advantage of this route was its short distance from Sagno to Cernobbio, and the relative inaccessibility of the frontier crossing – which meant few regular SS patrols. Even so the crossings took place at night as an additional security measure. Public transport in the area was efficient, with an electric bus service from Cernobbio to Como, from where it was possible to take one of two possible train routes to Milan. On the Swiss side, it was only a half an hour car journey from Sagno to Lugano. It made a perfect escape line and courier route.

Over the summer of 1944, a network was established of couriers who travelled undercover regularly from Vienna to Zurich via Salzburg, Innsbruck, over the Brenner Pass to South Tyrol, then on to Milan, Cernobbio on Lake Como and eventually over the mountain region near to Monte Bisbino. Molden commented on the importance: 'It meant that Austria's complete isolation that had begun in March 1938, and had lasted until the summer of 1944, was now finally at an end.'[72] It was also a route through which Allied agents could be smuggled across a border crossing. By 1945 it had become a safe route to escort Jewish refugees hiding in northern Italy and persecuted clergymen to the safety of Switzerland:

> It became the only illegal route from Switzerland into the German occupied parts of Europe that was never completely disrupted and always functioned without a hitch. In due course, it was used by Allied couriers – both French and American – as well as Papal messengers – usually Franciscan friars.[73]

An alternative route operated with special couriers via the joint border between Austria, Switzerland and Lichtenstein.[74] These were arduous routes and it was no small feat to trek through the mountain range for the weekly courier missions though, after the Allies built a small airfield for use by courier planes at Annemasse near the French-Swiss border, it became a bit easier. Weapons and equipment were also parachuted to the resistance groups in Italy.

The network had an effective communication centre in Zurich under the direction of Hans Thalberg who petitioned the Swiss authorities to allow him into the Swiss internment camps. There, he sought out Austrian internees and recruited them as guides and couriers – the Swiss agreeing to their release. Amongst them were three particularly experienced mountaineers who could tackle the most difficult tracks into Vorarlberg via Lichtenstein when the Germans had closed the Brenner Pass.[75]

Between September 1944 and May 1945, Molden made seven trips undercover to Vienna and twelve to Innsbruck. 'Somewhere at the back of my mind,' he wrote, 'was always the fear of being caught, a fear which did not grow less with experience.'[76]

His achievements for the Allies could not be overestimated. Molden had established an effective network that linked up with resistance cells in German military units in Vienna and Lower Austria. This would prove to be an important, well-established resistance base to aid the Allies during and after the liberation of Vienna. The courier routes operated successfully from July 1944 until

April 1945 when Vienna was liberated and just before the final collapse of the Third Reich.[77] Molden and his agents made the last crossings during March and April 1945. These were still dangerous times and they were often stopped by SS or Fascist patrols, encounters that often ended in a shoot-out and some casualties, but they always got through the border.[78]

Disruption of Stazione Goldoni

In the closing part of the war, Fritz Molden personally went from Italy into Nazi Germany on undercover missions, working closely with Austrian resistance groups which he united with sufficient foundations to enable a peaceful transition in post-war Europe. Due to heavy Allied bombing of railways, it could take Molden as much as a fortnight to travel from Vienna to Switzerland. He had also been working with a Croatian lieutenant (unnamed in the memoirs) who was stationed in Stockerau in Lower Austria recruiting Croatians for the network. In January 1945, the Croatian lieutenant was picked up by the Gestapo and under brutal interrogation gave away the name of agent Harald Frederiksen and also named Fritz Molden. This was to have consequences for the whole network and also led to the arrest of Molden's own parents in Vienna while Molden escaped across Austria and back into Italy.[79]

Once in Milan and fearing for Renata's safety, Molden escorted her over the border into Switzerland. Nam de Beaufort immediately took over the Milan intelligence headquarters and ran it from her rooms at the Grand Hotel. In Zurich, Renata became increasingly restless. In defiance of Molden's instructions she returned to Italy to help her beloved country, but in February 1945, while suffering a bout of influenza she woke to find the SS standing at the end of her bed, holding guns.[80] Renata and her mother Ida were arrested. Ida had no idea why she was being taken and, as she fetched her fur coat, said indignantly to the SS: 'You don't know who we are!' Renata reached for a toothbrush and the first volume of Voltaire.

In Molden's version of the arrest, he recounted how Renata had scribbled 'San Vittore' in lipstick on the mirror so that manservant Siro, who was out at the time, would know where they had been taken.[81] Although this part of Molden's version was not known to Renata's family, the accounts do agree that Renata and Ida were held in terrible conditions in separate cells in Milan's San Vittore prison. During a period of exercise in the yard, as Vanessa Clewes recounts, Renata met her mother again and whispered: 'You've got to get out of here! Then go to your dressing room and behind the curtain you will find incriminating evidence. Don't ask me any questions. Get rid of the lot!'[82]

Ida Faccincani was soon released, but at no point did she ever question what her daughter had been doing. She obeyed instructions and back in the apartment, she and Siro had a bonfire to destroy any trace of Renata's work.

'The bonfire lasted two days,' says Vanessa Clewes. 'My mother remained in prison, soon destined for transportation to Auschwitz. Her cellmate was sent to Auschwitz first. As they said their farewell in the cell, my mother handed her the first volume of Voltaire. Today our family has all the volumes of Voltaire except the first volume.'[83]

By this time, Renata's father had already died. Ida had taken a lover who bribed the prison guards with money, cigarettes and stockings just before Renata was due to be transported to Auschwitz.[84] On returning home after three weeks in San Vittore, she and her mother decided that she could not stay in Milan. Renata was smuggled out of Italy by a partisan on the same escape line that she and Molden had established: Milan – Como – Cernobbio – Monte Bisbino.

The precise timeline of subsequent events becomes unclear, but it is believed that it was at this point that Renata travelled to Berlin to finish off her pupillage under the direction of a German lawyer. This placed her at the heart of the Nazi regime and living right under the noses of the Germans. There may have been an ulterior reason for her being there. Molden oversaw covert missions involving Italian and Austrian Resistance movements working in coordination with Austrian émigrés living in Berlin. These Austrians were anti-Nazi but were working quietly and undetected in administrative posts within the city.[85] After a short time, and amidst the final disarray of the last days of the war and undiscovered by the authorities, Renata returned to Italy. But not, it seems, before the disruption of Stazione Goldoni forced Nam de Beaufort and Count Franz Otting to flee down the escape line in April 1945. Otting had been running a clandestine operation from Via Marconi in Milan.

After a mission in Austria, Molden had gone to see Nam at the Grand Hotel, not risking Stazione Goldoni for fear that the SS might still be conducting searches. Nam gave him the news that the SS commander in Italy had sent out a teleprint to all military headquarters for the immediate arrest of Franz Otting. Then she pulled out of a drawer a large 'wanted' poster for Lance Corporal Friedrich Molden, alias Pietro de Lago, alias Sergeant Hans Steinhauser. Molden had a reward of 20,000 lire on his head from the German military authorities on serious charges of desertion from the Wehrmacht and high treason. Nam had noticed that the Grand Hotel had been under surveillance for several days and it was fortunate for Molden that he had not walked into the police patrol.

Even at this stage Nam did not believe that her own life was in danger. Molden was not prepared to take the risk of her remaining in Milan because the Germans might discover that she was the traitor inside Abwehr headquarters. Finally, Nam relented and agreed to escape to Switzerland with Count Otting, escorted by Molden and Renata. Nam imposed one condition on her leaving Italy – that she be permitted to bring her luggage. Molden agreed, little suspecting that she would turn up at agent Pietro's house in Cernobbio with eight cabin trunks: 'I don't know how Nam had got her boxes up to Cernobbio,' he wrote, 'but I know only too well how, with the sweat of our brows, we lugged them as far as the frontier, heaved them over the barbed wire fence and lifted Nam after them.'[86]

The fact that Goldoni and the escape line had operated for so long and survived intact until a month before the end of the war without betrayal, given what had happened to other escape lines, was remarkable. Although it had closed, the undercover work continued and just two weeks after taking Nam and Otting to safety in Switzerland, Molden was on another mission. He and Renata, still in Switzerland after escorting Nam and Otting, headed south to the Gotthard Pass in the Alps. It was only a matter of time before the members of Allen Dulles's clandestine networks, which were deep undercover, would be mistaken for Nazi collaborators and executed or hanged by partisans. The city of Bologna had been taken by Allied forces as they continued their advance through Italy. In Piedmont, resistance groups were rebelling against Mussolini's Fascists who had hung onto power. At Lugano station, Renata and Molden were met by a military officer who advised them against crossing the frontier at Sagno because of the intense fighting between Fascists and partisans. They learned that the partisans had taken part of the shores of Lake Como and knew the end was nigh and that Italy would soon be completely liberated. All their work, the risks had been for this moment. As they sheltered in a frontier restaurant, they witnessed an entourage on the Italian side trying to cross the closed border into Switzerland. Amidst much shouting and gesticulation, they overheard the conversation and that Italy's fallen Fascist leader, Benito Mussolini himself, was rumoured to be in one of the vehicles, trying to seek sanctuary in Switzerland. The entourage was turned away and Mussolini was soon captured by partisans and shot. His body was transferred to Milan where it was strung up by the feet in the same square that had witnessed the killing of partisans during the war.

Molden had never given up on the central mission to fight the Nazis and see his beloved country – Austria – free from Nazi control. He lived to see that liberation and help the Allies to reconstruct a post-war democratic Austria, later serving in the Austrian Foreign Service and working as a journalist.

Later in 1945, Renata Faccincani met British officer Major Howard Clewes who was working as the press and information officer for northern Italy at the British embassy.[87] He had served in the Green Howards, seen action in North Africa and landed at Salerno to experience bitter fighting right up through Italy. Renata and Howard married in 1946 and eventually settled in England after Howard's career as a novelist and screenwriter took off.[88] Renata did not speak about her wartime work and much of the detail is still believed to be hidden in US archives.

After the war, Nam de Beaufort ran a perfume business in New York. Her particular hallmark was the use of copies of Roman glass bottles for the perfume, but the business was not successful. She became an American citizen after Foster Dulles (brother of Allen Dulles) gave her a new identity and passport and, recalls Vanessa Clewes, in typical Nam style, 'she asked him to take a few years off her date of birth'.[89] Allen Dulles went on to become the director of Central Intelligence from 1953 to 1961.

12

UNDER THE WINGS OF THE VATICAN

When Italy declared war on the side of Nazi Germany in June 1940, foreign diplomats to the Holy See in Rome were to retain their privileges under Article 12 of the Lateran Treaty which allowed them the right to live in the city.[1] The Italian government did not honour this and the British Legation and its minister to the Holy See, Sir D'Arcy Osborne, had to move into the precincts of the neutral Vatican. An Allied POW Relief Organisation was set up and originally was run by three individuals within the precincts of the 'neutral' Vatican. They were Monsignor Hugh O'Flaherty, John May and Count Sarsfield Salazar. All had been brought together by circumstances of war. John May was employed by Sir D'Arcy Osborne, His Majesty's representative to the Holy See. He had an excellent command of Italian and a friendly manner which immediately brought him a wide circle of friends in Rome and the Vatican City. He became the unofficial British representative for all escaped POWs, directed to him by the Swiss Guards who not only guarded the Vatican, but were sympathetic to the Allied cause. May acted as an intermediary for funds and supplies to Allied POWs as well as being the unofficial liaison officer between Sir D'Arcy Osborne and Monsignor Hugh O'Flaherty.

Count Sarsfield Salazar was already in Italy when war was declared in June 1940. He was first interned by the Italians in Turin for seventy-five days, then held in Camp Chieti and finally transferred to a concentration camp at Montechiarugol.[2] On the intervention of his distant Italian relative, General Salazar, the count was released in June 1941 and joined the staff of the American embassy in Rome. He was appointed Official Camp Inspector for the Americans and then for the Swiss Legation, in which capacity he visited POW and internment camps in Italy. After the Italian Armistice in 1943, Salazar was working for the Swiss Legation and became inundated with requests to help Allied POWs hiding in the city and surrounding countryside. He was denounced to the German authorities in Rome by an unknown traitor and on 12 December 1943, he went into hiding in a location not revealed in the official files. Two days later, the German SS raided his former apartment in Rome and destroyed all his belongings and furniture. From his secret place of hiding, Salazar continued to help POWs by coordinating the purchase and distribution of clothes, funds and food via Secundo Costantini, a caretaker at the British embassy in Rome. They successfully built up a branch of the organisation to help evaders hiding in the countryside. The work of John May and Count Salazar was made possible because of one man at the heart of it all: Monsignor Hugh O'Flaherty, a Roman Catholic priest based at the Teutonicum College, a German college just outside Vatican City State. For his work in helping Allied POWs and the escape line, O'Flaherty became known as the Scarlet Pimpernel.

The Scarlet Pimpernel

Hugh O'Flaherty was born in Lisrobin, County Cork, Ireland in 1898. In 1918 he attended Mungret College in Limerick to study for the priesthood in the Roman Catholic Church and was ordained in Rome in 1925. Prior to the Second World War he had held Vatican diplomatic posts in Palestine, Haiti and Santo Domingo. He first came into contact with Allied POWs at Easter 1941 after he had been appointed Secretary Interpreter to the Papal Nuncio, Monsignor Borgoncini Duca. O'Flaherty accompanied Duca on a tour of POW camps throughout northern Italy. Since the Papal Nuncio took a leisurely pace by visiting only one camp a day, it afforded time for O'Flaherty to link up with other POWs. He knew that the relatives of POWs would be worried about their safety. Journeying by train overnight between the POW camps and Rome, he gathered information and ensured it went out as messages about the prisoners' safety, transmitted by Vatican Radio as swiftly as possible. He made it his responsibility to speed up the despatch and delivery of Red Cross parcels and letters, and in wintertime ensured that prisoners had sufficient and warm clothing.[3]

Between 1941 and 1943, O'Flaherty collected and distributed over 10,000 books to the camps, the bulk of which were issued by local priests, thus obviating the delay that would occur had the books been sent via the usual channels and camp censors. He also compiled and arranged the printing of a prisoner of war prayer book and was given considerable assistance by Father Owen Sneddon, a New Zealander studying in Rome. Sneddon visited POWs in hospitals in Italy. The MI9 files pay tribute to three nurses of the Red Cross who acted as liaison with Sneddon and enabled him to bring cigarettes and parcels to the prisoners.[4] In one report, O'Flaherty noted that Sneddon was

> Instrumental in the removal of two undesirable commandants, the one from Camp 47, Modena, and the other from Piacenza Hospital, and through his personal intervention, doctors and Protestant chaplains from POW camps in northern Italy were posted to new ones in the south which were inadequately staffed in this respect. He carried this measure in the face of considerable opposition on the part of the Italian authorities.[5]

By Christmas 1942, O'Flaherty was asked to resign his post as Secretary Interpreter due to pressure being exerted on the Vatican by the Italian High Command. An intelligence report noted that he 'championed the cause of all Allied POWs, persecuted Jews, anti-Fascists and refugees and thus disturbed the Italian Fascists' conscience'.[6] He was known to hide Jews and anti-Fascists from the Gestapo, in his own residence, as well as monasteries and convents. O'Flaherty was a key founder of the Rome Escape Organisation.

One of the earliest prisoners to receive shelter in the Vatican precincts was Able Seaman Albert Penny, captured on 2 August 1940 in the Mediterranean. He was a crewmember of HM Submarine *Oswald* operating out of Alexandria in Egypt.[7] On the night of 1/2 August 1940, the submarine was on the surface charging its main batteries when it was rammed by an Italian destroyer, the

Ugolini Vivaldi, and depth-charged. The surviving crew were in the water for over two hours before being picked up by another destroyer and taken to Taranto in Italy. At Taranto, the crew were held in hospital for nine days, interrogated and transferred to a camp at Vetralia. Penny escaped from there on 5 October 1942 by passing through a gap in the fence. He had befriended the Catholic priest who visited the camp and learned that the British Minister to the Holy See could help POWs. He headed for Rome on a bicycle given by a sympathetic Italian.

Once in Rome he staked out which gate of the Vatican was the easiest to negotiate the guards. He discovered that workmen lived outside and went home for meals, that trains entered the Vatican City with their goods, and that all road transport went through the gates. Dressed in workman's overalls, he took a notebook out of his pocket and was busily writing as he walked passed the guards, unchallenged. He spent an hour walking around the Vatican precincts, looking for a Union Jack for the residence of the British Minister until finally an Italian workman showed him to the British Legation. D'Arcy Osborne suggested an exchange with the Vatican, though the precise nature of that exchange is unknown. Penny wrote a personal letter to Pope Pius XII to strengthen his case. It was two months before the Italians officially agreed to the exchange, during which time he was housed at the British Legation and permitted to walk around the Vatican precincts under escort. On 28 December 1942, he was granted a private audience with Pope Pius XII:

I waited for him in the Sala di Tronetto where he gave me his benediction. Conversing in English, which he did reasonably well, he said he was very pleased to be able to meet me and give me his blessing. He also gave me a rosary.[8]

Penny left Rome by air on 3 January 1943, flew via Palma, Majorca and Seville (delayed by fog) and arrived at Lisbon on 6 January.

Another early example of an Allied prisoner to come through the Rome Escape Organisation was Private Gino Rosati, a British soldier of Italian parentage. Serving in the Royal West Kents, he was wounded and captured at El Alamein on 4 September 1942, then transferred from North Africa to a military hospital near Naples in Italy. In April 1943, he was transferred to the Regina Coeli prison in Rome, escaping from there three months later, on 26 July. He was lucky to meet a friendly Italian corporal who recognised his British battledress. The corporal suggested that Rosati follow him at a distance towards the Vatican where he gave himself up to the Pontifical Gendarmes (police guards). After interrogation, he was taken into the Gendarmes' barracks where he was visited by Sir D'Arcy Osborne. Rosati was given shelter and remained in the Vatican until Allied forces liberated Rome in 1944.

On 11 September 1943, three officer POWs broke away from a party of prisoners who were being marched to Castro Pretorio Barracks in Rome.[9] They met a friendly Italian doctor, Luigi de Vita, who drove them in his car to the Vatican where the Gendarmerie took them in and sheltered them in their barracks. The British Legation began to receive letters from relatives of POWs who were enquiring as to their safety and survival. From within the walls of the Vatican, Captain Byrnes and Sub-Lieutenant Elliott were given the task of compiling lists of the names of Allied POWs known to be hiding in Italy. Unknown to the Vatican authorities who prepared the scripts, Father Owen Sneddon, now the Vatican Radio broadcaster, included news of ex-prisoners and surviving Allied POWs within his broadcasts which went out across several English-speaking countries. This was especially helpful for the next of kin of airmen who had made forced landings over enemy territory and could not easily communicate.

That same month, O'Flaherty received the sum of 150,000 lire (about £1,500) from Prince Filippo Doria-Pamphilli, an anti-Fascist who was hiding in the city of Rome. This was to fund O'Flaherty's work with POWs and refugees. Later, after liberation, Prince Doria-Pamphilli was appointed mayor of Rome by the Allied Military authorities.

During the German occupation, O'Flaherty risked his life by going to the train station personally to meet evaders known to be arriving at a certain time, and took them to a safe address in Rome. In the case of two American pilots who had been forced to land by parachute and evade capture, he personally escorted them to their billets to ensure they arrived safely. On another occasion he met British paratrooper Sergeant Horace Stokes who had evaded capture and reached St Peter's Square in an attempt to enter the Vatican. O'Flaherty placed him with a trusted family and arranged for his medical treatment whilst there in hiding.

On 14 September 1943, O'Flaherty received a phone call from a personal friend and anti-Fascist, Antonio Call, that he had met fourteen badly dressed and hungry British POWs. Call had explained to their leader, Sergeant J. Hand, how to pass the Swiss Guards to be given shelter by the Vatican and suggested that they presented themselves in groups of twos and threes to increase their chances of getting in. For fourteen POWs to turn up as one group would surely meet with failure. Call soon discovered that they had failed to be admitted and were being held in the barracks at the Caserma Vittorio Emanuele. He had gone to see them and learned that, although they had succeeded in getting past the Swiss Guards, the Gendarmes had expelled them. O'Flaherty agreed to support them and gave Call 3,000 lire to purchase extra food. The following morning, O'Flaherty was accompanied by Father Giuseppe Clozner to the barracks at the Caserma Vittorio Emanuele where they distributed Red Cross parcels to the evaders, who remained there for around six weeks, supported with food and clothing from O'Flaherty and John May. No attempt was made to gain their release because it was believed that the Allies were on their way. However, early one morning at the end of October 1943, the Germans took over the barracks. Only two of the fourteen POWs managed to escape.

Evaders continued to contact the British and Swiss Legations and the Vatican for help. O'Flaherty, John May and Count Salazar provided them with accommodation, food and clothing. Evader POWs were initially hidden by Mrs Henrietta Chevalier at her home at 12 Via Imperia in Rome until suitable long-term housing could be found. Her resourcefulness, courage and efforts on behalf of ex-POWs 'cannot be overestimated nor adequately rewarded'.[10] Her home became too small for the number of evaders and the Rome Escape Organisation acquired premises in Via Firenze, very close to SS headquarters.

The MI9 report stated that these premises were considered very secure because 'the Germans would hardly credit the enemy with the audacity to hide escapers in the neighbourhood of their SS quarters'.[11]

As numbers of evaders steadily increased, the organisation leased another apartment at 4 Via Chellini in the name of Dr Ubaldo Cippolla, a sympathiser. Although Sir D'Arcy Osborne supplied funds for the evaders, he was reluctant to keep financial records inside HM Legation for fear of a raid by the Germans.

During the middle of November 1943, O'Flaherty received a note 'To Whom it May Concern' from a Major Sam Derry requesting financial assistance for himself and a group of POWs whom he had collected together in the region of Salone, near Rome. O'Flaherty sent him 3,000 lire and an invitation to come alone to Rome for a meeting that would be an opportune moment for the Rome Escape Organisation. Samuel (Sam) Ironmonger Derry MC, of the Royal Artillery, had been reported missing in action since July 1942. Three months later, Vatican Radio had sent a coded message to London that Derry was alive in a POW camp in Italy. He was in Camp 21 at Chieti which had opened on 3 August 1942, reserved primarily for Allied POWs of officer rank.[12] The camp consisted mainly of sturdily built single storey bungalows. Senior officers were given small single rooms, but those in the rank of lieutenant and below were accommodated forty men to a dormitory, leading to overcrowding. The dormitories had two-tier wooden bunks just 20 inches apart, insufficient washing and toilet facilities, inadequate bedding and no heating. When Derry arrived, it already held 1,600 POWs from a total capacity of 1,800. Twelve hundred were British personnel of officer rank.[13] From March 1943 until September 1943, he took charge of the Escape Committee and oversaw the completion of five escape tunnels.

The 'Stay Put Order'

After Allied forces landed in southern Italy in the summer of 1943 Crockatt, as MI9 chief in London, issued a 'Stay Put Order' to all prisoners of war in Italy. It was a controversial decision. The reason he issued it was a desire to avoid the mistakes of the First World War when camps were opened and POWs swarmed out, causing chaos in terms of, for example, tracking their identities, providing food, shelter and clothing. Crockatt's 'Stay Put Order' was designed to manage the liberation of Allied personnel in POW camps, but it was based on an assumption that the rest of Italy would be swiftly liberated. The German resistance was much stronger than expected and the Allied advance temporarily halted. In many of the camps, after the Italian guards had abandoned their posts, the senior British officers ignored Crockatt's order and thousands of prisoners walked out of the gates. A new problem arose, as they were not, in fact, liberated and had to go into immediate hiding in the villages and hills to avoid recapture. Ultimately, they were safe because MI9 evacuated them after the liberation of Italy in 1944.

In some camps senior British officers like Derry, although disagreeing with Crockatt's order, decided to obey it and did not walk out although German guards then moved into the camps. In spite of obeying the 'Stay Put Order', Derry continued to organise for forty-seven prisoners in Camp 21 to hide in the escape tunnels, with three other POWs hidden elsewhere in the camp. With a total of fifty prisoners in hiding, the Germans could not take an accurate roll call each day. Between 23 and 25 September 1943, these fifty officers escaped from Camp 21 just as the Germans began to move their comrades to Sulmona, then on to Germany.

The 'Stay Put Order' became a controversial policy because it endangered the lives of prisoners in ways that Crockatt could not have foreseen. During September 1943, the Germans began to move POWs from all Italian camps to Germany and an unknown destination, feared to be concentration camps. Crockatt's order is therefore widely viewed today as a mistake. The prisoners had more chance of survival if they walked out of the camps and hid in the countryside, in spite of the delays in military progress by the Allies. But Italian networks needed to be in place to feed and shelter them until the arrival of the Allied troops. This required advance escape and evasion planning on the part of MI9 – something which Crockatt had not asked to be implemented. Neave and Langley would ensure the same mistakes were not made around D-Day.

The following month, October 1943 (eight months ahead of D-Day), they began planning for this scenario in France in a mission codenamed Operation Marathon. In spite of the controversy of the 'Stay Put Order' in Italy, Crockatt would once again issue the order in 1944.

Sam Derry's Escape

On 30 September 1943, Derry and a number of other prisoners were being transported from Camp 21 by train, under heavy German guard, to a concentration camp in Germany. Between Tivoli and Rome that day, Derry made a dramatic escape. He asked the guard if he could leave the carriage to use the toilet. Derry's chance of escape seemed unlikely as the German paratrooper followed him. Inside the toilet, Derry looked for a way of escape: the window was boarded up and too small for escape. He stepped out of the toilet compartment, turned in the opposite direction and darted for the nearest door. By now the train was moving at 30 to 40 miles an hour. He opened the door and jumped out in broad daylight:

> I still wince when recalling how the stony track rushed up to hit and bounce me, and then rose to hit me again, fearsomely close to the deafening roar and clanking of the carriage wheels. The air was blasted from my lungs in a sudden, overwhelming flash of multi-coloured pain. I first touched the ground in an ungainly crouch, pitched forward, skidded on all fours, and scraped to a spread-eagled halt.[14]

For the next few days Derry rested in a haystack, then walked to a farm not far from Rome where he stayed in hiding for about a month.[15] Whilst there, local Italians informed him that escaping Allied airmen and soldiers were sheltering nearby in the foothills. Derry agreed to see them and was accompanied by local Italians. He returned to the farm very concerned for their welfare and asked if a local priest would come and see him to take a message to the Vatican for help. Derry returned to the hills to discover double the number of evaders and POWs, all in hiding some 120 miles behind enemy lines. Derry's haystack on the farm became a temporary operational headquarters for overseeing the welfare, food and clothing of these men.

The Vatican responded via the priest to Derry's request for help and money to improve the conditions of the escapers. After further visits to bring more money, the priest informed Derry that his superior at the Vatican wanted to see him. On 19 November 1943, after the Germans occupied the district, Derry made his way to Rome at great risk of capture, with Pietro Fabri who was taking his farm produce to market. Derry was hidden in the back of the cart at key moments during the journey. Once in Rome, he bade farewell to Fabri and met O'Flaherty at the German Teutonicum College just outside the Vatican City State. With the intention of obtaining more funds and asking for advice, O'Flaherty and John May arranged for Derry to meet Sir D'Arcy Osborne, the British minister and diplomat to the Holy See. The report read: 'That night Major Derry, dressed as a Monsignor [bishop] entered the Legation with Mgr O'Flaherty and met HM Minister to the Holy See.'[16]

Sir D'Arcy Osborne and Derry had supper together during which time he gave Derry the sum of 50,000 lire for evaders in the Salone and Tivoli regions who were under Derry's jurisdiction. D'Arcy Osborne asked him if he would assume control of the Rome Escape Organisation but he felt obliged to go back to the men in the hills and left the Vatican after an overnight stay there, returning to the evaders.

On 2 December, Derry returned to Rome where he was again sheltered by O'Flaherty at the Teutonicum College. From this college they both now ran the Rome Escape Organisation – still relatively unknown today. Derry met with an MI9 agent, known only as 'Peter Tumiati of A Force'.[17] Tumiati told Derry that he had been sent up from Bari with 20,000 lire by a Commission for POWs to assist them in German-occupied parts of Italy. Derry needed maps of central Italy which Tumiati duly supplied, receiving in return a roll of film containing the names of all Allied POWs whom the Escape Committee had contacted and who were awaiting repatriation.[18] Tumiati smuggled the film into Bari inside a loaf of bread and passed it over to the Allied authorities. His mission was not yet complete as he was to secure a large (undisclosed) sum of money to be credited to His Majesty's Minister to the Holy See, and set up rendezvous places on both Italian coasts where ex-POWs could be evacuated by sea. He was also to coordinate the dropping of supplies by plane into areas where ex-POWs were known to be hiding.

The Rome Escape Organisation

Derry and O'Flaherty conducted secret communications with MI9 in London. They received help from an Italian parachutist, Major Umberto Losena, who became Derry's wireless operator and sent wireless messages about the drops of supplies into four regions for the POWs in hiding.[19] He met Derry three times a week and travelled all over the provinces of Lazio and Umbria to bring assistance to POWs. Losena was eventually captured by the Germans, imprisoned and shot on 24 March 1944 in the Ardeatine Cave Massacre.[20]

Derry's wife Nancy, whom he had married in 1939, did not know her husband was still alive until she received in the post a black and white photograph of the dome of St Peter's Cathedral (Vatican City) rising from a cluster of trees. In the foreground stood Derry in casual civilian clothes, looking like a tourist. Standing next to him was a priest.[21] Derry was still officially listed as missing in action so this showed Nancy that he was still alive, though not what he was doing in a German-occupied country.

Thirteen ex-POWs succeeded in sheltering in the guarded precincts of the Vatican and stayed in the Pontifical Gendarmerie barracks. All were eventually interrogated by MI9 on their return to England.[22]

That December 1943, O'Flaherty received a report from one of his contacts. Lieutenant Ristic Cedomier, a Jugoslav officer, had visited evaders in the Arda valley on O'Flaherty's instructions and noted there to be 600 POWs hiding in the region. A month later, this number had diminished to about a third because large groups of evaders were being escorted over the border into Switzerland. Evasion was made increasingly difficult by the establishment of the Republican Fascist militia who had been given instructions to search for and capture Allied prisoners of war as well as young Italians trying to avoid call-up into the Fascist Party. Special guides took the evaders over the Swiss frontier as well as professional smugglers who did so for money. One particular woman, Gianetta Augeri, was reported to have spent 260,000 lire of her private means on supporting prisoners of war to escape.

The local police discovered that Italians were distributing funds to prisoners in the area and arrested sixteen men and two women.[23] Six were later released, but a reward was issued for the capture of whoever was bringing money into the area. They failed to discover that it was Lieutenant Cedomier. He continued to move around the region on his business for O'Flaherty, avoiding areas like the woods where many prisoners were hidden. In Florence, he left 1,000 lire with the Serbian Orthodox bishop there, Inici Dordevic, for the support of two British officers and some Yugoslav officers in hiding. Cedomier was aware of the trust which O'Flaherty had bestowed on him and ended his report to him: 'I beg you accept the expression of my thankfulness for the confidence with which you have honoured me.'[24]

Derry and O'Flaherty worked closely with other diplomatic channels, including the American embassy. The American Chargé d'Affaires, Harold Tittmann, was kept informed of the whereabouts of all American POWs known to the Rome Escape Organisation. Two officials of the Vichy French embassy to the Holy See, de Blesson and de Vial, had about eighty French under their care. De Vial was permitted to leave the Vatican and became an invaluable agent for obtaining supplies for POWs.[25] Father Bezchctnoff, a Russian priest, was appointed by O'Flaherty to oversee some 400 Russian POWs. The Catholic newspaper, *The Tablet*, gave a report on life inside the Vatican City for Allied evaders and wrote that their presence had 'considerably enlivened diplomatic life'.[26] Though they were free to roam the Vatican gardens and took solace in reading and playing cards, they did complain about the unheated quarters in winter.

Various intermediaries kept up a roll of honour so the Escape Organisation could regularly track the whereabouts of POWs who often had to move from one location to another to avoid discovery. Funds, clothing, food and medicine were distributed to these groups wherever they were hiding in the countryside, considered to be 'one of the big achievements of the staunch band of helpers assisting the Organisation'.[27] These helpers risked their own lives for the Allies, such as Lita Ferrovante who was singled out in a report for making the rounds of about eighty escapers in the region of Montorio Romano, 35 kilometres north-east of Rome. She led a donkey, laden down with packs of food and clothing for the prisoners and fortunately managed to escape arrest.

Betrayal

Italy fared no differently to other escape lines and also risked betrayal. The Rome Escape Organisation was vulnerable and its eventual betrayal appeared to come from a young woman by the name of Irido Imperoli who had been travelling between Rome and Sulmona carrying funds to the area for POWs in hiding there. She had telephoned a POW, Private J. Pollak, and told him that she had to see him urgently with a message. Derry was cautious, but a curious Pollak insisted on going and left his forged documents behind. On 6 January 1944, Derry sent a young woman, Graziella, to accompany him and wait at a distance to check that Pollak was safe, but he was arrested and later released.

The motive was believed to be possible jealousy due to Imperoli's diminishing role in the organisation, but her version of events was somewhat different, as she outlined to 'Patrick' (aka Derry) in a letter.[28] She told him of her arrest by the Germans together with her baby, mother and sister:

I won't talk unless threatened that I endanger the life of my baby by not doing so – in which case I shall poison myself. I beg you, however, to save the lives of my baby and poor mother . . . They [German Command] only want to know who supplies the money and I repeat that they will never know from me – I prefer death.[29]

Two days later, on 8 January, the organisation suffered what was described as its worst blow.[30] The SS raided two apartments belonging to the organisation as well as an address where three British evaders were living. One report says they were betrayed by 'Captain Messenger', described only as working as a Red Cross orderly. Lieutenant Furman was arrested and held in Regina Coeli prison. At the end of that month, he would jump from a train in the vicinity of Verona, as it was taking captured POWs back to Germany. Lieutenant Simpson was left for a time as the sole billeting officer for the Rome Escape Organisation.[31] Derry's own life was at risk and on 12 January 1944 he was smuggled into rooms of the British Legation at the 'neutral' Vatican and secretly sheltered there.

Further arrests followed at the end of the month when one of the organisation's main helpers was arrested and also taken to Regina Coeli prison. Concetta Plazza was accused of helping Allied POWs. In prison she refused to give up and wrote a letter on toilet paper – the only item she could find – addressed to Field Marshal Kesselring, the German Commander of Italy. It was smuggled to Derry's headquarters where it was typed up. A priest took it to the Irish Legation who passed it to the German embassy. Her request succeeded because she was released from prison a few days later.

As MI9's man in Rome, Derry ran the Rome Escape Organisation from his new quarters. He was aided by Captain H. Byrnes and Sub-Lieutenant R. Elliott who kept POW records, dealt with correspondence and liaised with the Foreign Office and British Legation in Berne over POWs in hiding. John May was the main contact with the outside world. Ex-POWs Lieutenant W. Simpson, Lieutenant J. Furman and Private J. Pollak all spoke fluent Italian and arranged the billets in Rome for evaders.[32] They regularly risked their lives as they collected supplies, often via the black market, and delivered them to POWs wherever their place of hiding.[33]

O'Flaherty's office at the Teutonicum College became the operational headquarters of the Rome Escape Organisation and a 'clearing house' for agents. Count Sarsfield Salazar had taken up residence in the British embassy (now temporarily the Swiss Legation) which he used as a subsidiary clearing house for agents and from where he could contact Derry or Sir D'Arcy Osborne (the HM Minister to the Holy See) via O'Flaherty's office. The main individuals connected to the organisation all had code names: Derry's was 'Patrick' until it became known to the Germans and changed to 'Toni', O'Flaherty's was 'Golf', and Count Salazar's was 'Emma'. In total, thirty-six members of the network were given codenames.[34]

At this time Derry received a letter from Major General Michael Gambier-Parry requesting help to bring him into the Vatican for safety.[35] He had commanded the 2nd Armoured Division in North Africa before being captured by the Italians in April 1941 and was in hiding in the Italian countryside with five brigadiers and three other officers. Generals Neame and O'Connor and Air Marshal Boyd, who had been with him, had already got away. Gambier-Parry made a plea to Derry for money to be able to buy food without which 'the question of how we are going to live will arise shortly'.[36] Derry told him that their best chance of survival was to remain hidden in the countryside because the SS patrols had made Rome a dangerous place.[37]

An agent accompanied Gambier-Parry for three days across the countryside to Rome. They arrived on 13 January 1944. The General was lodged in a secret room in the home of the niece of Lord Strickland. The intelligence report described it: 'The door of this room which is on the fourth storey, had been walled up, and the only way of gaining entry was through the window of the General's room to the window of a passage at right angles to the room.'[38] Protocol dictated that, as the senior officer POW, Gambier-Parry should take over as head of the escape organisation but he was so pleased with its efficiency that he directed Derry to carry on. O'Flaherty arranged for Gambier-Parry to accompany him into the Vatican to attend the Pope's birthday celebration on 2 March 1944. He was smuggled out of his secret room to the Vatican in a tram and introduced to various diplomats and guests as an 'Irish doctor'.

Derry completed a report at the end of January 1944 for Sir D'Arcy Osborne informing him that the Rome Escape Organisation had 2,253 names of ex-POWs in Italy whom they were helping with shelter (in hiding) by paying rent, food and clothing. In Rome, there were twenty-six officers and fifty-nine other ranks. Derry commented: 'These figures do not include any personnel in the Vatican, in the Regina Coeli prison or in the Forte Boccea (military fort).'[39]

In March 1944, Peter Tumiati made contact again and was interviewed by John May as Derry was in hiding in the Legation and unable to leave. Tumiati claimed to have been to Bari, carried out his mission to secure money, set up evacuations from the east coast and arranged for supplies to be dropped by parachute.[40] For reasons not disclosed in the official files, neither May nor Derry believed his story and decided not to use him again.

By April 1944, a total of 3,975 Allied POWs were receiving assistance of food, clothing, shelter and supplies in the Rome area, while agents distributed further afield to evaders hiding in the Italian countryside; the careful records kept by the organisation provide evidence of all the assistance given.[41]

Dark Days

The German SS and Fascist network tried to close in on the Rome Escape Organisation. The morale of the Allied POW network was maintained because the Allied forces were advancing from southern Italy, albeit at a slow pace. The German embassy sent a warning to O'Flaherty that if he stepped outside the protected precincts of the Teutonicum College he would be arrested. He now delegated his outside visits to others who would be less conspicuous to the German authorities.

Catholic clerics who aided the Rome Escape Organisation were taking the same risks to their personal safety as others helping the Allies. On 16 March 1944, Brother Robert was arrested along with two Italians, named Andrea Casadei and Vittorio Fantini, in a small hut on the outskirts of Rome where they were to meet some American evaders and bring them under the protection of the organisation. At German headquarters they were separated. Casadei and Fantini were shot. Brother Robert endured a lengthy interrogation, and was then released with a caution that the authorities knew he lived in the Vatican and they would come for him if they needed to interrogate him further. Back at the Vatican, Brother Robert 'disappeared' into a convent from where he continued his escape work for POWs. Derry summed up this dark period in a letter:

We have had a very black time recently – eight chaps shot in the country (some 40 km north of Rome), no details yet, Bill Simpson and over forty chaps retaken . . . Added to these black times, a lot of our boys have been going out contrary to orders, getting drunk, etc. I think the waiting is getting them down.[42]

The situation for clerics aiding MI9 was becoming more dangerous because the German police were sending out their officers dressed as priests to find and befriend English ex-POWs, masking as their protectors and helpers and offering to find them safe houses. The intelligence file warned of this, stating that these spies were hard to detect, except that they were young and never over the age of thirty.

There was cause for some optimism, though, and Derry believed the Germans were now pulling a lot of their heavy war machinery out of Italy. The Swiss Legation had been providing practical support at this time by distributing money to POWs and evaders. The Germans knew this was happening and sent a warning via the German ambassador that any Legation staff found aiding Allied POWs would be arrested. The German ambassador added that there was no need for the Swiss Legation to help the Allies because the British were doing a good job of helping their POWs in Rome and 'on so generous a scale that British officers were often to be seen lunching luxuriously at Ranieri's and other expensive restaurants'.[43]

On 1 May 1944, Father Anselmo was accosted by a German SS agent and arrested. He had worked for the organisation since September 1943. He had been on his way to visit two Allied prisoners in hiding when stopped and asked for his identity papers by an SS agent who had been trailing him for a while. Anselmo managed to get to the top of the steps of Santa Maria Maggiore church to shelter within ecclesiastical property. The SS agent knocked him to the ground backwards into the church. A church guard came to his rescue and the SS agent ran off. A message was sent to alert the Vatican and Anselmo was told to stay in the church until he could be moved to a convent for hiding. Half an hour later, the church was surrounded by SS men under the command of a Captain Kehle. They stormed inside and found Anselmo in a quiet room. He refused to accompany them, at which point he was struck on the head with a machine gun by Kehle, dragged out of the church and taken to Via Tasso. The intelligence file read: 'His arrival there [Via Tasso] caused quite an atmosphere of triumph because the Germans thought they had arrested an English colonel disguised as a priest. His clothes were torn from him and thoroughly searched. All the seams of his garments were opened up, and his shoes were taken to pieces.'[44]

During his time in Via Tasso, Anselmo's feet were shackled and his hands tied behind his back. He was subjected to daily intensive interrogation about the Allied POW network, was flogged on several occasions for refusing to give any information, but gave nothing away. Just two days before the Allies liberated Rome, on 3 June 1944, he was put on a train bound for Germany. He managed to escape from the train at Florence, and made his way back to Rome.

Towards the end of 1943, Sir D'Arcy Osborne sent a message via the diplomatic bag to London that he had been alerted by Cardinal Tisserant to the existence of 91 Greek soldiers who had escaped an Italian camp and were hiding in Rome.[45] Osborne needed funds to feed them and asked the Foreign Office if he could borrow money locally to help them; he was also short of funds to support Russian prisoners of war in hiding in Italy.[46] The reply came back that the cost of supporting Greek and Russian POWs could ultimately be reclaimed from the Greek embassy and Soviet embassy. In a communication, the Soviet government agreed to repay expenses for all its POWs in hiding in Rome.[47]

Amongst the Greek POWs in hiding in northern Italy were Evangelos Averoff (the former Prefect of Corfu) and Theodore Meletiou (aka 'Mario'), a sergeant in the Greek army. They had formed a clandestine Greek organisation called Liberty or Death and Meletiou had carried out various acts of sabotage against the German occupying authorities.[48] This was Derry's opportunity to extend the work of the Rome Escape Organisation into the north, using Meletiou to distribute funds to POWs. In mid-March 1944, he and Averoff hired a car and made an extensive tour of northern Italy with a view to contacting British and Greek POWs in hiding. They returned to Rome the following month having travelled 3,000 kilometres and reported that a large number of POWs had made it over the border from Italy into Switzerland. Those who were still in northern Italy were well-organised armed bands which had been supplied with money, food and arms. Others had already made their way towards Rome for help.

The Rome Escape Organisation funded half of the expenses for this trip. Altogether, a sum of 100,000 lire was required to hire a car and distribute further funds to ex-POWs. Messages were also brought back for next of kin that could be taken to England via diplomatic channels.

Rome: 1943

By the winter of 1943, the Rome Escape Organisation was running short of funds to assist British prisoners in hiding. D'Arcy Osborne sent a telegram to Sir Ronald Campbell at Lisbon asking for credit from the War Office of £5,000.[49] Campbell subsequently wrote to the Foreign Office: 'In view of the crying and urgent needs and of demands, I should be grateful if credit might be raised to £5,000.'[50] He further wrote to the Foreign Office: 'the experiences which they are undergoing are very hard but they affirm that the majority of them would prefer to die of cold and hunger rather than give themselves up or accept re-internment. I have already learnt of some who have died and there are many who are sick.'[51] He asked whether the military attaché at Berne could help prisoners in the north of Italy.

British diplomat Sir Anthony Rumbold, working at the Foreign Office from 1942 to 1944, replied: 'It is worth taking a good many risks, including that of compromising his [D'Arcy Osborne] position in the Vatican, to send money to British prisoners wherever they may be in Italy.'[52]

The War Office and Foreign Office faced difficulty over converting so many Italian lire into cash during war, so special arrangements were made for a Vatican financial branch to loan the equivalent of £5,000 with interest at 4 per cent, to be repaid after the Allied occupation of Rome. During December, the sum was finally transferred to Sir D'Arcy Osborne via the Instituto Opere di Religione in the Vatican City.[53]

Osborne wrote to the Foreign Office: 'I am sure you will realise how painful it is to be unable readily and fully to meet the needs of people in the tragic situation of many. It is often a question of saving valuable lives.'[54] On 4 January 1944, Sir Anthony Rumbold finally approved the loan of a further £5,000 via the Amministrazione Speciale and three days later the funds were received in Italy. D'Arcy Osborne received yet further funds for British escapers until May 1944, including as much as £12,500 on 30 January 1944.[55]

The Role of the Vatican

In late spring 1943, three escapers arrived at the Vatican seeking shelter: Squadron Leader McAuley, Flight Sergeant Nightingale and CQMS Cook.[56] They were taken to Celio military hospital outside Rome from where they began to plan an escape. On 13 April 1943, they escaped through a window to the outside wall but because of an 8-metre drop could not proceed as Nightingale had a broken ankle. They returned inside to procure a rope by plaiting together string from Red Cross boxes and escaped successfully the following night. Cook walked ahead to Vatican City and asked for directions in German, whilst McAuley and Nightingale followed at a safe distance. Once at the Vatican, the Swiss Guards took them inside and to the Gendarmerie. When an Italian police officer arrived and asked for prisoners to be handed over, the Guards refused, thus ensuring the escapers were protected from arrest and sheltered inside the Vatican.

Ten days later, on 24 April, they were visited by Hugh Montgomery from the British Legation to the Holy See who gave them civilian clothes and shoes. The report by Cook for MI9 read: 'Arrangements were then put on foot for our exchange.'[57] No further details have emerged on what kind of exchange this was. The following day, they had an audience with Pope Pius XII who gave his benediction and good wishes. The three men were presented with rosaries, even though only Cook was a Roman Catholic. Cook told MI9: 'We left Rome by air on 7 June, via Barcelona and Madrid, where we spent the night. We then continued our journey by air to Lisbon where we arrived on 8 June and were taken to the British embassy.'[58]

By 4 June 1944, the number of escaped prisoners in the Vatican amounted to twelve: ten British and two American. A room in the legation apartment was put at their disposal, with a wireless set for messages and they slept and took their meals in accommodation in the barracks of the Papal Gendarmerie. After a time, they were allowed to walk in the gardens of the Vatican and museums. A number of Allied diplomats also showed kindness to them. 'The Vatican authorities did their best to exclude these unwanted guests, but once they had succeeded in entering, they were treated with every kindness, being lodged, fed, clothed and given the run of amenities.'[59]

Again, the Foreign Office commented on the situation in Italy:

Invaluable work outside the Vatican City was done by British officers and a number of young priests, Irish and Dominion, at considerable danger to themselves, while the generosity and kindness displayed at great personal risk, and on occasion at the cost of death, by great numbers of Italian peasants is above all praise.[60]

The Allied armies advanced up through Italy from the south. Pope Pius XII extended his charitable activities and expressed his sense of frustration and deep distress at the suffering caused under Nazi occupation. By 30 May 1944, the food situation in Rome became serious as food convoys were attacked en route to the city, and also as a result of intense bombing of road communications by the Allies. But Rome was spared by Hitler's commanders and was not destroyed during the retreat as were other cities in Italy. The Vatican Information Office continued its work of collecting and listing the names of prisoners of war. The Germans refused to give the Vatican any facilities in respect of Allied prisoners held by them. The nuncios and apostolic delegates abroad carried out Papal instructions to visit Allied POWs of all creeds. The Foreign Office files noted: 'Money, food stuff and medicines were distributed on behalf of the

Pope to sufferers outside Italy, including France, Holland, Belgium and Greece. This wide variety of expenditure on charitable objectives was a severe strain on the Papal resources, already greatly reduced by war.'[61]

By May/June 1944, the German forces were too exhausted to worry about prisoners and inmates in the prisons of Rome. Lieutenant Simpson, who had once worked for Derry and O'Flaherty, had been recaptured by the Germans and was being held in Regina Coeli prison. He and his fellow inmates knew the war in Italy could not last much longer and decided not to make escape attempts but wait for liberation. On 4 June 1944, Rome was liberated and they were finally able to walk out of Regina Coeli prison into the sunshine and freedom.

A Foreign Office report commented: 'After the liberation of Rome, the life and atmosphere of the Vatican changed with that of the city itself. The oppression of the Nazi and Republican Fascism terror was lifted and the relief was enormous.'[62] Refugees in the Vatican City and its extra-territorial properties emerged from their places of hiding, including Allied generals and officers, Jews, anti-Fascists, and youth who were evading military service.

It was also reported that 'The Pope received a remarkable and welcome tribute from the Allied armies.' British Prime Minister Winston Churchill visited Rome and it was reported that 'His Holiness was greatly impressed with the Prime Minister, and on several occasions expressed his admiration of Mr Churchill as a great and wise statesman.'[63]

The Legacy in Italy

The German surrender in Italy was finally secured in September 1944. Derry and O'Flaherty had kept the Rome Escape Organisation running until the Allies liberated the capital. They had saved over 4,000 Allied POWs. Derry was awarded the DSO for 'secret and perilous work which called for a leader endowed with the rare qualities of brilliant organising abilities, unlimited initiative, great tact and a sure and balanced judgement'. In addition, he received the Military Cross and Territorial Decoration, and the Gold Cross of the Royal

Order of George I from the King of the Hellenes. After the liberation of Rome, he had an audience with Pope Pius XII who apparently remained unaware that Derry had been his 'guest' in the Vatican for so long.[64] Derry served in the rank of brigadier in the Allied Forces HQ and then as the new head of MI9.[65] His duties included forming a nucleus of MI9/MI19 drawn from the three military services, to study the lessons of escape and evasion from 1939 to 1945 and to carry out research into tactics.[66] This involved preparing an entirely new set of codes and communication with POWs, new escape equipment, keeping abreast of wireless developments, and studying geography and politics. In civilian life, he served as a magistrate and conducted charitable work for hospitals and numerous other organisations. He died on 3 December 1996.[67]

At the end of the war, in a twist of fate, O'Flaherty visited German and Italian POWs being held in camps by the Allies to ensure they were being treated properly – including Colonel Herbert Kappler, former head of the Gestapo in Rome and his chief tormentor.[68] O'Flaherty's humanitarian work and bravery were honoured by many nations. In 1945, the British honoured him with a CBE and in 1946 he received the United States Medal of Freedom with Silver Palm. After an illness in 1960, he retired to Ireland and died there in 1963. A memorial to O'Flaherty in the form of a bronze figure by sculptor Alan Ryan Hall was unveiled in Killarney in October 2013. O'Flaherty is attributed with saving over 6,500 Jews and Allied POWs via the escape lines.[69]

Sir D'Arcy Osborne paid tribute to the ordinary Italian helpers without whom MI9 could not have operated in Italy. He wrote about the many helpers and agents 'without whose courage, charity and self-sacrifice the Organisation within the Vatican City could have achieved little'.[70] He went on to put on record his admiration and gratitude for

> ... the numberless Italians, mostly of the poorest peasant class in the country districts, who displayed boundless generosity and kindness to our men over a long and trying period ... in so doing ... they refuse[d] the financial rewards for the denunciation of British prisoners of war which the Germans offered and which would have been a fortune to them.[71]

Their sacrifice went much deeper too. They showed courage in sharing the few clothes and scanty food they had with evaders and, above all, in risking their lives and the lives of their families and friends by disregarding the increasingly severe German penalties for harbouring or helping prisoners of war. It was a self-sacrifice that was carried out in spite of the fact that some of their people were captured and shot.

The history of MI9 in Italy is one of pride and success. But these stories also raise new questions about the role of the Vatican. Was it quite as neutral as is traditionally believed? It is an area that would benefit from further research and a possible re-evaluation of Pius XII and the Vatican during the war. However, Italy was also one of the countries from where at the end of the war major Nazi war criminals evaded justice and escaped to freedom in South America along secret Nazi ratlines. The failure to catch the majority of these criminals continues to cast a long shadow over the Vatican and the question of its official role in the escape routes.

13

OPERATION MARATHON AND D-DAY

As preparations were being made by the Allies for the largest amphibious landing in history, Jimmy Langley moved across from Room 900 to jointly head a new Anglo-American section called IS9(WEA) with Lieutenant Colonel Richard Nelson of MIS-X. It was formally established on 14 January 1944 to be attached to Eisenhower's Supreme Headquarters Allied Expeditionary Force (SHAEF) to operate in Western Europe.[1] Crockatt outlined its brief in clear terms: 'The continuance of escape and evasion until the war in the west is over.'[2] Neave temporarily became head of Room 900 before himself joining IS9(WEA). In readiness for D-Day, being planned for early summer 1944, the work of MI9 was carved up into specific areas. MI9 and the War Office were responsible for Norway and Sweden. IS9 was responsible for Portugal, Spain, Switzerland and POW camps in Austria, Germany and Poland. IS9(WEA) covered Belgium, Denmark, France, Germany, Holland and Luxembourg (excluding POW camps). MI9 and MIS-X continued to be responsible for equipping units with escape aids as well as training in escape and evasion.

The focus turned to what might happen to Allied POWs when Germany realised it was losing the war. MI9 feared that captured airmen and soldiers would not be treated as POWs but could be subjected to brutality in reprisals and even executed.[3] Neave noted that with Germany losing the war the Gestapo behaved with 'vindictiveness and purposeless brutality'.[4] There was concern that during heavy fighting after D-Day in the campaign for Normandy, Allied evaders hiding in those areas would not be safe. It was too dangerous to move them by train from Paris to Spain. Plans began in October 1943 to make provisions for their safety in special hidden camps after the D-Day landings. This became known as Operation Marathon, aiming, now with the full backing of the Air Ministry, to hide Allied personnel in the countryside until they could be found by IS9(WEA).

Operation Marathon was intended to aid any Allied personnel evading capture in Belgium, France and Holland. Even with sea evacuations and escapes to Spain taking place as late as two days before D-Day, a plan was still required to hide other British and American airmen shot down on D-Day or afterwards. Neave was involved in planning the operation, and drew on the support of the French intelligence service BCRA and the Belgian Sûreté (intelligence service) to hide airmen away from the battle zones. Special camps for sheltering the airmen were set up in the countryside at Rennes and Châteaudun in France and the Belgian Ardennes, sites where it was possible to organise parachute drops of food and supplies.[5] Heavily wooded areas were deemed ideal locations for the camps because their existence could be camouflaged and protected from discovery by the Germans. The camp at Rennes would be used for those awaiting evacuation via the Shelburne Line.

The two designated leaders of Operation Marathon were Georges d'Oultremont (aka Ormonde), who had been brought out by the Comet Line earlier that year with his cousin Edouard and Peggy van Lier, and Corporal Conrad Lafleur (aka Charles) who had escaped the Dieppe Raid in 1942 with Dumais. D'Oultremont and Lafleur's mission was to organise pick-ups by Lysander aircraft and liaise with headquarters at Rheims. On 21 October 1943, they were parachuted into a field near Fismes, not far from Rheims, well armed and carrying a supply of whisky and cigarettes for bribes. Their drop came at a particularly difficult and sombre time for MI9 and the Comet Line – they were dropped during the night immediately after Nemo (Jean Greindl) and other members of the Swedish Canteen were executed in Brussels.

Lafleur, a French-Canadian, was to be d'Oultremont's radio operator, briefed to keep a low profile and move frequently from house to house to avoid being arrested. D'Oultremont went in under cover of being a lawyer by the name of Monsieur La Porte. His mission was to find a landing zone near Rheims for agents to be dropped and Allied evaders to be picked up. He landed with 3 million French francs given to him by Neave and headed straight for Paris to deposit it with a trustworthy banker. He made contact with a number of young French women who had already agreed to act as guides and couriers.

D'Oultremont sought out suitable landing zones for Lysanders near Coucy-le-Chateau-Auffrique in the Aisne region, after which the RAF flew over and photographed the sites for Room 900. In November 1943, two Lysanders landed agents there and picked up three US and two British pilots to return them to England. That same month, d'Oultremont found a safe reception place for Baron de Blommaert who was being dropped in France with a Belgian wireless operator, Lemaitre (aka London).[6] De Blommaert's code word to the reception committee on the ground was 'Napoleon', and their reply, 'Marie-Louise', assured him he was safe and had not dropped into the hands of the Abwehr. Apparently this idea came from the fact that Neave was called 'Napoleon' in his MI9 office.[7] De Blommaert then led a Belgian group to recruit additional helpers and was responsible for setting up a secret camp to hide Allied airmen in the forests near Châteaudun.

As a radio operator, Lafleur faced constant danger from mobile German radio vans. On one occasion, when his temporary hiding place was surrounded, Lafleur opened fire and killed two German patrol officers. He then jumped out of a window and fled to Reims where the Comet Line brought him safely down the line back to England.[8]

After Lafleur disappeared and Potier was arrested in Fismes, d'Oultremont, his wireless operator now lost, appeared on the German lists and the Gestapo were on his trail.[9] He headed for Paris where he met Nothomb (Franco) on 17 January 1944. It was a lucky escape for d'Oultremont but not so for Nothomb who was arrested the next day, betrayed by Jean Masson.

MI9's urgent priority was to get d'Oultremont out of France. Neave advised 'Monday' that their best agents must now be saved for Operation Marathon. He contacted d'Oultremont through the French Resistance and told him to come back to Britain; it was too dangerous to stay in Paris with so many people arrested and tortured. D'Oultremont left Paris for Poitier and moved north to find another escape route by air or sea. With false papers, he then took a train south to Bordeaux and from there to Pau where he had to find his guide.

Second Escape

Georges d'Oultremont was about to escape from France for a second time, having come out the previous year via a different route over the Pyrenees. He arrived at Oloron-St-Marie and was hidden for several days in a farm before the French network, Délégation Militaire Nationale, smuggled him into Spain on 10 February 1944.[10] It was an extremely difficult crossing over the Pyrenees at night, using a higher route to avoid detection. He was accompanied by Henri Garnier (a French colonel from the Resistance) and a small party of others.[11] After two days of walking, they reached snow on the high slopes where D'Oultremont slipped and fell, disappearing into the darkness and tumbling down the slope. It was pitch dark and the others had to go on without him, but two hours later, he managed to find them again and the guide then took them along an easier path. He suddenly stopped and said, 'Here you are in Spain, just go on by yourselves heading in that direction. Good luck.'[12] He disappeared on his skis into the night.

On 18 March, Garnier and d'Oultremont entered Ochagavia in northern Spain, not far from the French border, where they were confronted by Spanish police. They were taken to the prison in Ochagavia for interrogation, during which they both claimed to be Canadian. The police officers were sympathetic, phoned the British embassy and d'Oultremont was collected by Creswell two days later on 20 March.[13] Spain was already feeling the turn of the tide for the Nazi regime as the German armies suffered defeats by Allied forces and the Spanish government came to an agreement with the Allies that their police force would facilitate the quick liberation of evaders and escapers who came over the Pyrenees. D'Oultremont wrote:

One morning Michael Creswell appeared who immediately took me in his car and drove me to Madrid up to a little hotel Medroda. What a difference from my first passage where I was rather like a clandestine person – now I could go out – and I met my great friend Albert Greindl who was about to enter into France after the Pyrenees. We exchanged our hats. Albert would soon be arrested in the mountains, thanks to a traitor, and taken to Fresnes prison . . . he was violently tortured and finally, by huge chance, at the liberation of Paris, was forgotten by the Germans.[14]

From Madrid d'Oultremont was driven in an embassy car by Creswell to Gibraltar where Donald Darling greeted him. Figures from the past emerged again: whilst in Gibraltar, he met Gerard Greindl (a third brother of Nemo) who was an airman in the South African Air Force. Greindl had just returned from a dangerous low flying mission to drop food supplies over Poland, along with munitions for the Polish resistance, and was scheduled to pilot a Halifax plane to Britain the next day. He agreed to take d'Oultremont with him.[15] In his memoirs, d'Oultremont simply writes: 'Airey Neave came to collect me to London' where he was taken to MI9. He then joined 1st Belgian SAS Squadron in August 1944 and once again embarked on rescue missions.

Michou Saves the Comet Line

On 24 December 1943, twenty-year-old Michou (Aline Dumont) just escaped being arrested by the Gestapo and had to leave Belgium. She went to Paris on 8 January 1944 to ask for the reorganisation of the network between Paris, Brussels and the south of France. Within a few weeks she would be joined by another helper, Monique Hanotte. Having missed Franco on her arrival at Paris because he had gone to Belgium on a brief visit to reorganise contacts, Michou arranged to meet him at Saint-Jean-de-Luz in the south a few days later, but he never turned up. She returned to Paris to learn that Franco had been arrested by the Gestapo on 18 January 1944 along with the chief in Paris, le Grelle. Departures via the Comet Line were temporarily suspended. On 10 April 1944, in readiness for Operation Marathon, Jean de Blommaert and Albert 'Daniel' Ancia were dropped into France by Room 900 and took on the responsibility of the Comet Line in Paris, now liaising with Michou. Henri Crampon, le Grelle's second in command, had not been arrested and soon replaced him. But the Comet Line was not out of danger . . .

Crampon had already contacted the Abbé Beauvais who was an important link in Paris for lodging escapers and evaders. He introduced Beauvais to a young Belgian, Pierre (Paul) Boulain who would become an important guide. But Boulain was already known to MI9. After the second Brittany sea evacuation on 14/15 June 1942, Dumais had written to Neave and warned him that the Gestapo already knew of the identity of de Blommaert as an agent, although the name of the betrayer was not then known. Just before Franco's arrest Boulain had been working for him and had offered to set up a new escape line in northern France, for which Franco had given him 20,000 francs. De Blommaert had begun coordinating this escape line with Pierre Boulain.

Having made an appointment to meet with Boulain at the beginning of March, Michou first travelled back to the south to give 'Monday' in Madrid the devastating news from Paris of the arrests. She also returned to Saint-Jean-de-Luz where she learned that Abbé Beauvais had been arrested along with others in the network. Max Roger, a guide between Paris and the south and chief there, left immediately for Gibraltar and flew to London to make MI9 aware of the situation and discuss what to do next. Michou returned to Paris and telephoned her friend Martine for news, but a strange voice answered the phone.[16] She realised that Martine must have been arrested and feared the worst. There was only one place where Martine could be – Michou stood outside Fresnes prison and called up to the windows, 'Martine! Martine!'

Martine answered her and Michou shouted up, 'Martine, who is the traitor?'

She answered, 'It is Pierre, Pierre Boulain!' With the shouting outside, the guards came running and took Michou into the prison. She was interrogated but had the quick sense to speak like a child and act immaturely. She had gone there wearing white socks and two pink ribbons in her hair and proceeded to plead with the guards that she was alone at home after her aunt had been arrested, and she needed to see her. The commandant thought her too young to be any threat or part of the network and released her.[17]

Michou knew she must save the line from Boulain. She arrived at the prearranged meeting point with Boulain and waited in the shadows, watching de
Blommaert and Ancia speak with Boulain.[18] She attracted the attention of de
Blommaert and Ancia by making a strange face which they understood and
did not follow Boulain inside their meeting point, but slipped away. Michou
immediately warned de Blommaert of the dangers. The Comet Line and its
members, whom Boulain could have infiltrated, were saved. Boulain was in
fact working for a Gestapo team headed by Prosper Desitter, whose name had
appeared frequently in Room 900 reports for months.[19] It is still unclear why
MI9 had done nothing to alert the network.

Michou managed to evade any further encounter with Boulain. She saved
the Comet Line by passing over the Pyrenees a further three or four times to
keep in contact with 'Monday' until just before D-Day and kept communications open between the line, London and Madrid by passing on news, guiding
people to the south and bringing money back from Spain for the network.[20]
She escorted de Blommaert and Ancia south to Spain and the two men arrived
back in London on 9 March to meet Neave and plan the next moves. Plans
were also being put in place to liquidate Pierre Boulain.

MI9 became extremely concerned for Michou's own safety along with that
of Monique Hanotte and instructed them to come to England. It was felt that
they had done enough for the Comet Line and their safety was paramount. On
10 May 1944, Michou and Monique left the de Greef family home, Villa
Voisin in Anglet, where they had been staying and crossed into Spain. When
they arrived in London, it was clear that their work for the escape line over
five years had taken its toll. Both were burned out and exhausted. Neave noted
that Michou 'escaped literally by the skin of her teeth'.[21] Once she was safe
in England, she tried to persuade Neave to send her back but he refused. The
risk was too great and she would have suffered the same fate as her father and
sister.

Brigitte d'Oultremont comments, 'Michou saved the Comet Line in the end
but had to flee'.[22] Monique Hanotte had been working on the Belgian-French
border for the line, and was well known to MI9. When Monique arrived in

London she was required to go through the Royal Patriotic School and was interrogated by Langley. She instantly recognised him from when she had helped him in Belgium in 1940 and said, 'Hello! How are you?'

He answered, 'I don't know you!' Only at the end of all the questioning did he say to her, 'Hello Monique, of course I know you!'[23]

The Comet Line survived after Michou and Monique had left, but it had been a gruelling war for them. They had been inspiring women in the spirit of defiance against the Nazis. The de Greef family continued the work in the south, though the following month Freddy and Janine de Greef followed Michou and Monique for their own safety. Freddy was of an age when he could have been taken to Germany for forced labour. It was believed that he was ordered by Creswell to go to the UK and join the army. He crossed into Spain on 4 June 1944, according to the Little Black Books maintained by the Comet Line and arrived in the UK via Gibraltar on 12 July. Elvire de Greef stayed in Madrid for a week with Creswell until it was considered safe for her to go back home. On 25 June, she and her husband facilitated the crossing of a number of French agents through Saint-Jean-de-Luz and, on the instruction of Creswell, kept up the search for evaders who were reported as being in hiding in the area.

On the night of 23 August 1944, a German police vehicle was captured after a short fight in the area of Anglet. The car contained the identity documents of all German frontier guards passing into Spain. Fernand de Greef and his friend (the local commandant) took the documents into Spain, from where Elvire de Greef brought them to Creswell. It was then that Creswell asked Fernand to secure other information. Fernand started to receive a number of visits from military attachés from Madrid – army, navy and RAF. Elvire later wrote: 'They were interested in a prototype aeroplane with a moveable wing that the Luftwaffe had made in the Breguet factory at Anglet and which was able to be saved from destruction during the [German] retreat.'[24]

It was another example where the most trusted members of the escape line could be involved in intelligence work for MI9 alongside escape and evasion.

The 'Stay Put Order'

At the beginning of 1944, IS9 was in discussion with the Air Ministry and other departments about the security of Allied personnel after D-Day. The discussion raised the issue of the 'Stay Put Order' and whether personnel should return to the lines rather than remain in hiding. It was advocated that lessons should be learnt from North Africa (Western Desert) including that, in spite of capture, immediate escape was possible during the confusion of battle and counter-orders within enemy ranks.[25] It was argued that thousands of personnel could find themselves cut off from their units. Escaping back to their units was considered of prime importance because, if uninjured, these men were valuable fighting forces: 'It is once more pointed out that the experience of the battles fought in the Western desert taught us that, provided men are properly trained and briefed, it is surprising how many will be able to return to their own lines after being cut off from their units and being captured by the enemy.'[26] The point was made too that escapers could bring operational intelligence and by staying put valuable intelligence could be lost to the fighting units. This exchange demonstrated the belief that escapers were an important source of intelligence as well as fighting power.

Langley was also engaged in this correspondence on the safety of Allied personnel during heavy fighting. He was particularly concerned about the blurring of lines between evaders and the Special Operations Executive (SOE). He wrote to Lieutenant Colonel Maurice Buckmaster, head of SOE's F Section, that some evaders might link up with his agents and networks to take up arms to fight with them or join disparate local resistance fighters. Buckmaster provided reassurance that his trained groups (who had their own leader behind the line, usually a British officer) had been given set tasks for D-Day and beyond, and they would not be coming out into the open. The leading officer would make best use of the evader, but 'every care will be taken', wrote Buckmaster, 'to reintegrate them with their unit if this is possible'.[27]

The above discussion was overtaken by the 'great escape' from Stalag Luft III in March 1944 and subsequent shooting of fifty Allied airmen by the Germans.

There was concern within some MI9 quarters that the Germans would start shooting escapers in other breakouts. Crockatt issued the 'Stay Put Order' which discouraged prisoners from attempting any further escapes from POW camps. Evaders already in hiding were ordered not to leave their places of hiding but wait for liberation by the Allies after the D-Day landings. It is clear from correspondence in the MI9 files that the 'Stay Put Order' was an MI9 directive that was supported at the highest level by the director of Military Intelligence, Major General Francis H. Davidson.[28]

Neave disagreed with Crockatt over the order because he believed that, if Allied airmen were captured in the interim period with false papers on them, they would be shot by the Gestapo or SS, not treated as POWs and protected under the Geneva Convention. Neave argued that Allied personnel had a duty to take up arms with the local resistance fighters as long as they knew that the Allies were on their way. It was deemed extremely risky for local French people to shelter POWs when food was scarce and there would be hard-fought battles around them. There was also no way of knowing how heavily the Germans would defend Paris and Brussels, making it too dangerous to hide airmen in these capitals during the final battles. The airmen should be kept away from any areas of heavy fighting or concentrations of German troops to avoid recapture.[29]

In spite of Crockatt's 'Stay Put Order', a number of successful escapes occurred over the summer of 1944 primarily via the Baltic ports and with the help of French workers. Stettin proved to be the best Baltic port owing to the existence of a brothel, frequented by Swedish seamen, and of two or three camps of French dockers.

Forêt de Fréteval

After Michou and MI9 had brought de Blommaert and Ancia out of occupied France, Neave deliberated whether it was safe for them to be sent back on Operation Marathon. He needed leaders for the future operation of D-Day and eventually decided that as long as de Blommaert stayed out of Paris he would not be discovered. It was clear that d'Oultremont could not be sent back and it was arranged for him to meet personnel who would be involved in implementing Operation Marathon. They met at 22 Pelham Crescent, just off the Fulham Road where d'Oultremont and de Blommaert were lodging.[30] Attending the planning meeting were de Blommaert (aka Rutland), a Belgian operator named Lemaître (aka London), and a Belgian air force officer in France called Dominique Edgar Potier (aka Martin).

Neave trained Albert Ancia (aka Daniel Mouton) to link up with the Comet Line in command of camps in the Ardennes, and appointed a Belgian officer in the RAF, Squadron Leader Lucien Boussa (aka Belgrave), to take charge of the strict security that had to be adhered to in the hidden camps. All were part of Operation Marathon as agents or radio operators for Room 900, under the direction of Neave. The secret camp was to be located at Forêt de Fréteval between Châteaudun and Vendôme, a hundred miles south of Paris where the dense woodland was ideal for hiding escapers and evaders, with a clearing not far away for parachute drops of supplies. The camp was nick-named 'Sherwood' after Robin Hood's forest.

On 9 April 1944, de Blommaert and Ancia were accompanied by Neave to RAF Tempsford in readiness to be dropped back into France for Operation Marathon. The plan was not without risks as the Germans were camped just 3 miles away from the Forêt de Fréteval in the town of Cloyes. De Blommaert's task was to arrange for the transfer of airmen by train from Paris to Châteaudun, then drive them 10 miles along country roads to Forêt de Fréteval. He also had to recruit helpers and agents around Cloyes, relying mainly on local Resistance, priests and farmers, because one of the many chal-lenges was how to feed the men in hiding without being discovered. Neave anticipated that the airmen could be hidden in the camp for up to three months, depending on the progress of the Allies through Normandy after D-Day.

De Blommaert and Ancia landed at St Ambroise during the night of 10 April. Neave arranged for a message to be sent out on the BBC that they had arrived safely. They headed for Paris to link up with helpers, but initially their arrival caused some tension with the Comet and Shelburne Lines as decisions had been made autonomously and members had risked everything for years. De Blommaert had been given 2 million francs by Neave, which he promptly hid. He checked out his old flat and realised it had been untouched and therefore was not compromised as an address.

News arrived that the Comet Line was only intact in the south under Madame de Greef – the rest had been betrayed. Pierre Boulain and Prosper Desitter were still at large and constituted the gravest threat to Operation Marathon. Instructions had gone out to liquidate Boulain who soon reappeared in Paris and offered himself as a double agent for the Allies. On reaching the Forêt de Fréteval, de Blommaert, still wanted by the Gestapo and nicknamed 'The Fox', learned that Boulain had been killed. It turned out to be the wrong Pierre Boulain, but the real Boulain was found at the end of the war, tried and executed at Lille.

On 13 May Boussa arrived at the Forêt de Fréteval from Spain with his radio operator, Toussaint, and sent a message to Neave on 16 May that they had arrived safely. On 20 May the first airmen were brought from Paris by train and taken by road to the Cloyes region where they were hidden for two weeks in local villages. Virginia and Philippe d'Albert-Lake worked for the Comet Line in Paris and supported Operation Marathon by arranging transport for the airmen from Paris to Fréteval. Virginia was caught by the Gestapo, interrogated and transferred to Ravensbrück; she survived to be liberated the following year.

In the weeks immediately prior to D-Day, the Allies undertook an intensive bombing campaign of the French railways in preparation for the invasion. The Comet and Pat Lines had to cease bringing escapers down the line, a momentous temporary breaking of links between France and Brussels, and Marseille and the Pyrenees that had been virtually continuous since 1940. In the south, mountain guide Florentino and Elvire de Greef continued to walk evaders over the Pyrenees right up until 4 June 1944 – just two days prior to D-Day. The last party to be brought over the border were two RAF airmen. In July 1944, Florentino crossed the Pyrenees for the final time, carrying intelligence documents for the Allies.[31] He was badly wounded when shot in the leg by the Germans and captured, though he managed to hide the documents he was bringing from Creswell to Elvire de Greef. He was transferred to a hospital in Bayonne from where Elvire organised his rescue with her husband who drove to the hospital in an ambulance taken from the Town Hall, accompanied by two policemen from Biarritz. Fernand de Greef was carrying forged German identity papers for Florentino that authorised his removal from the hospital (under the false name of Urrestaratzu). Florentino was successfully escorted out of the hospital and was hidden in a garage, where a doctor came to treat him. He survived.

Back at Room 900, Neave decided that he would personally liberate the Forêt de Fréteval. Crockatt finally relented and agreed he could return to Europe for the first time since his escape from Colditz. Darling was brought back from Gibraltar to head Room 900. On his return he faced intense criticism from Sir Samuel Hoare that he had been involved with subversive and revolutionary elements in Spain. Darling defended himself, strongly justifying his actions, and eventually the accusations subsided.

D-Day

On 6 June 1944 the Allies landed on the beaches of Normandy in the largest amphibious, air and invasion operation in military history. Hard-fought battles had yet to be won and any progress through Normandy was slower than antic-ipated. In the early days after the invasion, at times the battle advanced little and the number of Allied personnel rescued by IS9(WEA) was small; but when the battle became more fluid, the IS9 teams went forward with the advance elements and were responsible for rescuing escapers and evaders from farms, woods and villages. The essential priority was to move the men away from areas which could become a battle ground for fierce fighting, where they risked being shot or recaptured. Although it was not the role of IS9(WEA), it found itself feeding and clothing escapers and evaders until they could be handed over to the relevant teams evacuating them from occupied Europe. IS9(WEA) and IS9(D) rescued around 2,000 Allied servicemen who might not have been successfully evacuated otherwise.[32] They all had to be interrogated and the reports distributed to the relevant services, including MI9 in London. It was noted that 'a considerable amount of tactical information has been obtained'.[33]

Airmen were sheltering in 'Sherwood Camp' and awaiting liberation. Conditions in occupied France were grave; there was a severe shortage of basic food, and items such as fuel or petrol, rice, coffee or chocolate were only available on the black market. De Blommaert had established a network of helpers and local farmers who supplied fresh vegetables, eggs and milk, and a young girl brought bread to the camp. Within 3 weeks of D-Day, over 100 airmen were being sheltered at 'Sherwood Camp' and the number would rise to 152 by mid August. The paths into the forest were guarded and each airman had an MI9 escape kit in case of emergency evacuation from the area. The airmen slept under the parachutes, slung across the trees. Severely wounded men were hidden and given medical treatment in the home of a local Frenchwoman; the less injured were tended by a local French doctor from Cloyes who was smuggled in and out of the camp.

On 6/7 July, Room 900 arranged for the parachute drop of twenty-five tents into Forêt de Fréteval in Operation Jupiter. Boussa took command of the camp while de Blommaert set up another camp 6 miles away in the forest at Richeray. It was a short distance from a German ammunition centre which was heavily guarded, but this also meant that not many Germans would stray too far from the centre to discover the hidden camp. By the end of July 1944 the Germans had put into place a plan in occupied France that restricted three-quarters of civilian travel, including via the train networks.[34] An application for travel had to be approved by the local mayor and in some areas by the German authorities too. Travel to the north and west was severely restricted and in Normandy was impossible.[35] Neave came up with a plan to infiltrate the German lines in Normandy and bring back airmen via agents in civilian clothes called 'Retrievers'.[36] One of those earmarked to be a Retriever was Georges d'Oultremont, but the mission was deemed too risky and Neave pulled back. He then suggested sending Retrievers into no-man's-land to retrieve airmen and soldiers once the Allied forces had advanced into Normandy after D-Day and set up their centre at Bayeux. It was still too hazardous and Langley evacuated the Retrievers to London; some would eventually be used by Neave in France and Belgium.

The escape lines were still not safe and were penetrated leading to the arrest of many helpers, yet in the spirit of resistance, they continued to work with those who had managed to escape arrest. Smaller camps were set up in Normandy after the Allied landings to enable some Allied evaders to be evacuated via the Shelburne Line. As German forces began to be pushed back, the French Resistance needed new supplies, which MGBs from Cornwall landed on the islands of Ushant and L'Aberwarch off the Brittany coast as part of Operation Knockout. Supplies were also brought by sea by the Inshore Patrol Flotilla which was based at the Helford river in Cornwall under the command of Nigel Warrington Smythe. Operation Knockout saw the delivery of hundreds of pairs of boots to the French via the island of Ushant, west of Brest to remedy the shortage of boots for soldiers. These sea operations continued to drop spies into France and returned with SOE agents, intelligence officers and escapees.

The report for the week ending 12 August 1944 noted:

Numerous escapers and evaders are being collected up in the Brittany Peninsula. Despite the fact that Brittany is cut off from the rest of German occupied France, and escapers and evaders in this area will ultimately be picked up by American troops, reports from the field show that the Germans are acting with considerable brutality towards inhabitants, and escapers and evaders must be considered to be in danger until they are actually in the hands of Allied Troops.[37]

Two hundred escapers and evaders were successfully collected in the Châteaudun area and around a hundred in Brittany. One rescue team was 'still in the area of Caen, and owing to the fierceness of the fighting is for the moment unable to operate'. The report, which was compiled by Jimmy Langley, concluded that 'interrogators should have a busy week'.[38]

The success achieved by Creswell in Spain was also highly significant by autumn 1944. He had continued to organise the escape of Allied airmen and other POWs from the Spanish frontier. Sir Samuel Hoare at the British embassy at San Sebastian was able to report to Anthony Eden (Secretary of State for Foreign Affairs) of Creswell's work that 'with the growing intensity of our air offensive, the number of air force personnel passing through Spain reached a figure of great military importance'.[39] Up to August 1944 this figure reached a thousand. Hoare concluded, 'It is principally to the courageous men and women of Holland, Belgium and France that we owe the safe arrival of this great company of airmen.'[40] Without these escape lines through Spain, MI9 estimated that less than 1 per cent of airmen would have reached the Pyrenees.[41]

Until the hidden camps in France could be liberated, the airmen remained at risk. After leaving Room 900, Neave landed at Arromanches by motor torpedo boat and set up headquarters at Caen. All was set for the liberation of the hidden camps at Rennes and Forêt de Fréteval.

Neave first turned his attention to the camp at Rennes and led an American team to liberate the airmen but when he arrived he discovered that the men had already left. He sent some Retrievers to Plouha to link up with the Shelburne Line, placed an American section in charge of evaders in Brittany, and headed for Forêt de Fréteval. He made his way through the carnage and devastation of the fierce fighting of previous days and weeks to set up headquarters at Le Mans. Neave knew that to get to Forêt de Fréteval would mean passing close to retreating enemy forces. He had no personal armoured protection and had difficulty gaining it. Much to Neave's relief, de Blommaert emerged at Le Mans but was disconcerted to hear that Forêt de Fréteval had not yet been liberated. Of the 152 men 20 had become impatient and difficult and had broken out of the camp, disappeared into hiding in new places or had joined liberated towns and villages for celebrations. With Captain Coletta of MIS-X, Neave liberated 132 men at Forêt de Fréteval with his team on 14 August 1944.[42] The majority of the airmen returned to flying duties until the end of the war; thirty-eight of them died in action.

Escaper Peter Baker returned to the Forêt de Fréteval with de Blommaert and a group of SAS to retrieve any further evaders and searched local farmhouses and villages.[43] Baker had transferred to the Intelligence Corps in 1942 and joined a clandestine reconnaissance unit called 'Phantom', serving first in North Africa and Italy, then with MI9/IS9(WEA) rescuing Allied airmen. On 17/18 August, de Blommaert, Baker and Boussa moved to the Chartres area but were unable to make progress because of the fighting.

Neave was able to recover more airmen between Châteaudun and Paris. During the final stages of the battle for Paris, he succeeded in entering the city near the Arc de Triomphe and set up interrogation headquarters at the Hotel Windsor. He located helpers of the Comet Line and Shelburne Line. It was in Paris that Revd Donald Caskie sought out Neave, Caskie now looking pale and thin from his treatment at the hands of the Gestapo and time in a civilian internment camp, but he had survived.[44] Meanwhile, Jimmy Langley had reached Rambouillet with his staff, passing through liberated towns and villages amidst scenes of jubilation and celebration. Langley and his staff conducted interrogations and began to compile a list of helpers in readiness for the awards and compensation at the end of the war. Within a matter of weeks, Crockatt set up the Awards Bureau to compensate the helpers. Neave moved on to Belgium and found no hidden camps there.

For their leadership and work in Operation Marathon, de Blommaert and Boussa were recommended by Neave for immediate awards and received the DSO and MC respectively. They were both awarded the French and Belgian Croix de Guerre. It would be twenty-two years before a plain memorial column was placed at Forêt de Fréteval to commemorate this liberation.[45]

14

IS9(WEA) WESTERN EUROPE

Over the summer of 1944 the Allied armies made progress through France, including the liberation of Paris in August, and continued on to the liberation of Belgium. MI9's work with POWs was far from over and continued until the end of the war in May 1945. Much of the practical work would be carried out in Western Europe in recently liberated areas of France and Belgium, and shortly Holland. Langley and Nelson set up their new headquarters at Bayeux in Normandy. Langley communicated back to Camp 20 at Wilton Park and Nelson with MIS-X, while Neave, after joining IS9(WEA) and a short time with Major James Thornton (US), communicated directly with Room 900 in London.

In the period immediately after D-Day, IS9(WEA) took the lead in overseeing the rescue of Allied POWs. Initially its personnel consisted of 14 officers and 26 other ranks, but later rose to 40 of each from MI9 and MIS-X.[1] Each team was equipped with a No. 22 radio set, weapons and supplies, enabling them to communicate with advancing fighting forces. The duties of IS9(WEA) mirrored those of MI9: it was to brief personnel on escape and evasion techniques, equip them with escape aids and organise the return of escapers and evaders from enemy territory – including those in hiding since Dunkirk in 1940 or in hiding in Belgium and Holland. It also brought personnel out from German and Italian POW camps after liberation, and sent Retrievers behind enemy lines to bring out escapers and evaders. IS9(WEA) was responsible for setting up interrogation centres to process returning escapers and evaders, and distribute intelligence gained from their interrogations.[2] Prisoners liberated from camps in Germany were interrogated by IS9(WEA) and asked to complete a range of different forms: white for all POWs, pink if they had served on Escape Committees, and a Q form if they had knowledge of atrocities committed by the Germans.[3]

Three Witches on Broomsticks

Personnel attached to special missions with IS9(WEA) had a particular insignia of three witches on broomsticks, designed by Captain Leo Fleskins who had been in the Dutch Resistance since 1941. The badge was only used for ten months and today is extremely rare.[4] The highly significant symbolism of three witches on broomsticks was no coincidence and, in the author's view, was probably drawn from Shakespeare's *Macbeth*, although other theories suggest it may be derived from a poem by Rudyard Kipling or is a tribute to a British escaper in the First World War whose account is titled *The Road to Endor*. The Macbeth symbolism seems the most probable as, like the witches in Macbeth, the special missions intended to bring 'toil and trouble' to the enemy.

IS9(WEA) personnel wore this insignia if involved in Operation Blackmail – a top secret mission involving Dutchmen, the RAF and the army – and other missions in Holland and Germany in 1944/45. The special teams flew from an airfield at Gilze-Rijen over occupied Holland day and night in Mosquito aircraft of RAF 264 Squadron to maintain wireless contact with agents and the Resistance movement on the ground. In late March 1945 these duties were taken over by 664 Squadron Air Observation Post, Royal Canadian Air Force, flying Austers.[5] RAF aircraft used in Operation Blackmail had the three witches on broomsticks tattooed on the nose of the plane. To liaise with agents of the Dutch Resistance, a Dutch-speaking officer was always on board, using a secure S-Phone.[6] Leo Fleskins, Hilda Bergsma and Jaap Ludolph were the officers who worked alongside IS9(WEA). After US forces moved beyond Eindhoven, Leo Fleskins acted as liaison and interpreter.[7] As part of Operation Blackmail, vital target intelligence was secured from the Dutch Resistance about which German artillery barrages to attack and where, the status of retreating German troops and which bridges and routes to sabotage.

Working with them and attached to IS9(WEA) was John (Jimmie) Smith of the Royal Engineers, the senior NCO in charge of liaison and clerical duties at the operational headquarters in the field.[8] His efficiency in being able to relocate headquarters at very short notice earned him the respect of his commanding officer Jimmy Langley: 'He showed all the expected qualities of loyalty and trustworthiness and handled unexpected situations with great tact and intelligence.'[9]

Arnhem and Operation Pegasus

The next challenging evacuation came in the wake of Operation Market Garden at Arnhem from 17 to 25 September 1944. This was the Allied airborne drop and battle of Arnhem which, had it been successful, would have brought about the liberation of the north of Holland much sooner and brought the war to a close by the end of the year. The ensuing battle at Arnhem led to casualties on a massive scale and was a military disaster, with 13,226 British casualties. British Forces from XXX Corps tried to break through to Arnhem to provide relief but were hampered by German troops. They arrived at the southern bank of the river Rhine too late to provide help to the beleaguered airborne forces, the remnants of which were evacuated across the river on the night of 26 September. The Allies had failed to hold a bridgehead over the Rhine and the British army was stuck between the rivers Rhine and Waal. Several hundred paratroopers had evaded capture and gone into hiding; many were badly wounded. They were saved by the courage of the local Dutch people who hid them in farmhouses and small villages. Initially the plan was for the troops north of the Rhine to be re-equipped to provide a force to support any attempted crossing, but as the prospects of this diminished and the risks encountered by the Dutch in hiding the evaders increased, the order was given to get them back across the river.

As the Allies advanced towards Holland, Peter Baker made contact with the Dutch Resistance to facilitate the rescue of Allied evaders. This work was being undertaken by a Belgian SAS team. On 11 October, Baker and American paratrooper Theodore Bachenheimer crossed the river Waal in a canoe in a risky mission to link up with the Dutch Resistance. They managed to evacuate to Allied lines the Dutch diplomat Herman van Roijen, who later became the country's foreign minister. However they disregarded the instructions that they were to remain in uniform at all times. On 16 October Baker and Bachenheimer were arrested at their safe house when the Germans raided it after observing a supply of weapons and explosives being delivered. Baker and Bachenheimer were saved when their hidden uniforms were discovered and they were treated as POWs but their hosts (the Ebbens family) were arrested. Whilst being transferred by train, Bachenheimer escaped, was recaptured and shot on 23 October. Baker suffered violent interrogation and narrowly avoided the death sentence.[10]

Neave was joined at IS9(WEA) by Major Hugh Fraser (SAS).[11] They mounted Operation Pegasus – a mission to rescue some of the approximately five hundred paratroopers known to be in hiding behind enemy lines across the banks of the river Rhine after the failure at Arnhem. The Germans were aware of these evaders and had drafted in additional troops in an attempt to find them, along with those responsible for sheltering them. To help organise the Pegasus operations, MI9 borrowed two ex-SOE agents, Raymond Holvoet and Abraham DuBois, to be dropped into Holland but both were captured – a vivid reminder of the disaster that had beset SOE agents there in the previous year.[12]

On 22/23 October 1944 Operation Pegasus was executed as an incredibly successful joint operation between IS9(WEA), SAS, the Dutch Resistance, and British and American troops.[13] Fraser and Neave set up a command centre in a deserted farmhouse near Randwijk for the operation. The lack of any proper escape organisation in Nazi-occupied Holland had necessitated a change in methods and IS9(WEA) relied on local people to help evacuate Allied personnel from enemy territory. The Dutch Underground agreed to move evaders from their places of hiding to the banks of the Rhine near Wageningen. From the Allied side opposite, assault boats which had been provided by 210 Field Company, Royal Engineers, left to pick them up, accompanied by members of the American 506th Parachute Infantry Regiment providing fighting support.[14] Fraser and Neave waited on the bank of the Allied side to help men out of the boats and to quickly take cover. Operation Pegasus resulted in the rescue of 138 evaders who were brought safely across the lower Rhine. The operation was assessed as a success, especially as a joint operation with British and American personnel:

> Pegasus 1 had been a striking, indeed memorable performance, thought by Langley to be the best in which IS9(WEA) ever took part. Not only had it recovered highly trained airborne troops, but they brought with them important information about the Battle of Arnhem, and ideas for organising new escapes for those who remained in Holland.[15]

River evacuations relied on short-range communication and this was where S-Phones were used again. S-Phones were particularly good because they were light, easy to conceal and only needed three days of training to learn how to operate them. The disadvantage was that they could not be used in bad weather. SAS HQ 21 Army Group were able to use S-Phones to communicate with sections who had been dropped at the time of Arnhem and were not yet under Allied Occupation.[16] Those sections passed on SAS operational messages to agents using S-Phones and communication was possible with evaders from Arnhem.

Small boats for five or six personnel were used to avoid detection by the enemy. This led to the establishment of a special boating school at Tholen Island to train personnel in the use of the small craft. They operated at night, including moonlit periods. The official file reported: 'On several occasions, the boats penetrated to some miles up the river in enemy territory, and although the enemy on a number of occasions fired on the boats and took defensive measures in the form of blocking the river, they never succeeded in capturing or sinking a single boat.'[17]

A plan was put in place for Pegasus II but it was beset with difficulties because it took at least three weeks to plan such an operation and it was already the end of October, with the height of the river rising, which made it impossible to use rowing boats. A decision was taken to use flat-bottomed storm boats for the evacuation with the noise of the motors disguised by using a diversion of artillery gunfire. The operation was set for 16 November 1944:

sixty-three evaders were ready for evacuation, but the water was rising further and even the storm boats were going to struggle.

Pegasus II was rescheduled for 22 November. It had a major disadvantage compared to Pegasus I in that the Germans had an exclusion zone which was patrolled. Neave and his team were heavily shelled from the enemy side, sustaining one casualty amongst the Canadian officers. The following day the wind had dropped and all seemed calm. A voice called across the river and a boat was sent over. It brought out only 3 evaders with tales of how the party of 120 had been challenged on the Ede–Arnhem road and fired upon. The men had scattered, some were killed and others taken prisoner but luckily many were able to return to the locations where they had previously been hidden and many were able to escape in the coming weeks and months. For Neave, it was a depressing time and dashed any real hopes of bringing evaders out of Holland before the spring. In the weeks after Operation Market Garden, and in spite of the failure of Pegasus II, it was estimated that teams of IS9(WEA) saved around 500 evading troops and brought them back to Allied lines. Small groups were still extricated until the end of the war through the Biesbosch National Park.[18]

By 1944 the Germans had discovered MI9's escape and evasion aids going into the camps and compiled a list of the kind of gadgets being used, but they did not realise the sheer scale of the operation.[19] MI9 was sending so many thousands of gadgets and escape aids in parcels that they could not all be intercepted by the Germans, and it was too late in the war to make any difference.

In October 1944, IS9(WEA) sent a message into Stalag Luft II that prisoners no longer had a duty to escape – they were to wait for liberation by Allied armies.[20] Another tunnel had been completed in the camp but was only to be used for mass escape if German forces or camp guards were exterminating POWs because Germany was losing the war.[21] Special squadrons of commandos or airborne forces were ready to overpower the Germans, take control of the camp, and facilitate a mass escape to join the nearest Allied forces. The situation never arose and the tunnel was not used.

Neave was back in London in February 1945 and busy with training new radio operators and organisers who could be sent over to IS9(WEA) as they moved further into Germany. Improved weather conditions in the spring of 1945 augmented the chances of more evacuations. The Canadian Army gave extra boats to be used by IS9(WEA) as transport. Various field sections of IS9(WEA) continued to work close to the Dutch front, mounted successful infiltration missions to bring out escapers and evaders, and carried out missions on the rivers Waal, Maas and Rhine. It was uncertain whether German troops would evacuate Holland or begin to heavily fortify the big towns and cities and hold out. In the end, owing to the rapid advance of Allied armies and the complete disorganisation of the German military machine, Allied POWs were rescued more easily than anticipated. The closing operations of IS9(WEA) in Holland led to the successful evacuation of eighty escapees and evaders there.

Plan Endor

In the same way as MI9 planned for the rescue of evaders after D-Day in Operation Marathon, planning began for the invasion of Germany and was codenamed 'Plan Endor'. It ran from August 1944 until June 1945, and was to be implemented by IS9(WEA) on the collapse of Germany.[22] The operation was directed by Jimmy Langley, and again the choice of symbolism of 'Endor' was deliberate. It harked back to the city of Endor in the Bible that represented the end of King Saul's monarchy and the beginning of David's reign. Plan Endor therefore symbolised the end of the Nazi regime and the beginning of a new era. It involved the evacuation of all British and American POWs within the Allied occupied sectors of Germany. At the end of the war, the Allied occupying powers would divide Germany into four sectors – British, American, French and Russian – for military governance during the reconstruction of Germany. If liberated Allied POWs fell inside the Russian zone of occupation, it was agreed under Plan Endor that they would be sent to four staging camps in West Germany.

IS9 personnel were divided into interrogation teams to process the prisoners of war liberated from camps in Germany. All prisoners were asked to complete a questionnaire and, on a separate form known as a Q form, provide any information about the concentration camps and any atrocities committed by the Germans. This was with a view to bringing Nazi war criminals to justice. Interrogators were to record any prisoner who may have cooperated with the Germans or acted against the Allies as traitors. Where possible, at least one German-speaking officer was to be attached to each interrogation team. To aid this task, thirty officers were attached from MI9(UK) and HQ of Dominion Forces in London. IS9(WEA) personnel who were not on interrogation duties gathered information on the whereabouts of British and American POWs ahead of the liberation of the POW camps. In March 1945, teams interrogated 1,330 escapers and evaders – it was quite a workload.

The task of repatriating Allied prisoners of war on the collapse of Germany was equally colossal. In the zone occupied by the British forces, it was believed that there were 20,981 British and Commonwealth POWs and 1,651 American.[23] Most British and Commonwealth POWs were thought to be within the Russian zone of occupation and totalled 106,547, with 23,263 American POWs. The ports for evacuation were agreed as Hamburg, Rotterdam and Le Havre. The IS9 liaison officers for the Forward Unit were Major P.S. MacCallum and US First Lieutenant E.H. Tiffany. Accompanying the Forward Unit were two Liaison Officers and fifteen interrogation officers. A further ten officers were stationed at four POW camps as base camps from which the unit would operate. To aid the interrogation of 7,500 RAF prisoners of war of officer rank, MI9 attached a number of RAF interrogators to IS9(WEA). An estimated 2,500 Canadian POWs were in German camps and to help process them, three Canadian officers were despatched to IS9(WEA).[24] The Director of Military Intelligence wrote to Canadian Military Headquarters at 2 Cockspur Street, London:

You will see from a perusal of these documents [plans for Operation Endor] that IS9(WEA) acting as agents for MI9, PW2, MI6 and MIS-X is charged with the interrogation of all British Commonwealth and US prisoners of war in Greater Germany.[25]

Plan Endor included provision for all Allied POWs wherever located – whether in camps, wounded in hospitals or placed in work detachments (hard labour) by the Nazi regime. All had to be liberated and processed in an orderly manner to avoid a descent into chaos and itinerant displaced POWs straying around the countryside. It was estimated that at the end of the war a total of 160,000 British Commonwealth POWs were distributed throughout Germany and German-occupied territories, and an estimated 350,000 Russian POWs within the British and American zones of occupation. Towards the end of the war, MI9 issued the 'Stay Put Order' for prisoners in Germany, the same order that had proved so controversial when used in Italy in 1943. It meant that there were to be no more escape attempts by POWs: 'All prisoners of war and internees should be required to remain in their camps or other places of confinement on the cessation of hostilities until arrangements can be made for their evacuation.'[26]

The last months of the war were spent trying to safeguard, protect and rescue British POWs from Nazi reprisals when the final collapse came. One by one the prisoner of war camps were liberated by the Allied armies. Colditz, from which Neave had been the first British soldier to escape and return to England, was finally liberated by the Americans on 16 April 1945 without a single shot being fired. As the unconditional surrender was signed on 7 May 1945, there was relief across Europe. Plan Endor closed a few weeks later on 15 June 1945; it had deployed interrogators at Brussels, Rheims, Namur, Luneburg, Barth and Halle. In a huge administrative undertaking between April 1945 and 10 June 1945, IS9 had processed a staggering 54,645 interrogation questionnaires from POWs. MI9 also received 1,358 completed 'Q Forms' on Nazi atrocities.

With the end of hostilities, personnel of IS9(WEA) returned to the UK to Camp 20 at Beaconsfield on 31 July 1945 and IS9(WEA) was disbanded.[27] Now another huge administrative task was about to unfold for MI9 – the identification and reward of all helpers from throughout the war who had aided the Allies in sheltering airmen and soldiers, acting as guides, couriers and running the escape lines.

15

A MATTER OF HUMANITY

At the end of the war, MI9 promised to track down every helper in Europe and reward them for aiding the Allies and in August 1944 had already set up the Awards Bureau to operate in France, Belgium and Holland. The Allied Screening Commission carried out the same work in Italy. The brief was to investigate, assess and pay out claims submitted by helpers of British and American evaders.[1] The equivalent of millions of pounds was paid in compensation through these two organisations, while MIS-X also handled the payment of compensation to helpers.

Tracking down the tens of thousands of individuals who aided the Allies in the occupied countries of Europe was a significant challenge. Some estimates place the number of helpers across France, Belgium and Holland at over 12,000.[2] The interrogation reports of escapers and evaders enabled the Bureau to piece together the evidence and announcements were made in the press and radio, appealing for helpers to come forward so they could be given appropriate recognition with awards or letters of thanks and financially compensated for their wartime expenses.[3] IS9(Z) provided very practical aid as countries were suffering from a shortage of basic items, and despatched thousands of food parcels containing tins of meat, tea, coffee, sugar, salt, biscuits and jam, as well as items of clothing, to the helpers. The official file notes, 'Many people owed their lives and liberty to the equipment devised and issued by this Section IS9(Z).'[4]

Depending on the level of work that had been carried out for MI9, the Awards Bureau and Allied Screening Commission could award a number of medals.[5] Citations and testimonies were taken down from eyewitnesses and collated by IS9 before awards could be made. MI9 had a duty to fiercely protect the identity of the helpers and did so even after the war. Today, the British government has still not released the files relevant to helpers and apart from a few well-known individuals who appear in books and other files, the names of the majority of them remain classified. It is estimated that over 500 civilian helpers died in concentration camps or were shot for helping evaders. Soldiers and airmen were deeply affected by the experiences of war, not only the emotional trauma of battles and loss of comrades, but also the humanitarian efforts of ordinary people in Europe who had helped them. Those who returned and were debriefed by MI9 spoke of the courage of men and women of all ages from all corners of occupied North-West Europe and could never forget what they had done to save them. The helpers saw their role in giving help and shelter as a matter of humanity and an action against the brutal occupying forces.

The work of the Awards Bureau in compensating the helpers was extensive. From the end of the war until 31 July 1946, a total of 112,570 cases of compensation were settled in Europe, a task that required sufficient personnel to deal with the claims.[6] In February 1946, 19 officers were posted abroad consisting of 8 WAAF, 3 RAF, 6 army and 2 Royal Navy.

After the liberation of Paris, Donald Darling ('Sunday') was despatched to the capital to oversee the Paris Awards Bureau to verify the credentials of helpers who claimed to have assisted the escape lines. He was headquartered for this work at the Hotel Palais Royal. One female member of MI9 who joined the Awards Bureau in Paris during the autumn of 1944 was Miss M.K. Howat, though she travelled frequently between Paris and London.[7] In spring 1945, her unit of military intelligence was concerned with tracing the whereabouts of missing British POWs and she was also responsible for debriefing returning wounded POWs in their hospital beds, some of whom were extremely sick.[8] She recounts a very moving human encounter that took place on a visit to Connaught Military Hospital near Woking in Surrey. The hospital commandant sent a message around the wards that Miss Howat would be available to speak to any of the former POWs if they wished. A twenty-three-year-old New Zealand sergeant, who was very ill and about to undergo surgery, insisted that he spoke to someone. Howat was diverted from a particular ward to see him. She wrote: 'The young sergeant put his hand under the pillow and brought out a dirty, scruffy little notebook. He talked urgently in a weak voice.' He explained which POW camp he had been in and how the prisoners had been evacuated by the Germans and put on a death march through thick snow. With no food, many men fell and died where they fell. There was nothing that could be done for them, but this young sergeant checked the identity of each man who fell, where it happened and wrote it all down in a notebook which he had kept hidden for the whole of the death march. 'Will you please take it and deal with it for me?' he said.

Howat recalled: 'As I sat beside him, listening to him, I looked at his thin, drawn face with dark circles under his eyes, and I thought of him with his home thousands of miles away on the other side of the world, refusing to undergo an operation until he had completed the discharge of his self-imposed responsibility for his men, even in captivity.'[9]

The Awards Bureau carried out work in Denmark and Holland to recognise helpers there.[10] Leading helpers in Denmark have been named in files as Leif Hendil and Werner Christiansen.[11] The Danish Resistance had been particularly helpful in compiling a list of Danish helpers, but not everyone in Denmark wished to be compensated by the Allies. A report, dated February 1946, of a visit made by Sam Derry to Copenhagen noted: 'Colonel Derry had the pleasure of meeting Professor Ege, an outstanding helper who, like other Danish helpers, is very reticent about his fine record and will offer no information.'[12] The Danes were not the only nation not to want recognition. In Greece, under the command of Lieutenant Colonel James Rydon, monks had sheltered escapers and evaders in the Preveli Monastery in Crete after 1941, saving 680 Allied forces by evacuating them by fishing boats or submarine to Egypt.[13]

Most of the sections of the Awards Bureau closed between June 1946 and September 1946. Camp 20 Beaconsfield closed in July 1946 and personnel transferred to the War Office in London.

A MATTER OF HUMANITY

Allied Screening Commission

The Rome Escape Organisation had assisted 3,975 Allied escapers and evaders during 1944.[14] In Rome alone it had sheltered and supported approximately 200 British and American escapers. After the liberation of Rome on 5 June 1944, at a conference between Her Majesty's Minister to the Holy See and General Alexander, the question of recognition of Italian helpers was discussed. As a result General Alexander nominated the leaders of the Rome Escape Organisation as the nucleus of an Allied Screening Commission. Sam Derry, the escaper from Camp Chieti in Italy and who had run an escape line from within the walls of Vatican City, established the Allied Screening Commission in Rome. It was then headed by Lieutenant Colonel H. de Burgh after Derry departed for a mission in Greece. Many of the peasants and ordinary women of Italy did not seek compensation from the Allies. They remained humble in the face of their actions, as one report commented: 'The Italians who have risked their lives to help Allied prisoners, and who today find themselves in poverty, rarely ask for money. The most they do is to ask for work. In this, they are a symbol of the true Italy.'[15]

The case of Lieutenant Colonel Vicedomini, Italian commander of the POW camp at Fontanellato, Parma, was singled out for public recognition. MI9 issued a special broadcast across Italy about his work because it wanted the Italian people to recognise his sacrifice. Vicedomini had made a conscious decision to protect the prisoners under his care.[16] The highest British officer in the camp, Lieutenant Colonel H. de Burgh, testified to Vicedomini's self-sacrifice in allowing prisoners to escape. De Burgh and others tried to persuade Vicedomini to escape with them but he refused, preferring to stay in his post to protect others. When the Germans arrived at the camp, Vicedomini was caught, tortured and transferred to Mauthausen concentration camp. Vicedomini survived but was in terrible health at the time of liberation and died soon afterwards. De Burgh testified that Vicedomini had saved 600 Allied POWs by permitting them to escape.[17]

Derry's career took an interesting turn. In January/February 1945, letters refer to him meeting Winston Churchill and Anthony Eden in Greece and he spent time with the Greek government. He was later awarded the Greek Gold

Cross. From March to June 1945, he appeared to be dropping agents behind enemy lines, visiting POW camps and travelling around Austria and Yugoslavia.[18] In June 1945, Derry returned to the War Office in London and in November was promoted to brigadier, becoming the new head of MI9 on the retirement of Norman Crockatt. In February 1946, he was flown in a Stirling bomber to Western Europe on a 10-day tour handing out awards in Belgium, Denmark and Holland. He met Dédée and other notable people who helped escapers and wrote: 'Time after time, helpers have expressed surprise and pleasure that their services should have been recorded . . . these helpers remarked that Britain was the only country which took the trouble to say thank you.'[19]

Derry's warm and dynamic personality contributed in no small way to MI9 in the early post-war period. He transferred from MI9 to become MI19's caretaker in peacetime and on the instructions of Winston Churchill founded the Territorial SAS.[20]

A charity called the Monte San Martino Trust was set up by Allied ex-POWs who had been helped by ordinary Italians during the war. It commemorates their sacrifices and gives something back by way of bursaries for Italian students to come to the UK. Many of the students have been descendants of families who helped Allied prisoners during the Second World War. In Belgium, an organisation called Comète Remembrance is active in keeping alive the memory, stories and legacy of the Comet Line.

Special Ceremonies

Across Europe special ceremonies were held in recognition of the helpers. On 6 July 1946, a ceremony and reception were held in Palazzo Vecchio in Florence to present certificates to helpers who had aided British and American POWs in escape and evasion. On 18 July, thirty French helpers were received at the British embassy in Paris and awarded the King's Medal for Courage. On 27 July 1946, a special ceremony was held in Brussels at the Palais des Sports, at which 1,300 Belgian helpers received certificates. The armed forces were represented by Air Marshal Sir Arthur Coningham (UK) and US General McNarney.[21] Dédée said a few words at the ceremony, and she and Baron Nothomb ('Franco') were amongst those receiving the first certificates as leaders of the Comet Line. The following day, a ceremony was held at Château de la Houssaye near Gisors (Oise) to commemorate those who died for the Comet Line, the Shelburne and Alsace escape organisations, and to decorate thirteen members who had survived.

The awards are too numerous to mention for the thousands of individuals involved in the escape lines across Western Europe, but Dédée, Elvire de Greef (Tante Go) and Micheline Dumont (Michou) all received the George Medal. Jean-Francois Nothomb (Franco), who had once been condemned to death by the Nazis, survived to be liberated by the Allies on 17 April 1945. He was awarded the Distinguished Service Order.[22] The exact number of helpers of the Comet Line is not known, but 156 members died helping Allied servicemen to escape. Of Dédée's colleagues, 88 perished in camps for helping MI9 – a vivid reminder of the cost and sacrifice.[23] Dédée, like so many others, had survived torture and inhumane conditions. She returned to Belgium on 7 May 1945 via Switzerland 'greatly weakened by her experiences but with her morale unbroken'.[24] As well as receiving the George Medal, the King of Belgium honoured her with the title of countess. Unlike her father who did not survive, she lived to see the results of the Comet Line, her own work and the successes of her colleagues across Europe, achieved during her absence since her arrest in January 1943. The mountain guide Florentino also received the George Medal. During the presentation, King George VI asked what he did for a living. Florentino replied: 'I am in the import-export business!'[25]

There were decorations too for MI9's main personalities. Jimmy Langley was decorated with a Croix de Guerre (French), MBE and Military Cross. At the end of the war, he became town mayor of Antwerp in Belgium. His wife Peggy Langley (née van Lier) was awarded the Croix de Guerre twice, an MBE and the Netherlands Resistance Cross. Airey Neave headed up the IS9 station in Wassenaar for a couple of months before being sent to the Nuremberg Trials as a prosecutor. There, in Nuremberg prison, he read out the indictments to the leading Nazi war criminals in their cells.[26] Neave went on to become a politician and in Parliament worked with others to secure justice for the British victims of

Nazi brutality. It was a huge struggle and finally in 1964, the Foreign Office secured an agreement from the Federal German Republic to pay £1 million in compensation. In his view, it was 'a sad reflection in our sense of priorities that the fear of embarrassing our former enemies, for reasons of foreign policy, should take precedence over the fate of those they maltreated'.[27] It did not bring compensation for the British prisoners who suffered in Sachsenhausen concentration camp and elsewhere.

Neave, Peter Baker, Hugh Fraser (Phantom and SAS) and Maurice Macmillan (the wartime liaison officer between MI9 and the government) all took up political careers and became Members of Parliament. Neave was the force behind Margaret Thatcher becoming the first female Prime Minister in Britain.[28] To the shock of the nation, Neave was assassinated on 30 March 1979 in the car park of the House of Commons by the Irish republican group, the Irish National Liberation Army.

Michael Creswell became a diplomat serving in Egypt and South America. Christopher Clayton Hutton who had retired from MI9 for health reasons, died in 1965 and is buried in Ashburton cemetery in Devon.[29] The interesting inscription on his tombstone reads: 'Major. MI9. 1939–1945 whose escape devices aided so many prisoners of war'.[30]

In the spring of 1946, Donald Darling was transferred to Germany to investigate and track down the escape routes – known as ratlines – that were being used to smuggle leading Nazi war criminals to South America, Iraq and Egypt. In 1947, he was transferred to Brazil on government work for the UK Central Office of Information. He died in London in 1980.

With the closure of MI9, its personnel went their separate ways, the majority into civilian life. There were reunions because of the deep friendships made through their part in the fight against Nazism. For them, there was 'a sense of pride in having contributed in some measure to a notable achievement without precedent in history'.[31] That pride lived with them for the rest of their lives. Although there was much about MI9's work that they could never talk about and took with them to the grave, they had the knowledge that together they had helped to liberate Europe.

16

THE FAR EAST AND OTHER THEATRES OF WAR

The escape work of MI9 extended to the Middle East, Far East, Eastern Europe, Greece and Greek islands as well as the Balkans, Poland, Hungary and Palestine. In these regions, the campaigns were complex and had their own unique challenges and complications. MI6 and SOE arrived in North Africa at the same time as its invasion in Operation Torch in November 1942, although Room 900 had already been gaining operational intelligence from the region via agents and informers.[1] MI9 came on the scene later and also found itself lagging behind in operations into Italy, Sicily, Sardinia, Corsica and southern France. An MI9 file comments that this was due to lack of preparation and training arrangements of personnel in sufficient time.[2] SOE had already established contact with the Resistance movement in Corsica, which enabled MI9 to gain its assistance in linking up with local resistance groups in readiness for escape arrangements to assist a number of commando raids on Corsica and Sardinia.[3] Cooperation with SOE appears to have been limited to contacts to help infiltrate MI9 agents and create links with Resistance movements, rather than a combined operation on running escape lines – something which Dansey had always avoided.

Clandestine operations, including those by MI9, were extremely complex in Greece and the Balkans. MI9 operations in Greece were divided into three main phases.[4] The first period was from October 1941 when the Greek Intelligence Service tried to organise and control evacuations from Greece and Greek islands on its own. From March 1942, in the second phase, the Greek Intelligence Service attempted operations in liaison and with the help of MI9, and it was concluded that 'these operations of the H.I.S [Greek Intelligence Service] would have to be coordinated with those of the British secret organisations'.[5] During these first two phases, evaders were evacuated largely by individuals on their own initiative rather than via a formal network or escape line.[6] The final phase was from March 1943 when MI9 formally took over all rescue operations of British escapers and evaders from Greece. A complicating factor had been that the Greek Intelligence Service was combining intelligence work with sabotage in the country and the rescue of escapers and evaders. Matters were complicated further by the thousands of refugees who were fleeing to the beaches, estimated at between 1,000 and 2,000 a day. This threatened to confuse the rescue efforts of Allied personnel, and also potentially complicate the situation for agents operating in the area – causing the crossing of a number of lines, and hence security concerns for the secret organisations.[7] MI9 could have left evacuations to the Greek Intelligence Service who, however, were altogether inadequately equipped to organise, administer or carry out escape operations unaided. An Anglo-Greek Escape Committee had already been formed to coordinate escape work and manage the refugee situation and it passed a resolution that Lieutenant Colonel Simonds of MI9 would undertake the whole organisation of Greek escape operations.[8]

The signing of Germany's unconditional surrender on 7 May 1945 ended the war in Europe and led to celebrations in the streets of Britain the following day – Victory in Europe Day. But the war in the Far East was far from over and continued for another three months, often with scenes of bloody warfare.

The Far East

The conflict of the Second World War had widened to the Far East after the Japanese bombed the US base at Pearl Harbour on 7 December 1941: this had the immediate consequence of bringing America into the war. Japan believed that America was obstructing its imperial ambitions in the region and trying to block its control of Southeast Asia and the Western Pacific. The day after Pearl Harbour, Japanese troops landed on the northern part of the US-held

Philippines and, with the conflict widening, Germany declared war on America. On 25 December 1941, the British colony of Hong Kong surrendered to the Japanese and by the end of the year, most of northern and eastern China had been overrun by their troops. Between the end of 1941 and 31 January 1942, the Japanese also led assaults on Malaya and Burma and attacked the Dutch East Indies. There appeared to be no limit to their expansion in the Far East. On 24 January, the Japanese took the northern region of Australia and the following month, on 15 February, the British colony of Singapore also fell to them. On 20 May 1942, Japan finally conquered the British colony of Burma, occupying it and thereby cutting off British supply routes to India. The Japanese attacks across Asia had been extensive and impeccably planned.

The conflict in the Far East inevitably led to the capture of Allied soldiers and airmen. MI9 and its American counterpart, MIS-X, both operated in the Far East, where their main role was to distribute MI9 maps and deliver escape briefings to personnel before they went into combat.[9] When initially assessing the situation in the region, both agencies believed it would be impossible to set up escape and evasion there because of the great distances to Asia, and the Pacific Ocean. In the end, some success was achieved, although MI9 acknowledged that in the early days of the war in the Far East, an evader might find himself on his own because assistance was not then as organised as in Western Europe.[10]

The basic philosophy remained the same as for Western Europe: do not be captured.[11] If aircrew bailed out over enemy territory or seamen were captured, then it was recognised that surrender might be the only option. For soldiers, however, the order from MI9 was different and they were instructed to fight to the last round and be prepared to die. In cases where they were wounded in action, or there was a shortage of ammunition or food, then evasion was the next step. If, however, capture was unavoidable, then it was the duty of a prisoner to escape at the earliest opportunity, bearing in mind that as a trained soldier or pilot, they could not be replaced as easily as a tank or gun. MI9 reminded them: 'Your battle experience can never be replaced if you are taken prisoner.'[12]

The war in the Far East differed significantly from Western Europe and thus warranted separate survival training by MI9 to all operational crews and personnel going into action there. The terrain was vast and the jungle environment so hostile that the survival of escaped prisoners was considered by the Japanese to be virtually impossible.

Although there were some basic shared principles in escape and evasion for all theatres of war, MI9's training gave different practical information and advice for the Far East. The training covered survival in different scenarios for capture in Burma, China, Hong Kong, Japan, Taiwan or Thailand. The lectures, training manuals and bulletins were tailored to survival in those countries and became part of the manual for physical survival. It formed, arguably, the most important aspect of MI9's work relating to the Far East operations. The primary focus for MI9 and troops in the Far East was on survival in completely unfamiliar, even hostile and alien, environments where climate, habitats and creatures were completely different from Western countries. MI9 issued the following in training:

> Throughout the whole area of Burma, Thailand, Malaya, Sumatra and French Indo-China, the rule in any area occupied by the enemy is to get to the hills. There is no opportunity whatsoever for an unassisted evader to travel far in the plains by himself.[13]

An evader had more chance of meeting a friendly native in the hills than enemy troops who were much too occupied with holding the vast plains and valleys. Advice if found alone in the jungle was: 'Do not Panic – there is food and water all around you'.[14] The jungle provided many opportunities for concealment from the enemy and evading capture. The advice was to rest in a safe place, hidden, and gather thoughts and confidence for survival and construct a plan on which direction to walk, how to ration food, where to obtain water, and how long to walk before taking a break. It was important to become familiar with the sounds of the jungle, which could initially be frightening or hostile, but also to obliterate one's own noise so as not to be recaptured.

Japanese troops, like natives, laugh and chatter when marching in the jungle, and only keep silent on a definite operation. They leave their cigarette butts on the trail. Sometimes they wear canvas or rubber boots with the big toe separate. Avoid giving them any [clues] by your cigarette ends or the ashes of your fires.[15]

A separate section of training covered the background to Japan, including understanding the Japanese psyche as regards family, the individual, religion (Buddhism and Shinto), feudal groups and divinity of the Emperor.[16] It was impressed on personnel that the Japanese considered being taken prisoner as the greatest possible disgrace and in their culture, release after capture by the enemy entailed execution by their own country.[17] Suicide instead of execution was said to remove the guilt from the family.

Particular attention was paid to the battledress for troops in the Far East: the dress blouse and trousers were made of green cellular material. Suede or leather boots were useless in the jungle because they would eventually disintegrate, so a stronger ammunition boot was issued by the army for jungle warfare. To militate against personnel forgetting their escape aids during an escape – as Winston Churchill had in the Boer War – MI9 arranged for the design and production of a Beadon suit, which was made of light material so as not to overheat the body, and could be worn over battledress. It had several buttoned pockets which held a compass, hacksaw, maps, a machete, anti-malarial tablets and an escape kit.

MI9 recognised that hiding in hostile territory was not in itself sufficient to survive. Specialist survival training was required. A series of instructions and photographs were issued to demonstrate how to make essential items from the most common commodity in the jungle – bamboo. This could be used to make cooking utensils, drinking cups, rafts to cross rivers and shelter. The jungle had an abundance of food: frogs, bats, pigeons, iguanas, crocodiles and their eggs, fish, sweet potato and yam, wild grapefruit, papaya, mangoes and bananas. Unlike Western Europe, where aircrew and agents dropped behind enemy lines were advised to bury their parachute on landing, in the jungle this was the best equipment for erecting a tent or protection against rain, mosquitoes and insects. An appendix to the training manual provided photographs of how to make items from bamboo and a parachute.[18]

At the end of a training lecture, the necessity for total secrecy was impressed on all personnel. Nothing about escape and evasion was to be discussed in a bar or restaurant or at home because it jeopardised the chances of a successful escape and evasion. They were never to speak about who or where they had been helped. The only authorisation to talk about their escape and evasion experience was solely to the intelligence officer who debriefed them on their return.

Bulletins were issued with updated information to help escapers and evaders in the Far East, including survival techniques and how to identify badges of rank and uniforms of enemy units.[19]

Interrogation

The Japanese viewed surrender as dishonourable and thus had a brutal view of their prisoners, often subjecting them to savage treatment, torture, then death. Allied personnel were given instructions on this during escape and evasion training. It was known that recaptured POWs were publicly executed or beheaded or buried alive, but there was little MI9 or MIS-X could do to combat this kind of enemy. The War Office and MI9 prevented such news from leaking into the public sphere via newspapers because it could break morale.[20]

If captured, personnel were to remember any military information observed during capture or transfer between places and were to resist interrogation.[21] The instruction regarding interrogation was the same for all theatres of war: personnel were to give only their name, rank and number – according to the requirements of the Geneva Convention (1929). However, during the Second World War, Japan had not signed the Geneva Convention putting prisoners in a difficult situation, as a refusal to talk at all might anger the interrogator and result in violence.[22]

Resisting interrogation was a fundamental order from MI9 however, and part of the tactic was to understand the mind-set of the interrogators. A section of the training was on Japanese civilisation and underlined, in particular, that although emotion might not show on an interrogator's face this does not mean he is cold and unfeeling.[23] However, the trainees were reminded that arrogance provoked violence: 'The Japanese instinctively admire a man who is without fear . . . and a dignified military bearing is of such importance to them that they respect it even in their enemies.'[24]

Japanese interrogators asked many unimportant questions, for example on a prisoner's family and upbringing. MI9 conceded that in these circumstances, it was safe to answer these questions to appear cooperative. On non-operational matters the Admiralty, War Office and Air Ministry had a policy of allowing prisoners to give some information in interrogation, and therefore for the Far East the command to only give name, rank and number in interrogation was modified.[25]

Personnel were reminded that once in a POW camp, they would encounter fellow prisoners who had been there for months or longer. The war was not over for the newly arrived POW and another direct instruction from MI9 was that he had to instil hope and boost morale within the camp until escape or liberation.[26] As with training for Western Europe, men were warned about the use of hidden microphones, stool pigeons, befriending a prisoner, use of drugs and clever cross-examination.[27]

In summarising the situation for POWs in Japanese captivity, MI9 issued a number of key principles: never cease to study the Japanese character – the more you learn of them the more you will be aware of their uncomplicated nature; know the enemy ranks; be polite and correct; maintain dignity, military bearing and fearlessness; avoid arrogance, sarcasm, mention of the Emperor or of the Geneva Convention or prisoners' rights; and make use of any opportunity to escape.[28]

Escape Aids and Survival

MI9 issued escape and evasion maps of the Far East and Pacific regions and these were to become as vital to survival as those used in Western Europe.[29]

Training lectures and a manual on the Far East included a number of examples of real-life escapes in the region.[30] The purpose was to provide knowledge to personnel on how hardships could be overcome and to encourage a mind-set that would be determined to succeed in an escape. MI9 advised evaders to wait in hiding from an observation point and assess whether the local population might be friendly. The training lecture stated that 'Broadly speaking, most of them are friendly if you approach them properly.'[31] There were instructions on understanding the culture and psychology of people in the Far East and the kind of behaviour to avoid that could provoke hostility: 'Don't show any interest in their womenfolk; any approach of that kind, however innocently meant, may very likely be misinterpreted, with possibly unfortunate results. Their ideas and ours do not coincide on the subject.'[32]

It was said that if approached correctly, locals would offer an evader food and drink – both were safe as long as cooked or boiled. Money should be offered to pay for food and drink because it was customary and evaders were not to expect this for free.

A heavy knife was issued to be able to cut through tough bamboo and thick vegetation. Particular attention was paid in training to personal health: what to do in the case of jungle fever, tick and insect bites, snake bites or chafes that could become septic. A special warning was given about leeches and ticks which had to be removed quickly and carefully because they dig their heads into the skin; if pulled off, the heads can remain embedded and go sceptic. The advice was to smoke them out with a cigarette near them so they loosen their grip with their eight legs, and then they can be flicked off. 'For a problem with leeches and sleeping, burn a pile of dead leaves and sprinkle the ashes on the ground around where an evader will sleep, and the leeches will not cross the ash.'[33]

If the natural ecosystem of the jungle could be survived, there was always the risk of contracting yellow fever, cholera, fungal infections or malaria. Some evaders had died from these illnesses or from malnutrition and dehydration. Sometimes, after they discovered an escape, the Japanese might appear unconcerned because they believed that the chances of an escaper surviving the jungle were almost zero.

THE FAR EAST AND OTHER THEATRES OF WAR

Escape Lines

Formal MI9 escape lines could not be established in the Far East in quite the same way as in Western Europe, because it was much harder to carve out a definite route, especially through jungle regions. That did not prevent ad hoc escape routes from being used. Help was available to escapers and evaders in Burma from the hill tribes. Many tea planters were also prepared to assist them. Most of the Burma escape routes ran through India and necessitated crossing the dangerous Irrawady, Chindwin and Dapha rivers. These routes were possibly the most hazardous of the war – and of anywhere in the world: one escape line ran from Burma to India using elephant routes. Navigating through the thick bamboo vegetation in the jungle was a major challenge, so evaders walked along trails left by elephants that had trampled down the vegetation. One organiser of an escape route was Geoff Bostock who worked for the Bombay Burma Trading Corporation. He had already set up a secret escape route for the employees and their families if the war should become difficult. Geoff knew the jungle well, and how to survive in it, having lived in the region for a number of years. He was assisted by Jim ('Elephant Bill') Williams who had worked for the same company for over twenty years and also had experience with elephants. Williams organised for a caravan (of elephants) to be assembled, the first of which consisted of 56 elephants and their Burmese drivers. It started out with 22 women and 15 children and successfully trekked 300 miles to India. It meant that it was possible to use remote routes to evacuate escapers too.

Gyles Mackerall, a tea planter in Assam, assisted the escape lines by taking a caravan of elephants into Burma to rescue Allied escapers across the raging torrents of the Dapha river. He took his 20 elephants and their Indian handlers through the jungle to the river over 100 miles away: 'The elephants took to the water and edged along the water up to their tusks. The 68 soldiers were rescued after a number of attempts to cross. Many were suffering from starvation and jungle diseases.'[34]

Mackerall knew many of the natives of the hills who helped him along the route with food and water for the escapers. At one point the column ran short

275

of food, was spotted by an Allied aircraft and food supplies were dropped to them from the air. Mackerall was awarded the George Cross for his rescue work.

Some of the most successful escapes through occupied areas of China were by boat with the aid of the Chinese. Once an evader reached the shoreline, he could be smuggled out in a boat, covered in a blanket and feigning tuberculosis, or in a coffin or under a load of fish.

Accounts of individual escapes were used in MI9 lectures.[35] One example was an airman simply known as 'X' in the files. His Hurricane had been shot down over the Mayu Peninsula in April 1943. He was injured, swam ashore and was taken by the Japanese to a field tent where his leg was dressed. He was interrogated through an interpreter, primarily about the strength of the Allied troops and number of aircraft. His captors frequently threatened to kill him, but did not carry out the threats. Instead, they harangued him on his lack of fighting spirit, and told him if they had been him, they would have dived the plane into the ground and committed suicide. This is an interesting example of the kind of psyche that Allied prisoners might encounter if captured. He was asked if he would fight for the Japanese, but X did not reply.[36] He was taken daily to a hospital for his wounds and used the opportunity to observe any possible way of escape. After being transferred to a convalescent camp, he waited for a day when it was less guarded. One evening he witnessed some commotion with the new arrival of Japanese soldiers from the frontline. He took the opportunity of the confusion to walk out of the camp at night, navigated his way by the stars and rested in hiding during the day. In a small quiet village he approached a Muslim who proved friendly and who offered him fruit, water and cigarettes. The man hid him in bushes and brought him food every day until a small party of Arakanese could take him to the British lines. X later told MI9 that the Japanese seemed to be ill informed about the progress of the war.

The Jungle Queen

Pioneering anthropologist Ursula Graham Bower, who was born in London, was living in the Naga Hills in Burma in the 1930s.[37] At the outbreak of war in

Europe in 1939 she came back to England temporarily but decided to return to Burma. In the Naga Hills region there had been a rebel sixteen-year-old woman called Gaidiliu who had been active against the British. Gaidiliu had been captured, but the local tribes believed that her spirit could not be repressed and that a reincarnation of Gaidiliu would reappear. When Ursula Bower returned after 1939, she encountered local people in the jungle territories who mistakenly thought she was a reincarnation of Gaidiliu. They saw her as a goddess and called her the Naga Queen. Bower worked with them in the coming months during times of famine and illness and petitioned government officials to provide food and supplies for them. The Nagas were fiercely independent and loyal, especially to Bower now considered to be the reincarnation of Gaidiliu who had helped them through hardship.

As the war developed in the Far East – Burma, Malaya and Singapore – Bower stayed with the Nagas. With British and Indian troops retreating, she began to assist evading soldiers and civilians. The environment was uncompromising for the withdrawing troops as they found themselves crossing the deep jungle, their clothes and footwear ripped by the natural elements, sustaining cuts from the bamboo, which were difficult to heal causing infestations of mosquitos and leeches to occur in the wounds. With Bower, the Nagas assisted the soldiers, but also began to gain intelligence on the Japanese for the British. An intelligence unit was formed called V Force within the British army, which operated under the control of Special Forces and British officers who had been trained in jungle warfare.[38] The role of V Force was to patrol particular regions either side of the border and send intelligence back to the British. The specific detachment working with Bower was nicknamed 'Bower Force' and was responsible for patrolling 800 square miles of jungle. Bower was armed with a Sten gun, and it was said that she got through two of them in the war.[39]

During 1944, as the Japanese troops were heading for Bower's region, the local tribesmen told her they were ready to fight and to die with her. They moved out of their villages and into the jungle where they dug holes in the dense foliage to hide and constructed communication tunnels across the jungle. Three Japanese divisions, amounting to 80,000 men, reached India and overran other sections of V Force. They continued south to Imphal and north to Kohima where they vastly outnumbered the British who had only 1,500 soldiers, though they held out for six weeks until reinforcements arrived from India. The Japanese eventually withdrew but left terrible casualties. The battles of Imphal and Kohima were amongst the most savagely fought battles of the Second World War. During this period of the fighting, Bower had garnered assistance from Ghurkha troops to defend the villages and organise patrols to engage the enemy.[40] In the process, they encountered Allied airmen, mainly American, who had been shot down in combat and were evading capture. Bower, christened the Jungle Queen by the American pilots, organised their food, shelter and return to India. By now, the Japanese were offering rewards for her capture, dead or alive. During the Japanese retreat from Imphal and Kohima, Bower organised detachments to harass and ambush their troops. Her V Force detachment was disbanded in November 1944.

Bower was awarded an MBE for her bravery and the rare Lawrence of Arabia Medal. She went on to marry a former V Force officer and returned to England in 1948 where she died in 1989.[41]

British Army Aid Group

The British Army Aid Group (BAAG) was a charitable aid organisation that became part of MI9's contribution in the Far East.[42] Its headquarters was based in Kwangtung, then Kweilin, and headed by Lieutenant Colonel Leslie Ride, of the Hong Kong Volunteers Field Ambulance Unit, who had escaped from Sham Shui Po Camp in Hong Kong in mid-January 1942.[43] He escaped with the aim of setting up a network to help other POWs who were at risk after the surrender to the Japanese on 25 December 1941. Ride had been born in Australia, was twice wounded in the First World War whilst serving in the Australian army, and prior to the Second World War was professor of physiology at the University of Hong Kong. After breaking out of the POW camp with a small number of Hong Kong volunteers, and evading recapture, he made contact with Chinese guerrillas in the Sai-kung area. The guerrillas formed a route for the evasion party across Mirs Bay, evading Japanese patrols, and to safety in China.

On his way to Chungking, Rice began to formulate an idea for an aid organisation for escape and evasion. This became the British Army Aid Group, with the mission of providing medical and welfare assistance to Allied troops. He was joined by another escaper from Sham Shui Po Camp, Captain Clague of the Royal Engineers, and the personnel whom they enlisted into BAAG were mainly Hong Kong Volunteers. In the latter part of 1942, Ride set up forward posts to liaise and share intelligence with the Chinese authorities on the enemy positions. BAAG was involved in three main areas of work: escape and evasion, welfare, and intelligence gathering, despite the fact that MI9 had always tried to resist the merging of these specific areas.[44] Ride smuggled messages, written in invisible ink, into the POW camps, but he found that POWs in the war in the Far East had no 'escape-minded' philosophy and decided this needed to change. BAAG soon therefore came under the auspices of MI9 in London.

The biggest hurdle facing escapers was their inability as Europeans to blend into the background. The Far East was as much beset by the risk of traitors as in Western Europe. With the number of escapers from Sham Shui Po Camp increasing and successfully reaching China, the Japanese enlisted Chinese traitors to roam the areas where escapers and evaders were thought to be hiding to rout out the helpers and escape routes. Some of this was successful and some helpers were betrayed and tortured to death by the Japanese secret police. A line roughly from Hong Kong – China – Shanghai was operated by BAAG and then run by MI9.

BAAG had excellent relations with SOE operating in the region, however, its relations with MI6 were less favourable.[45] Ride believed that he and BAAG had almost exclusive control over intelligence gathering in the region, but MI6 was busy counteracting this notion.[46] He had difficulties too with the OSS who appeared cooperative but were bribing the intelligence runner for information before it reached Ride and before it was published in the MI9 bulletins.[47]

By the end of the war in the Far East, BAAG had established escape routes throughout the Far East, working alongside Force 136 (SOE), gathering information and intelligence for the Allies but placing assistance to escapers and evaders as a higher priority.

After VE Day, there still appeared to be no end in sight to the war in the Far East. The Japanese believed in fighting to the death and surrender was unthinkable. The war finally ended in the Far East because the Americans dropped atomic bombs on the Japanese cities of Hiroshima and Nagasaki on 6 and 9 August 1945. This brought the war to a close and saw the final surrender of the Japanese a few days later on 15 August, known as VJ Day – Victory over Japan Day. One unexpected outcome of the war in the Far East was the decolonisation of Asia and independence for Asian nations.

EPILOGUE
THE LEGACY

How successful was MI9 and what was its significance within the wider intelligence operations of the Second World War?

The history of MI9 is as much about those who made up this highly secret branch of military intelligence as the daily workings and structure of the organisation itself. Its success was largely due to the diversity of people who came together quite by chance in wartime and who would probably never have crossed paths in peacetime.

From its beginnings in 1939, the nascent organisation evolved into a highly efficient branch of military intelligence. The success of the escape lines would only be realised at the end of the war when it became known that, after the evacuation of Dunkirk in May/June 1940 and in spite of the dangers and difficulties of German occupation, MI9 managed to smuggle back to the UK all except 300 of the several thousand soldiers who had not been evacuated then.

The achievements went further: in the course of the war around 35,000 Allied soldiers and airmen eventually made it back to Allied Lines – 23,000 of whom were escapers. Due to the direct intervention of MI9, a total of 21,533 British and 4,657 Commonwealth escapers came out of Nazi-occupied Europe, totalling 26,190 airmen and soldiers. It is estimated that 90 per cent of those who evaded capture were successfully rescued by MI9. As an inter-service section of the War Office, MI9 had successfully brought together the air force, army, navy, WRNS, ATS and WAAF, as well as American forces. Its wartime operations extended beyond Western Europe to Eastern Europe, Greece and the Aegean region, the Middle East and Far East.

Thousands of interrogation reports of returning escapers and evaders survive today in the National Archives. A study of these reveals how no two escape stories were the same – each had a unique set of circumstances behind it. These debriefings provided intelligence of the situation behind enemy lines and enabled MI9 to include updated information in bulletins to help others. From 1942 to March 1945, IS9(Z) was responsible for the issue and manufacture of 1.3 million round brass compasses; 65,096 tunics; 13,242 pencils; 9,519 pipes, and 1.6 million maps concealed in purses and pouches; 7,039 flying boots that converted into civilian shoes; 348,102 phrase books and 560,200 aid boxes. The rapid production of escape devices in large quantities was essential to escape and evasion, and the MI9 maps and escape boxes were particularly important for survival.

Whilst MI9 worked in utmost secrecy to bring personnel out of occupied countries, this was only possible because of local helpers. People living under Nazi occupation were prepared to risk their own lives for Allied airmen and soldiers to return to England.[1] They represent individual stories of courage and sacrifice – men and women of all ages secretly helping the Allies, often at great personal risk to themselves and their families. The helpers' spirit of resistance is the inspirational backdrop to the story of MI9 and their ethos of defiance sustained their silent fight for freedom. No evasion line could have operated without them. Neave spoke of their 'courage and sacrifice . . . in defiance of the Gestapo'.[2]

Neave was correct. It has been clear from the research for this book that, with the exception of the betrayers, the helpers undertook to save airmen and soldiers because they thought it the right action. It was to be a common theme in the stories of the helpers. Langley wrote:

Hundreds of men and women were arrested and condemned to death under the charge of having helped the Allied cause, with no specific details given. That for every successful evader a Belgian, Dutch or French helper gave his or her life would be a fairer estimate of the price paid.[3]

But MI9 faced serious challenges. In occupied Europe a major failure came from the betrayal of the escape lines and networks by a small number of agents who were believed to be working for MI9. Men like Harold Cole and Christiaan Lindemans sabotaged the escape lines for their personal gain, often for money. When Langley raised concerns over Cole, MI9 arguably could have done more to terminate him. Dansey, however, failed to take action and it has been suggested that he was running Cole as a double agent. Dansey was ruthless, capable of making decisions that could compromise the lives of others as part of a wider plan. He, and not the head of MI6, was said to hold the power within MI6.

The escape lines stretched hundreds of miles across enemy territory, often operating within close proximity of the occupying authorities and German patrols. Paris was a good example of this – where evaders were escorted right through the patrolled city, blending into the background to shelter in safe houses, then boarding a train south towards the Pyrenees and Spain. They could be penetrated at any point. Was it reasonable to expect every part of the escape line could be protected from 1940 until D-Day? Neave criticised the MI9 leadership and said that 'the real blame lay with those who, despite the efforts of Monday and Darling, for so long refused to allow sufficient recruits and wireless communications to Room 900 to create new lines'.[4] Neave believed that, in spite of its achievements, MI9's main failure was not to establish new escape lines to relieve the older lines which were becoming vulnerable, arguing that new lines would substitute a compromised escape route. He was right in this respect. MI9 in London and Beaconsfield failed to implement what he, Langley, Darling and Creswell were asking for. But was this failure due to Dansey or Crockatt?

Crockatt was a straightforward man of the old military school, kind, yet efficient at overseeing the administration of an organisation for escape and evasion. But his 'Stay Put Order' – that POWs should remain in their camps until the liberating Allied armies arrived – remains a controversial point in MI9's history, particularly in the case of Italy. His overriding concern had been for the protection and welfare of the prisoners. To sanction them walking out of camps to an unknown fate in parts of Europe, to go into further hiding without support networks for food and shelter, placed them at risk. But he did have options and could have, for instance, implemented an operation like Operation Marathon with dedicated hidden camps for prisoners to seek safe haven until areas were totally liberated. Crockatt was the right man to head MI9, cleverly instilling his organisation with a philosophy of 'escape-mindedness' which underpinned MI9's modus operandi. However, he did not have Dansey's tough character and ability to make the difficult and controversial decisions around agents in the field. For that, MI9/Room 900 needed Dansey.

In my view, the failure to implement the recommendations of Neave, Langley, Darling and Creswell was due to Dansey who, for the higher reasons of MI6 operations, placed MI6 above MI9. At the end of the war Crockatt himself felt a sense of disappointment that MI6 had hampered MI9's work on the escape lines in an attempt to protect its own:

> The oft repeated statement that nurse Edith Cavell, who apparently worked for SIS, or MI6 during the last war, had been discovered through assisting a prisoner of war seemed to dictate the whole attitude of SIS towards the section [MI9]. They were determined to prevent evaders and escapers from involving them in any way. This attitude may have been correct from their own security aspect, but it was a terrific hardship to those trying to build up an organisation.[5]

Dansey was the limiting factor in MI9's work because of his power in overseeing the escape lines for both MI6 and MI9. Interestingly, his name does not appear in declassified MI9 files, nor those of Room 900. He is surprisingly 'absent' from the files, but this could be due to the fact that he was deputy head of an organisation – MI6 – which until the late 1990s did not officially acknowledge that it existed. In the end, Dansey's insistence on keeping the MI6 and MI9 operational lines apart from each other and from SOE, saved MI6 and MI9 from becoming completely non-operational. SOE was betrayed in France – many of its agents dropped into enemy territory and were immediately picked up by the Gestapo, tortured and killed or sent to a concentration camp. The agents of MI9, MI6 and SOE were all beset by similar risks, particularly that of penetration, therefore it made practical sense to separate them. Dansey's intention was for total non-cooperation between SOE, MI9 and MI6, but this failed in some cases, like Italy, Greece and the Far East, where a level of cooperation occurred.

However, although Dansey wanted to separate SOE from MI9 and MI6, I contend that behind the scenes the work of MI6 and MI9, and particularly that of Room 900, merged. I have been able to reveal for the first time that MI9/Room 900 was firmly involved in intelligence gathering and counter-espionage under the auspices of MI6. The two organisations – MI6 and MI9 – were separate from each other on the surface and for their escape lines, yet closer analysis has shown that in the area of intelligence, they were not so independent. It was desirable for them to appear as two separate organisations as Britain would have had no Secret Intelligence Service if MI6 was compromised (as it had been after the Venlo incident in 1939). Already, in the 1930s, Dansey had overseen one such form of a contingency plan, the Z Organisation, in which he ran agents to penetrate Germany and Italy for intelligence. It might have been a substitute for SIS/MI6 if the latter was compromised, although this is unproven. The question remains – could MI9/Room 900 have been used as a back-up in the same way? It is impossible to say for certain, but it seems likely.

The history and inter-connectedness of MI9 and MI6 are fascinating, if complex. This book has shown that IS9(D) and Room 900 were in fact part of MI6, as well as part of MI9. Room 900 was firmly engaged in obtaining intelligence along the same lines as MI6. Their sources were agents behind enemy lines, refugees and civilians coming into Britain and interrogated by MI9 and MI5, and members of various escape lines who were at risk and had to be smuggled out. All intelligence was provided overtly, or inadvertently, from occupied Europe as well as neutral countries, like Spain (from where many Axis spies and agents were operating).

The lasting legacy of MI9 has, on the one hand, been in the rescue of thousands of Allied personnel but, on the other, it can now be firmly seen as an intelligence gathering organisation. MI9/Room 900 was, arguably, as significant as other secret intelligence organisations – MI5, MI6 and today's GCHQ – in gaining vast quantities of intelligence during the war. This is attested by the tens of thousands of detailed interrogation reports at the National Archives, many providing information which fed into escape and evasion operations, and by running agents along the same lines as MI6 and engaging in counter-intelligence work. MI9 also undertook the interrogation of thousands of civilians entering Britain throughout the war – and these files, primarily in War Office archives WO 208, contain copious material on the situation in enemy occupied countries, such as the positions of German patrols, safe border crossing points, and details of the German defences in ports. Another branch of MI9 – the M Room – was amassing vast intelligence from the interrogation and bugging of the conversations of Axis prisoners of war at its secret sites in London and Buckinghamshire.[6] When taken all together, this amounts to an extensive, multi-faceted intelligence database that was shared with other branches of military intelligence and armed services, such as the Air Ministry and Bomber Command, even if the original source was sometimes obscured to protect its origin. The impact MI9 had on different aspects of the war deserves much more analysis from historians today.

At the end of the Second World War, Europe entered the Cold War and faced new threats from the Soviet Union. Stay-behind units were hidden across Europe in the event of a need for escape and evasion again. But there were lessons to be learned from MI9's wartime operations. At this time, MI9 made a number of strong recommendations for a future conflict: that escape and evasion should be studied as a special form of intelligence and separate subject within intelligence training. It recommended that MI6 training should be the model for preparing agents, pointing out that wireless transmission, codes, parachuting and pick up training would be particularly relevant. Finally, it recommended that a separate MI9 organisation be established with its own communications and agents.

Whilst today MI9 might not traditionally be understood as a spying organisation – like MI5, MI6 or Bletchley Park (later GCHQ) – the espionage and intelligence gathering it undertook were arguably just as significant. This, I believe, has been its undiscovered legacy and one which continues to be overlooked or forgotten in scholarship and the vast map of Second World War intelligence studies.

Perhaps the final word on MI9's history must be recognition of its helpers. To them is owed a debt of gratitude by the Western world which should not forget the tens of thousands of ordinary men and women across Europe who participated in the spirit of resistance. Today, Elsie Maréchal still bears the physical scars of her incarceration in two Nazi concentration camps. When asked why she risked her life, she replied: 'We had to do something against the Nazi occupation. That's why my family fought back and was involved with the escape line. For me, democracy is essential everywhere.'[7] That fight for and guardianship of democracy is as true today as then. In the words of Peggy van Lier:

> The despair, the humiliation, the anger [at German occupation] was so deep that one felt ready to do anything to regain the priceless treasure of freedom. It is only when one has lost freedom that one realises it is the most precious thing.

NOTES

Author's Note

1. Foot and Langley, *MI9*; Darling, *Secret Sunday*; Darling, *Sunday at Large*.
2. WO 208/3242, WO 208/3428, WO 165/39 and AIR 40/2432.
3. For example, Neave, Foot and Langley were unable to assess the extent, or otherwise, of the involvement of the Vatican with Allied escapers because those files had not been released into the public domain.
4. At the time of writing this book, the Vatican's Second World War archives had not been opened.
5. Janes, *Express Delivery*; Richards, *Secret Flotillas*.
6. Winston Churchill's letter of 3 August 1941, copy in WO 208/3242.
7. MI9 bulletin, WO 208/3268.
8. With the exception of Greece, Holland and the Far East later in the war.
9. Foot and Langley's entry on MI9 in *Oxford Companion to the Second World War*, p. 747.

Prologue: Red Carnation

1. Langley, *Fight Another Day*, p. 129.
2. Ibid.
3. Read and Fisher, *Colonel Z*, pp. 43–7.
4. Foot and Langley, *MI9*, p. 36.

Chapter 1: The Creation of MI9

1. WO 165/39, 23 December 1939.
2. The meeting included two deputies at the Directorate of Military Intelligence, Air Commodore K. Buss (Air Ministry) and Major General Sir Noel Mason-Macfarlane (director of Military Intelligence British Expeditionary Force, and later Governor of Gibraltar).
3. Memo dated 23 December 1939, signed by Colonel J. Spencer for DMI, in WO 208/3242.
4. Ibid. See also 'MI9 Historical Record', p. 2, WO 208/3242.
5. Founding charter of MI9, in Per Ardua Libertas, copy in the archives of the Military Intelligence Museum.
6. 'Prisoner of War Interrogation 1939–1945', ADM 223/475.
7. In brief, MI9(a) worked on the idea that if Axis prisoners were handled appropriately they could yield significant intelligence. The unit worked first from the Tower of London, Trent Park at Cockfosters in North London, and later Latimer House and Wilton Park in Buckinghamshire – the history of this aspect of MI9's work, under the auspices of Colonel

Thomas Joseph Kendrick, can be read in detail in Fry, *The Walls Have Ears*. Linked to the latter, and still part of MI9(a), was a secret interrogation centre located at Nos 6-7 and Nos 8 and 8a Kensington Palace Gardens, known as the London Cage. Prisoners were taken there for interrogation if 'their will to resist could not be broken' at other sites. That history has been told in Fry, *The London Cage* and the unpublished memoirs of its commanding officer, Colonel Alexander Scotland, in the National Archives, ref: WO 208/5381.

8. See also 'MI9 Historical Record', p. 2, WO 208/3242.
9. Examples of these First World War codes survive in the Imperial War Museum in the papers of La Dame Blanche network (not yet catalogued). For examples of POW escape accounts for the First World War, see AIR 1/2251/209/54/25 and AIR 1/2251/209/54/29. The First World War debriefings / interrogations are quite basic in the level of information and are stamped MI.1.
10. Foot and Langley, *MI9*, p. 2.
11. In the inter-war period, Rawlinson had worked as a scriptwriter; his work included the script for the 1934 British film *The Man Who Knew Too Much*.
12. WO 165/39, 28 March 1940.
13. Foot and Langley, *MI9*, p. 23. On 28 September 1939, Templer wrote from France to Major-General Beaumont-Nesbitt (the then director of Military Intelligence) about establishing mechanisms to communicate with British personnel in German POW camps. The matter was swiftly referred to the Joint Intelligence Committee.
14. Foot and Langley, *MI9*, p. 26.
15. Ibid. p. 44.
16. Ibid. p. 14.
17. Neave, *Saturday at MI9*, p. 24.
18. Langley, *Fight Another Day*, p. 136.
19. Susan Broomhall joined MI9 in October 1940.
20. These lectures took place in Room 660 of the Metropole Building. Johnny Evans was soon joined by Major E. Christie-Miller, Mr W.E. Butler and L.J. Bennett, MC. See WO 165/39, 29 February 1940. The pool of lecturers then increased to include Lieutenant Colonel M.C.C. Harrison DSO, MC; W.E. Butler; Brian Manning; Gilbert Beyfus, KC; L.A. Wingfield MC, DFC; Squadron Leader E.H. Keeling; A.Q. Robinson; and Captain Cyril Strong.
21. Amongst the ranks of senior officers in the early days of MI9 were former escapers of the First World War: Major C.M. Rait MC of the Artists Rifles, and Lieutenant Commander Philip Wood Rhodes RN who had been a German prisoner of war. Rait and Rhodes joined MI9 in February 1940; see WO 165/39, 10 February 1940. Rhodes became a liaison officer between MI9 and the Director of Naval Intelligence and an instructor in escape and evasion training at naval bases. Others joining the ranks were Leslie Winterbottom; Chief of Staff V.R. Isham; Pilot Officer H.E. Hervey; and Second Lieutenant H.B.A. de Bruyne (Royal Artillery).
22. Foot and Langley, *MI9*, pp. 50–1.
23. WO 165/39, 27 April 1940. The film *Name, Rank and Number* (1940) is available to view on YouTube.
24. Fry, *The Walls Have Ears*.
25. De Bruyne joined on 15 March 1940 and Hervey on 8 May 1940. Isham was invalided out in 1942 and replaced by K.R. Stirling Wylie of the Royal Scots who later became head of MI9.
26. Administrative clerks were drawn from the Royal Engineers and worked out of Room 805, a small office on the 8th floor of the Metropole Buildings. They were Sappers W. Ward, F. Astill, W.L. Whitmarsh and C.R. Townrow.
27. S/O Hughes drafted a summary report on behalf of Major I/O, dated 23 January 1944 for IS9(W), WO 208/3248.
28. Fry, *The Walls Have Ears*, p. 50.
29. They were Miss P. Madge and Miss V. Robbins (stenographers) and four (unnamed) shorthand typists who worked out of Room 662. See MI9 war diary, January 1940, WO 165/39.

Miss Matthews joined from MI8 as a shorthand typist on 6 May 1940, and is noted in the war diary on 10 June 1940, WO 165/39.

30. Fry, *The Walls Have Ears*.
31. WO 165/39, 10 February 1940. Fraser-Smith, *The Secret World of Charles Fraser-Smith*; and Clayton Hutton, *Official Secret*.
32. Foot and Langley, *MI9*; Neave, *Saturday at MI9*.
33. Porter, *The Man who Was Q*.
34. Later in the war, Clayton Hutton provided gadgets for 30 Assault Unit, the brainchild of Ian Fleming, for their special commando missions.
35. WO 165/39, 26 February 1940.
36. Clayton Hutton, *Official Secret*, pp. 5–7.
37. Ibid.
38. Ibid. p. 8.
39. Ibid. p. 11.
40. Foot and Langley, *MI9*, p. 30.
41. Clayton Hutton, *Official Secret*, p. 13.
42. Baker, *Confession of Faith*, p. 27.
43. Jestin, *A War Bride's Story*, pp. 216–17.
44. Fraser-Smith, *The Secret War*, p. 22.
45. Fraser-Smith moved his wife and son to his original family home at Croxley Green in Herefordshire and commuted into London every day.
46. Fraser-Smith, *The Secret War*, p. 24.
47. Froom, *Evasion and Escape Devices*, pp. 107–27 and pp. 277–301; Bond, *Great Escapes*.
48. Interview with son Rolf Steiner.
49. Rolf Steiner remembers the visit of two strangers to the house who took away his father's German clothes and typewriter. Rolf was hurried into another room because of the mysterious men but heard what was happening. There were days when it was known that his father did not always go straight to work in Upper Thames Street and was probably visiting MI9.
50. Clayton Hutton, *Official Secret*, p. 40.
51. Ibid.
52. Ibid. p. 167.
53. Ibid. p. 157.
54. Information supplied to the author by Phil Froom.
55. Clayton Hutton, *Official Secret*, p. 40.
56. Foot and Langley, *MI9*, p. 51.
57. Fraser-Smith, *The Secret War*, pp. 57–58.
58. Ibid. p. 56.
59. Foot and Langley, *MI9*, p. 53.
60. Bentine, *The Reluctant Jester*, p. 181–2.
61. Ibid.
62. Fraser-Smith, *The Secret War*, p. 62.
63. Other fictitious charities included the British Local Ladies Comforts Society, C&H Sports (Exeter), East Street Sports Shop (Brighton), Empire Service League, Jigsaw Puzzle Club, Lancashire Penny Fund, League of Helpers, Prisoners Leisure Hours Fund and The Wilberforce Foundation.
64. Bond, *Great Escapes*, pp. 87–8.
65. Fraser-Smith, *The Secret War*, p. 62.
66. Christopher Bowes, archivist for Waddington in 1999, quoted by Bond, *Great Escapes*, p. 91, see also pp.78–80.
67. Bond, *Great Escapes*, p. 91.
68. Ibid. p. 52.
69. A list of MI9 maps is given in ibid. pp. 216–41.
70. Clayton Hutton, *Official Secret*, pp. 18–24.
71. Froom, *Evasion and Escape Devices*, p. 87.

72. Ibid. p. 87.
73. WO 165/39, 14 August 1940.
74. Bond, *Great Escapes*, p. 50.
75. Froom, *Evasion and Escape Devices*, p. 88.
76. Neave's escape account is ref: MI9/S/P.G.(G) 676 in WO 208/3242.
77. Froom, *Evasion and Escape Devices*, p. 89.
78. Phil Froom, correspondence with the author, 2018 and 2019.
79. See also Froom *Evasion and Escape Devices*, p. 92.
80. Bond, *Great Escapes*, p. 79.
81. Ibid. p. 70.
82. Ibid.
83. WO 165/39, entry for March 1943.
84. Likely to have been series GSGS 3982. Bond, *Great Escapes*, p. 59.
85. Bond, *Great Escapes*, pp. 67–71.
86. Ibid. p. 70. MI9 maps were also produced for Africa and the Far East.
87. Bond, *Great Escapes*, p. 115.
88. Clayton Hutton, *Official Secret*, p. 10. Winterbottom was aided by Johnny Evans and Lt. Comdr. Rhodes who provided instruction in the use of codes to RAF and naval personnel, on the advice of Mr Hooker of the Foreign Office.
89. WO 165/39, 30 April 1940.
90. Examples of coded messages are in Appendix P, WO209/3242. See also Bond, *Great Escapes*, pp. 242–246.
91. Bond, *Great Escapes*, p. 116.
92. Ibid. p. 143.
93. Ibid. pp. 129–43.
94. Ibid.
95. Ibid. p. 143.
96. WO 165/39, April 1940.
97. Bond, *Great Escapes*, p. 113.

Chapter 2: Europe under Occupation

1. The Vemork site was the subject of Operation Freshman, a raid in October 1942 by Allied Combined Operations. See also Lewis, *Hunting Hitler's Nukes*.
2. Kiszely, *Anatomy of a Campaign*.
3. Lieutenant Colonel E.J. King-Salter was appointed the British military attaché to Norway on 1 March 1940.
4. Orders received on 11 April 1940, see E.J. King-Salter's MI9 escape report in WO 208/3297.
5. Ibid.
6. Ibid.
7. Ibid.
8. See JIC/1373/43, Folio 79, 11 September 1943, WO 208/5622.
9. WO 165/39, entry for 10 May 1940.
10. 'Specimen Lecture for Army Units on Conduct if Cut Off from Unit or Captured', in WO 208/3242.
11. Fry, *The Walls Have Ears*; Fry, *The London Cage*.
12. Interviews with the author in 2006 and 2007. See also Fry, *Churchill's German Army*.
13. Clayton Hutton, *Official Secret*, p. 44.
14. Ibid. p. 50.
15. Ibid. p. 51; Froom, *Evasion and Escape Devices*, pp. 196–219.
16. Clayton Hutton, *Official Secret*, p. 59.
17. Clayton Hutton's health finally overtook him. In 1943 he had to retire from MI9 with mental health problems. He had been central in the invention of MI9's escape and evasion

gadgets. The vast array of impressive gadgets and miniature inventions provided immeasurable assistance to escapers and evaders and became affectionately known as 'Churchill's toyshop'.

18. WO 165/39, 10 June 1940.
19. Ibid. 30 June 1940.
20. Bloch, *The Secret File of the Duke of Windsor*, p. 147.
21. 'Intelligence Liaison between the War Office, GHQ, Field Force and French Military Authorities', in WO 193/826.
22. Bloch, *The Secret File of the Duke of Windsor*, p. 149.
23. Having escaped occupied Europe, the Duke and Duchess remained in Lisbon whilst the British government discussed their future. On 4 August 1940, Prime Minister Winston Churchill offered the Duke the governorship of the Bahamas which he accepted. See Bloch, *The Secret File of the Duke of Windsor*, p. 171.
24. Historical Record of MI9, WO 208/3242.
25. WO 165/39, 31 July 1940.
26. Historical Record of MI9, WO 208/3242.
27. Neave, *Saturday at MI9*, p. 69.
28. Confirmed in interviews with the author by veterans and families involved in the escape lines in occupied Western Europe.
29. Special Order of the Day, August 1941. Brigadier Dudley Clarke was born in South Africa in 1899. He was partly responsible for forming the British Commandos, Special Air Service and US Rangers. In the First World War, he served in the Royal Artillery, then the Flying Corps. In 1936, he was in Palestine where he helped quell the Arab uprising. In 1940, in the rank of Lieutenant Colonel, he operated under the cover of MI9 and was sent to Cairo. In 1941, he set up Advanced Headquarters 'A' Force where he ran a number of deception operations. He ended up running MI9's Middle East department alongside his deception work until August 1944. He appointed Captain Ogilvie-Grant of the Scots Guards to manage the escape and evasion work in his region. See Rankin, *Churchill's Wizards*, pp. 158–163.
30. Lieutenant Colonel Blake's escape report is in WO 208/3297.
31. Ibid.
32. Ibid.
33. Ibid.
34. Ibid.
35. Mackenzie trained at HMS *King Alfred* and HMS *Vernon* (the naval and torpedo mining schools), then at Chatham. Mackenzie, unpublished memoirs, IWM, ref: 15/12/1.
36. Mackenzie already knew Pat Whinney's father-in-law because his own father had served under him on a destroyer in the First World War and the family had kept in contact during the inter-war years.
37. See Mackenzie, unpublished memoirs, p. 6.
38. Ibid. p. 10.
39. WO 165/39, 31 July 1940.

Chapter 3: Gateway to Freedom

1. Langley, *Fight Another Day*, p. 136.
2. Read and Fisher, *Colonel Z*, p. 269.
3. Langley, *Fight Another Day*, p. 132. See also Read and Fisher, *Colonel Z*, pp. 268–269.
4. Darling, *Sunday at Large*, p. 9 and p. 17. See also Neave, *Saturday at MI9*, p. 75.
5. In 1941, 4Z left Lisbon for an unknown destination, thought to be Chile, and was replaced by Jimmy Langley.
6. 'Donald Darling – MI9 Escape Lines 1940–1947,' article in escape line society papers, ELMS newsletter No. 30, 2012.
7. Langley, *Fight Another Day*, p. 136.

8. WO 165/39, 31 July 1940–6 August 1940.
9. Neave, *Saturday at MI9*, p. 78.
10. Ibid.
11. Pitchfork, *Shot Down and on the Run*, p. 43.
12. 'Memorandum of the Services Rendered to the Allied Cause and to British Subjects in France: June 1940–January 1945', p. 5, FO 371/49176.
13. Neave, *Saturday at MI9*, p. 79. See also Darling, *Sunday at Large*.
14. Foot and Langley, *MI9*, p. 38.
15. Interview with the author, October 2019.
16. 'Memorandum of the Services Rendered to the Allied Cause and to British Subjects in France: June 1940–January 1945,' by Revd Donald Caskie in FO 371/49176.
17. Ibid. p. 4. See also WO 361/24.
18. Information from Lord Rooker, interview and correspondence with the author in 2018.
19. See Fry, *The London Cage*, pp. 135–139.
20. Ibid.
21. WO 165/39, 31 August 1940.
22. Letter of 12 March 1941, CAB 301/90.
23. Fry, *Surrender on Demand*, p. 31.
24. Ibid. pp. 23–4, 33.
25. Ibid. pp. 35–6, 39–40.
26. Ibid. pp. 128–9.
27. Ibid. p. 81.
28. Varian Fry also saved the painter Marc Chagall, writer Lion Feuchtwanger, and sculptor Jacques Lipchitz.
29. A letter dated 12 March 1941 makes clear that Varian Fry had been helping MI9 since 1940, CAB 301/90.
30. Fry, *Surrender on Demand*, pp. 76–9.
31. Letter from Hopkinson (Foreign Office) to Sir Harry Brittain, 12 March 1941, CAB 301/90.
32. Fry, *Surrender on Demand*, p. 77.
33. Ibid.
34. WO 165/39, 13 September 1940.
35. The move took place on 14 October 1940.
36. Foot and Langley, *MI9*, p. 66.
37. Ibid. p. 67. This was corroborated by Dick Smith who was interviewed by the author.
38. Walton had been appointed to MI9 in April 1940, see WO 165/39. Miss B. Peechey and Miss Humble joined as shorthand typists, and the following month saw the arrival of Susan Broomhall as personal assistant to Crockatt. See WO 165/39, entry for 16 November 1940.
39. Shean Block opened in 1942 and was demolished by developers in autumn 2014.
40. WO 165/39 entry for 30 November 1940.
41. Ibid.
42. Jestin, *A War Bride's Story*, pp. 216–17.
43. Ibid. p. 217.
44. Foot and Langley, *MI9*, p. 65.
45. Ibid. p. 218.
46. WO 165/39, December 1940.
47. As in the case of a party of three officers and 108 other ranks who returned to Britain from Sweden via Iceland. See WO 165/39, 28 September 1940.
48. Jestin, *A War Bride's Story*, p. 217.
49. Fry, *Surrender on Demand*, p. 87.
50. Cypher from Hoare, 23 November 1940, CAB 301/90.
51. Cypher from Hoare to Cadogan, 2 December 1940, CAB 301/90.

52. Confirmed in a cypher of 16 December 1940, and another dated 9 January 1941, CAB 301/90.
53. Cypher, 9 December 1940, CAB 301/90.
54. Letter from the Foreign Office, 16 December 1940, CAB 301/90.
55. Fry finally received the funds in February 1941. See cypher from Foreign Office to Hoare, 24 February 1941, CAB 301/90.
56. Cypher No. 338 from Foreign Office to Sir Samuel Hoare, 24 February 1941, CAB 301/90.
57. Ibid.
58. Cypher 398, 4 March 1941, CAB 301/90.
59. Letter of 12 March 1941, CAB 301/90.
60. Cypher 536, 1 April 1941, CAB 301/90.
61. Letter from Norman Crockatt (head of MI9) to Mr W. Mack at the Foreign Office, 20 March 1941, CAB 301/90.
62. Ibid.
63. Ibid.
64. Letter from the Foreign Office to Sir Henry Brittain, 17 July 1941, CAB 301/90.
65. Letter from Peter Loxley to Sir Henry Brittain, 17 July 1941, CAB 301/90. Sir Harry Brittain agreed that the expenditure in Spain should be financed through C (i.e. MI6), memo of 19 July 1941, CAB 301/90.
66. Summary report dated 13 February 1945, FO 371/49176.
67. 'Memorandum of the Services Rendered to the Allied Cause and to British Subjects in France: June 1940-January 1945', pp. 5–6, in FO 371/49176.
68. Ibid. p. 7.
69. In December 1942, he published an article, 'The Massacre of the Jews: The Story of the Most Appalling Mass Murder in Human History'.
70. 'Memorandum of the Services Rendered to the Allied Cause and to British Subjects in France: June 1940–January 1945', FO 371/49176.
71. Ibid. p. 8.
72. Summary report dated 13 February 1945, FO 371/49176.
73. 'Memorandum of the Services Rendered to the Allied Cause and to British Subjects in France: June 1940–January 1945', p. 9 in FO 371/49176.
74. Letter of 9 March 1945 from Mr. M. Maude at the Foreign Office to Colonel Rait at MI9, FO 371/49176. See also 'Memorandum of the Services Rendered to the Allied Cause and to British Subjects in France: June 1940-January 1945', p. 12 in FO 371/49176. The list also included two escapers whom Caskie had helped: Commander Redvers Prior, MP and Air Marshal Whitney Straight.
75. *London Gazette*, 12 June 1945. See also memo MI9/E/6/8084, 14 June 1945, FO 371/49176.
76. Langley was educated at Aldeburgh Lodge in Suffolk, then a school at Uppingham from 1929, and went to Cambridge University in 1934. Langley's father had served and been wounded in the First World War, then was appointed assistant military attaché in Berne, a cover for his SIS activities and worked for Claude Dansey. The family joined him in Switzerland in 1918.
77. Foot and Langley, *MI9*, p. 16.
78. Langley, *Fight Another Day*, p. 120.
79. Foot and Langley, *MI9*, p. 65.
80. Langley, *Fight Another Day*, p. 135.
81. Ibid. p. 136.
82. Foot and Langley, *MI9*, p. 38.
83. Langley, *Fight Another Day*, p. 133.
84. Ibid. p. 138.
85. Ibid. p. 140.
86. Precise dates can vary in sources, but Langley wrote that he was sent to Gibraltar by Dansey in May 1941, see *Fight Another Day*, p. 140.
87. Langley, *Fight Another Day*, p. 145.

Chapter 4: The Pat Line

1. Brome, *The Way Back: The Story of Pat O'Leary, One of the Most Celebrated Mysterious Secret Operatives of World War II*.
2. Neave, *Saturday at MI9*, p. 79.
3. Ibid. p. 80.
4. Foot and Langley, *MI9*, p. 72.
5. Neave, *Saturday at MI9*, p. 81.
6. Ibid. p. 75.
7. Read and Fisher, *Colonel Z*, p. 260.
8. Neave, *Saturday at MI9*, p. 76.
9. Ibid. p. 77.
10. Ibid. p. 19.
11. 'Historical Record of MI9, IS9 and RAF Intelligence Course B', WO 208/3243.
12. Ibid.
13. Langley, *Fight Another Day*, p. 152.
14. Ibid. p. 153.
15. Neave, *Saturday at MI9*, p. 68.
16. Stalag Luft, Dulag Luft, Oflag VIIC, Oflag IVC, Stalag XXIC and Sulmona (Italy) and at the internment camp at Curragh (Ireland) in 'Historical Record of MI9', in WO 208/3242.
17. WO 165/39, July 1941.
18. Neave, *Saturday at MI9*, p. 109.
19. WO 165/39, August 1941. By January 1942, the complement of female staff at MI9 was still relatively small: 2 WRNS, 6 ATS and 3 WAAF officers from a total of 33, as indicated in the war diary entry that same month.
20. Harold Cole's MI5 security files are declassified in KV2/415, KV2/416 and KV2/417. These contain investigations into Cole as a traitor, eyewitness reports of helpers in France given to MI9, and correspondence between MI5 and Special Branch.
21. As in the case of Agent Celery who worked for MI5 as a double agent in the Second World War. See Carolinda Witt, *Double Agent Celery*.
22. Neave, *Saturday at MI9*, pp. 83–4.
23. Harold Cole's personal files are KV 2/415 – KV 2/417.
24. Dear, *Escape and Evasion*, p. 40.
25. Langley, *Fight Another Day*, p. 160.
26. Ibid. p. 83.
27. Neave, *Saturday at MI9*, p. 307.
28. Langley, *Fight Another Day*, pp. 160–2.
29. Ibid. pp. 250–1.
30. Ibid.
31. Brome, *The Way Back*, p. 242.
32. Neave, *Saturday at MI9*, p. 85.
33. Another safe house in the city was owned by Madame Mongelard.
34. Neave, *Saturday at MI9*, p. 124.
35. Ibid.
36. Fry, *The Walls Have Ears*, pp. 95–98.
37. MIS was an abbreviation for Military Intelligence Service.
38. See Foot and Langley, *MI9*, p. 39. The number of personnel in the US Military Intelligence Division was initially modest. In 1941, it had 200 officers and 656 civilian aides. By 1945, that figure rose to 575 officers and 931 aides.
39. Froom, *Evasion and Escape Devices*, p. 31.
40. Winfrey survived several attempted journeys across the Atlantic in ships that were torpedoed by U-boats. His survival was remarkable.
41. Froom, *Evasion and Escape Devices*, p. 32.

42. Foot and Langley, *MI9*, p. 43.
43. He also liaised with Major Arthur Richard (Dick) Rawlinson, the British Deputy Director of Military Intelligence (Prisoners of War).
44. Dear, *Escape and Evasion*, p. 72.
45. Foot and Langley, *MI9*, pp. 44–5.
46. 'Historical Record of MI9', p. 2, WO 208/3242.
47. For MIS-X and gadgets, see Froom, *Evasion and Escape Devices*, p. 31.
48. Ibid. p. 34.
49. Fry, *The London Cage*, pp. 158–160.
50. Dear, *Escape and Evasion*, p. 72.
51. For more details on MIS-X and radios, see Froom, *Evasion and Escape Devices*, pp. 36–38.
52. The Scoville Company in Waterbury, Connecticut manufactured buttons with a compass in the back. The button unscrewed anti-clockwise. The company produced a staggering 5 million escape buttons for MIS-X. Dear, *Escape and Evasion*, p. 75.
53. Froom, *Evasion and Escape Devices*, p. 39.
54. See Fry, *The Walls Have Ears*.
55. Froom, *Evasion and Escape Devices*, p. 30.
56. Dear, *Escape and Evasion*, pp. 76–9. The statistics are as follows: 3,069 from Belgium and Germany, 47 from Holland and Denmark, 6,335 from Italy, 18 from North Africa, 100 from Greece, 1,333 from Albania and Yugoslavia, 218 from Japanese occupied areas and 853 from China.
57. Foot and Langley, *MI9*, p. 44.
58. Ibid. p. 2.
69. 'Camp History of Oflag IVC: Colditz, November 1940–April 1945', p .9, AIR 40/1910.
60. Ibid.
61. Ibid.
62. Ibid. p. 4.
63. His escape report is in WO 208/3242.
64. His experiences are described in his autobiography, *The Real Enemy*. D'Harcourt was captured in July 1941.
65. Neave's escape report, MI9/S/P.G(G) 676, AIR 27/2104.
66. 'Camp History of Oflag IVC: Colditz, November 1940–April 1945', p. 27, AIR 40/1910.
67. Neave, *Saturday at MI9*, p. 36.
68. Ibid. p. 37.
69. Froom, *Evasion and Escape Devices*, p. 88.
70. Colonel Henry Cartwright served as the British attaché in Berne from 1939 to 1945.
71. Cartwright wrote up his experiences of escape during the Second World War in his book, *Within Four Walls*.
72. Neave, *Saturday at MI9*, p. 42.
73. Ibid. p. 40.
74. Ibid. p. 47.
75. Ibid. p. 52.
76. Ibid. p. 54.
77. Darling had a flat on the main street in Gibraltar where agents who had to swiftly get out of Europe, including SOE personnel, could stay overnight before being flown back to Britain. Information provided by Roger Stanton in 2019 and 2020.
78. Neave and Woollatt's return is noted in the MI9 war diary, WO 165/39, March 1943.
79. Copies of his debrief interrogation were sent to IS9, MI9(d), MI6(D) and the chief training instructor of IS9 at Harrow. His interrogation report survives in AIR 27/2104.
80. Neave, *Saturday at MI9*, p. 57.
81. Ibid. p. 62.
82. Ibid. p. 60.
83. Ibid. p. 82.

84. Appendix O of WO 208/3243 gives the organisations which operated in Western Europe under the direction of IS9(D) / Room 900. In 1945 this consisted of Major Neave, Captain Windham-Wright and Captain Zundel who ran agents in the field.
85. 'Historical Record of MI9, IS9 and RAF Intelligence Course B', WO 208/3243.
86. Reports contained in WO 204/12900.
87. Room 900 intelligence reports contained in WO 204/12900. It is the author's belief that other files from Room 900 may be declassified but have not yet been found amongst the thousands of G-2 intelligence files at the National Archives.
88. Report, 16 October 1942, WO 204/12900.
89. Ibid. 7 October 1942.
90. Ibid.
91. Ibid.
92. Ibid. p. 2.
93. Ibid. p. 3.
94. One-page report, 9 October 1942, WO 204/12900.
95. Ibid.
96. Report, 7 October 1942, p. 6, WO 204/12900.
97. Ibid. p. 9.
98. Ibid. p. 11. There are two separate reports, with the same date of 7 October 1942, in WO 204/12900 and both deal with these named individuals and the French Naval Security Control at the port of Oran.
99. Ibid. p. 10.
100. Report of 24 October 1942, WO 204/12900.
101. Report of 20 October 1942, WO 204/12900.
102. Report to the Joint Intelligence Committee, 23 November 1942, WO 204/12900.
103. Ibid.
104. Memo from Darling to G2 Section (Intelligence) Allied Force Headquarters, 18 November 1942, WO 204/12900.
105. The author has not yet been able to uncover further intelligence reports issued by Room 900 or Kim Philby.
106. Report in WO 204/12900.
107. Report, 14 November 1942, WO 204/12900.
108. Ibid. 15 November 1942.
109. Ibid. Report, 14 November 1942.
110. Jeffery, *MI6*, p. 768, endnote 27.

Chapter 5: The Comet Line

1. Foot and Langley, *MI9*, p. 79.
2. Cavell is now widely believed to have been a British MI6 spy.
3. Unpublished notes entitled 'Detail of the Activity of M. Fernand de Greef from 26 June 1940 to the end of the War', report of Tante Go about the Comet Line.
4. Citation for George Medal for Elvire de Greef, WO 208/5451.
5. Foot and Langley, *MI9*, p. 139.
6. Interview and correspondence with Anne and Chris Lyth, February 2020.
7. Pte Cromar was interrogated by MI9 on 7 October 1941, ref: MI9/S/P.G(B)514, WO 208/3306. His report was copied only to MI6(D).
8. Andrée De Jongh, citation for George Medal, no date, WO 208/5452.
9. Neave, *Little Cyclone*, p. xxii.
10. Ibid. pp.3–5.
11. Foot and Langley, *MI9*, p. 80.
12. Fourcade, *Noah's Ark*.
13. Citation for George Medal, WO 208/5452.

14. Dear, *Escape and Evasion*, p. 138.
15. Foot and Langley, *MI9*, p. 79.
16. Sergeant Cowan's interrogation report, ref: MI9/S/P.G(B)656, WO 208/3307. Private Conville's interrogation report, ref: MI9/S/P.G(B)658, WO 208/3307. He had been captured near Cherbourg in July 1940. Both were interrogated by MI9 on 7 January 1942 and their reports copied to MI6(D), MI9(d) and MI9(I.S). In an appendix to Cowan's interrogation report, MI9 wrote that it cost 10,000 French francs each man to bring them out: 1,000 French francs for the journey from Belgium to Spain, 1,000 French francs to cross the Somme, and 8,000 French francs for the Spanish guide over the Pyrenees.
17. Information provided by Brigitte d'Oultremont.
18. Interview with Brigitte d'Oultremont, October 2019.
19. Author's interviews with Brigitte d'Oultremont, October 2019.
20. Foot and Langley, *MI9*, p. 132.
21. Author's interview with Elsie Maréchal, October 2019.
22. Dear, *Escape and Evasion*, p. 135.
23. Foot and Langley, *MI9*, p. 138.
24. Copies of the Little Black Books in the family papers.
25. Dear, *Escape and Evasion*, p. 139. Johnson died in 1954 with little recognition and scant details of his efforts for the Comet Line.
26. Correspondence with Brigitte d'Oultremont.
27. Unpublished notes by Fernand de Greef. Copy given to the author by the family.
28. Foot and Langley, *MI9*, p. 139.
29. Dear, *Escape and Evasion*, p. 139.
30. The first route, and the one always used by Florentino, crossed the Bidassoa river and on to San Sebastian. The second route used over the Pyrenees by other guides was down to Sutar, continuing to Larressore and Espelette, crossing at Jauriko-Borda and on to a safe house near Gaineko-Borda in Spain. Other neighbouring villages were sometimes used to vary the route.
31. Count Antoine d'Ursel, personal citation for posthumous award of Certificate No.17, no date, WO 208/5452.
32. Neave, *Saturday at MI9*, pp.141–2.
33. Citation for George Medal, no date, in WO 208/5452.
34. Dear, *Escape and Evasion*, p. 136.
35. Neave, *Saturday at MI9*, p. 155.
36. Foot and Langley, *MI9*, p. 134. Baron Jean Greindl took over the network in April 1942.
37. Interview with the author, October 2019.
38. *Twenty Thousand Leagues under the Sea* (1870), and *The Mysterious Island* (1874).
39. Etherington, *A Quiet Woman's War*, p. 42.
40. Peggy Langley (née van Lier), Unpublished Reminiscences, pp. 2–3, copy given to the author by Roddy Langley.
41. Ibid. p. 1.
42. Ibid.
43. Eugenie De Jongh was arrested on 27 March 1943 for writing a veiled letter on evasion to Nemo. She denied all charges, was imprisoned at St Gilles in Brussels and released on 12 August 1943.
44. Andrée Dumont ('Nadine') was arrested on 11 August 1942.
45. Nadine survived and returned to Belgium in May 1945.
46. Peter Verstraeten, *The US Medal of Freedom Awarded to Belgians*, p. 41.
47. Written correspondence with Brigitte d'Oultremont, November 2019.
48. At the arrest of Frederic De Jongh in Paris, on 9 June, Michou quit work at the hospital and put herself totally at the disposal of the Comet Line. She took care of RAF lodging, food and clothing and organised their departure. She guided them to various train stations.
49. Interview with the author, October 2019.
50. Etherington, *A Quiet Woman's War*, p. 22, and pp. 39–40.

51. After being invalided out of the army in the First World War, Georges Maréchal was sent to the UK to recover with the Belgian forces-in-exile. He met his future wife, British born Elsie Bell, then. By 1929 he was back in Belgium, eventually working for the Ministry of Economics to travel to Flanders to control prices in the area. He travelled daily from their home.
52. Etherington, *A Quiet Woman's War*, p. 33.
53. Elsie Maréchal, interview with the author in Belgium, October 2019.
54. Ibid.
55. Ibid. See also Etherington, *A Quiet Woman's War*, pp. 47–48.
56. Their names are listed in ibid. p. 49.
57. Ibid. p. 52.
58. Elisabeth Constance Liegeois, unpublished memoir (1958) entitled *L'Enchainement 1940–45*, extract from chapter 3, translated by Angela Hammond whose father was hidden by the two Elisabeths. Translation used by kind permission of Angela Hammond and the Comète Line Remembrance.
59. Information provided by Angela Hammond, daughter of Ronald Shoebridge, December 2019.
60. Peggy Langley, Unpublished Reminiscences, p. 1.
61. Foot and Langley, *MI9*, p. 153.
62. Peggy Langley, Unpublished Reminiscences.
63. Ibid. p. 13.
64. Georges d'Oultremont also helped in a different soup kitchen from headquarters at the Swedish Canteen.
65. Interview with the author, October 2019.
66. Elisabeth Liegeois/Elisabeth Warnon worked with Georges d'Oultremont and sheltered airmen during 1942. She was arrested at the beginning of 1943.
67. Peggy Langley, Unpublished Reminiscences, p. 6.

Chapter 6: Escape Lines under Attack

1. Etherington, *A Quiet Woman's War*, p. 56. The incident is also recounted in Foot and Langley, *MI9*, pp. 146–148. Also interview with the author, October 2019.
2. The whole betrayal is also described in detail by Neave in *Little Cyclone*, pp. 62–73.
3. Etherington, *A Quiet Woman's War*, pp. 57–58.
4. Ibid. p. 59.
5. Interview with the author, October 2019. See also Etherington, *A Quiet Woman's War*, pp. 60–61.
6. Neave, *Saturday at MI9,* p. 150.
7. Etherington, *A Quiet Woman's War*, p. 61.
8. Peggy Langley, Unpublished Reminiscences, pp. 9–11.
9. Obituary, *The Guardian*, 17 August 2000.
10. Peggy Langley, Unpublished Reminiscences, p. 13.
11. Ibid.
12. Address by Secretary-General Baron Snoy et d'Oppuers at the inauguration ceremony of a plaque to commemorate eight officers of the Department of Economic Affairs, including Georges Maréchal, who died for their country in 1940–1945. Full text reproduced in Etherington, *A Quiet Woman's War*, p. 129.
13. Georges Maréchal was also posthumously awarded the Croix de Guerre with Palm, the Resistance medal and the Croix du Prisonnier Politique.
14. Etherington, *A Quiet Woman's War*, pp. 81–93.
15. Ibid. p. 83.
16. Interview with the author, October 2019. Her incarceration in Ravensbrück is described in detail in Etherington, *A Quiet Woman's War*, pp. 94–108.

17. Elisabeth Constance Liegeois, unpublished memoir (1958) entitled *L'Enchainement 1940–45*, extract from chapter 3, translated by Angela Hammond. Used by kind permission of Angela Hammond and the Comète Line Remembrance.
18. Ibid.
19. Interview and correspondence with Roddy Langley between 2017 and 2019.
20. See MI19 RPS report 1202, 15 January 1943, and report 1206, 16 January 1943 in WO 208/3694.
21. Extract translated by Brigitte d'Oultremont from her father's unpublished memoirs. This was Fontarabie, the first village in Spain.
22. Hendon aerodrome is today the site of the RAF Hendon Museum. Peggy was later debriefed by Neave in a flat in Ebury House, 39 Elizabeth Street, near Victoria Station. The flat belonged to the aunt of Neave's wife.
23. Peggy and Jimmy Langley married in November 1942. Mention is made in the minutes of a meeting on 7 November 1942, WO 208/3510.
24. Letter dated 21 January 1944 from Neave to the Belgium Government in Exile, Report in Peggy van Lier's personal file, Belgium Military Archives, ref: Comète/I/B/3.
25. Georges d'Oultremont, unpublished memoirs.
26. On arriving back at London, they were held at the Royal Victoria Patriotic School (RPS) in London and interrogated as non-British nationals. Neave described the RPS as a 'forbidding interrogation centre ... It tried to break professional German agents who had entered Britain ... and wore down the suspect by patience, suspense and boredom, mixed with cigarettes and endless cups of official tea.' See Neave, *Saturday at MI9*, pp. 87–8. The premises had been founded in 1857 as an orphanage for girls whose fathers had been killed in the Crimean War. In the Second World War its primary purpose was catching enemy spies and interrogating civilians from enemy territories for information. Its interrogation files exist in the National Archives in series WO 208.
27. Foot and Langley, *MI9*, pp. 158–9.
28. Ibid. p. 160.
29. Ibid. p. 157.
30. Verstraeten, *The US Medal of Freedom Awarded to Belgians*, p. 36.
31. Dédée's citation for the George Medal, no date. WO 208/5452 describes her work in detail for MI9 and cites that 112 men were saved by her. A list of names of men and dates that she saved them is appended to her citation with an acknowledgement that it is not a complete list.
32. Dédée's citation for the George Medal, no date. WO 208/5452.
33. Neave, *Saturday at MI9*, pp. 168–170.
34. Ibid. p. 137.
35. Dear, *Escape and Evasion*, p. 143.
36. Citation for award of MBE, no date, in WO 208/5452.
37. Ibid.
38. Sophie Grandjean's personal citation, no date, in WO 208/5452.
39. Baroness de Ruyter's personal citation, no date, in WO 208/5452.
40. Neave, *Saturday at MI9*, p. 173.
41. It is not clear where exactly they flew from in the Bideford area. Northam Burrows in Bideford Bay was used as an airfield in the First World War, so it is possible that clandestine missions may have taken off from there in the Second World War.
42. Neave, *Saturday at MI9*, p. 176.
43. Ibid.
44. Foot and Langley, *MI9*, pp. 156–7.
45. Information provided by Peter Verstraeten, January 2020.
46. Bernstein, *Hitler's Uranium Club*. See also Fry, *The Walls Have Ears*.
47. Neave, *Saturday at MI9*, p. 163.
48. Information provided by Peter Verstraeten, January 2020.

49. Peggy Langley, Unpublished Reminiscences, p. 3.
50. Neave, *Saturday at MI9*, p. 164.
51. Dear, *Escape and Evasion*, p. 143.
52. Neave, *Saturday at MI9*, p. 151.
53. Ibid. p. 170.
54. Ibid.
55. Nemo's colleagues were executed on 20 October 1943. They were Jean Ingels, Albert Maréchal, Eric de Menten de Hornes, Henri Rasquin, Gaston Bidoul, Robert Jones and Ghislain Neybergh.
56. MI9 bulletin, Advice memo No.4, section 'Letter written by a Belgian officer on the eve of his execution', in WO 208/3428.
57. Foot and Langley, *MI9*, p. 93.
58. Neave, *Saturday at MI9*, pp. 115–16.
59. Ibid. p. 111.
60. Ibid.
61. Ibid. p. 127.
62. Ibid. p. 122.
63. Unpublished notes by Fernand de Greef.
64. Ibid.
65. Etherington, *A Quiet Woman's War*, p. 38.
66. Ibid.
67. They were Ligne Nanson, Service Martiny-Daumerie, Jam (linked with network Francis-Daniel), Group 'M' of the resistance organisation MNB (Mouvement National Belge), Mane Thecel Phares of the resistance organisation Armée de le Libération, Groupe Franck-Deprez, Dragon, Tempo and Catherine. Correspondence with Peter Verstraeten, October 2019 and January 2020.
68. For more information, see military archives in Belgium (VSSE, Belgian State Security), references: Cegesoma AA1333/298 Réseau Jam; Cegesoma AA1333/198 Réseau Martiny-Daumerie; Cegesoma AA1333/114 Réseau Sabot – ligne Nanson; Cegesoma AA1333/174 Réseau Francis-Daniel and Cegesoma AA1333/230 Réseau Tempo.
69. Charles de Hepcée formed an underground network called Pyrenees-Orientales in France in 1943 to establish a new escape route called l'Iraty, which operated between France and Spain. He also smuggled secret reports across the Pyrenees to Lisbon for MI9.
70. Interview for this book with Monique Hanotte conducted by Brigitte d'Oultremont, November 2019.
71. Ibid.

Chapter 7: Great Escapes

1. Colditz Camp History, p. 40, AIR 40/1910.
2. Ibid.
3. Ibid. p. 41.
4. For other tunnelled escape attempts in Colditz, see Colditz Camp History, pp. 39–42, AIR 40/1910.
5. Reid, *The Colditz Story*.
6. Colditz Camp History, p.20, AIR 40/1910.
7. Colditz Camp History, pp. 47–8, AIR 40/1910. A full account of Reid's escape is contained in his MI9 debriefing report, ref: MI9/S/PG 995 in WO 208/3311.
8. Colditz Camp History, AIR 40/1910.
9. Ibid. p. 9.
10. Ibid. p. 25.
11. Camp History of Oflag IVC: Colditz, November 1940–April 1945, p. 39, AIR 40/1910.
12. Copy of message dated 17 January 1942, in Historical Record of MI9, WO 208/3242.
13. Ibid. message dated 22 January 1942.

14. Ibid., message dated 24 January 1942.
15. 'Specimen Lecture for Army Units on Conduct if Cut Off from Unit or Captured', in WO 208/3242.
16. Historical Record of MI9, p. 27, WO 208/3242.
17. Ibid. p. 25.
18. 'Extract Appendix ZG of report submitted by Group Captain A. Kellett, 27 June 1945', p. 1, in Air 40/2614.
19. Ibid. p.2.
20. Colditz Camp History, p. 27, AIR 40/1910.
21. Ibid. p. 29.
22. This process was used in Colditz, Stalag Luft III and other POW camps. See Stalag Luft III camp history April 1942–January 1945, p. 27, WO 208/3283.
23. Ibid. p. 38.
24. *The Wooden Horse* (1950) and *The Great Escape* (1963) were based on the escapes from Stalag Luft III in autumn 1943 and March 1944 respectively.
25. Stalag Luft III camp history, April 1942–January 1945, WO 208/3283.
26. Ibid. p. 7.
27. Ibid. pp. 7–8.
28. Stalag Luft III camp history, p. 25, WO 208/3283.
29. Ibid. p. 25.
30. From April 1942 this department was headed by Flight Lieutenant G. Walenn (RAF); Stalag Luft III camp history, p. 27.
31. Ibid. pp. 33–4.
32. Ibid. pp. 23–7. See also p. 34 which lists the personnel who constructed it.
33. Ibid. pp. 23–7.
34. Lieutenant Richard Michael Codner (Royal Artillery) had been captured at Medjez-el-Bad on 14 December 1942. He was sent as a POW via Rome then to Dulag Luft interrogation centre at Frankfurt am Main, and transferred to Stalag Luft III.
35. For their escapes see Stalag Luft III camp history, p. 39, WO 208/3283.
36. Copy of Lieutenant Richard Codner's escape report No. MI9/S/PG/1619 in WO 208/3242.
37. Ibid.
38. Stalag Luft III camp history, pp. 37–8, WO 208/3283.
39. Ibid. pp. 40–4.
40. See Fry, *The London Cage*, pp. 158–60.
41. Alexander Scotland's *Unpublished Memoirs*, pp. 274ff in WO 208/5381.
42. William Broomhall, unpublished short manuscript 'The Show Which Didn't Come Off', copy given to the author. His German POW cards (captured at the end of the war from German records) survive in WO 416/47/427.
43. William Broomhall, unpublished short manuscript, 'The Show Which Didn't Come Off', p. 3.
44. Ibid. p. 5.
45. Interviews with Dick Smith and the author between 2017 and 2019.
46. William Broomhall, unpublished short manuscript, 'The Show Which Didn't Come Off', p. 4.
47. Escape Report: MI9/S/P/G/LIB/258, interviewed by IS9(W) on 12 July 1945, WO 208/3336/258.
48. William Broomhall, unpublished short manuscript, 'The Show Which Didn't Come Off', p. 7.
49. Colditz Camp History, p. 94 AIR 40/1910.
50. Escape Report: MI9/S/P/G/LIB/258, WO 208/3336/258.
51. Ibid. pp. 38–9. Flight Lieutenant Goldfinch aided by Flight Lieutenant J. Best (RAF), Lieutenant A. Rolt (Rifle Brigade), Captain D. Walker (Black Watch) and Lieutenant G. Wardle (RN).
52. Obituary for Roger Rolt in *The Guardian*, 9 February 2008.

53. Mention in Despatches in WO 373/100/541. Two photographic portraits of Major General William Broomhall survive in the National Portrait Gallery, and his papers, interview and uniforms are in the National Army Museum.
54. Foot and Langley's entry on MI9 in *Oxford Companion to the Second World War*, p. 747.
55. 'Section IS9(D) /P.15', in 'History of IS9', WO 208/3242.
56. A large bound volume of the intelligence from MI9's interrogation of returning escapers and evaders is in ADM 199/2484.
57. MI9 bulletin, WO 208/3268.
58. RPS interrogation 631, 24 March 1942, WO 208/3673.
59. ADM 199/2478.
60. 'Camp History of Oflag IVC: Colditz, November 1940–April 1945', pp. 30–1, AIR 40/1910.
61. Ibid. p. 31.
62. Ibid. p. 86.

Chapter 8: Intelligence School 9 (IS9)

1. The first course was given on 20 September 1939.
2. Copy of the history in AIR 40/2432.
3. Bentine, *The Reluctant Jester*, p. 181.
4. Courses were given at Station X in Harrow from 28 October 1940. Not to be confused with Bletchley Park which was also known as Station X.
5. The lectures were initially delivered by Johnny Evans (RAF) and Philip Wood Rhodes (RN). The strength of RAF Intelligence School began with 1 commander (RN), 1 RNVR officer, 11 army officers, 3 RAFVR officers, 2 WRNS officers, 6 ATS officers and 5 WAAF officers.
6. 'Specimen Lecture for Army Units on Conduct if Cut Off from Unit or Captured', in WO 208/3242.
7. Re-Capture Training, IS9, WO 208/3428.
8. Ibid.
9. 'Specimen Lecture for Army Units on Conduct if Cut Off from Unit or Captured', in WO 208/3242. This advice was also given in 'Commando Lecture on Evasion', Ref: DB/E/a in WO 208/3264. This lecture was given to commandos ahead of the raid on St Nazaire in 1942.
10. Ibid.
11. Lectures on enemy POWs and interrogation were given by Wing Commander Denys Felkin who was head of Air Intelligence, linked to the bugging operation and Combined Services Detailed Interrogation Centre. See Fry, *The Walls Have Ears*.
12. British intelligence was doing the same to Axis prisoners of war. See Fry, *The Walls Have Ears*.
13. Re-Capture Training, IS9, WO 208/3428.
14. IS9(TA) War Training, Precis of POW Preventative Training World Wars I and II, p. 7. Ref: 08/44/1, IWM archives.
15. ADM 116/6266.
16. The full transcript of a lecture given on 'The Organisation of the German Air force' survives in AIR 40/1323.
17. MI9 handbook in WO 208/3428.
18. 'Specimen Lecture for Army Units on Conduct if Cut Off from Unit or Captured', in WO 208/3242.
19. Foot and Langley, *MI9*, p. 59.
20. RN special lecture in WO 208/3242.
21. Ibid.
22. Interview with the author, October 2019.
23. 'Summary of Work by IS9(WEA) British and American elements from April–December 1944', WO 208/3428.

24. Training lecture, February 1944.
25. WO 165/39, March 1942. See also WO 208/3449.
26. Information for RAF Highgate survives in AIR 29/715 and WO 208/3242.
27. Bentine, *The Reluctant Jester*, p. 174.
28. 'MI9 Intelligence Courses,' in WO 208/3242.
29. 9 September 1942, AIR 40/280. The wartime commanding officer and chief instructor in 1942 was Squadron Leader H.M. Parson, with assistant instructor Ft. Lt. L.H. Graham, and adjutant Ft. Lt. A.J. Cobb. Assistant instructor and security officer was Ft. Lt. A. Duxbury and WAAF officer S/O C. Potter.
30. 'Operational Training Unit, RAF School of Intelligence, Highgate', AIR 29/715.
31. Ibid.
32. RAF Highgate was first commanded by Philip Rhodes (RN). The chief instructor was Squadron Leader Johnnie Evans who also drew up the syllabus for the course. The administrative organisation of the courses was arranged by Squadron Leader H.M. Parsons. See 'MI9 Intelligence Courses' in WO 208/3242.
33. See ADM 116/6266. Lectures on interrogation techniques of Allied POWs by the enemy were given by Wing Commander Denys Felkin of AI1(K); on conditions in Europe by Major de Bruyne (IS9); camp conditions by Major Winterbottom (IS9); survival at sea by S/Lt the Lord Holden (MI9); and propaganda by Mr. Richard Hottelet. In February 1943, F/Lt H.E. Hervey was appointed assistant instructor to Evans. Hervey first joined MI9 in 1940.
34. Lectures to naval personnel were given by Lieutenant Commander C.P. Wade who had been appointed to MI9 in 1942.
35. English Heritage publication, *Kenwood: The Iveagh Bequest*, p. 47.
36. 'Operational Training Unit, RAF School of Intelligence, Highgate', AIR 29/715.
37. Bentine, *The Reluctant Jester*, p. 176.
38. Escape and Evasion Bulletins, AIR 40/1832.
39. Ibid.
40. Ibid.
41. Ibid.
42. At 0730 hrs on 16 June 1944, Caen Wood Towers was hit by a German bomb and sustained damage to four large plate glass windows, a smaller window and a broken skylight. Its operational capacity was unaffected.
43. Appendix G, 'Historical Record of MI9, IS9 and RAF Intelligence Course B', WO 208/3243. Up to April 1944 the commander of RAF Highgate was Wing Commander C.W. Pollock (RAFVR). He was replaced temporarily by Acting Wing Commander J.B. Newman, OBE. From mid-1944 until December 1945 it was Wing Commander L.H. Graham who was then succeeded by Wing Commander F.K. Kennedy.
44. Interrogation section in paper entitled 'No.9 Intelligence School', in WO 208/3242.
45. Fry, *The Walls Have Ears*, p. 50.
46. Interrogation section in paper entitled 'No.9 Intelligence School,' in WO 208/3242. Examples of Hughes's interrogation reports survive in WO 208/5583.
47. 'Historical Record of MI9', in WO 208/3242.
48. Ibid.
49. FO 898/321.
50. Message from Colditz, dated 28 August 1941, FO 898/321.
51. History of IS9, in WO 208/3242.
52. Detailed examples of the codes and how they work are given in WO 208/3242.
53. M.K. Howat, unpublished memoirs, IWM, 08/111/1.
54. Ibid.
55. During 1942 Captain Winfrey of USAAF was attached to IS9(Z), see WO 208/3428.
56. Other items included railway maps of Germany, German uniform badges, overalls, buttons, make-up boxes for disguises, razors and blades, raincoats, special rope, brief cases.
57. Foot and Langley, *MI9*, p. 28.
58. History of IS9, in WO 208/3242.

59. Operation Cornet, WO 208/3262.
60. Appendix O of WO 208/3243 gives the organisations which operated in Western Europe under the direction of IS9(D) Room 900. In 1945 this consisted of Major Neave, Captain Windham-Wright and Captain Zundel who ran agents in the field.
61. 'Section IS9(D) /P.15', in 'History of IS9', WO 208/3242.
62. History of IS9, in WO 208/3242.
63. Appendix O in WO 208/3242.
64. Ibid.
65. 'Section IS9(D) /P.15', in 'History of IS9', WO 208/3242.

Chapter 9: Sea Evacuations

1. Mackenzie, unpublished memoirs, p. 13, IWM, ref: 15/12/1.
2. The former was destroyed in a German daylight raid on Portsmouth during August 1940 at the height of the Battle of Britain. MDV 2 was sunk in 1942.
3. Schneidau's work is outlined in Mackenzie, pp. 16–18, IWM, ref: 15/12/1. Schneidau was awarded the DSO.
4. Mackenzie, unpublished memoirs, p. 18.
5. Ibid. p.21.
6. Ibid. p.24. Much of that information came to R.V. Jones via a branch of MI9 at the clandestine bugging of German prisoners and officers at Trent Park in North London, or Latimer House and Wilton Park in Buckinghamshire. See Helen Fry, *The Walls Have Ears*.
7. Mackenzie, unpublished memoirs, Appendix II.
8. In April 1943, Pat Whinney and Mackenzie were awarded the Croix de Guerre.
9. By the end of 1942, two motor gunboats were operating out of Dartmouth with navigators Commander Ted Davis and Angus Letty.
10. Mackenzie, unpublished memoirs, pp. 29–38, IWM, ref: 15/12/1.
11. Ibid. p. 36.
12. Ibid. p. 29.
13. Ibid. p. 36.
14. Ibid. p. 38.
15. For Operation Marie-Louise, see Richards, *Secret Flotillas*, vol 1, pp. 125–36.
16. Mackenzie, unpublished memoirs, p. 53, IWM, ref: 15/12/1I.
17. Richards, *Secret Flotillas*, vol. 2, pp. 346–9.
18. Ibid. pp.185–186.
19. Ibid. pp. 288–289, and pp. 368–9.
20. His escape report is No. 787 in WO 208/3309.
21. Mackenzie, unpublished memoirs, pp. 91–2.
22. Dr Rodocanachi is commemorated by the naming of Boulevard Dr Rodocancachi in Marseille.
23. For the account of his escape, see report No.787 in WO 208/3309.
24. Neave, *Saturday at MI9*, p. 87. The telegram went on to read: 'Please remind Saturday [Neave] Madame Savinos is German repeat German.' On board were Leoni Savinos (a Greek) and his German-born wife Madame Savinos. Leoni Savinos had worked for Pat O'Leary.
25. Neave, *Saturday at MI9*, p. 88.
26. Ibid. p. 93.
27. Higginson was interrogated three times by MI9 on his return. His escape reports were given the same number MI9/S/PG(F) 872 in WO 208/3310.
28. An account of the breakout of Higginson is also given in Brome, *The Way Back*, pp. 100–4.
29. Escape report MI9/S/PG(F) 872, WO 208/3310.
30. Ibid.
31. Brooks Richards, *Secret Flotillas*, vol. 2, pp. 364–7 and pp. 370–5.
32. Neave, *Saturday at MI9*, p. 94.

33. Navigators with the Inshore Patrol Flotilla included Angus Letty and David Birkin.
34. Mackenzie, unpublished memoirs, Appendix II, IWM, ref: 15/12/1.
35. Hemingway-Douglass, *The Shelburne Escape Line*.
36. Mitterand was landed from MGB 502 at Beg-an-Fry during Operation Easement II on 26 February 1944, accompanied by Peter Harratt. The latter served with SOE from late 1942 until the end of the VAR escape line in April 1944. Information provided by David Hewson.
37. ADM 1/16951.
38. Other vessels in the fleet included P.11, MFV 2020, and *Sunbeam*. In 1943, *Angèle Rouge* was captained by a Frenchman, Jean Jacques Allen.
39. Hemingway-Douglass, *The Shelburne Escape Line*, pp. 17–21.
40. St Ermin's Hotel has a history of clandestine activities for British intelligence. See Matthews, *House of Spies*.
41. Neave, *Saturday at MI9*, p. 220.
42. Dear, *Escape and Evasion*, p. 152.
43. Neave, *Saturday at MI9*, p. 223.
44. Ibid. p. 224.
45. Dumais's MI9 escape report is MI9/S/PG(F) 932, WO 208/3311, interrogated on 22 October 1942.
46. Fry, *The Walls Have Ears*, p. 10; Fry, *The London Cage*, p. 32.
47. Ref DB/E/a in WO 208/3264.
48. Escape report MI9/S/PG(F) 932, WO 208/3311.
49. Ibid.
50. Appendix to original interrogation report MI9/S/PG(F) 932, WO 208/3311.
51. Neave, *Saturday at MI9*, p. 227.
52. Hemingway-Douglass, *The Shelburne Escape Line*, p. 13.
53. Ibid. p. 19; Neave, *Saturday at MI9*, p. 227.
54. Hemingway-Douglass, *The Shelburne Escape Line,* p. 33.
55. Neave, *Saturday at MI9*, p. 235.
56. The mine detector was parachuted into the area on the night of 23 March 1944.
57. Neave, *Saturday at MI9*, p. 237.
58. The evacuation was executed under the direction of Acting Lieutenant Commander R.M. Marshall (DSC) who was aided by Lieutenant Andrew Smith (RNVR). See report in ADM 1/16951.
59. In July 1944 Broussine was captured as he tried to cross into Allied lines. Neave recommended him for an MC. Broussine was also awarded the Croix de Guerre by the French.
60. There were SOE escape lines, in which Lesley Humphreys and the Clandestine Communications Section played an important part. The major circuits were in France with the Vic Line, organised by Victor Gerson. There were other smaller lines: Greyhound and Woodchuck, and Alibi which operated for SIS. Information provided by David Hewson; for the Vic Line, see HS 8/174.
61. Dear, *Escape and Evasion*, p. 56ff.
62. Birdsall and Plisko, *500 Spy Sites of London*, pp. 252–3.
63. Neave, *Saturday at MI9*, p. 226. For a definitive history of the Burgundy Line, see Janes, *They Came from Burgundy*.
64. Richards, *Secret Flotillas*, vol. 1, p. 209.
65. A list survives in ADM 1/30197.
66. ADM 1/30197.

Chapter 10: Secret Intelligence Service (SIS) Escape Lines

1. Jeffery, *MI6*, pp. 382–6.
2. Fourcade, *Noah's Ark*.

3. One soldier Mary Lindell rescued was Captain James Windsor-Lewis of the Welsh Guards whom she escorted from Paris to Limoges.
4. Neave, *Saturday at MI9*, p. 190.
5. Ibid. p. 189.
6. Ibid.
7. Foot and Langley, *MI9*, pp. 87–8.
8. Neave, *Saturday at MI9*, p. 194.
9. Hasler's escape report is in WO 208/3312, No. 1140. Spark's escape report is in WO 208/3313, No.1162. Both were interrogated by Commander M.S. Jackson (ATS) at IS9(W).
10. Hasler, escape report 1140 in WO 208/3312, Appendix C.
11. Ibid.
12. Ibid.
13. Ibid.
14. The other escapers were P/O Spittal, Sgt Dawson and Sgt Hodgson. Sparks arrived at Liverpool on 12 April 1943. Hasler arrived at Portreath on 2 April 1943.
15. Mary Lindell's personal file, FO 950/1898.
16. Ibid.
17. Ibid.
18. Ibid.
19. Neave, *Saturday at MI9*, p. 204.
20. Details in FO 950/1898.
21. Nigel Morgan, correspondence with the author, 2017 whose father Kenneth Morgan translated the book into English.
22. HS 9/1452/8.
23. Neave, *Saturday at MI9*, p. 205.
24. Personal file, HS 6/762. Trix trained from 1 December 1942 at a number of Special Training Schools, including STS 5 (Wanborough Manor, Putteham, Surrey) and STS 51 (Dunham House, Altrincham near RAF Ringway).
25. Personal file, HS 6/762.
26. Ibid.
27. Neave, *Saturday at MI9*, p. 206.
28. Ibid. pp. 207–8.
29. Ibid. p. 207.
30. Confirmed by a memo dated 31 January 1945 that she was sent behind enemy lines on 13/14 February 1943 for IS9. Operation Chicory in HS 6/762.
31. HS 9/1452/8.
32. Neave, *Saturday at MI9*, p. 208.
33. M.R.D. Foot, *SOE in the Low Countries*, and Leo Marks, *Between Silk and Cyanide*.
34. Dourlien, *Inside North Pole*.
35. Scharrer, *The Dutch Resistance Revealed*, pp. 112–13. Christiaan Lindemans' MI5 files have now been declassified – KV 2/31 – KV 2/37.
36. Neave, *Saturday at MI9*, p. 213.
37. On 22 June 1945 Airey Neave asked in a letter to Captain W.E. Mills in Holland: 'Have you any news of PANDER?' The identity of PANDER is still not known, but was possibly linked to Trix's mission.
38. Neave, *Saturday at MI9*, p. 205.
39. Chicken I is mentioned in Froom, *Evasion and Escape Devices*, p. 363, but no further details given.
40. Her record states: Army No. 2992382, date of birth 17 June 1921, born Budapest; branch of service: WAAF.
41. Letter to The Jewish Agency from IS9(ME), dated 5 July 1945, in personal file WO 208/3401.
42. Personal file, WO 208/3415.

43. AIR 40/1533 contains limited details of her mission, including a letter dated 12 April 1945 from Flight Officer Neville to Crockatt at MI9. Appendix A describes the torture she suffered from the Gestapo. Personal file WO 208/3505. It contains graphic details of her mistreatment and torture.

Chapter 11: Italy

1. The type codes used by MI9 in Italy up to the Armistice were No. II & III, and to a limited degree Code VI.
2. Molden, *Exploding Star*, p. 135.
3. Operations in Italy, p. 6, HS 7/172.
4. Ibid. p. 7.
5. Molden, *Fires in the Night*, p. 69.
6. Escape and Evasion Bulletins, AIR 40/1832.
7. Letter from Major Irving-Bell, Advanced HQ Allied Screening Commission (Italy) to General Staff Officer, Allied Screening Commission (Italy), 2 August 1946, WO 208/5479.
8. Peter Barshall escaped from Capua camp dressed in Italian uniform but was immediately recaptured; then evacuated from Camp 49 at Fontanellato at the time of the Italian Armistice in September 1943. See his personal card, ref: WO 373/100/473.
9. Peter Barshall, unpublished memoirs entitled *Peter's Story*.
10. In 1916, Allen Dulles had been attached to the US embassy in Vienna.
11. Molden, *Exploding Star*, pp. 177–8.
12. Ibid.
13. Ibid.
14. Ibid.
15. Letter dated 7 January 1946 from Brigadier General Barnwell Legge, Military Attaché USA at American Legation in Berne, to Captain Peter Barshall c/o of the British Legation at Berne. Copy given to the author, and quoted, by kind permission of son James Barshall. Information also provided by David Margulies.
16. See WO 373/100/473. Copy of the original certificate given to the author by the family.
17. See Fritz Molden's autobiographical books *Fires in the Night* and *Exploding Star* for a brilliant and detailed study of the Switzerland – Italy – Austria clandestine missions and Italian escape lines in the war.
18. Molden, *Exploding Star*, p. 177.
19. Molden, *Fires in the Night*, p. 100.
20. Molden, *Exploding Star*, pp. 151–6.
21. Molden, *Fires in the Night*, p. 70.
22. Ibid. p. 91. Nam de Beaufort was also known as Nan Brauer de Beaufort.
23. Molden, *Exploding Star*, p. 182.
24. Ibid. p. 138.
25. Also helping the network were young Italian friends of Renata Faccincani.
26. Molden, *Exploding Star*, p. 156.
27. Ibid. p. 138.
28. Ibid.
29. Ibid. p. 139.
30. Ibid. p. 141.
31. Report by Guido Calogero entitled 'The Handful of Flour', in WO 208/5479, p.1.
32. Ibid.
33. Ibid.
34. Ibid. p. 2.
35. Notes on Italian helper Volumia Ugolotti in WO 208/5479.
36. The Escape Committee consisted of Lieutenant General Sir Richard O'Connor, Major General Adrian Carton de Wiart, Air Marshal Owen Boyd, Brigadier J. Combe, Brigadier

Reginald Miles and Brigadier Hargest. They were assisted by General Philip Neame VC, Brigadier Douglas Sterling and Lieutenant Lord Ranfurly.

37. Brigadier Hargest's escape report No. MI9/S/PG (Italy) 1587, copy in WO 208/3242.
38. Letter from IS9(CMF) to Allied Forces Headquarters, 14 November 1944, WO 208/5479.
39. Hargest's account of the escape was published posthumously as 'Farewell Camp 12' in 1945.
40. Operation Simcol, p. 16, HS 7/172.
41. Ibid. pp. 16–19.
42. Appendix to 1st Parachute Brigade War Diary for November 1943, in WO 169/8837.
43. Harvey Grenville, *Tim's Tales*. See also Appendix to No. 1 Parachute Brigade War Diary for November 1943, in WO 169/8837.
44. Ibid.
45. For his leadership in Operation Simcol, Major John Timothy was awarded a Bar to his Military Cross. *London Gazette*, 20 April 1944.
46. 'E&E Bulletin No.30: Plan Gooseberry', 3 April 1944 in AIR 20/8532. See also history of operations in Italy in HS 7/172.
47. Letter to Allied Forces Headquarters from 5 Field Section of IS9, 6 February 1945, WO 208/5479.
48. Letter from IS9(CMF) to Allied Forces Headquarters, 4 June 1945, WO 208/5479.
49. Memo, no date, WO 208/5479.
50. Ibid.
51. Memo about Aristide Silenzi, no date, WO 208/5479.
52. Memo about Giuseppe de Eise, no date, WO 208/5479.
53. Citation for Nanni Giovanetta, no date, WO 208/5479.
54. Citation for Hugh Raniere Bourbon del Monte, no date, WO 208/5479.
55. Interview with Vanessa Clewes, September 2019.
56. Obituary in *The Times*, 18 July 2009 and also interviews with Vanessa Clewes during 2019.
57. Interview with Vanessa Clewes, September 2019.
58. Molden, *Exploding Star*, p. 158.
59. Ibid. pp. 157–8.
60. Interview with Vanessa Clewes, September 2019.
61. Ibid.
62. Ibid.
63. Molden, *Exploding Star*, p. 193.
64. Canaris, whom Hitler believed was the 'spiritual leader' behind the assassination plot, was executed at Flossenbürg concentration camp on 9 April 1945.
65. Molden, *Exploding Star*, p. 193.
66. Interviews with Vanessa Clewes between 2017 and 2019.
67. Molden, *Exploding Star*, p. 141.
68. Ibid. p. 174.
69. Ibid.
70. Ibid. pp. 174–9.
71. Molden, *Fires in the Night*, p. 70.
72. Ibid. p. 72.
73. Molden, *Exploding Star*, p. 176.
74. For penetration operations into Austria and OSS missions, see Molden, *Fires in the Night*, pp. 86–90.
75. The experienced mountaineers were Lieutenant Hans Berthold, Herwig Wallnöfer and Louis Mittermayer.
76. Molden, *Exploding Star*, p. 194.
77. For details of Molden's network of operations in the final stages of the war, see Molden, *Exploding Star*, pp. 195–201.
78. Ibid. pp. 175–6.
79. Ibid. pp. 224–6.
80. Interviews with Vanessa Clewes.

81. Molden, *Exploding Star*, p. 245.
82. Interviews with the author, September 2019.
83. Ibid.
84. Molden, *Exploding Star*, p. 225 and interviews with Vanessa Clewes.
85. Molden, *Fires in the Night*, pp. 101–2.
86. Molden, *Exploding Star*, p. 249.
87. Obituary in *The Times*, 18 July 2009. Howard Clewes worked for the Foreign Office after the war before his successful writing career, including a period living in the Mato Grosso state in Brazil in 1952. There he worked as a cowboy for the Vestey family whose ranches in South America and Australia supplied prime beef around the world and created a vast fortune for the family. Renata worked for a time for the Foreign Office paper *Union Jack*.
88. Howard Clewes wrote a number of books and novels, including *The Long Memory*, *The Man on a Horse*, *I, the King*, and film scripts including *The One That Got Away*, *The Day They Robbed the Bank of England*, and *Mutiny on the Bounty*.
89. Interviews with Vanessa Clewes and her son Toby between 2017 and 2019.

Chapter 12: Under the Wings of the Vatican

1. Special Foreword in WO 208/3396.
2. Untitled report, WO 208/3396.
3. Ibid.
4. The nurses were Sister Josephine Vella, Countess Armallini and Princess Potenziani.
5. Untitled report, WO 208/3396.
6. Ibid.
7. MI9 debriefing report, No.1038 in WO 208/3312.
8. Ibid.
9. The three POWs were Major John Sym (Seaforth Highlanders), Captain Henry Byrnes (RCASC) and Sub-Lieutenant Roy Elliott (RNR). See untitled report, WO 208/3396. Elliott died in the Vatican on 15 March 1944 in tragic circumstances. While sleep walking during the night, he walked through a low window and fell three storeys to his death.
10. Untitled report, WO 208/3396.
11. Ibid.
12. The Italian commander of Camp 21 was Lieutenant Colonel Mario Barela.
13. 'Report on Prisoners of War Camp No.21', October 1942, WO 32/18499. 386 of the others held in the camp were South African POWs.
14. Derry, *The Rome Escape Line*, p. 1.
15. Ibid. pp. 11–14.
16. Untitled report, WO 208/3396. See also Derry, *The Rome Escape Line*, pp. 44–5.
17. Prisoners of War papers, WO 204/1012. See also Derry's account in *The Rome Escape Line*, p. 64.
18. 'Report on the Activities of British Organisation in Rome for Assisting Allied Escaped Prisoners of War', WO 208/3396.
19. These areas were 2 kilometres north, east and south of Montorio Romano, and 1.5 kilometres south of Nerola. 'Report on the Activities of British Organisation in Rome for Assisting Allied Escaped Prisoners of War', WO 208/3396.
20. Prisoners of War papers, WO 204/1012. See also Fry, *The London Cage*.
21. Interviews with daughter Claire Derry between 2017 and 2019. Derry's wife never discovered who had sent it but it had been smuggled to her in England at Christmas 1943.
22. They were Major John Sym (Seaforth Highlanders), Captain Henry Byrnes (RCASC), Sub-Lieutenant Roy Elliott (RNR), Capt. T. Roworth (RE), Lieut. H. Stevens (RNVR), Lieut. P. Freyberg (Grenadier Guards), C. Buxton (RN), Staff Sergeant P. Grimmer (RE), Sergeant C. Johnston (no service given), Private G. Rosati, Lance Corporal L. O'Sullivan (RTR), and Sergeant B. Scalisi and Staff Sergeant A. Brodniak from US forces. A party was sheltered in the American College under Lieut. C. Lesslie of the Irish Guards.

23. 'Report on the Activities of British Organisation in Rome for Assisting Allied Escaped Prisoners of War', WO 208/3396.
24. Report dated 22 December 1943 within 'Report on the Activities of British Organisation in Rome for Assisting Allied Escaped Prisoners of War', WO 208/3396.
25. Ibid.
26. *The Tablet*, 8 April 1944.
27. Summary report, no date, WO 204/1012.
28. Ibid.
29. Copy of letter from Irido Imperoli to Sam Derry, 6 January 1944, WO 204/1012.
30. Report in WO 204/1012.
31. Lieutenant Simpson, who was operating under the false name of O'Flynn and masking as a Vatican librarian, was arrested in April 1944.
32. Pte J. Pollak was from 604 Palestine Pioneer Coy.
33. The interrogation of evaders was conducted for MI9 by Captain B. Ryan who was attached to Combined Services Detailed Interrogation Centre (CMF). 'Report on the Activities of British Organisation in Rome for Assisting Allied Escaped Prisoners of War', WO 208/3396.
34. Amongst them were: HM Minister at the Legation was 'Mount'; Mr Hugh Montgomery (secretary to HM Minister) was 'Till'; John May was 'Giovanni'; Secundo Costantini was 'Sek'; and Lieut. J. Furman was 'John'. These are listed in 'Report on the Activities of British Organisation in Rome for Assisting Allied Escaped Prisoners of War', WO 208/3396.
35. Letter from Gambier-Parry to Derry, 13 January 1944, WO 204/1012. He was the brother of Brigadier Sir Richard Gambier-Parry who headed the Communications Section VIII of SIS in Britain during the war. Its headquarters were at Whaddon Hall in Buckinghamshire, originally with a radio station known as 'Station X' in the tower of the mansion house at Bletchley Park.
36. Letter from Gambier-Parry to Derry, 13 January 1944, WO 204/1012.
37. Letter from Derry to Gambier-Parry, no date, WO 204/1012.
38. 'Report on the Activities of British Organisation in Rome for Assisting Allied Escaped Prisoners of War', WO 208/3396.
39. Appendix A, dated 31 January 1944, Prisoners of War papers, WO 204/1012.
40. Ibid.
41. Citation for Sam Derry's Distinguished Service Order, WO 208/18499.
42. Letter dated 23 April 1944 from Derry to Lieutenant C. Lesslie (Irish Guards), copy in WO 204/1012.
43. Summary report, no date, WO 204/1012.
44. Ibid.
45. Telegram sent to London, 10 December 1943, FO 371/44215.
46. Telegram, 4 February 1944, FO 371/44215.
47. Memo, 21 March 1944, FO 371/44215.
48. Derry later received a Gold Cross for his part as one of only three British officers to join this Greek underground Resistance movement in Italy.
49. FO 371/12486.
50. Telegram from Sir R. Campbell to the Foreign Office, 27 November 1943, FO 371/12486.
51. Telegram, 10 December 1943, FO 371/12486.
52. Sir Anthony Rumbold, reply dated 11 December 1943 in FO 371/12486.
53. Copy of bank transfer dated 16 December 1943 in FO 371/12486. Subsequent correspondence about the bank transfer is also in this file.
54. Sir D'Arcy Osborne to the Foreign Office, 28 December 1943, FO 371/12486.
55. Sir D'Arcy Osborne also received funds of £4,000 on 1 May 1944 and another £2,000 on 10 May 1944. Copies of correspondence in FO 371/44215.
56. Flight Sergeant Nightingale was captured near Cuneo (Piedmont) in December 1942, and CQMS Cook near Medjez-el-Bab (Tunisia) in November 1942. See Cook's escape report in WO 208/3313.
57. Cook's escape report for MI9 in WO 208/3313.

58. Ibid.
59. Annual Report for Italy for 1944, written by Sir D'Arcy Osborne, British Legation to the Holy See, copy in FO 371/50084.
60. Ibid.
61. Ibid.
62. Ibid.
63. Ibid.
64. *The Times*, 27 December 1996.
65. Copy of Derry's personal army record, courtesy Claire Derry. See also MI9 war diary, WO 165/39.
66. 'Escape and Evasion – MI9, Post War Policy', AIR 40/2457.
67. Derry's autobiography, *The Rome Escape Line*, was published in 1960. In 1963, his life was honoured in the television series *This is Your Life* hosted by presenter Eamon Andrews. *The Times*, 27 December 1996.
68. It was on Kappler's orders that the Ardeatine Cave Massacre was carried out. See Fry, *The London Cage*.
69. Walker, *Hide and Seek: The Irish Priest in the Vatican who Defied the Nazi Command*.
70. Note by H.E. Sir D'Arcy Osborne, K.C.M.G, no date, WO 208/3396.
71. Ibid.

Chapter 13: Operation Marathon and D-Day

1. History of IS9(WEA) in WO 208/3246. Also relevant is 'History of Intelligence School No.9(WEA) from 14 January 1944 to 25 June 1945' in WO 208/3569. See also Froom, *Evasion and Escape Devices*, pp. 24–6.
2. Dear, *Escape and Evasion*, p. 25. Guidelines on escape and evasion were given to personnel involved in the D-Day and post D-Day forces; see lecture 'Briefing of Army Personnel by Lecturers of IS9(WEA)', WO 208/3424.
3. 'Position of Imperial and American POWs on Collapse of Germany', in AIR 40/280.
4. Neave, *Saturday at MI9*, p. 261.
5. Reports from evaders who sheltered in one of these special camps at Bohan (Ardennes) are in National Archives Research Center (NARA), Washington; references MIS-X 1632 and MIS-X 1671.
6. Neave, *Saturday at MI9*, p. 244.
7. Correspondence with Brigitte d'Oultremont.
8. Lafleur received the Distinguished Conduct Medal.
9. Georges d'Oultremont, *Souvenirs d'Oultre-Bombes*, translated for the author by Brigitte d'Oultremont.
10. Correspondence with Brigitte d'Oultremont.
11. Georges d'Oultremont, *Souvenirs d'Oultre-Bombes*.
12. Ibid.
13. Confirmed by an official letter dated 18 February 1944 from the War Office in the family archives of Georges d'Oultremont.
14. Georges d'Oultremont, *Souvenirs d'Oultre-Bombes*.
15. For his active service, Gerard Greindl received the Distinguished Flying Cross.
16. Information provided by Brigitte d'Oultremont from archives of the Comet Line.
17. Obituary, *The Times*, 24 November 2017.
18. Correspondence with Brigitte d'Oultremont, and this story is also told by Neave in *Saturday at MI9*.
19. Neave, *Saturday at MI9*, p. 249.
20. Interviews and correspondence with Brigitte d'Oultremont.
21. Neave, *Saturday at MI9*, p. 247.
22. Correspondence with Brigitte d'Oultremont, November 2019.
23. Interview with Monique Hanotte for this book by Brigitte d'Oultremont, November 2019.

24. Elvire de Greef, unpublished memoirs.
25. Correspondence from unnamed Flight Lieutenant, MI9(d), dated 31 December 1943.
26. Ibid.
27. Buckmaster to Langley, 1 January 1944, WO 208/3424.
28. Undated correspondence around January 1944 in WO 208/3424.
29. Neave, *Saturday at MI9*, pp. 242–3.
30. Georges d'Oultremont and Jean de Blommaert lived at 22 Pelham Crescent, off the Fulham Road, London.
31. Elvire de Greef, unpublished memoirs.
32. 'Summary of Work by IS9(WEA) British and American elements from April–December 1944', written by Jimmy Langley in WO 208/3428.
33. Ibid.
34. Escape and Evasion Bulletin, 30 July 1944, AIR 40/1832.
35. Ibid.
36. Neave, *Saturday at MI9*, p. 263.
37. History of IS9(WEA), WO 208/3246. Copies sent to Lieutenant Colonel C. Rait (MI9) and US Lieutenant Colonel J. Starr (MIS-X). See also reports in WO 208/3428.
38. Ibid.
39. Written by Sir Samuel Hoare (Lord Templewood) from the British embassy at San Sebastian to Anthony Eden (Secretary of State for Foreign Affairs), 21 September 1944, ref: C 13479/40/G, copy in Dédée's personal file, Belgium military archives.
40. Ibid.
41. Ibid.
42. Froom, *Evasion and Escape Devices*, p. 25.
43. Peter Baker's wartime exploits are told in *Confession of Faith*.
44. Revd Caskie's account is held in FO 371/49176.
45. Neave, *Saturday at MI9*, p. 271.

Chapter 14: IS9(WEA) Western Europe

1. Froom, *Evasion and Escape Devices*, p. 24.
2. The Allied interrogation section of IS9(WEA) was commanded by Major C. Fraser of the Lovat Scouts that had seen action in Italy.
3. 'History of Intelligence School No.9(WEA) from 14 January 1944 to 25 June 1945', p. 6. WO 208/3569.
4. Froom, *Evasion and Escape Devices*, pp. 193–194.
5. Information provided by John Howes.
6. An 'S-Phone' section was set up at Tilburg that consisted of 3 officers and 2 OR's from IS9(WEA) and 2I(U), a technical team of 2 officers and 14 ORs from special forces, plus 4 Dutch air interpreters. During the last month of the campaign (1945), 250 contacts were made using S-Phones, of which 189 were successful. Those that were not successful were due to bad weather.
7. Leo Fleskins provided support for Operation Pegasus I and II for IS9(WEA) and SHAEF.
8. See also www.mi9-is9.com
9. Testimonial by Jimmy Langley of John Smith, 27 December 1945, copy given to the author by Barbara Smith and Sarah Hardcastle.
10. Peter Baker was liberated by the Americans on 12 April 1945, and awarded the Military Cross on 2 August 1945.
11. Hugh Fraser, originally of Lovat Scouts, was dropped into the Ardennes on 1 September to act as liaison officer with the Belgian SAS and special forces.
12. Marks, *Between Silk and Cyanide*; also files of Trix, HS 6/762.
13. With the exception of Leo Heaps working with IS9, there were no Canadians involved in Pegasus I. Information kindly provided to the author by John Howes from his extensive decades of research in the UK and Netherlands.

14. American 506th Parachute Infantry Regiment (Easy Company, Band of Brothers).
15. Neave, *Saturday at MI9*, p. 294.
16. S-Phones were organised in Holland by Captain Newell. Signalmen Baker and Craig were trained codists and W/T operators; see WO 208/3255 and History of IS9(WEA), WO 208/3246.
17. 'Use of S-Phones', in History of IS9(WEA), WO 208/3246.
18. Warrack, *Travel by Dark*.
19. Froom, *Evasion and Escape Devices*, p. 334.
20. Stalag Luft III camp history April 1942–January 1945, p. 40, WO 208/3283.
21. Ibid.
22. Material for Plan Endor is contained in WO 208/3432.
23. In the American zone it was believed there were 14,847 British and Commonwealth POWs and 1,795 American POWs. See Plan Endor in WO 208/3432.
24. They were Capt. F.A. Burrell, Capt. D.K. Drury, Lieut. J. Surprenant.
25. Letter dated 13 September 1944 from Director of Military Intelligence to the Military Liaison Officer at Canadian Military HQ, in WO 208/3432.
26. Plan Endor, WO 208/3432.
27. Disbandment of IS9, WO 208/3255.

Chapter 15: A Matter of Humanity

1. A list of names of those who received awards up to 31 March 1947 is contained in WO 208/5479. It also includes a list of posthumous awards.
2. Hemingway-Douglass, *The Shelburne Escape Line*, p. 1.
3. Report entitled 'Escape and Evasion – MI9 Post War Policy' in AIR 40/2457.
4. History of IS9, in WO 208/3242.
5. The George Medal was given for outstanding and exceptional gallantry, and OBE, MBE or BEM for great gallantry or service, the King's Medal for gallantry or service, and Certificate of No.17 which was a King's Commendation for Brave Conduct. See 'Awards to Foreign Civilians', 11 April 1945, WO 208/5479.
6. 'Escape and Evasion – MI9 Post War Policy' paper in AIR 40/2457.
7. Also based at the Awards Bureau in Paris were Squadron Leader Gil Wills, Major Headley White, Captain A. Johnson, and Staff Officer Wendy Charnier.
8. M.K. Howat, unpublished memoirs, IWM, 08/111/1.
9. Ibid. p. 2.
10. The work of the Awards Bureau in Denmark and in Holland was covered by Captain de Cent, Flight Lieutenant Dowler and US parachutist, Lieutenant Jack Horner.
11. Lieutenant Colonel Sam Derry's papers, IWM 08/44/1; M.K. Howat, unpublished memoirs, IWM, 08/111/1. Major Pat Windham-Wright, involved in sea evacuations in the war, headed the Awards Bureau in the Hague with Liaison Officer Jack Bottenheim. Also amongst those working for the Bureau was S/O Baring-Gould who was in Air Intelligence in the war attached to MI9 and later married Jack Bottenheim.
12. Lieutenant Colonel Sam Derry's papers, IWM 08/44/1.
13. Ibid.
14. Citation for Sam Derry's DSO, WO 373/96/573.
15. Report by Guido Calogero entitled 'The Handful of Flour', in WO 208/5479, p. 3.
16. Broadcast by Radio Tricolore, 15 March 1945, WO 208/5479.
17. Ibid.
18. Information from daughter Claire Derry.
19. Lieutenant Colonel Sam Derry's papers, IWM 08/44/1.
20. A copy of Derry's personal army record given to the author by the family. Interestingly this records his specialist knowledge as 'escapology'.
21. Also present at the ceremony in an official capacity were Brigadier Page (War Office), Colonel Furman (MI9/MI19), Wing Commander Harrison, and Lieutenant Orchard,

RNVR. IS9 Awards Bureau was represented by Squadron Leader Ellen, Miss M. Jackson and Squadron Leader Wills.

22. Nothomb was also awarded the Croix de Guerre with Palm and Commander Class of the Order of Leopold II with Palm.
23. Appendix in Neave, *Little Cyclone.*
24. Citation in WO 208/5452.
25. Harrison and Langley, *An Orange Boat from Seville,* unpublished manuscript, p. 5.
26. Fry, *Inside Nuremberg Prison.*
27. Neave, *Saturday at MI9,* p. 24.
28. Bishop, *The Man Who Was Saturday.*
29. Froom, *Evasion and Escape Devices,* p. 49.
30. Ibid. p. 341.
31. October newsletter, 1946 in Sam Derry's papers, IWM 08/44/1.

Chapter 16: The Far East and Other Theatres of War

1. HS 7/172, p. 7.
2. Ibid.
3. Ibid.
4. 'MI9 Mediterranean Area, March 1943–December 1943', p. 42, HS 7/172.
5. Ibid.
6. Ibid. p. 43.
7. Ibid. p. 44.
8. Ibid. resolution dated 10 March 1943.
9. MI9 Bulletin Far East, WO 208/5191. In late 1943, a joint Australian-American-British MIS-X headquarters was set up at Brisbane to cover the South-West Pacific. A detachment of MIS-X was based at New Delhi (India), the US sphere of China and South-West Pacific (addresses not given). This was headed by Wing Commander Lamb (RAAF) and Major Kraus (USAF).
10. Far East Section 1, p. 2 in WO 208/3268.
11. 'Specimen Lecture on Escape and Evasion in the Far East', p. 1, in AIR 23/2934. Also contained in WO 208/3424.
12. Ibid. p. 6, WO 208/3424.
13. MI9 Bulletin Far East, Chapter 1: Evasion and Escape, pp. 8–9, WO 208/5191.
14. 'Specimen Lecture on Escape and Evasion in the Far East', p. 1, WO 208/3424.
15. Ibid. p. 2.
16. MI9 Bulletin Far East, Chapter 2, pp. 1–5, WO 208/5191.
17. Ibid. p. 3.
18. 'Appendix B, Specimen Lecture on Evasion and Escape in the Far East', WO 208/3424.
19. MI9 Bulletin Far East, WO 208/5191.
20. Foot and Langley, *MI9,* p. 293.
21. 'Specimen Lecture on Escape and Evasion in the Far East', p. 4, WO 208/3424.
22. MI9 Bulletin Far East, Chapter 3, p. 1, WO 208/5191.
23. Ibid. p. 5.
24. Ibid. p. 11.
25. Ibid.
26. Ibid.
27. Ibid. p. 13. See also security briefing dated 22 June 1944 from Air Liaison at MI9 to Air Intelligence Section 2, AIR 40/2450.
28. MI9 Bulletin Far East, Chapter 3, p. 15, WO 208/5191.
29. MI9's maps for the Far East, including Burma, China, Hong Kong, Taiwan and Thailand are in WO 418/67-80.
30. Ibid. p. 9ff. Other examples of escapes in the Far East are found in AIR 40/2462.
31. 'Specimen Lecture on Escape and Evasion in the Far East', p. 3, WO 208/3424.

32. Ibid.
33. Ibid. p. 3.
34. Information provided by Roger Stanton from ELMS newsletter No.29.
35. MI9 Lecture for Troops for the Far East, AIR 23/2934. Other examples of escape stories are in 'Specimen Lecture on Escape and Evasion in the Far East', p. 17, WO 208/3424 and in AIR 40/2450.
36. MI9 Lecture for Troops for the Far East, AIR 23/2934. Other examples of escapes in this file include one entitled 'Extreme Courage and Endurance' and focuses on a case of physical brutality during interrogation.
37. Thomas, *The Naga Queen*.
38. For V Force war diary, see WO 172/10045. For the organisation and correspondence of V Force, see WO 203/2694, WO 203/2695 and WO 203/1064.
39. Information provided by Roger Stanton from ELMS newsletter No.29.
40. For Burma Special Forces, V Force HQ, see WO 172/4585. For other clandestine operations in Burma, see WO 106/5838.
41. Ursula Graham Bower's archive and photographs, including her Naga headhunter's shield, are held by the Pitt Rivers Museum in Oxford.
42. Foot and Langley, *MI9*, pp. 295–303.
43. An example of another escape from Sham Shui Po Camp is given in the MI9 training bulletin. See 'Naval Officer's Escape from Hong Kong and His Journey Back to Allied Territory', in AIR 23/2934.
44. See a number of relevant files: HS 1/166, HS 1/167, WO 203/5766, WO 208/452A and WO 208/3762.
45. Foot and Langley, *MI9*, p. 302. SOE in South-East Asia was headed by Colin Mackenzie. See his personal file: HS 9/964/2.
46. Ibid. p. 302.
47. Ibid.

Epilogue: The Legacy

1. Foot and Langley, *MI9*, p. 5.
2. Neave, *Saturday at MI9*, p. 16.
3. Langley, *Fight Another Day*, p. 251.
4. Ibid. p. 127.
5. Foot and Langley, *MI9*, p. 35.
6. Fry, *The Walls Have Ears*; Fry, *The London Cage*.
7. Interview with the author, October 2019.

BIBLIOGRAPHY

National Archives

ADM 1/16951, ADM 1/30197, ADM 116/6266, ADM 199/2478, ADM 199/2484, ADM 223/475, AIR 1/2251/209/54/25, AIR 1/2251/209/54/29, AIR 23/2934, AIR 27/2104, AIR 29/715, AIR 40/280, AIR 40/281, AIR 40/282, AIR 40/1323, AIR 40/1533, AIR 40/1832, AIR 40/1910, AIR 40/2327, AIR 40/2335, AIR 40/2432, AIR 40/2450, AIR 40/2451, AIR 40/2457, AIR 40/2462, AIR 40/2614, CAB 121/304, CAB 154/55, CAB 301/90, DO 35/1454, FO 371/12486, FO 371/44215, FO 371/49176, FO 371/50084, FO 898/321, FO 950/1898, HS 1/166, HS 1/167, HS 6/762, HS 7/172, HS 8/174, HS 9/771/4, HS 9/964/2, HS 9/1452/8, IWM 08/44/1, IWM 08/111/1, KV 2/415, KV 2/416, KV 2/417, WO 32/18499, WO 106/5838, WO 165/39, WO 169/8837, WO 169/24879, WO 172/4585, WO 172/10045, WO 193/826, WO 203/1064, WO 203/2694, WO 203/2695, WO 203/5766, WO 204/1012, WO 204/12900, WO 205/24, WO 208/3242, WO 208/3243, WO 208/3246, WO 208/3264, WO 208/3265, WO 208/3268, WO 208/3269, WO 208/3283, WO 208/3297, Wo 208/3306, WO 208/3309, WO 208/3310, WO 208/3311, WO 208/3312, WO 208/3313, WO 208/3336/258, WO 208/3396, WO 208/3401, WO 208/3415, WO 208/3424, WO 208/3428, WO 208/3449, WO 208/3450, WO 208/3505, WO 208/3510, WO 208/3569, WO 208/3572, WO 208/3673, WO 208/3694, WO 208/3762, WO 208/452A, WO 208/452B, WO 208/5191, WO 208/5381, WO 208/5451, WO 208/5452, WO 208/5479, WO 311/632, WO 361/24, WO 373/18/147, WO 373/96/573, WO 373/100/473, WO 373/100/541, WO 416/47/427, WO 418/67-80

Archives

Archives and collection of RAF Medmenham
Belgian Military Archives (VSSE): files of the Felix network and Peggy van Lier
Imperial War Museum: papers of Miss M.K. Howat, ref: 08/111/1 and Lieutenant Commander S.M. Mackenzie, ref: 15/12/1
Military Intelligence Museum archives (Chicksands): *Special Duties and the Intelligence Corps 1940 to 1946* by Fred Judge
National Army Museum: cassette tape oral history interview with Major General William Broomhall, ref: 1992-09-175
RAF Hendon

Published Works

Absalom, Roger. *A Strange Alliance: Aspects of Escape and Survival in Italy 1943–45*, Olschki, 1990.

BIBLIOGRAPHY

Baker, Peter. *Confession of Faith*, Falcon Press, 1946.

Bentine, Michael. *The Reluctant Jester*, Bantam Press, 1992.

Bernstein, Jeremy. *Hitler's Uranium Club: The Secret Recordings at Farm Hall*, Copernicus Books, 2001.

Birdsall, Mark and Deborah Plisko. *The Insider's Guide to 500 Spy Sites in London*, Eye Spy Publishing Ltd, 2015.

Bishop, Patrick. *The Man Who Was Saturday*, William Collins, 2019.

Bloch, Michael. *The Secret File of the Duke of Windsor*, Harper & Row, 1988.

Bond, Barbara. *Great Escapes: The Story of MI9's Second World War Escape and Evasion Maps*, Time Books, 2015.

Brome, Vincent. *The Way Back: The Story of Pat O'Leary, One of the Most Celebrated Mysterious Secret Operatives of World War II*, Vail-Ballou Press, 1957.

de Burgh, Lucy. *My Italian Adventures: An English Girl at War 1943–47*, The History Press, 2013.

Cartwright, Henry. *Within Four Walls*, Edward Arnold, 1930.

Castle, John. *The Password is Courage*, Souvenir Press, 1954.

Clayton Hutton, Christopher. *Official Secret: The Remarkable Story of Escape Aids, Their Invention, Production and the Sequel*, Max Parrish, 1960.

Darling, Donald. *Sunday at Large: Assignments of a Secret Agent*, Harper Collins, 1977.

Darling, Donald. *Secret Sunday*, Harper Collins, 1975.

Deane-Drummond, Anthony. *Return Ticket*, The Popular Book Club, 1952.

Deane-Drummond, Anthony. *Arrows of Fortune*, Leo Cooper, 1992.

Dear, Ian. *Escape and Evasion: POW Breakouts in World War Two*, Cassell, 1997.

Dear, Ian. *Oxford Companion to the Second World War*, Oxford University Press, 1995.

Derry, Sam. *The Rome Escape Line*, George Harrap, 1960.

Dourlien, Pieter. *Inside North Pole: A Secret Agent's Story*, William Kimber, 1968.

Etherington, William. *A Quiet Woman's War*, Mousehold Press, 2002.

Evans, Alfred John. *The Escaping Club: Escape and Liberation 1940–45*, Fonthill Media, 2012.

Foot, M.R.D. *SOE in the Low Countries*, St Ermin's Press, 2001.

Foot, M.R.D. and Jimmy Langley. *MI9: Escape and Evasion 1939–1945*, Bodley Head, 1979.

Fourcade, Marie-Madeleine. *Noah's Ark*, Dutton, 1974. Translated by Kenneth Morgan.

Fraser-Smith, Charles. *The Secret War of Charles Fraser-Smith*, Michael Joseph, 1981.

Fraser-Smith, Charles. *Secret Warriors: Hidden Heroes of MI6, OSS, MI9, SOE and SAS*, Paternoster Press, 1984.

Froom, Phil. *Evasion and Escape Devices Produced by MI9, MIS-X and SOE in World War II*, Schiffer Publishing Ltd, 2015.

Fry, Helen. *The Walls Have Ears: The Greatest Intelligence Operation of World War II*, Yale University Press, 2019.

Fry, Helen. *The London Cage: The Secret History of Britain's World War II Interrogation Centre*, Yale University Press, 2017.

Fry, Helen. *Inside Nuremberg Prison*, Thistle Publishing, 2015.

Fry, Helen. *Churchill's German Army*, Thistle Publishing, 2015.

Fry, Helen. *Spymaster: The Secret Life of Kendrick*, Thistle Publishing, 2015.

Fry, Varian. *Surrender on Demand*, Atlantic Books, 1999.

Furman, John. *Be Not Fearful*, Anthony Blond, 1959.

Grenville, Harvey. *Tim's Tale: A Wartime Biography of Major John Timothy*, privately published, 2008.

d'Harcourt, Pierre. *The Real Enemy*, Longmans, 1967.

Heaps, Leo. *The Grey Goose of Arnhem*, Littlehampton, 1976.

Hemingway-Douglass, Reanne and Don Douglass. *The Shelburne Escape Line*, Cave Art Press, 2014.

Houliston, Laura and Susan Jenkins. *Kenwood: The Iveagh Bequest*, English Heritage, 2014.

Janes, Keith. *Express Delivery*, Matador, 2019.

Janes, Keith. *They Came from Burgundy: A Study of the Bourgogne Escape Line*, Matador, 2017.

BIBLIOGRAPHY

Jeffery, Keith. *MI6: The History of the SIS, 1909–1949*, Bloomsbury, 2010.

Jestin, Catherine. *A War Bride's Story*, Briarwood Print Co., 1995.

Kiszely, John. *Anatomy of a Campaign: The British Fiasco in Norway, 1940*, Cambridge University Press, 2017.

Koreman, Megan. *The Escape Line: How the Ordinary Heroes of Dutch-Paris Resisted the Nazi Occupation of Western Europe*, Oxford University Press, 2018.

Lewis, Damien. *Hunting Hitler's Nukes: The Secret Race to Stop the Nazi Bomb*, Quercus, 2016.

Macintyre, Ben. *Operation Mincemeat*, Bloomsbury, 2016.

McLachlan, Donald. *Room 39: Naval Intelligence in Action 1939–45*, Weidenfeld, 1968.

Marks, Leo. *Between Silk and Cyanide*, HarperCollins, 2000.

Matthews, Peter. *House of Spies: St Ermin's Hotel, the London Base of British Espionage*, The History Press, 2016.

Molden, Fritz. *Fires in the Night*, Westview Press, 1989.

Molden, Fritz. *Exploding Star*, Weidenfeld & Nicolson, 1978.

Morgan, Janet. *The Secrets of Rue St Roch: Intelligence Operations behind Enemy Lines in the First World War*, Allen Lane, 2004.

Neame, Philip. *Playing with Strife*, George Harrap, 1946.

Neave, Airey. *Little Cyclone*, Biteback Publishing, 2016.

Neave, Airey. *Saturday at MI9: The Classic Account of the WWII Allied Escape Organisation*, Pen & Sword, 2010.

Pitchfork, Graham. *Shot Down and on the Run: The RAF and Commonwealth Aircrews who got home from behind enemy lines 1940–1945*, The National Archives, 2003.

Porter, David. *The Man who Was "Q": The Life of Charles Fraser-Smith*, Paternoster Press, 1989.

Rankin, Nicholas. *Defending the Rock: How Gibraltar Defeated Hitler*, Faber & Faber, 2017.

Rankin, Nicholas. *Churchill's Wizards: The British Genius for Deceptions, 1914–1945*, Faber & Faber, 2008.

Read, Anthony and David Fisher. *Colonel Z: The Life and Times of a Master of Spies*, Hodder & Stoughton, 1984.

Reid, P.R.. *The Colditz Story*, Cassell, 1952.

Richards, Brook. *Secret Flotillas: Clandestine Sea Operations to Brittany 1940–1944*, Frank Cass, 2004.

Sands, Monica. *The MK Story. Code Name: The Black Cat*, Seaside Press, 2019.

Scharrer, Jos. *The Dutch Resistance Revealed: The Inside Story of Courage and Betrayal*, Pen & Sword, 2018.

Stourton, Edward. *Cruel Crossing: Escaping Hitler across the Pyrenees*, Doubleday, 2013.

Thomas, Vicky. *The Naga Queen: Ursula Graham Bower and her Jungle Warriors*, The History Press, 2012.

Vernoy, Alec de. *No Drums, No Trumpets*, Michael Joseph, 1988.

Verstraeten, Peter. *The US Medal of Freedom Awarded to Belgians for Services during the Second World War*, privately published.

Walker, Stephen. *Hide and Seek: The Irish Priest in the Vatican who Defied the Nazi Command*, Lyons Press, 2012.

Walters, Guy. *The Real Great Escape*, Bantam Press, 2013.

Warrack, Graeme. *Travel by Dark*, Harvill, 1963.

West, Nigel (ed.). *The Guy Liddell Diaries, Vol 1, 1939–1942*, Routledge, 2009.

West, Nigel (ed.). *The Guy Liddell Diaries, Vol 2, 1942–1945*, Routledge, 2009.

Witt, Carolinda. *Double Agent Celery: MI5's Crooked Hero*, Pen & Sword, 2017.

Wynne, Barry. *No Drums, No Trumpets: The Story of Mary Lindell*, Arthur Barker Ltd, 1961.

Unpublished Manuscripts

Barshall, Peter. Unpublished memoirs, *Peter's Story* used by kind permission of James Barshall.

Broomhall, William. 'The Show Which Didn't Get Off', unpublished reminiscences of his escape.

de Greef, Elvire (Tante Go). Unpublished notes entitled 'Detail of the Activity of M. Fernand de Greef from 26 June 1940 to the End of the War', used by kind permission of Anne and Chris Lyth.

Harrison, Ian and Roddy Langley. *An Orange Boat from Seville*, unpublished manuscript for film.

Jestin, Helmwarth. *A Memoir 1918–1946*, unpublished memoirs.

Langley, Peggy. *Unpublished Reminiscences* (copy lent to the author).

Liegeois, Elisabeth Constance. Unpublished memoir (1958) entitled *L'Enchainement 1940–45*, translated by Angela Hammond. Used by kind permission of Angela Hammond and the Comète Line Remembrance.

d'Oultremont, Georges. 'Souvenirs d'Oultre-Bombes', unpublished memoirs written in 1991.

INDEX

INDEX

INDEX